Fodor's

PRAGUE

D0033063

WELCOME TO PRAGUE

One of Europe's best-preserved cities, Prague has a romantic riverside location enhanced by graceful bridges and a magnificent skyline punctuated with medieval church spires. Its historic Old Town follows a plan laid out 1,000 years ago, with ancient squares and winding cobblestone streets. Haunting Prague Castle looms large across the Vltava River, rising above the exquisite Charles Bridge. Add extravagant, fairy-tale architecture; memorable classical music; and, these days, good food and drink, and it's easy to see why Prague charms everyone who visits.

TOP REASONS TO GO

★ **Historic architecture:** Gothic, baroque, Renaissance, Art Nouveau—it's all here.

★ **Prague Castle:** This Gothic fortress and soaring cathedral were Kafka's inspiration.

★ **Jewish heritage:** Historic synagogues and sights reflect an 800-year-old legacy.

★ **Old Town Square:** The city's pulsing heart fans out below the twin-spired Týn church.

★ **Excellent beer:** Czechs brew the best pilsner, and Prague pubs know how to pour it.

★ **Classical music:** Musicians from Dvořák to Mozart made their mark in Prague.

Fodor's PRAGUE

Design: Tina Malaney, *Associate Art Director*; Erica Cuoco, *Production Designer*

Photography: Jennifer Arnow, *Senior Photo Editor*

Maps: Rebecca Baer, *Senior Map Editor*; David Lindroth, Mark Stroud (Moon Street Cartography), *Cartographers*

Production: Angela L. McLean, *Senior Production Manager*; Jennifer DePrima, *Editorial Production Manager*

Sales: Jacqueline Lebow, *Sales Director*

Business & Operations: Chuck Hoover, *Chief Marketing Officer*; Joy Lai, *Vice President and General Manager*; Stephen Horowitz, *Head of Business Development and Partnerships*

Writers: Raymond Johnston, Jennifer Rigby, Will Tizard

Editors: Margaret Kelly (lead editor), Alexis Kelly, Amanda Sadlowski

Production Editor: Elyse Rozelle

Copyright © 2017 by Fodor's Travel, a division of Internet Brands, Inc.

Fodor's is a registered trademark of Internet Brands, Inc. All rights reserved. Published in the United States by Fodor's Travel, a division of Internet Brands, Inc. No maps, illustrations, or other portions of this book may be reproduced in any form without written permission from the publisher.

2nd edition

ISBN 978-0-14-754662-3

ISSN 2230-0639

All details in this book are based on information supplied to us at press time. Always confirm information when it matters, especially if you're making a detour to visit a specific place. Fodor's expressly disclaims any liability, loss, or risk, personal or otherwise, that is incurred as a consequence of the use of any of the contents of this book.

SPECIAL SALES

This book is available at special discounts for bulk purchases for sales promotions or premiums. For more information, e-mail specialmarkets@penguinrandomhouse.com.

PRINTED IN THE UNITED STATES OF AMERICA

10 9 8 7 6 5 4 3 2 1

CONTENTS

1 EXPERIENCE PRAGUE 9
Prague Today.................................10
Prague Planner..............................12
What's Where 14
Prague Top Attractions 16
Prague Like a Local 19
Prague Top Experiences................20
Great Itineraries............................22
Best Festivals in Prague 24
Best Tours in Prague 26

2 EXPLORING PRAGUE 27
Karlův most (Charles Bridge).........28
Staré Město (Old Town).................32
Josefov (Jewish Quarter)...............43
Malá Strana (Lesser Quarter).........48
Hradčany (Castle Area)..................57
Pražský Hrad (Prague Castle).........61
Nové Město (New Town)
and Vyšehrad.................................73
Vinohrady and Žižkov....................83
Letná, Holešovice, and Troja 87

3 WHERE TO EAT 91
Eating and Drinking Well
in Prague.......................................92
Planner..97
Restaurant Reviews 100
Best Bets for Prague Dining.........101

4 WHERE TO STAY 123
Planner..124
Hotel Reviews..............................127

5 PERFORMING ARTS 139
Planner..141
Classical Music............................142
Film..146
Performance Arts Centers
and Major Venues........................147

Puppet Shows and Black-Light
Theater..150
Theater and Dance 154

6 NIGHTLIFE 155
Prague's Beer Culture..................156
Planner..160
Staré Město.................................161
Josefov...163
Malá Strana.................................165
Hradčany 166
Nové Město..................................166
Vinohrady.....................................169
Žižkov 170
Smíchov.......................................171
Letná, Holešovice, and Troja........172

7 SHOPPING 173
Planner..175
Staré Město.................................176
Malá Strana.................................187
Hradčany 190
Nové Město..................................190
Vinohrady.....................................195
Žižkov 196
Smíchov.......................................196

8 DAY TRIPS FROM PRAGUE 197
Day Trips from Prague.................198
Planning 201
Kutná Hora...................................202
Karlštejn......................................208
Křivoklát 210
Mělník..211
Český Šternberk..........................213
Konopiště Castle..........................214
Lidice 215
Terezín 217

CONTENTS

9 SOUTHERN BOHEMIA............ 221
Welcome To Southern Bohemia ... 222
Planning 224
Český Krumlov 225
Tábor 233
Písek 236
Třeboň 237
Jindřichův Hradec 239
Hluboká nad Vltavou 242
České Budějovice 244

10 WESTERN BOHEMIA 247
Welcome To Western Bohemia 248
Planning 251
Karlovy Vary 252
Cheb 260
Františkovy Lázně 264
Mariánské Lázně 265
Plzeň 270

11 MORAVIA 275
Welcome To Moravia 276
Planning 279
Třebíč 280
Telč 281
Mikulov 284
Brno 287
Olomouc 296

TRAVEL SMART PRAGUE 301

INDEX 323

ABOUT OUR WRITERS 335

MAPS

Staré Město (Old Town) 34
Josefov (Jewish Quarter) 45
Hradčany (Castle Area) 59
Pražský hrad (Prague Castle) 63
Nové Město (New Town) and
Vyšehrad 75
Vinohrady and Žižkov 85
Letná, Holešovice, and Troja 89
Prague Dining 98
Where to Eat in Prague 104
Where to Stay in Prague 128
Kutná Hora 203
Český Krumlov 228
Karlovy Vary 256
Prague Metro 336

ABOUT THIS GUIDE

Fodor's Recommendations

Everything in this guide is worth doing—we don't cover what isn't—but exceptional sights, hotels, and restaurants are recognized with additional accolades. **Fodor's Choice** ★ indicates our top recommendations; and **Best Bets** call attention to notable hotels and restaurants in various categories. Care to nominate a new place? Visit Fodors.com/contact-us.

Trip Costs

We list prices wherever possible to help you budget well. Hotel and restaurant price categories from **$** to **$$$$** are noted alongside each recommendation. For hotels, we include the lowest cost of a standard double room in high season. For restaurants, we cite the average price of a main course at dinner or, if dinner isn't served, at lunch. For attractions, we always list adult admission fees; discounts are usually available for children, students, and senior citizens.

Hotels

Our local writers vet every hotel to recommend the best overnights in each price category, from budget to expensive. Unless otherwise specified, you can expect private bath, phone, and TV in your room. For expanded hotel reviews, visit Fodors.com.

Top Picks

★ Fodor's Choice

Listings

✉ Address
✉ Branch address
☎ Telephone
📠 Fax
🌐 Website
📧 E-mail
🎟 Admission fee
🕒 Open/closed times
[M] Subway
✥ Directions or Map coordinates

Hotels & Restaurants

🏨 Hotel
🛏 Number of rooms
🍽 Meal plans
🍴 Restaurant
✍ Reservations
👔 Dress code
💳 No credit cards
[$] Price

Other

⇨ See also
☞ Take note
🏌 Golf facilities

Restaurants

Unless we state otherwise, restaurants are open for lunch and dinner daily. We mention dress code only when there's a specific requirement and reservations only when they're essential or not accepted.

Credit Cards

The hotels and restaurants in this guide typically accept credit cards. If not, we'll say so.

EUGENE FODOR

Hungarian-born Eugene Fodor (1905–91) began his travel career as an interpreter on a French cruise ship. The experience inspired him to write *On the Continent* (1936), the first guidebook to receive annual updates and discuss a country's way of life as well as its sights. Fodor later joined the U.S. Army and worked for the OSS in World War II. After the war, he kept up his intelligence work while expanding his guidebook series. During the Cold War, many guides were written by fellow agents who understood the value of insider information. Today's guides continue Fodor's legacy by providing travelers with timely coverage, insider tips, and cultural context.

EXPERIENCE PRAGUE

PRAGUE TODAY

The "City of a Hundred Spires" is staggeringly beautiful, but it seems to have lost a bit of the swagger it had a decade ago, when it was the travel industry's golden child. But that's not such a bad thing, because there's a new air of maturity, and people are realizing that the city can no longer rest on its architectural and historical laurels. Part of this renewed sensibility can be traced to the death of former president Václav Havel—an international icon and hero of the 1989 Velvet Revolution—in 2011. The second came in 2013, when Prague experienced another major flood in little more than a decade. Both events were a reminder that good things should never be taken for granted. The result is a city that's palpably more introspective, and perhaps a bit more appreciative of the thousands of visitors who come here each year.

Today's Prague...

...is constantly beautifying itself. Deep down, Prague must have some kind of inferiority complex. What else could explain the perpetual need to make a beautiful city even more beautiful? A few years ago, city officials closed Charles Bridge for a two-year makeover, and then they worked on Prague Castle's Golden Lane.

Now, they've set their targets on the very emblem of the city atop Wenceslas Square: the National Museum. The grande dame of city museums will be shuttered for a little while to make way for a thorough renovation inside and out. And just down the road from the museum, the main train station (Hlavní nádraží) is freshly spiffed up following a multiyear rehab that has restored some beauty and dignity to a station, that for years, truth be told, had been something of an eyesore.

...is feverishly building for the future. For city planners, it seems, there's no rest for the weary. After spending the first decade post–Velvet Revolution apparently pondering what capital improvements might be needed, planners have seemingly embarked on everything—at the same time. So while metro builders are busy extending metro Line A (eventually) to the airport (and ripping up the main access road, Evropská, in the process), highway construction crews have at last finished the massive Blanka Tunnel. This is just one component of a road system that is starting to relieve traffic (a real issue in consumer-mad Prague of recent years). Most visitors to the center won't notice much of this, but for residents all the

WHAT'S HOT IN PRAGUE

Fresh food, slow food, locally grown, organic...call it what you want, Praguers have fully embraced the notion that food should be healthy, tasty, and sustainable. Weekend farmers' markets are all over town, bringing fresh, locally sourced fruits, vegetables, meats, and cheeses to the urban masses. Restaurateurs have gotten in on the act too, rewriting menus to embrace domestic ingredients and old-fashioned Czech cooking.

Watch out for that bike! Prague residents are taking to cycling in greater and greater numbers. For years, Czechs have enjoyed pedaling through their lush countryside, but more cyclists than ever are turning to bikes for everyday commuting. Credit Berlin and Vienna for showing how cycling can work as a viable urban transport model in rebuilding sometimes adds up to one big *bordel* (literally "bordello"—Czech slang for "big mess").

...is reviving proud traditions. From Bohemia-made toys to craft gin and a return to 19th-century butchery traditions, Czechs are actively returning to native skills and showing off the results at shops, eateries and studios all over the capital. Beer, too, is now widely served in unpasteurized, natural, and flavor-packed varieties. Meanwhile, artisanal textiles, clothing, decor and art are also filling locally owned, surprisingly affordable specialty shops.

...is still paying for everything with korunas. The Czech Republic was among the first of the former Eastern Bloc nations to be admitted into the European Union, in 2004. At the time, it was the shining star of the former communist countries (in yearbook terms, the country would have been voted "most likely to succeed"). The Czechs, however, have yet to adopt the euro despite innumerable promises and passed deadlines. Politicos have said adoption won't come until 2017 (and the governor of the Czech National Bank said that 2019 is more realistic). So what gives? Well, mostly, the euro crisis of the past few years greatly dented the euro's prestige. With the Czechs by and large recovered from the economic crisis, there's no great push to join the common currency. And really, they probably don't need to. Prices are stable and the country's accounts are still solid.

Central Europe. But maybe it's just all that road construction around town.

The cocktail craze has washed up on the city's shores. Across town, a new generation of cocktail bars has opened up, and gone are those glitzy, ultra-posh places of yesteryear. The new places emphasize civility and feature virtuoso drinks fashioned from artisan spirits and classic recipes.

Along with the cocktail craze comes a caffeine cornucopia. Since the fall of communism, coffee in Prague has evolved from a cup of low-quality grind doused with hot water, to Italian imports like Illy and Lavazza, to Starbucks, and now to local roasters, fancy French presses, and vacuum pots. It's not quite Brooklyn, but we love it.

PRAGUE PLANNER

Prague Weather

Winters here can be bone-chillingly cold, with days that are overcast and dark (the sun tends to set by 5 pm). Maximum average temperatures in December and January are in the mid-30s F, and the mercury frequently drops to the low 20s F. Things improve substantially in spring and summer. By July you can expect around 10 hours of sunshine per day. Showers, moreover, are infrequent and usually light and short. Temperatures hover in the mid-70s F, although summer heat waves seem to be increasingly common. Fall brings comfortably cool temperatures, as well as a riotous display of autumn foliage in parts of the city and countryside.

The words we use to designate different months are derived from Latin names and numbers. Czechs, on the other hand, use native words for climate-related events to reflect the importance of the four seasons. For instance, *únor* (our February) means "melting ice," and *listopad* (our November) means "falling leaves."

When to Go

Beautiful year-round, Prague is busiest over the Christmas and Easter holidays and during the summer months. Spring generally offers good weather, with a more relaxed level of tourism: flowers are blossoming, historic sites are open for business, and the Prague Spring International Music Festival is in full swing. Once fall arrives the trees are decked out with gold and scarlet leaves, and Czechs head to the woods in search of mushrooms (picking fungi is a time-honored pursuit here). In winter, crowd sizes and hotel costs drop along with the temperatures. You'll get a chance to see the photogenic capital blanketed in snow—the drawback is that some castles and museums (especially those outside of town) do close for the season. January and February usually bring the best skiing to Bohemian slopes, and finding a room at area ski resorts can be difficult. If you're not a skier, try visiting the mountains in late spring (April or May) or in fall, when the countryside is ablaze with brilliant colors and you have hotels and restaurants pretty much to yourself.

Hours

April through October, most of the city attractions open each day save Monday. Notable exceptions are the Jewish Museum (which shuts Saturday instead) and Prague Castle (which opens daily). Hours vary off-season, and many outlying sites close completely November through March.

Czech stores traditionally open weekdays from 9 am to 6 pm and Saturday from 9 am to 1 pm. Yet a growing number (including Prague's larger department stores, malls, and supermarkets) now boast extended evening and weekend hours. Ditto for shops in key tourist zones.

Restaurants typically welcome diners from 11 am to 11 pm and start dishing out dinner around 6. Pubs have a similar schedule, but clubs are another matter altogether. Though they open a few hours earlier, clubs rev up around midnight, and don't close until 4 or 5 am.

As for other services, most banks are open weekdays from 8 am to 5 pm. Most pharmacies are open weekdays from 9 am to 6 pm (some maintain 24/7 hours for emergencies).

Getting Around

Central Prague is ideal for walking—provided you have enough leg muscle to handle the hills. If not, there's reliable **public transit**. Tourists will typically use one of three types of transferable tickets when riding subways, buses, and trams. The "Basic" is valid for 90 minutes and costs 32 Kč: the "Short Term" is good for 30 minutes and costs 24 Kč; while the "1 Day" covers 24 hours of unlimited rides and costs 110 Kč. Tickets are available from dispensing machines located in all metro stations and at select surface transit stops. They may also be purchased at tourist information centers, as well as at designated tobacco shops and newsstands. After buying your ticket you must time-stamp it at one of the machines found inside metro stations or aboard buses and trams. Miss this step and you potentially face a 1,000 Kč fine.

Trams are frequently rerouted to accommodate construction and general maintenance. Check the civic transit authority's website (⊕ *www.dpp.cz*) for English-language updates.

Prefer taxis? Be warned. Local cabbies are notorious for overcharging, especially if hailed on the street or from a stand in touristy areas. Scams include doctoring the meter or "forgetting" to turn it on, then demanding an exorbitant sum. (FYI, most rides within the tourist zone should cost no more than 150 Kč to 250 Kč.) To avoid rip-offs, confirm an approximate fare up front. Better yet, call an honest radio-operated firm like

AAA Radiotaxi. ⊠ *Prague* ☎ *222–333–222* ⊕ *www.aaataxi.cz.*

If you're interested in exploring beyond the city, check our "Top Tours" or review the train and bus schedules at ⊕ *www. idos.cz.*

Prague by the Numbers
Prague neighborhoods are sometimes referred to by numbers corresponding to their postal district:

Prague 1: Staré Město (Old Town), Josefov (the Jewish Quarter), Hradčany (the Castle Area), Malá Strana (the Lesser Quarter), Northern Nové Město (New Town)

Prague 2: Southern Nové Město (New Town), Vyšehrad, Western Vinohrady

Prague 3: Eastern Vinohrady, Žižkov

Prague 5: Smíchov

Prague 7: Letná, Holešovice

Safety
Although crime rates in Prague are relatively low, this is a major city, and travelers should exercise the usual precautions. For starters, that means being careful at night—even when visiting spots that seem safe by day. Prostitutes and drug dealers can make parts of Wenceslas Square feel sketchy after dark, and stag parties comprised of rowdy beer-addled lads can appear anywhere.

Regardless of the hour, be wary of pickpockets at crowded sites (like the Charles Bridge) and on public transit (the Tram No. 22, being popular with tourists, is a favorite among the sticky fingered). To be on the safe side, always keep your hands on purses, backpacks, cameras, and such, rather than leaving them placed beside you.

Distribute cash, credit cards, ID, and other valuables between a deep front pocket, an inside jacket or vest pocket, and a discreet money pouch—please, no in-your-face fanny packs. Don't rifle in that pouch or flash wads of cash once you're in public. If you need an ATM top-up, choose a machine inside a bank building. One further tip: Ignore those ubiquitous guys offering to exchange currency at great rates on the street unless you want to end up with worthless bills.

WHAT'S WHERE

1 **Staré Město (Old Town).** Prague's historic heart is "tourist central," so it's often jam-packed with people. Most gather in Old Town Square to marvel at the architecture and watch the astronomical clock strike, then wander the narrow streets.

2 **Josefov (Jewish Quarter).** The original Jewish Ghetto was largely razed in the 19th century, and art nouveau structures replaced many of its buildings. Yet the past is still apparent in the restored sites that comprise the Jewish Museum and the active synagogues.

3 **Malá Strana (Lesser Quarter).** This neighborhood is filled with hilly cobblestone streets edged with baroque buildings. The stunning Church of St. Nicholas dominates the district.

4 **Hradčany (Castle Area).** The highlight here is Pražský Hrad. It shelters a Romanesque basilica, a Gothic cathedral, a Renaissance garden, and a baroque palace.

5 **Nové Město (New Town) and Vyšehrad.** Prague's "New Town" was laid out in the 14th century. Its focal point is Wenceslas Square: a grand boulevard lined with shops, restaurants, and hotels. Upriver from the Charles Bridge, compact Vyšehrad contains the remains of Prague's "other castle."

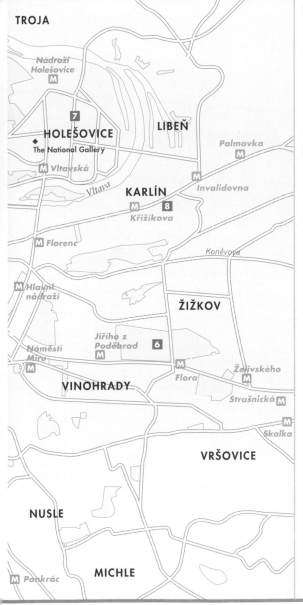

6 Vinohrady and Žižkov. As its name implies, Vinohrady began as a wine-producing region and the lovely, leafy neighborhood is still intoxicating. Žižkov retains its counter-culture reputation despite increasing gentrification. It reputedly has the most drinking spots in Prague.

7 Letná, Holešovice, and Troja. Known for its park, Letná is where some of the largest Velvet Revolution marches took place. Now protesters have been replaced by locals out for a stroll. Major redevelopment continues in Holešovice, where the chief attraction is the National Gallery's collection of art. With its zoo, botanical garden, and eponymous château, Troja feels like a day trip destination inside the city.

8 Karlín. The former industrial district is a warren of bars, galleries and start-up workspaces inside of repurposed factories and pre-war tenement buildings. The birthplace of the electric tram, an 1880s wonder from inventor František Křižík, Karlín is now the place to sip an espresso with hip urbanites.

9 Smíchov. Mostly malls, multiplex theaters, and office complexes, Smíchov now has new bars and eateries moving into the neighborhood.

PRAGUE
TOP ATTRACTIONS

Pražský Hrad (Prague Castle)

(A) The nation's most-visited site draws more than 1.6 million people per year, and Czech history has been irrevocably deeply intertwined with it from the 10th century onward. Attractions set inside the castle's imposing walls range from grand churches, manicured gardens, and regal abodes—including the official presidential residence—to the higgledy-piggledy little cottages that prettily line Golden Lane. To set this all in context, it helps to make "The Story of Prague Castle" your first stop. It's an engaging multimedia display located in the Old Royal Palace.

Chrám Svatého Víta
(St. Vitus Cathedral)

(B)"The City of a Hundred Spires" has more than its fair share of churches. None, however, can top this glorious Gothic structure on the grounds of Prague Castle. Almost six centuries in

the making (the cornerstone was laid in 1344, and work was finally completed in 1929), St. Vitus is a place of superlatives. It is both the largest church in the Czech Republic and—as the country's spiritual center and the final resting place for many of its beloved kings and saints—the most important.

Karluv Most (The Charles Bridge)

(C) When it was built in the mid-14th century, Europe's longest medieval bridge (a 1,700-foot span supported by 16 graceful arches) was an engineering triumph, and it remained the only boat-free way to cross the Vltava until the mid-19th century. Assuming that you can navigate through the crowds, it is still a convenient way to get from Staré Město to Malá Strana. Being studded by statues on both sides, it's also a veritable gallery, and a magnet for romantics, history buffs, buskers, and tourists.

Staromestské Námestí (Old Town Square)

(D)Dating back to the Middle Ages, this massive town-square-cum-marketplace in the heart of Staré Město is rimmed with postcard-perfect sites. The most striking of these—quite literally—is the Astronomical Clock on the Old Town Hall tower, which marked its 600th birthday in 2010. Operating like a giant cuckoo clock, its meticulously carved wooden figures of the Twelve Apostles appear on the top of the hour from 9 am to 11 pm. One legend has it that local officials were so impressed by the mechanical marvel that they blinded the clockmaker to ensure that he could never duplicate it.

Židovské Muzeum (The Jewish Museum)

(E)Rather than being a single bricks-and-mortar building, this museum is made up of six sites in the Josefov district. These include a Ceremonial Hall as well as four historic synagogues that house themed exhibits. The Pinkasova, with its Holocaust memorial, is most moving: the names of 77,297 Czech Jews murdered by the Nazis are inscribed on the main-floor walls, while impossibly poignant drawings made by children at the Terezín "transit" camp are displayed in its gallery. The museum also administers the Old Jewish Cemetery, which contains some 12,000 tilting headstones.

Chrám Svatého Mikuláse (Church of St. Nicholas)

(F)Not to be confused with the 18th-century edifice in Staré Město that is dedicated to the same saint, this domed beauty dominates the Malá Strana district. A prime example of "high baroque," its extravagant interior features a gilded statue of St. Nick plus frescos depicting his life in addition to the usual paintings and putti. The

church also hosts evening concerts from late March through early November, and again in the Christmas season (most showcase the music of Mozart, who himself played the organ here). Those who prefer the sound of pealing bells are welcome to climb the adjacent bell tower.

Obecní Dům (Municipal House)
(G) Prague is a compendium of architectural styles, and the remarkable range inevitably draws stares. For fans of art nouveau, though, this building takes the cake. Municipal House was built with nationalist zeal when the Austro-Hungarian Empire was waning. So it is no coincidence that the era's preeminent Czech artists were hired to decorate it, or that the main concert venue (Smetana Hall, home to the Prague Symphony Orchestra) was named for the "Father of Czech Music." Fittingly, the Republic of Czechoslovakia declared its independence from the balcony of Obecní dům in 1918.

Chrám Svaté Barbory (St. Barbara's Cathedral)
(H)"Heigh-Ho, Heigh-Ho, it's off to church we go" could have been the theme song for the silver miners of Kutná Hora who financed the building of this grand cathedral to honor their patron saint. Like St. Vitus Cathedral (aesthetically, its only rival), St. Barbara's was for centuries a work in progress: construction went on intermittently from 1388 to 1905. What makes this church so unusual, though, is the way metallurgy and liturgy intersect inside. Paying homage to both the blue collar and the clerical collar, it contains frescoes portraying both religious scenes and scenes of mining and minting.

PRAGUE LIKE A LOCAL

With the capital so full of foreign visitors, it can be a little hard to uncover what life for residents is like. So put the sightseeing on hold for a while and try these activities, beloved by locals.

Beer

Every discussion about this republic begins and ends with beer. That seems fair, given that Czechs aren't only the world's largest per capita consumers of *pivo*, they also invented the modern pilsner, and their national brews set the gold standard globally. They are so good, in fact, that beer here commands the type of reverence usually reserved for fine wine. But if you want to drink it like a native, don't chug from a bottle or a can. Head to the nearest *pivnice*, or pub, grab a seat at a communal table, and wait for the waiter to plunk down a mug in front of you. Turn to your neighbor, raise your glass, and say, "*Na zdraví!*" (To your health!)—any pronunciation suffices when you say it with feeling. Congratulations: you are now an honorary citizen.

Culture

Czechs survived three centuries of Austrian occupation (from 1620 to 1918) with nothing but a shared culture to unite them; and right across the class continuum they remain committed to the performing arts. Opera and orchestral music are the biggest draws, and you'll likely encounter touts advertising quick "greatest hits"–style concerts in churches all over town. However, these are targeted squarely at tourists, with nary a native in sight. So save your koruny for the real deal, like a performance by the Prague State Opera or the Czech Philharmonic. The comprehensive online listings at ⊕ *www.prague. eu* cover classical acts, plus concerts and club shows, where you can rub elbows with local music enthusiasts. The quality of the performances is high, and the audience reaction is invariably heartfelt.

Parks

Like many city dwellers, residents of Prague are fond of their green spaces, which serve as a sort of communal backyard. Formal gardens—like Vrtba in Malá Strana—offer a grassy respite when leisure time is limited. Yet lounging in a park is preferable. Two of the most popular are Letenské Sady and Riegrovy Sady. Aside from walking shoes, follow the locals' lead by coming equipped with a book, blanket, and picnic. Since both parks have huge beer gardens, you should be prepared to stay awhile, too. Rather take a walk on the wild side? At Divoká Šárka (literally, "Wild Sarka"), open fields, wooded paths, and a stream-fed pool lure nature lovers; conversely, Petřínské Sady, on Prague's highest hill, appeals to the upwardly mobile.

Spas

Praguers love spa resorts, and there are plenty of Bohemian ones to pick from. The most famous of the bunch are concentrated in the so-called Spa Triangle made up of Karlovy Vary, Mariánské Lázně, and Františkovy Lázně, where mineral springs are abundant. Other prized resources also come into play. In addition to water, spas build their treatments around peat, natural gas, and even beer. Czech spas have a long tradition of welcoming visitors (past guests at Karlovy Vary, for example, include Peter the Great, Beethoven, Tolstoy, and Freud). However, one legacy of the communist era is that many still present treatments as medical procedures. In short, they focus on health more than hedonism. If you want full-on pampering, choose your locale carefully.

PRAGUE TOP EXPERIENCES

Classic Music

Mozart is a civic obsession, so you can't leave Prague without hearing his music. The obvious choice is to attend an opera at the opulent Estates Theatre, where *Don Giovanni* (personally conducted by the maestro) premiered to an appreciative audience in 1787. Anyone who fears that opera may be a bit uppity can enjoy a more accessible performance—albeit with some strings attached—at the National Marionette Theatre. Tickets will cost anywhere from 290 Kč to 1,100 Kč at the former, about 600 Kč at the latter.

Excellent Beer

The king of beers in this part of the globe isn't Budweiser—though Czech Budvar runs a close second—but Plzeňský Prazdroj (aka Pilsner Urquell). The word *prazdroj* means "source," and you can go straight to that source by visiting the legendary brewery complex and adjacent brewery-themed museum in Plzeň, 55 miles southwest of Prague. The world-renowned pale lager was invented here in 1842. One taste and you'll understand why Czechs have an old proverb that goes, "Where beer is brewed, life is good."

Curative Waters

A different kind of beverage is the drink du jour in Karlovy Vary. Accidentally discovered by Emperor Charles IV in the 1300s, the hot springs here provide water for sipping as well as spa-ing—which explains why most folks tote porcelain cups that they fill for free at thermal fountains. You can buy your own for a few bucks (the unique little handle that doubles as a straw makes it a fun spa souvenir). Even without one, though, you will remember the experience. The curative water's sulfuric taste is unforgettably awful.

Fine Glassworks

The Czech Republic is synonymous with fine cut crystal, and purists contend that the very best is created by Moser, a glassmaker that has been operating in Karlovy Vary since 1857. Moser also has two Prague locations: the flagship store at Na Příkopě 12 (itself a work of art) and a second shop on Old Town Square. Looking for something more modern? Function coupled with contemporary form makes Artěl, also in Old Town, a sound choice. Wherever you shop, be sure that pieces bear an official "Bohemia Crystal" sticker.

Discover Kafka

Paging all literature lovers! Czech-born author and existentialist poster boy Franz Kafka lived out his life in Prague, and retracing his footsteps offers a surprisingly comprehensive city tour. Former homes, for example, include buildings on Old Town Square and in Prague Castle (Dům U Minuty and 22 Golden Lane respectively). A suitably surreal bronze statue of him stands in the Jewish Quarter, where he worshiped; plus, there's a whole Kafka museum in Malá Strana. Organized Kafka walks are also broadly touted.

Explore the Vltava River

The Vltava River (this country's longest) slices through Prague, offering ample on-the-water opportunities in the process. That's a good thing, because some people like standard-issue outings on big sightseeing vessels and some prefer a bit more quirkiness. Those who fall into the second category may sign on with Prague-Venice Cruises and tool around in a little 19th century–style canal boat. If you're eager to break free entirely and paddle your own rowboat, there are several waterfront rental companies that can set you up.

Picturesque Castles

Bordering Germany and the former Austro-Hungarian Empire, Southern Bohemia long held a strategically important position that needed to be defended with a series of fortifications. Today that makes it a popular locale among castle connoisseurs. If you can see only one, make it Hrad Krumlov, which, in Czech terms, is second only in size to Pražský Hrad in Prague. Positioned high above the fairytale town of Český Krumlov, this fanciful castle comes complete with a tower, a dungeon, and a moat.

Christmas Market

Christmas markets, which generally start four Saturdays before Christmas Eve and run daily until New Year's, are hugely popular in Prague. One well-stocked market sets up on Wenceslas Square (named for the "good king" of carol fame). But Old Town Square's wins the "most festive" prize, because St. Nick appears on the afternoon of December 5 to separate the naughty children from the nice. After stocking up on crafts, carp, and cups of mulled wine, revelers return to the square December 24 for a candlelit evening mass.

Spring International Music Festival

Since 1946 the Prague Spring International Music Festival has been the most noteworthy event on the Czech cultural calendar. Opening with a tribute to native composer Bedřich Smetana on May 12 (the anniversary of his death), it features three weeks of A-list performances. Musicians gather in concert halls and churches to play from the entire classical repertoire; hence the demand for tickets is high. So, too, are some of the ticket prices. The upside is that others are affordable and, on occasion, available the day of.

Comfort Food

This country's old-school comfort food is notoriously rich. On cool evenings, however, it's hard to beat sustaining, stick-to-your-ribs dishes like *vepřo-knedlo-zelo* (a fatty roast pork and cabbage concoction served with dumplings) or *vepřový řízek* (a variation on schnitzel) with crisp deep-fried potato pancakes on the side. Cap your meal with a crepe-style *palačinky* or fruit-filled *ovocné knedlíky*. If you're concerned about packing on pounds, just remind yourself that eating heavy food here is all part of the cultural experience.

GREAT ITINERARIES

Laid out on a bend of the Vltava River, Prague has always been a gathering place on the fringe of great powers, but just remote enough to allow it a bit of rugged independence (and so much of its unique, fringe character). Even in one day, it's clear that the city personifies the bohemian ideal of living for art, for life, and for love. Improbably gorgeous architecture houses venues for fine arts and culture, and there's no shortage of seriously romantic spots. Five days is barely time to scratch this beautful city's surface.

PRAGUE IN 1 DAY

Start with a classic coffee in a stunning setting, the art nouveau–style Municipal House kavarna. Walk down Celetna street past the cubist House of the Black Madonna to Old Town Square, where the Atronomical Clock chimes in each hour with a mechanical morality play opposite the haunting Tyn Church. Head down Parizska to the Old-New Synagogue, the oldest surviving medieval sacred structure in the city's former Jewish ghetto district, Josefov. This ¾-mile walk will take about 90 minutes at a leisurely pace with stops to take in interiors and tower views.

Now gear up for an afternoon across the river, strolling the postcard-perfect Charles Bridge to Malostranske namesti, once the heart of Prague's coffeehouse culture. Hop Tram No. 22 for a breathtaking view on your ride to the Prague Castle grounds in Hradcany, where you'll tour St. Vitus' Cathedral, the ancient St. George's Basilica and relax in the Royal Gardens. Wrap up the journey with a traditional Czech dinner at U Modre Kachnicky or dine riverside at Kampa Park on first-class gourmet cuisine.

PRAGUE IN 5 DAYS

Day 1: Arrival, Pražský Hrad (Prague Castle)

Even jet lag can't dampen the allure of Pražský Hrad, so it is a perfect place to hit on your first day in the city. The castle's ancient 17-acre property contains a slew of individual attractions conveniently linked by internal courtyards. The show-stopper is St. Vitus Cathedral (wherein lie the remains of fabled Czechs like Charles IV and St. Wenceslas). But don't forget to hit the Royal Palace and Lobkowicz Palace, too. Also worth a gander is Golden Lane: a row of crooked cottages, one of which was once occupied by Kafka. Diminutive to begin with, they look like dollhouses when compared with the supersize surrounding structures. Before calling it a day and descending from the castle, remember to take in the city view: aside from offering a photo op, it will also help you get your bearings!

Day 2: Josefov and Staré Město (Old Town)

Begin your day early in the Jewish Quarter. (Because it is best approached with a certain solemnity, arriving ahead of the tour groups is a definite advantage.) Here you will find Europe's oldest active synagogue—the Staronová, erected in 1270—as well as the Jewish Museum. Once you've seen the latter's evocative exhibits and paid your respects at the topsy-turvy Old Jewish Cemetery, saunter over to Staré Město to explore its centuries-old—and certifiably touristy—tangle of streets. Prepare to linger around Old Town Square, ideally timing your arrival to coincide with the striking of the Astronomical Clock. Later you can retrace the "Royal Way" (so named for the kings who trod it) that links the square with the Powder Tower. The Municipal House, an eye-popping 20th-century addition to Staré Město's medieval streetscape, is right beside it.

Day 3: Malá Strana

You shouldn't be surprised if the neighborhood you visit today looks vaguely familiar: after all, it has been featured in a glut of period movies, ranging from *Amadeus* to *Van Helsing*. Filmmakers come because its cobbled streets, beautifully preserved baroque buildings, and gorgeous formal gardens conjure up a long-ago time. Since the area seems to have a surprise at every turn, aimless wandering is Malá Strana's main pleasure; however, there is one site that deserves thorough investigation: St. Nicholas Church—an 18th-century beauty dedicated to Ol' Saint Nick. If you choose to climb the 215 steep steps of the church bell tower, you can reward your aching feet afterward by resting in Vrtba Garden or taking an extended break in leafy Kampa Island Park before returning to Staré Město via the Charles Bridge.

Day 4: Day Trip Outside
Prague to Kutná Hora

If you are ready for a break from the city, Kutná Hora—44 miles east of Prague—is a memorable destination for day-trippers. Rich deposits of silver put this town on the map in the 12th century, and the premiere local attractions are still tied to them. Chances are you will start your visit at St. Barbara's Cathedral, a divine Gothic sanctuary that was built with miners' donations. Afterward you can get the lowdown on mineralogy at the Czech Museum of Silver, then tour portions of an original silver mine and restored mint. (For a real heavy-metal experience, try coming in late June, when the town relives its glory days during the annual Royal

Silvering Festival.) When in the area, it is also worth making a detour to suburban Sedlec to see the somewhat spooky Kostnice Ossuary, a bizarre church decorated with human bones.

Depending on what time you get back to Prague, you might explore a new neighborhood or just rest up for a big night on the town. One tempting alternative is to indulge in some last-minute shopping, whether opting for upscale items on Pařížská Street or folksy mementos in Havelske Trziste. (Admit it. You're *dying* to have one of those omnipresent Mozart marionettes!) Before bedding down, revisit the Charles Bridge for a final floodlighted look at Golden Prague. Although you'll be hard pressed to take your eyes off the illuminated castle in the background, do take a moment to search among the many statues that decorate the span for the one depicting St. John Nepomuk. It's the eighth on the right, and—according to legend—travelers who rub it are bound to return.

BEST FESTIVALS IN PRAGUE

Although festival season is essentially a year-round phenomenon in Prague these days, things really take off in April and there's hardly a weekend that passes by through October without a music, food, film or arts festival taking over colorful venues.

4+4 Days in Motion (4+4 *dny v pohybu*). One of the more creative festivals on the Prague circuit, the 4+4 Days in Motion festival offers art projects, installations, performances, and discussions in venues across the city. The venues are half the fun—think reclaimied, little-used palaces surrounding Old Town. The festival is themed around contemporary dance and usually takes place in the fall. ☎ *224–809–116* ⊕ *www.ctyridny.cz*.

Days of European Film. Fans of foreign films have a chance to catch up on recent English-subtitled efforts in Days of European Film, which happens every April in Prague and other locations around the Czech Republic. A week of films play at two cinemas; there are also some panel discussions and seminars. Tickets are inexpensive, and the theaters used for screenings are beautiful and historic. ☎ *603–844–811* ⊕ *www.eurofilmfest.cz*.

Febiofest. One of the largest film festivals in Central Europe, with hundreds of screenings in Prague and its sister festival in Slovakia, Febiofest runs for about a week at the end of March and beginning of April. Films—both premieres and retrospectives—come from virtually all over the world, and a number of directors and stars, including Roman Polanski and Peter Mullan, come to introduce their work. As a side to the festival, world-music bands also perform for free in the garage of the multiplex where the festival is held. ☎ *221–101–111* ⊕ *www.febiofest.cz*.

International Organ Festival. The lovely organ in Bazilika sv. Jakuba attracts noted international musicians for the annual International Organ Festival, which runs from August to September with weekly concerts. ✉ *Malá Štuparská, Staré Mesto* ☎ *224–826–440* ⊕ *www.auditeorganum. cz/festival.html*.

Karlovy Vary International Film Festival. The most important film festival in the Czech Republic is in an ornate spa town in West Bohemia. The Karlovy Vary International Film Festival ranks with Cannes, Berlin, and Venice among major European festivals. Visitors to the gala, which rolls out in late July or early July, have included Lauren Bacall, Morgan Freeman, Michael Douglas, and Robert De Niro. This is one of the most publicly accessible film festivals around. ☎ *221–411–011* ⊕ *www. kviff.com*.

Khamoro Festival. Celebrating Roma culture and diversity, the Khamoro Festival offers music, dance, and film. Romany (Gypsy) bands have become a hot item on the world-music scene, and groups from all over Europe gather in Prague at the end of May for a week of merrymaking. Check out contemporary Roma music, Gypsy Jazz, exhibitions, and dance performances, as well as the crowning glory—a parade. ☎ *222–518–554* ⊕ *www.khamoro.cz*.

Mezi ploty. From amateur to professional, entertainers of all kinds descend on the grounds of a mental health institution for Mezi ploty—the festival between the fences. The two-day festival has some of the best local bands, plus theater acts and art workshops, but be aware that only nonalcoholic beer can be sold on the grounds. It takes place at the beginning of June and aims to raise awareness of issues concerning mental illness. ✉ *Ústavní ulice, Bohnice* ⊕ *www.meziploty.cz.*

One World Human Rights Film Festival (*Jeden svět*). The One World Human Rights Festival could be handily subtitled "films that will make you think." It showcases work dedicated to human rights and other social and political issues, offering a glimpse of the world through a filmmaker's eye along with many post-screening director chats and workshops. The festival runs in March at various theaters, usually including Lucerna, Světozor, and Atlas. Nearly all films are in English or with English subtitles. ⊕ *www.oneworld.cz.*

Prague Fringe Festival. There isn't much English-language theater in the Czech capital. An exception is the annual Prague Fringe Festival, which began in 2002 and has visiting acts from Scotland, New Zealand, Australia, and the United States. The venues are scattered around Malá Strana; performances, which range from Shakespeare to avant-garde cabaret, are staggered so that you could conceivably see five a day. The Fringe takes place in May. ⊕ *www.praguefringe.com.*

Prague Spring (*Pražské jaro*). Since 1946 Prague Spring has been the main event of the classical season, and usually runs from the end of May to the start of June. Conductors such as Leonard Bernstein and Sir Charles Mackerras have been among the guests. Important anniversaries of major composers, especially Czech ones, are marked with special concerts and the gala increasingly features hot international jazz talents. Orchestra performances, operas, and church recitals make up the bulk of the schedule. The competition element gives attendees the opportunity to see the next big star. Typically around 60 concerts are spread over more than 10

venues during the nearly three-week run. Bedřich Smetana's *Ma vlást* (*My Country*) usually opens the festival. Major events can sell out months in advance; tickets usually go on sale mid-December. If you miss the big one, don't despair—the festival does have a younger brother taking place later in the year, the Prague Autumn. ☏ *257–312–547* ⊕ *www.festival.cz.*

Tanec Praha. European contemporary dance and movement is celebrated at Tanec Praha. Lasting for about a month every May–June, renowned companies from all over the world strut their stuff in a renovated Prague 3 venue. ☏ *222–721–531* ⊕ *www.tanecpraha.cz.*

United Islands of Prague. Rockers, this festival is for you! Located on the peaceful, pretty islands of the Vltava, an often underutilized aspect of Prague, the festival brings international rock, blues, and world-music acts to several waterside venues for a weekend at the end of June, and entry is free. In the evenings performances by additional bands take place in nearby clubs. ☏ *220–951–432* ⊕ *www.unitedislands.cz.*

BEST TOURS IN PRAGUE

Sightseeing Tours

The most reliable operators—among them Čedok, Martin Tour, and Premiant City Tour—are a competitive lot, with an extensive menu that covers everything from the standard "top sites" tours to pub crawls and folkloric evenings. Most of these options are offered year-round, with some including a walking component and occasionally a boat trip. Full-day excursions to outlying areas are typically available, too.

Contacts Čedok. ☎ 221–447–242 ⊕ www. cedok.com. **Martin Tour.** ☎ 224–212–473 ⊕ www.martintour.cz. **Premiant City Tour.** ☎ 606–600–123 ⊕ www.premiant.cz.

Boat Tours

Of the numerous companies running Vltava River trips 12 months of the year, two stand out. The Prague Steamboat Company, established in 1865, scores points for being the biggest and oldest. Hour cuises on large-capacity vessels feature multilingual commentary. Longer meal-and-music junkets are regularly scheduled as well. For a more intimate experience, try a Prague–Venice cruise aboard a vintage-style canal boat that holds fewer than three dozen passengers.

Contacts Prague Steamboat Company. ☎ 224–931–013 ⊕ www.praguesteamboats.com. **Prague-Venice Cruises.** ☎ 776–776–779 ⊕ www.prague-venice.cz.

Specialized Walking Tours

Themed strolls are hugely popular, especially during the peak tourist season, and several providers (Guide-Prague, Prague Walks, and Prague Tours being only three examples) lead tours focusing on, say, local authors, civic architecture, or different historical eras. For visitors specifically interested in Prague's Jewish heritage, Wittmann Tours is your best bet. It organizes informative walks through the Josefov, plus day trips to related sites such as Terezín.

Contacts Guide-Prague. ☎ 776–868–770 ⊕ www.guide-prague.cz. **Praguer Tours.** ☎ 608–200–912 ⊕ www.praguertours. com. **Prague Walks.** ☎ 608–973–390 ⊕ www.praguewalks.com. **Wittmann Tours.** ☎ 222–252–472 ⊕ www.wittmann-tours. com.

Fun Alternatives

There are lots of cool conveyances that allow you to see Prague in style, at least in the warmer months. Consider a traditional horse-drawn carriage tour, or up the horsepower by riding an antique car (bookable in advance through Prague PG), a nostalgia-inducing tram, a Jetsons-worthy Segway, or an eco-friendly electric train. Praha Bike offers cycling tours in and around the city, along with straightforward bike rentals for independent types.

Contacts Ekoexpres. ☎ 602–317–784 ⊕ www.ekoexpres.cz. **Nostalgic Tram Line No. 91.** ☎ 296–191–817 ⊕ www.dpp. cz. **Pony Travel.** ☎ 736–752–671 ⊕ www. ponytravelsro.cz. **Prague on Segway.** ☎ 775–588–588 ⊕ www.pragueonsegway.com. **Prague PG.** ☎ 222–518–259 ⊕ www.guidingprague.com. **Praha Bike.** ☎ 732–388–880 ⊕ www.prahabike.cz.

Private Guides

Eager to take a private tour with a tailor-made itinerary? Lots of locals advertise themselves as guides. So it's wise to choose one registered by Prague Information Service.

Contacts Prague.eu. ☎ 236–002–569, 236–002–562 ⊕ www.prague.eu.

EXPLORING
PRAGUE

KARLŮV MOST (CHARLES BRIDGE)

This is Prague's signature monument. The view from the foot of the bridge on the Old Town side, encompassing the towers and domes of the Lesser Quarter and the soaring spires of St. Vitus Cathedral, is nothing short of breathtaking.

Above: View of the Charles Bridge, busy with pedestrians. Top right: Vendors on the bridge; Bottom right: Street-level photo of the Charles Bridge

This heavenly vista subtly changes in perspective as you walk across the bridge, attended by a host of baroque saints that decorate the bridge's peaceful Gothic stones. At night its drama is spellbinding: St. Vitus Cathedral lit in a ghostly green, the Castle in monumental yellow, and the Church of St. Nicholas in a voluptuous pink, all viewed through the menacing silhouettes of the bowed statues and the Gothic towers. Night is the best time to visit the bridge, which is choked with visitors, vendors, and beggars by day. The later the hour, the thinner the crowds—though the bridge is never truly empty, even at daybreak. Tourists with flash cameras are there all hours of the night, and in the wee hours revelers from the dance clubs at the east end of the bridge stumble across for breakfast.

The bridge is open all day, every day, and entry is free. The easiest way to find the bridge from Old Town Square is to follow the narrow, winding Karlova lane, which begins on the western end of Malé náměstí, just next to Old Town Square, and takes you, twisting and turning, to the foot of the bridge. From the Malá Strana side, start from central Malostranské náměstí and follow the street Mostecká directly to the bridge (you can't miss it).

A BRIEF HISTORY OF THE BRIDGE

When the Přemyslid princes set up residence in Prague during the 10th century, there was a ford across the Vltava here—a vital link along one of Europe's major trading routes. After several wooden bridges and the first stone bridge washed away in floods, Charles IV appointed the 27-year-old German Peter Parler, the architect of St. Vitus Cathedral, to build a new structure in 1357. It became one of the wonders of the world in the Middle Ages.

After 1620, following the disastrous defeat of Czech Protestants by Catholic Hapsburgs at the Battle of White Mountain, the bridge became a symbol of the Counter-Reformation's vigorous re-Catholicization efforts.

The religious conflict is less obvious nowadays, leaving behind an artistic tension between baroque and Gothic that gives the bridge its allure.

ABOUT THE TOWER

Staroměstská mostecká věž (Old Town Bridge Tower), at the bridge entrance on the Old Town side, is where Peter Parler, the architect of the Charles Bridge, began his bridge building. The carved façades he designed for the sides of the tower were destroyed by Swedish soldiers in 1648, at the end of the Thirty Years' War. The sculptures facing the Old Town, however, are still intact (although some are recent copies). They depict an old and gout-ridden Charles IV with his son, who became Wenceslas IV. Above them are two of Bohemia's patron saints, Adalbert of Prague and Sigismund. The top of the tower offers a spectacular view of the city for 70 Kč; it's open daily from 10 to 10, year-round.

TOURING THE BRIDGE, STATUE BY STATUE

Take a closer look at some of the statues while walking toward the Lesser Quarter. The third one on the right, a bronze crucifix from the mid-17th century, is the oldest of all. The fifth on the left, which shows St. Frances Xavier carrying four pagan princes (an Indian, Moor, Chinese, and Tartar) ready for conversion, represents an outstanding piece of baroque sculpture. Eighth on the right is the statue of St. John of Nepomuk, who according to legend was wrapped in chains and thrown to his death from this bridge. Touching the statue is supposed to bring good luck or, according to some versions of the story, a return visit to Prague. On the left-hand side, sticking out from the bridge between the 9th and 10th statues (the latter has a wonderfully expressive vanquished Satan), stands a Roland (Bruncvík) statue. This knightly figure, bearing the coat of arms of the Old Town, was once a reminder that this part of the bridge belonged to the Old Town before Prague became a unified city in 1784.

Updated by
Will Tizard

Full of fairy-tale vistas, Prague is beautiful in a way that makes even the most jaded traveler stop and snap pictures. The city is physically divided in two by the Vltava River (also sometimes known by its German name, the Moldau), which runs from south to north with a single sharp turn to the east.

Originally, Prague was composed of five independent towns: Hradčany (the Castle Area), Malá Strana (Lesser Quarter), Staré Město (Old Town), Nové Město (New Town), and Josefov (Jewish Quarter), and these areas still make up the heart of Prague—what you think of when picturing its famed winding cobblestone streets and squares.

Hradčany, the seat of Czech royalty for hundreds of years, centers on the Pražský hrad (Prague Castle)—itself the site of the president's office. A cluster of white buildings yoked around the pointed steeples of a chapel, Prague Castle overlooks the city from a hilltop west of the Vltava River. Steps lead down from Hradčany to the Lesser Quarter, an area dense with ornate mansions built for the 17th- and 18th-century nobility.

The looming Karlův most (Charles Bridge) connects the Lesser Quarter with the Old Town. Old Town is hemmed in by the curving Vltava and three large commercial avenues: Revoluční to the east, Na příkopě to the southeast, and Národní třída to the south. A few blocks east of the bridge is the district's focal point: Staroměstské náměstí (Old Town Square), a former medieval marketplace laced with pastel-color baroque houses—easily one of the most beautiful central squares in Europe. To the north of Old Town Square the diminutive Jewish Quarter fans out around a tony avenue called Pařížská.

Beyond the former walls of the Old Town, the New Town fills in the south and east. The name "new" is a misnomer—New Town was laid out in the 14th century. (It's new only when compared with the neighboring Old Town.) Today this mostly commercial district includes the city's largest squares, Karlovo náměstí (Charles Square) and Václavské náměstí (Wenceslas Square).

PHOTO OP

As you walk uphill from Malá Strana to the Castle Area, you'll get glorious views over the Prague rooftops. Many of the restaurants and hotels in this area have terraces where you can snap a photo, but you can also climb up the "Royal Way" or head to Petřín sady for more accessible vistas.

STARÉ MĚSTO (OLD TOWN)

Old Town is usually the first stop for any visitor. Old Town Square, its gorgeous houses, and the astronomical clock are blockbuster attractions. On the other hand, the north end of Wenceslas Square—its base, the opposite end from the statue and the museum—is also a good place to begin a tour of Old Town. This "T" intersection marks the border between the old and new worlds in Prague. A quick glance around reveals the often jarring juxtaposition: centuries-old buildings sit side by side with modern retail names like Benetton and Starbucks.

GETTING HERE AND AROUND

There's little public transit in the Old Town, so walking is really the most practical way to get around; you could take a cab, but it's not worth the trouble. It takes about 15 minutes to walk from Náměstí Republiky to Staroměstská. If you're coming to the Old Town from another part of Prague, three metro stops circumscribe the area: Staroměstská on the west, Náměstí Republiky on the east, and Můstek on the south, at the point where Old Town and Wenceslas Square meet.

TIMING

Wenceslas Square and Old Town Square teem with activity around the clock almost year-round. If you're in search of a little peace and quiet, you can find the streets at their most subdued on early weekend mornings or when it's cold. Remember to be in Old Town Square just before the hour if you want to see the astronomical clock in action.

TOP ATTRACTIONS

Clementinum. The origins of this massive complex—now part of the university—date back to the 12th and 13th centuries, but it's best known as the stronghold of the Jesuits, who occupied it for more than 200 years beginning in the early 1600s. Though many buildings are closed to the public, it's well worth a visit. The Jesuits built a resplendent **Baroque Library**, displaying fabulous ceiling murals that portray the three levels of knowledge, with the "Dome of Wisdom" as a centerpiece. Next door, the **Mirror Chapel** is a symphony of reflective surfaces, with acoustics to match. Mozart played here, and the space still hosts chamber music concerts. The **Astronomical Tower** in the middle of the complex was used by Johannes Kepler, and afterward functioned as the "Prague Meridian," where the time was set each day. At high noon a timekeeper would appear on the balcony and wave a flag that could be seen from the castle, where a cannon was fired to mark the hour. ⊠ *Mariánské nám. 5, Staré Mesto* ☎ *222–220–879* ⊕ *www.klementinum.com* ✉ *220 Kč, includes tour* Ⓜ *Line A: Staroměstská.*

Dům U černé Matky boží (*House of the Black Madonna*). In the second decade of the 20th century, young Czech architects boldly applied cubism's radical reworking of visual space to architecture and design. This building, designed by Josef Gočár, is a shining example of this reworking. While there is no longer a museum here, you are free to admire the characteristic geometric lines and sharp angles of the building's exterior. ⊠ *Ovocný trh 19, Staré Mesto* Ⓜ *Line B: Náměstí Republiky.*

Jan Hus monument. Few memorials in Prague elicited as much controversy as this one, dedicated in July 1915, exactly 500 years after Hus was burned at the stake in Constance, Germany. Some maintain that the monument's Secessionist style (the inscription seems to come right from turn-of-the-20th-century Vienna) clashes with the Gothic and baroque style of the square. Others dispute the romantic depiction of Hus, who appears here as tall and bearded in flowing garb, whereas the real Hus, as historians maintain, was short and had a baby face. Either way, the fiery preacher's influence is not in dispute. His ability to transform doctrinal disagreements, both literally and metaphorically, into the language of the common man made him into a religious and national symbol for the Czechs. ⊠ *Staroměstské nám., Staré Mesto* Ⓜ *Line A: Staroměstská.*

Kostel Matky Boží před Týnem (*Church of Our Lady Before Týn*). The twin-spired Týn Church is an Old Town Square landmark and one of the city's best examples of Gothic architecture. The church's exterior was in part the work of Peter Parler, the architect responsible for the Charles Bridge and St. Vitus Cathedral. Construction of the twin black-spire towers began a little later, in 1461, by King Jiří of Poděbrad, during the heyday of the Hussites. Jiří had a gilded chalice, the symbol of the Hussites, proudly displayed on the front gable between the two towers. Following the defeat of the Czech Protestants by the Catholic Hapsburgs in the 17th century, the chalice was melted down and made into the Madonna's glimmering halo (you can still see it resting between the spires). Much of the interior, including the tall nave, was rebuilt

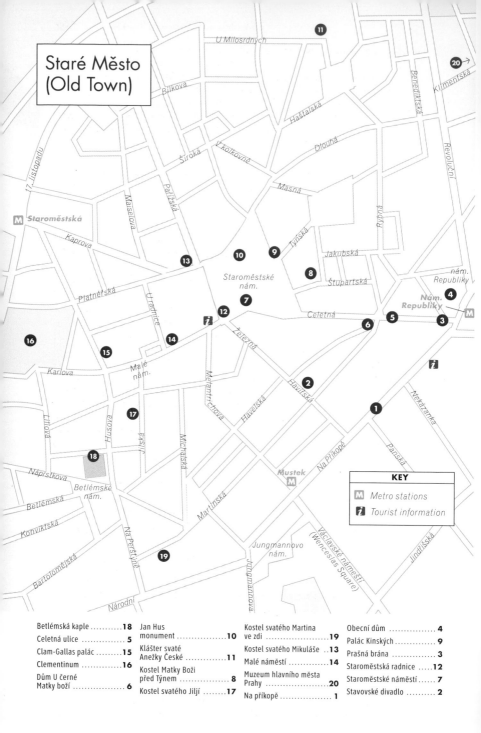

Staré Město
(Old Town)

KEY

Ⓜ Metro stations

🛈 Tourist information

Betlémská kaple **18**

Celetná ulice **5**

Clam-Gallas palác **15**

Clementinum **16**

Dům U černé
Matky boží **6**

Jan Hus
monument **10**

Klášter svaté
Anežky České **11**

Kostel Matky Boží
před Týnem **8**

Kostel svatého Jiljí **17**

Kostel svatého Martina
ve zdi **19**

Kostel svatého Mikuláše ..**13**

Malé náměstí **14**

Muzeum hlavního města
Prahy **20**

Na příkopě **1**

Obecní dům **4**

Palác Kinských **9**

Prašná brána **3**

Staroměstská radnice **12**

Staroměstské náměstí **7**

Stavovské divadlo **2**

in the baroque style in the 17th century. Some Gothic pieces remain, however: look to the left of the main altar for a beautifully preserved set of early carvings. The main altar itself was painted by Karel Škréta, a luminary of the Czech baroque. The church also houses the tomb of renowned Danish (and Prague court) astronomer Tycho Brahe, who died in 1601. ✉ *Staroměstské nám. between Celetná and Týnská, Staré Mesto* ☎ *222–318–186* 🌐 *www.tyn.cz* ⏲ *Closed Mon.–Tues. in July and Aug.* Ⓜ *Line A: Staroměstská.*

Na příkopě. The name means "At the Moat" and harks back to the time when the street was indeed a ditch separating the Old Town from the New Town. Today the pedestrian-only Na příkopě is prime shopping territory. Sleek modern buildings have been sandwiched between baroque palaces, the latter cut up inside to accommodate casinos, boutiques, and fast-food restaurants. The new structures are fairly identical inside, but near the eastern end of the block, Slovanský dům (No. 22) is worth a look. This late-18th-century structure has been tastefully refurbished and now houses fashionable shops, stylish restaurants, and one of the city's best multiplex cinemas. ✉ *Na příkopě, Staré Mesto.*

Obecní dům (*Municipal House*). The city's art nouveau showpiece still fills the role it had when it was completed in 1911 as a center for concerts, rotating art exhibits, and café society. The mature art nouveau style echoes the lengths the Czech middle class went to at the turn of the 20th century to imitate Paris. Much of the interior bears the work of Alfons Mucha, Max Švabinský, and other leading Czech artists. Mucha decorated the Hall of the Lord Mayor upstairs with impressive, magical frescoes depicting Czech history; unfortunately it's visible only as part of a guided tour. The beautiful Smetanova síň (Smetana Hall), which hosts concerts by the Prague Symphony Orchestra as well as international players, is on the second floor. The ground-floor restaurants are overcrowded with tourists but still impressive, with glimmering chandeliers and exquisite woodwork. There's also a beer hall in the cellar, with decent food and ceramic murals on the walls. Tours are normally held at two-hour intervals in the afternoons; check the website for details. ✉ *Nám. Republiky 5, Staré Mesto* ☎ *222–002–101* 🌐 *www.obecnidum.cz* 💴 *Guided tours 380 Kč* Ⓜ *Line B: Náměstí Republiky.*

NEED A BREAK

Hotel Paříž. Head around the corner from Obecní dům to the café at the Hotel Paříž for the café analog of the Municipal House. It's a Jugendstil jewel tucked away on a quiet side street. The lauded, haute-cuisine Restaurant Sarah Bernhardt is next door. At the café, the "old Bohemian" omelet with potatoes and bacon is enough fuel for a full day of sightseeing. ✉ *U Obecního domu 1, Staré Mesto* ☎ *222–195–195* 🌐 *www.hotel-paris.cz* Ⓜ *Line B: Náměstí Republiky.*

Palác Kinských (*Kinský Palace*). This exuberant building, built in 1765 from Kilian Ignaz Dientzenhofer's design, is considered one of Prague's finest rococo, late baroque structures. With its exaggerated pink overlay and numerous statues, it looks extravagant when contrasted with the marginally more somber baroque elements of other nearby buildings. (The interior, alas, was "modernized" under communism.) The palace once contained a German school—where Franz Kafka studied for nine misery-laden years—and now holds the National Gallery's permanent collection of art and artifacts of ancient cultures of Asia and Africa. Communist leader Klement Gottwald, flanked by comrade Vladimír Clementis, first addressed the crowds from this building after seizing power in February 1948—an event recounted in the first chapter of Milan Kundera's novel *The Book of Laughter and Forgetting.* ⊠ *Staroměstské nám. 12, Staré Mesto* ☎ *224–810–759* ⊕ *www. ngprague.cz* ⊠ *100 Kč* ☉ *Closed Mon.* Ⓜ *Line A: Staroměstská.*

> ### SAVING FACE
>
> In the Church of Our Lady Before Týn, find the grave marker (tucked away to the right of the main altar) of the great Danish astronomer Tycho Brahe. Tycho had a firm place in history: Johannes Kepler used his observations to formulate his laws of planetary motion. But it is legend that has endeared Tycho to the hearts of Prague residents. The robust Dane supposedly lost part of his nose in a duel. He quickly had a wax nose fashioned for everyday use but preferred to parade around on holidays and festive occasions sporting a bright metal one.

Prašná brána (*Powder Tower or Powder Gate*). Once used as storage space for gunpowder, this dark, imposing tower—covered in a web of carvings—offers a striking view of the Old Town and Prague Castle from the top. King Vladislav II of Jagiello began construction—it replaced one of the city's 13 original gates—in 1475. At the time, kings of Bohemia maintained their royal residence next door, on the site now occupied by the Obecní dům. The tower was intended to be the grandest gate of all. Vladislav, however, was Polish, and somewhat disliked by the rebellious Czech citizens of Prague. Nine years after he assumed power, and fearing for his life, he moved the royal court across the river to Prague Castle. Work on the tower was abandoned, and the half-finished structure remained a depository for gunpowder until the end of the 17th century. The golden spires were not added until the end of the 19th century. The ticket office is on the first floor, after you go up the dizzyingly narrow stairwell. ⊠ *Nám. Republiky 5/1090, Staré Mesto* ☎ *725–847–875* ⊕ *www.muzeumprahy. cz* ⊠ *75 Kč* Ⓜ *Line B: Náměstí Republiky.*

Fodor's Choice ★ **Staroměstské náměstí** (*Old Town Square*). The hype about Old Town Square is completely justified. Picture a perimeter of colorful baroque houses contrasting with the sweeping old-Gothic style of the Týn church in the background. The unexpectedly large size gives it a majestic presence as it opens up from feeder alleyways. As the heart of Old Town, the square grew to its present proportions when Prague's original marketplace moved away from the river in the 12th century. Its shape and appearance have changed little since that time (the monument to religious reformer Jan Hus, at the center of the square, was erected in the early 20th century). During the day the square pulses with activity, as musicians vie for the attention of visitors milling about. In summer the square's south end is dominated by sprawling outdoor restaurants. During the Easter and Christmas seasons it fills with wooden booths of vendors selling everything from simple wooden toys to fine glassware and mulled wine. At night the brightly lighted towers of the Týn church rise gloriously over the glowing baroque façades.

But the square's history is not all wine and music: During the 15th century the square was the focal point of conflict between Czech Hussites and the mainly Catholic Austrians and Germans. In 1422 the radical Hussite preacher Jan Želivský was executed here for his part in storming the New Town's town hall three years earlier. In the 1419 uprising a judge, a mayor, and seven city council members were thrown out the window—the first of Prague's many famous defenestrations. Within a few years the Hussites had taken over the town, expelled many of the Catholics, and set up their own administration.

> ## PRAGUE PLAYS WITH PLASTER
>
> *Sgraffiti*, plural for *sgraffito,* is a process where two contrasting shades of plaster are used on the façade of a building. Often the *sgraffiti* serve to highlight the original architecture; other times they can produce an optical illusion, painting brickwork and balconies from thin air. Walls can also be covered with lively classical pictures, which make houses resemble enormous Grecian vases. One of the best examples of *sgraffiti* is on Kafka's former residence, U Minuty, just next to the clock tower on Old Town Square.

Twenty-seven white crosses embedded in the square's paving stones, at the base of Old Town Hall, mark the spot where 27 Bohemian noblemen were killed by the Austrian Habsburgs in 1621 during the dark days following the defeat of the Czechs at the Battle of White Mountain. The grotesque spectacle, designed to quash any further national or religious opposition, took about five hours to complete, as the men were put to the sword or hanged one by one. ⊠ *Staroměstské nám., Staré Mesto* Ⓜ *Line A: Staroměstská.*

NEED A BREAK

Café au Gourmand. Just outside of Old Town Square on Dlouhá Street, Café au Gourmand has a delightful selection of authentic French pastries, salads, and sandwiches. There's also a small garden in the back where you can sit with your snacks. ⊠ *Dlouhá 10* ☏ *222–329–060* ⊕ *www.augourmand.cz* Ⓜ *Line A: Staroměstská.*

Fodor'sChoice
★

Staroměstská radnice (*Old Town Hall*). This is a center of Prague life for tourists and locals alike. Hundreds of visitors gravitate here throughout the day to see the hour struck by the mechanical figures of the **astronomical clock.** At the top of the hour, look to the upper part of the clock, where a skeleton begins by tolling a death knell and turning an hourglass upside down. The 12 apostles promenade by, and then a cockerel flaps its wings and screeches as the hour finally strikes. To the right of the skeleton, the dreaded Turk nods his head, almost hinting at another invasion like those of the 16th and 17th centuries. This theatrical spectacle doesn't reveal the way this 15th-century marvel indicates the time—by the season, the zodiac sign, and the positions of the sun and moon. The calendar under the clock dates to the mid-19th century.

DID YOU KNOW?

Yes, the skyline is stunning, but also look down. Old Town Square is marked with 27 white crosses in the paving stones that commemorate the spot where 27 noblemen were killed by the Austrian Hapsburgs in 1621.

Old Town Hall served as the center of administration for Old Town beginning in 1338, when King John of Luxembourg first granted the city council the right to a permanent location. The impressive 200-foot **Town Hall Tower**, where the clock is mounted, was first built in the 14th century. For a rare view of the Old Town and its maze of crooked streets and alleyways, climb the ramp or ride the elevator to the top of the tower.

Walking around the hall to the left, you can see it's actually a series of houses jutting into the square; they were purchased over the years and successively added to the complex. On the other side, jagged stonework reveals where a large, neo-Gothic wing once adjoined the tower until it was destroyed by fleeing Nazi troops in May 1945.

Tours of the interiors depart from the main desk inside (most guides speak English, and English texts are on hand). There's also a branch of the tourist information office here. Previously unseen parts of the tower have now been opened to the public, and you can now see the inside of the famous clock. ⊠ *Staroměstské nám., Staré Mesto* ⊕ *www.staromestskaradnicepraha.cz* 🖃 *130 Kč* Ⓜ *Line A: Staroměstská.*

■ NEED A BREAK

Hotel U Prince. With an entrance diagonally opposite the astronomical clock, Hotel U Prince has an impressive rooftop view. Go through the arched entryway to the right and walk all the way to the back, where you'll find a glass-door elevator. Take the elevator to the rooftop bar, which has covered seating and portable heaters running in cold weather. Be forewarned though: the view doesn't come cheap. ⊠ *Staroměstká nám. 29* ☎ *224–213–807* ⊕ *www.hoteluprince.com* Ⓜ *Line A: Staroměstská.*

WORTH NOTING

Betlémská kaple (*Bethlehem Chapel*). The original church was built at the end of the 14th century, and the Czech religious reformer Jan Hus was a regular preacher here from 1402 until his exile in 1412. Here he gave the mass in "vulgar" Czech—not in Latin as the church in Rome demanded. After the Thirty Years' War in the 17th century, the chapel fell into the hands of the Jesuits and was demolished in 1786. Excavations carried out after World War I uncovered the original portal and three windows; the entire church was reconstructed during the 1950s. Although little remains of the first church, some remnants of Hus's teachings can still be read on the inside walls. ⊠ *Betlémské nám. 3, Staré Mesto* ☎ *224–248–595* 🖃 *60 Kč* Ⓜ *Line A: Staroměstská.*

Celetná ulice. This is the main thoroughfare, which connects Old Town Square and Náměstí Republiky; it's packed day and (most of the) night. Many of the street's façades are styled in classic 17th- or 18th-century manner, but appearances are deceiving: nearly all of the houses in fact have foundations that date back to the 12th century. Be sure to look above the street-level storefronts to see the fine examples of baroque detail. ⊠ *Celetná ulice, Staré Mesto.*

Clam-Gallas palác (*Clam-Gallas Palace*). The work of Johann Bernhard Fischer von Erlach, the famed Viennese baroque virtuoso of the day, is showcased in this earth-tone palace. Construction began in 1713 and finished in 1729. Clam-Gallas palác serves as a state archive, but is also occasionally used to house temporary art exhibitions and concerts. If the building is open, try walking in to glimpse the Italian frescoes depicting Apollo and the battered but intricately carved staircase, done by the master himself. ✉ *Husova 20, Staré Mesto* 🎫 *Free* Ⓜ *Line A: Staroměstská.*

Klášter svaté Anežky České (*St. Agnes's Convent*). Near the river between Pařížská and Revoluční streets, in the northeastern corner of the Old Town, this peaceful complex has Prague's first buildings in the Gothic style. Built between the 1230s and the 1280s, the convent provides a fitting home for the National Gallery's marvelous collection of Czech Gothic art, including altarpieces, portraits, and statues from the 13th to the 16th century. ✉ *U Milosrdných 17, Staré Mesto* ☎ *224–810–628* ⊕ *www.ngprague.cz* 🎫 *150 Kč* Ⓜ *Line A: Staroměstská.*

Kostel svatého Jiljí (*Church of St. Giles*). Replete with buttresses and a characteristic portal, this church's exterior is a powerful example of Gothic architecture. An important outpost of Czech Protestantism in the 16th century, the church reflects baroque style inside, with a design by Johann Bernhard Fischer von Erlach and sweeping frescoes by Václav Reiner. The interior can be viewed during the day from the vestibule or at the evening concerts held several times a week. ✉ *Husova 8, Staré Mesto* ☎ *224–220–235* ⊕ *www.praha.op.cz* 🎫 *Free* Ⓜ *Line A: Staroměstská.*

Kostel svatého Martina ve zdi (*Church of St. Martin-in-the-Wall*). It was here in 1414 that Holy Communion was first given to the Bohemian laity in the form of both bread and wine. (The Catholic custom of the time dictated only bread would be offered to the masses, with wine reserved for priests and clergy.) From then on, the chalice came to symbolize the Hussite movement. The church is sometimes open for evening concerts, held often in summer, or for Sunday service, but that's the only way to see the rather plain interior. ✉ *Martinská 8, Staré Mesto* ⊕ *www.martinvezdi.eu* Ⓜ *Lines A & B: Můstek.*

Kostel svatého Mikuláše (*Church of St. Nicholas*). Designed in the 18th century by Prague's own master of late baroque, Kilian Ignaz Dientzenhofer, this church is probably less successful in capturing the style's lyric exuberance than its namesake across town, the Chrám svatého Mikuláše. But Dientzenhofer utilized the limited space to create a well-balanced structure. The interior is compact, with a beautiful, small chandelier and an enormous black organ that overwhelms the rear of the church. Afternoon and evening concerts for visitors are held almost continuously—walk past and you're sure to get leafleted for one. ✉ *Staroměstské nám., Staré Mesto* ⊕ *www.svmikulas.cz* 🎫 *Free, fee for concerts* Ⓜ *Line A: Staroměstská.*

Malé náměstí (*Small Square*). Note the iron fountain dating to around 1560 in the center of the square. The colorfully painted house at No. 3 was originally a hardware store (and now, confusingly, is the site of a Hard Rock Cafe). It's not as old as it looks, but you can find authentic

Gothic portals and Renaissance *sgraffiti* that reflect the square's true age in certain spots. ⊠ *Malé náměstí, Staré Mesto* Ⓜ *Line A: Staroměstská.*

Muzeum hlavního města Prahy (*Museum of the City of Prague*). This museum is dedicated to the history of the city, and though it's technically in Nové Město, it's relatively easy to reach from Old Town because it's near the Florenc metro and bus stations. The highlight here is a cardboard model of the historic quarter of Prague; it shows what the city looked like before the Jewish ghetto was destroyed in a massive fire in 1689 and includes many buildings that are no longer standing. ⊠ *Na Poříčí 52, Nové Mesto* ☎ *224–816–772* ⊕ *www.muzeumprahy. cz* ✉ *120 Kč* ☉ *Closed Mon.* Ⓜ *Lines B & C: Florenc.*

Stavovské divadlo (*Estates Theater*). Built in the 1780s in the classical style, this opulent, green *palais* hosted the world premiere of Mozart's opera *Don Giovanni* in October 1787 with the composer himself conducting. Prague audiences were quick to acknowledge Mozart's genius: the opera was an instant hit here, though it flopped nearly everywhere else in Europe. Mozart wrote some of the opera's second act in Prague at the Villa Bert, where he was a frequent guest. The program these days is mostly demanding Czech drama, though you can occasionally catch a more accessible opera or musical performance. You must attend a performance to see inside; buy tickets at the Narodní Divadlo. ⊠ *Ovocný trh 1, Staré Mesto* ☎ *224–901–448 for box office* ⊕ *www. narodni-divadlo.cz* Ⓜ *Lines A & B: Můstek.*

JOSEFOV (JEWISH QUARTER)

For centuries Prague had an active, vital Jewish community that was an exuberant part of the city's culture. Much of that activity was concentrated in Josefov, the former Jewish ghetto, just a short walk north of Old Town Square. This area first became a Jewish settlement around the 12th century, but it didn't actually take on the physical aspects of a ghetto—walled off from the rest of the city—until much later.

The history of Prague's Jews, like those of much of Europe, is mostly a sad one. There were horrible pogroms in the late Middle Ages, followed by a period of relative prosperity under Rudolf II in the late 16th century, though the freedoms of Jews were still tightly restricted. It was Austrian Emperor Josef II—the ghetto's namesake—who did the most to improve the conditions of the city's Jews. His "Edict of Tolerance" in 1781 removed dress codes for Jews and paved the way for Jews finally to live in other parts of the city.

The prosperity of the 19th century lifted the Jews out of poverty, and many of them chose to leave the ghetto. By the end of the century the number of poor gentiles, drunks, and prostitutes in the ghetto was growing, and the number of actual Jews was declining. At this time, city officials decided to clear the slum and raze the buildings. In their place they built many of the gorgeous turn-of-the-20th-century and art nouveau town houses you see today. Only a handful of the synagogues, the town hall, and the cemetery were preserved.

World War II and the Nazi occupation brought profound tragedy to the city's Jews. A staggering percentage were deported—many to Terezín, north of Prague, and then later to German Nazi death camps in Poland. Of the 40,000 Jews living in Prague before World War II, only about 1,200 returned after the war, and merely a handful live in the ghetto today.

The Nazi occupation contains a historic irony. Many of the treasures stored away in Prague's Jewish Museum were brought here from across Central Europe on Hitler's orders. His idea was to form a museum dedicated to the soon-to-be extinct Jewish race.

Today, even with the crowds, the ghetto is a must-see. The Old Jewish Cemetery alone, with its incredibly forlorn overlay of headstone upon headstone going back centuries, merits the steep admission price the Jewish Museum charges to see its treasures. Don't feel compelled to linger long on the ghetto's streets after visiting, though—much of it is tourist-trap territory, filled with overpriced T-shirt, trinket, and toy shops—the same lousy souvenirs found everywhere in Prague.

A ticket to the Židovské muzeum v Praze (Prague Jewish Museum) includes admission to the Old Jewish Cemetery and collections installed in four surviving synagogues and the Ceremony Hall. The Staronová synagóga, or Old-New Synagogue, a functioning house of worship, does not technically belong to the museum, and requires a separate admission ticket.

GETTING HERE AND AROUND

The Jewish Quarter is one of the most heavily visited areas in Prague, especially in peak tourist seasons, when its tiny streets are jammed to bursting. The best way to visit is on foot—it's a short hop over from Old Town Square.

TIMING

The best time for a visit (read: quiet and less crowded) is early morning, when the museums and cemetery first open. The area itself is very compact, and a fairly thorough tour should take only half a day. Don't go on the Sabbath (Saturday), when all the museums are closed.

TOP ATTRACTIONS

Klausová synagóga (*Klausen Synagogue*). This baroque synagogue displays objects from Czech Jewish traditions, with an emphasis on celebrations and daily life. The synagogue was built at the end of the 17th century in place of three small buildings (a synagogue, a school, and a ritual bath) that were destroyed in a fire that devastated the ghetto in 1689. In the more recent **Obřadní síň** (Ceremony Hall) that adjoins the Klausen Synagogue, the focus is more staid. You'll find a variety of Jewish funeral paraphernalia, including old gravestones, and medical instruments. Special attention is paid to the activities of the Jewish Burial Society through many fine objects and paintings. ⊠ *U starého hřbitova 3A, Josefov* ☎ *222–317–191* ⊕ *www.jewishmuseum.cz* ✍ *300 Kč museums only, 200 Kč Old-New Synagogue* ۞ *Closed Sat. and during Jewish holidays* Ⓜ *Line A: Staroměstská.*

NEED A BREAK

Les Moules. Crave a culinary change from constant meat and potatoes? Try the Belgian-styled bistro Les Moules, at the end of Maiselova. There's a nice open terrace and a fine selection of mussels, as you'd expect from

Klausová
synagóga 2
Maiselova
synagóga 7
Pinkasova
synagóga 6
Rudolfinum 5
Španělská
synagóga 9
Staronová
synagóga 1
Starý zidovský
hřbitov 3
Uměleckoprůmys-
lové museum v
Praze 4
Židovská
radnice 8

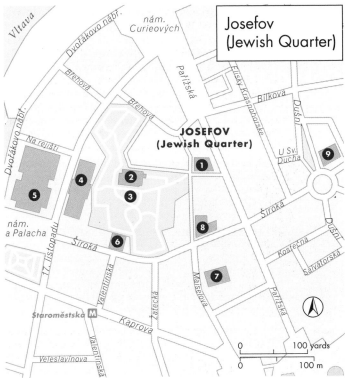

the name. If you're tired of Pilsner Urquell, too, they have a variety of Belgian Trappist beers. ✉ *Pařižská 19, Staré Mesto* ☎ *222-315-022* ⊕ *www. lesmoules.cz* Ⓜ *Linc A: Staroměstská.*

Maiselova synagóga. The history of Czech Jews from the 10th to the 18th century is illustrated, accompanied by some of the Prague Jewish Museum's most precious objects. The collection includes silver Torah shields and pointers, spice boxes, and candelabra; historic tombstones; and fine ceremonial textiles—some donated by Mordechai Maisel to the very synagogue he founded. The glitziest items come from the late 16th and early 17th centuries, a prosperous era for Prague's Jews. ✉ *Maiselova 10, Josefov* ☎ *222-317-191* ⊕ *www.jewishmuseum.cz* 🎫 *300 Kč museums only, 200 Kč Old-New Synagogue* ☉ *Closed Sat. and during Jewish holidays* Ⓜ *Line A: Staroměstská.*

Pinkasova synagóga (*Pinkas Synagogue*). Here you'll find two moving testimonies to the appalling crimes perpetrated against the Jews during World War II. One astounds by sheer numbers: the walls are covered with nearly 80,000 names of Bohemian and Moravian Jews murdered by the Nazis. Among them are the names of the paternal grandparents of former U.S. Secretary of State Madeleine Albright. The second is an exhibition of drawings made by children at the Nazi concentration camp Terezín, north of Prague. The Nazis used the camp for propaganda purposes to demonstrate their "humanity" toward Jews, and for a time the prisoners were given relative freedom to lead "normal" lives. However, transports to death camps in Poland began in earnest in 1944, and many thousands of Terezín prisoners, including most of these children, eventually perished. The entrance to the Old Jewish Cemetery is through this synagogue. ⊠ *Široká 3, Josefov* ☎ *222–317– 191* ⊕ *www.jewishmuseum.cz* ⊠ *300 Kč museums only, 200 Kč Old- New Synagogue* ☉ *Closed Sat. and during Jewish holidays* Ⓜ *Line A: Staroměstská.*

Rudolfinum. This 19th-century neo-Renaissance monument has some of the cleanest, brightest stonework in the city. Designed by Josef Zítek and Josef Schulz and completed in 1884—it was named for then Hapsburg Crown Prince Rudolf—the low-slung sandstone building was meant to be a combination concert hall and exhibition gallery. After 1918 it was converted into the parliament of the newly independent Czechoslovakia until German invaders reinstated the concert hall in 1939. Now the Czech Philharmonic has its home base here. The 1,200-seat **Dvořákova síň** (Dvořák Hall) has superb acoustics (the box office faces 17 Listopadu Street). To see the hall, you must attend a concert. ⊠ *Alšovo nábřeží 12, Josefov* ☎ *227–059–227* ⊕ *www.rudolfinum.cz* Ⓜ *Line A: Staroměstská.*

Staronová synagóga (*Old-New Synagogue, or Altneuschul*). Dating to the mid-13th century, this is the oldest functioning synagogue in Europe and one of the most important works of early Gothic in Prague. The name refers to the legend that the synagogue was built on the site of an ancient Jewish temple, and the temple's stones were used to build the present structure. Amazingly, the synagogue has survived fires, the razing of the ghetto, and the Nazi occupation intact; it's still in use. The entrance, with its vault supported by two pillars, is the oldest part of the synagogue. Note that men are required to cover their heads inside, and during services men and women sit apart. ⊠ *Červená 2, Josefov* ☎ *222–317–191* ⊕ *www.jewishmuseum.cz* ⊠ *200 Kč* ☉ *Closed Sat. and during Jewish holidays* Ⓜ *Line A: Staroměstská.*

Fodor'sChoice
★

Starý židovský hřbitov (*Old Jewish Cemetery*). An unforgettable sight, this cemetery is where all Jews living in Prague from the 15th century to 1787 were laid to rest. The lack of any space in the tiny ghetto forced graves to be piled on top of one another. Tilted at crazy angles, the 12,000 visible tombstones are but a fraction of countless thousands more buried below. Walk the path amid the gravestones; the relief symbols you see represent the names and professions of the deceased. The oldest marked grave belongs to the poet Avigdor Kara, who died in 1439; the grave is not accessible from the pathway, but the original tombstone can be seen in the Maisel Synagogue. The best-known marker belongs to Jehuda ben Bezalel, the famed Rabbi Loew (died 1609), a chief rabbi of Prague and a profound scholar, credited with creating the mythical Golem. Even today, small scraps of paper bearing wishes are stuffed into the cracks of the rabbi's tomb with the hope that he will grant them. Loew's grave lies near the exit. ✉ *Široká 3, enter through Pinkasova synagóga, Josefov* ☎ *222-317-191* ⊕ *www.jewishmuseum.cz* 💳 *300 Kč museums only, 200 Kč Old-New Synagogue* ⊘ *Closed Sat. and during Jewish holidays* Ⓜ *Line A: Staroměstská.*

Uměleckoprůmyslové museum v Praze (*Museum of Decorative Arts or U(P)M*). In a custom-built art nouveau building from 1897, this wonderfully laid-out museum of exquisite local prints, books, ceramics, textiles, clocks, and furniture will please anyone from the biggest decorative arts expert to those who just appreciate a little *Antiques Roadshow* on the

TOURIST TRAPS

Walking through Old Town Square and on Celetná it's almost impossible not to be accosted by men in Mozart costumes or guides selling hour-long bus tours. Just know: Most of the concerts are dismissed as "tourist music" by locals. There are better performers in the city's much more authentic classical music venues. As for the tours, remember that Prague is blessed with a fantastic and efficient public transportation system—why shell out to take a bus when you can ride a tram with the same view?

weekend. Superb rotating exhibits, too. ✉ *17. listopadu 2, Josefov* ☎ *251-093-111* ⊕ *www.upm.cz* 💳 *120 Kč* ⊘ *Closed Mon.* Ⓜ *Line A: Staroměstská.*

WORTH NOTING

Španělská synagóga (*Spanish Synagogue*). This domed, Moorish-style synagogue was built in 1868 on the site of an older synagogue, the Altschul. Here the historical exposition that begins in the Maisel Synagogue continues to the post–World War II period. The attached Robert Guttmann Gallery has historic and well-curated art exhibitions. The building's painstakingly restored interior is also worth experiencing. ✉ *Vězeňská 1, Josefov* ☎ *222-317-191* ⊕ *www.jewishmuseum.cz* 💳 *300 Kč museums only, 200 Kč Old-New Synagogue* ⊘ *Closed Sat. and during Jewish holidays.*

Židovská radnice (*Jewish Town Hall*). The hall was the creation of Mordechai Maisel, an influential Jewish leader at the end of the 16th century. Restored in the 18th century, it was given a clock and bell tower at that time. A second clock, with Hebrew numbers, keeps time counterclockwise. Now a Jewish Community Center, the building also houses Shalom, a kosher restaurant. Neither the hall nor the restaurant is open to the public, but the beautiful building is worth seeing from the outside. ✉ *Maiselova 18, Josefov* Ⓜ *Line A: Staroměstská.*

MALÁ STRANA (LESSER QUARTER)

Established in 1257, this is Prague's most perfectly formed— yet totally asymmetrical—neighborhood. Also known as "Little Town," it was home to the merchants and craftsmen who served the royal court. Though not nearly as confusing as the labyrinth that is Old Town, the streets in the Lesser Quarter can baffle, but they also bewitch, and today the area holds embassies, Czech government offices, historical attractions, and galleries mixed in with the usual glut of pubs, restaurants, and souvenir shops.

GETTING HERE AND AROUND

Metro Line A will lead you to Malá Strana, the Malostranká station being the most central stop (from here, take Tram No. 12, 20, or 26 one stop to Malostranké náměstí). But there's no better way to arrive at Malá Strana than via a scenic downhill walk from the Castle or a lovely stroll from Old Town across the Charles Bridge.

TIMING

Note that the heat builds up during the day in this area—as do the crowds—so it's best visited before noon or in early evening. On literally every block there are plenty of cafés in which to stop, sip coffee or tea, and people-watch, and a wealth of gardens and parks ideal for resting in cool shade. As with the other most popular neighborhoods of Prague—Old Town, New Town, and the Castle Area—there are fewer crowds in the early morning or in the bitter cold. (The former is preferable over the latter.)

TOP ATTRACTIONS

Chrám svatého Mikuláše (*Church of St. Nicholas*). With its dynamic curves, this church is arguably the purest and most ambitious example of high baroque in Prague. The celebrated architect Christoph Dientzenhofer began the Jesuit church in 1704 on the site of one of the more active Hussite churches of 15th-century Prague. Work on the building was taken over by his son Kilian Ignaz Dientzenhofer, who built the dome and presbytery. Anselmo Lurago completed the whole thing in 1755 by adding the bell tower. The juxtaposition of the broad, full-bodied dome with the slender bell tower is one of the many striking architectural contrasts that mark the Prague skyline. Inside, the vast pink-and-green space is impossible to take in with a single glance. Every corner bristles with life, guiding the eye first to the dramatic statues, then to the hectic frescoes, and on to the shining faux-marble pillars. Many of the statues are the work of Ignaz Platzer and constitute his last blaze of success. Platzer's workshop was forced to declare bankruptcy when the centralizing and secularizing reforms of Joseph II toward the end of the 18th century brought an end to the flamboyant baroque era. The tower, with an entrance on the side of the church, is open in summer. The church also hosts chamber music concerts in summer, which complement this eye-popping setting but do not reflect the true caliber of classical music in Prague. For that, check the schedule posted across the street at **Líchtenský palác,** where the faculty of HAMU, the city's premier music academy, sometimes also gives performances. ⊠ *Malostranské nám., Malá Strana* ☏ *257–534–215* ⊕ *www.stnicholas. cz* 🎫 *Tower 70 Kč, concerts 490 Kč* Ⓜ *Line A: Malostranská plus Tram No. 12, 20, or 22.*

Franz Kafka Museum. The great early-20th-century Jewish author Kafka wasn't considered Czech and he wrote in German, but he lived in Prague nearly his entire short, anguished life, so it's fitting that he's finally gotten the shrine he deserves here. Because the museum's designers believed in channeling Kafka's darkly paranoid and paradoxical work, they created exhibits true to this spirit. And even if the results are often goofy, they get an "A" for effort. Facsimiles of manuscripts, documents, first editions, photographs, and newspaper obits are displayed in glass vitrines, which in turn are situated in "Kafkaesque" settings: huge open filing cabinets, stone gardens, piles of coal. The basement level of the museum gets even freakier, with expressionistic representations of Kafka's work itself, including a model of the horrible torture machine from the "Penal Colony" story—not a place for young children, or even lovers on a first date, but fascinating to anyone familiar with Kafka's work. Other Kafka sites in Prague include his home on Golden Lane, his Old Town birthplace at Náměstí Franze Kafky 3, and Jaroslav Rona's trippy bronze sculpture of the writer on Dušní Street in the Old Town. (Speaking of sculptures, take a gander at the animatronic *Piss* statue in the Kafka Museum's courtyard. This rendition of a couple urinating into a fountain shaped like the Czech Republic was made by local enfant terrible sculptor David Černy, who also did the babies crawling up the Žižkov TV Tower.) ⊠ *Hergetova Cihelna, Cihelna 2b, Malá*

Strana ☎ *257–535–507* ⊕ *www.kafkamuseum.cz* 📖 *180 Kč* Ⓜ *Line A: Malostranská.*

FAMILY **Kampa.** Prague's largest "island" is cut off from the "mainland" by the narrow Čertovka streamlet. The name Čertovka, or "Devil's Stream," reputedly refers to a cranky old lady who once lived on Maltese Square. During the historic 2002 floods, the well-kept lawns of the **Kampa Gardens,** which occupy much of the island, were covered as was much of the lower portion of Malá Strana. Evidence of flood damage occasionally marks the landscape, along with a sign indicating where the waters crested. ✉ *Kampa, Malá Strana* Ⓜ *Line A: Malostranská.*

Fodor's Choice **Karlův most** *(Charles Bridge).* This is Prague's signature monument. The
★   view from the foot of the bridge on the Old Town side, encompassing the towers and domes of the Lesser Quarter and the soaring spires of St. Vitus's Cathedral, is breathtaking. After several wooden bridges and the first stone bridge washed away in floods, Charles IV appointed the 27-year-old German Peter Parler, the architect of St. Vitus's Cathedral, to build a new structure in 1357. It became one of the wonders of the world in the Middle Ages. Its heavenly vista subtly changes in perspective as you walk across the bridge, attended by a host of baroque saints from the late 17th century (most now copies) that decorate the bridge's peaceful Gothic stones. *For more information, see the highlighted feature in this chapter.*

█ NEED A
BREAK

Bohemia Bagel. This informal breakfast and sandwich spot is just steps away from the Charles Bridge. When it opened more than a decade ago, it was a welcome addition for homesick expats as it was the first chain in town to offer homemade bagels, along with soups and salads. ✉ *Lázenská 19, Malá Strana* ☎ *257–218–192* ⊕ *www.bohemiabagel.cz* Ⓜ *Line A: Malostranská plus Tram No. 12, 20, or 22.*

Kostel Panny Marie vítězné *(Church of Our Lady Victorious).* This aging, well-appointed church on the Lesser Quarter's main street is the unlikely home of Prague's most famous religious artifact, the Pražské Jezulátko (Infant Jesus of Prague). Originally brought to Prague from Spain in the 16th century, the wax doll holds a reputation for bestowing miracles on many who have prayed for its help. A measure of its widespread attraction is reflected in the prayer books on the kneelers in front of the statue, which have prayers of intercession in 20 different languages. The "Bambino," as he's known locally, has an enormous and incredibly ornate wardrobe, some of which is on display in a museum upstairs. Nuns from a nearby convent change the outfit on the statue regularly. Don't miss the souvenir shop (accessible via a doorway to the right of the main altar), where the Bambino's custodians flex their marketing skills. ✉ *Karmelitská 9A, Malá Strana* ☎ *257–533–646* ⊕ *www.pragjesu.cz* 📖 *Free* Ⓜ *Line A: Malostranská plus Tram No. 12, 20, or 22.*

Malostranské náměstí *(Lesser Quarter Square).* Another one of the many classic examples of Prague's charm, this square is flanked on the east and south sides by arcaded houses dating from the 16th and 17th centuries. The Czech Parliament resides partly in the gaudy yellow-and-green palace on the square's north side, partly in a building on

Sněmovní Street, behind the palace. The huge bulk of the Church of St. Nicholas divides the lower, busier section—buzzing with restaurants, street vendors, clubs, and shops—from the slightly quieter upper part. ✉ *Malá Strana.*

Museum Kampa. The spotlighted jewel on Kampa Island is a remodeled flour mill that displays a private collection of paintings by Czech artist František Kupka and first-rate temporary exhibitions by both Czech and other Central European visual wizards. The museum was hit hard by flooding in 2002 and 2013, but rebounded relatively quickly on both occasions. The outdoor terrace offers a splendid view of the river and historic buildings on the opposite bank. ✉ *U Sovových mlýnů 2, Malá Strana* ☎ *257–286–113* ⊕ *www.museumkampa.cz* 💰*240 Kč* Ⓜ *Line A: Malostranská plus Tram No. 12, 20, or 22.*

Nerudova ulice. This steep street used to be the last leg of the "Royal Way," the king's procession before his coronation. As king, he made the ascent on horseback, not huffing and puffing on foot like today's visitors. It was named for the 19th-century Czech journalist and poet Jan Neruda, after whom Chilean poet Pablo Neruda renamed himself. Until Joseph II's administrative reforms in the late 18th century, house numbering was unknown in Prague. Each house bore a name, depicted on the façade, and these are particularly prominent on Nerudova ulice. AT No. 6, U červeného orla (At the Red Eagle) proudly displays a faded painting of a crimson eagle. Number 12 is known as U tří housliček (At the Three Fiddles); in the early 18th century three generations of the Edlinger violin-making family lived here. Joseph II's scheme numbered each house according to its position in the "town" (here, the Lesser Quarter) to which it belonged, rather than its sequence on the street. The red plates record the original house numbers, but the blue ones are the numbers used in addresses today. Many architectural guides refer to the old, red-number plates, much to the confusion of visitors.

Two large palaces break the unity of the houses on Nerudova ulice. Both were designed by the adventurous baroque architect Giovanni Santini, one of the popular Italian builders hired by wealthy nobles in the early 18th century. The **Morzin Palace,** on the left at No. 5, is now the Romanian Embassy. The fascinating façade, created in 1713 with an allegory of night and day, is the work of Ferdinand Brokoff, of Charles Bridge statue fame. Across the street at No. 20 is the **Thun-Hohenstein Palace,** now the Italian Embassy. The gateway with two enormous eagles (the emblem of the Kolovrat family, who owned the building at the time) is the work of the other great Charles Bridge statue sculptor, Mathias Braun. Santini himself lived at No. 14, the **Valkoun House.**

The archway at No. 13 is a prime example of the many winding passageways that give the Lesser Quarter its captivatingly ghostly character at night. Higher up the street at No. 33 is the **Bretfeld Palace,** a rococo house on the corner of Jánský vršek. The relief of St. Nicholas on the façade was created by Ignaz Platzer, a sculptor known for his classical and rococo work. But it's the building's historical associations that give it intrigue: Mozart, his librettist partner Lorenzo da Ponte, and the aging but still infamous philanderer and music lover Casanova

DID YOU KNOW?

According to popular super-
stition, touching the eighth
statue on the right of the
Charles Bridge, St. John of
Nepomuk, is said to bring a
return visit to Prague.

stayed here at the time of the world premiere of *Don Giovanni* in 1787. ⊠ *Nerudova ulice.*

FAMILY **Petřínské sady** (*Petřín Park or Petřín Gardens*). For a superb view of the city—from a slightly more solitary perch—the park on top of Petřín Hill includes a charming playground for children and adults alike, with a miniature (but still pretty big) Eiffel Tower. You'll also find a mirror maze (*bludiště*), as well as a working observatory and the seemingly abandoned Svatý Vavřinec (St. Lawrence) church. To get here from Malá Strana, simply hike up Petřín Hill (from Karmelitská ulice or Újezd) or ride the funicular railway (which departs near the Újezd tram stop). Regular public-transportation tickets are valid on the funicular.

TAKING YOU FOR A RIDE

Sadly, Prague has a deserved reputation for dishonest taxi drivers. In an honest cab, the meter starts at 40 Kč and increases by 28 Kč per km (½ mile) or 6 Kč per minute at rest. A typical ride around the center, depending on the distance, of course, should cost no more than 280 Kč. The best way to avoid getting ripped off is to ask your hotel or restaurant to call a cab for you. (AAA Taxi is the best-known and most trustworthy company.) The good news is that big improvements have been made and the chance of hailing an honest cab on the street has greatly improved.

From the Castle district, you can also stroll over from Strahov klášter (Strahov Monastery), following a wide path that crosses above some fruit orchards and offers some breathtaking views out over the city below. ⊠ *Petřín Hill, Malá Strana* ⊕ *www.muzeumprahy.cz* ✉ *Observatory 65 Kč, tower 120 Kč, maze 90 Kč* Ⓜ *Line A: Malostranská plus Tram No. 12, 20, or 22 to Újezd (plus funicular).*

Valdštejnska Zahrada (*Wallenstein Palace Gardens*). With its idiosyncratic high-walled gardens and superb, vaulted Renaissance *sala terrena* (room opening onto a garden), this palace displays superbly elegant grounds. Walking around the formal paths, you come across numerous fountains and statues depicting figures from classical mythology or warriors dispatching a variety of beasts. However, nothing beats the trippy "Grotto," a huge dripstone wall packed with imaginative rock formations, like little faces and animals hidden in the charcoal-colored landscape, and what's billed as "illusory hints of secret corridors." Here, truly, staring at the wall is a form of entertainment. Albrecht von Wallenstein, onetime owner of the house and gardens, began a meteoric military career in 1622, when the Austrian emperor Ferdinand II retained him to save the empire from the Swedes and Protestants during the Thirty Years' War. Wallenstein, wealthy by marriage, offered to raise an army of 20,000 men at his own cost and lead them personally. Ferdinand II accepted and showered Wallenstein with confiscated land and titles. Wallenstein's first acquisition was this enormous area. After knocking down 23 houses, a brick factory, and three gardens, in 1623 he began to build his magnificent palace. Most of the palace itself now serves the Czech Senate as meeting chamber and offices. The palace's cavernous former Jízdárna, or riding school, now hosts art exhibitions.

✉ *Letenská 10, Malá Strana* ☎ *257-075-707* ⊕ *www.senat.cz* 🎫 *Free* Ⓜ *Line A: Malostranská.*

Vrtbovská zahrada (*Vrtba Garden*). An unobtrusive door on noisy Karmelitská hides the entranceway to a fascinating sanctuary with one of the best views of the Lesser Quarter. The street door opens onto the intimate courtyard of the Vrtbovský palác (Vrtba Palace). Two Renaissance wings flank the courtyard; the left one was built in 1575, the right one in 1591. The original owner of the latter house was one of the 27 Bohemian nobles executed by the Habsburgs in 1621. The house was given as confiscated property to Count Sezima of Vrtba, who bought the neighboring property and turned the buildings into a late-Renaissance palace. The Vrtba Garden was created a century later. Built in five levels rising behind the courtyard in a wave of statuary-bedecked staircases and formal terraces reaching toward a seashell-decorated pavilion at the top, it's a popular spot for weddings, receptions, and occasional concerts. (The fenced-off garden immediately behind and above belongs to the U.S. Embassy—hence the U.S. flag that often flies there.) The powerful stone figure of Atlas that caps the entranceway in the courtyard and most of the other statues of mythological figures are from the workshop of Mathias Braun, perhaps the best of the Czech baroque sculptors. ✉ *Karmelitská 25, Malá Strana* ☎ *272-088-350* ⊕ *www.vrtbovska.cz* 🎫 *65 Kč* Ⓜ *Line A: Malostranská plus Tram No. 12, 20, or 22.*

WORTH NOTING

Palácové zahrady pod Pražským hradem (*Gardens Below Prague Castle*). A break in the houses along Valdštejnská ulice opens to a gate that leads to five beautifully manicured and terraced baroque gardens, which in season are open to the public. A combined-entry ticket allows you to wander at will, climbing up and down the steps and trying to find the little entryways that lead from one garden to the next. Each of the gardens bears the name of a noble family and includes the Kolowrat (Kolovratská zahrada), Ledeburg (Ledeburská zahrada), Small and Large Palffy (Malá a Velká Pálffyovská zahrada), and Furstenberg (Furstenberská zahrada). You can also enter directly from the upper, south gardens of Prague Castle in summer. ✉ *Valdštejnská 12–14, Malá Strana* ☎ *257-214-817* ⊕ *www.palacove-zahrady.cz* 🎫 *90 Kč* Ⓜ *Line A: Malostranská.*

Schönbornský palác (*Schönborn Palace*). Franz Kafka had an apartment in this massive baroque building at the top of Tržiště ulice in mid-1917, after moving from Zlatá ulička, or Golden Lane. The U.S. Embassy and consular office now occupy this prime location. Although security is stepped down compared with a few years ago, the many police, guards, and jersey barriers don't offer much of an invitation to linger. ✉ *Tržiště 15, at Vlašská, Malá Strana* Ⓜ *Line A: Malostranská plus Tram No. 12, 20, or 22.*

Velkopřevorské náměstí (*Grand Priory Square*). This square is south and slightly west of the Charles Bridge, next to the Čertovka stream. The Grand Prior's Palace fronting the square is considered one of the finest baroque buildings in the Lesser Quarter, though it's now part of the

The John Lennon Peace Wall on Kampa Island continues to be marked with free-spirited, antiwar graffiti years after his death.

Embassy of the Sovereign Military Order of Malta—the contemporary (and very real) descendants of the Knights of Malta. Alas, it's closed to the public. Opposite is the flamboyant orange-and-white stucco façade of the Buquoy Palace, built in 1719 by Giovanni Santini and the present home of the French Embassy. The so-called **John Lennon Peace Wall**, leading to a bridge over the Čertovka, was once a kind of monument to youthful rebellion, emblazoned with a large painted head of the former Beatle. But Lennon's visage is seldom seen these days; the wall is usually covered instead with political and music-related graffiti. ⊠ *Velkopřevorské náměstí, Malá Strana* Ⓜ *Line A: Malostranská plus Tram No. 12, 20, or 22.*

FAMILY **Vojanovy sady** (*Vojan Park*). Once the gardens of the Monastery of the Discalced Carmelites, later taken over by the Order of the English Virgins, this walled garden is now part of the Ministry of Finance. With its weeping willows, fruit trees, and benches, it provides another peaceful haven in summer. Exhibitions of modern sculpture are occasionally held here, contrasting sharply with the two baroque chapels and the graceful Ignaz Platzer statue of John of Nepomuk standing on a fish at the entrance. At the other end of the park you can find a terrace with a formal rose garden and a pair of peacocks that like to aggressively preen for visitors under the trellises. The park is surrounded by the high walls of the old monastery and new Ministry of Finance buildings, with only an occasional glimpse of a tower or spire to remind you of the world beyond. ⊠ *U lužického semináře 17, between Letenská ulice and Míšeňská ulice, Malá Strana* ⊕ *www.vojanovysady.cz* Ⓜ *Line A: Malostranská.*

2

HRADČANY (CASTLE AREA)

To the west of Prague Castle is the residential Hradčany (Castle Area), a town that during the early 14th century emerged from a collection of monasteries and churches. The concentration of history packed into Prague Castle and Hradčany challenges those not versed in the ups and downs of Bohemian kings, religious uprisings, wars, and oppression—but there's no shame in taking it all in on a purely aesthetic level.

GETTING HERE AND AROUND

There's a rise from river level of nearly 1,300 vertical feet to get to the Castle Area, so if you're on foot, be prepared for a climb. The best Metro approach is via Line A. ■ **TIP→ Don't get off at the Hradčanská stop (as the name might imply).** Instead, take the metro to Malostranská, and after exiting the station, take Tram No. 22 running north (uphill) to the stop Pražský hrad (Prague Castle). The tram leaves you about 200 yards north of the Castle.

TIMING

To do justice to the subtle charms of Hradčany once you arrive, allow at least two hours just for ambling and admiring the passing buildings and views of the city. The Strahovský klášter halls need about a half hour to take in, more if you tour the small picture gallery there, and the Loreta and its treasures need an equal length of time at least. The Národní galerie in the Šternberský palác deserves a minimum of a couple of hours. Keep in mind that several places are not open on Monday, and that early morning is the least crowded time to visit.

TOP ATTRACTIONS

Hradčanské náměstí (*Hradčany Square*). With its fabulous mixture of baroque and Renaissance houses, topped by the Castle itself, this square had a prominent role in the film *Amadeus* (as a substitute for Vienna). Czech director Miloš Forman used the house at No. 7 for Mozart's residence, where the composer was haunted by the masked figure he thought was his father. The flamboyant rococo Arcibiskupský palác (Archbishop's Palace), on the left as you face the Castle, was the Viennese archbishop's palace. For a brief time after World War II, No. 11 was home to a little girl named Marie Jana Korbelová, better known as former U.S. Secretary of State Madeleine Albright. ✉ *Hradčanské náměstí, Hradcany* Ⓜ *Line A: Malostranská plus Tram No. 22.*

Schwarzenberský palác (*Schwarzenberg Palace*). A boxy palace with an extravagant façade, this space is home to the National Gallery's permanent exhibition of baroque sculpture and paintings. Among the masters featured are Peter Brandl, Maximilian Brokof, and the sculptor Mathias Braun (whose work you've seen on the Charles Bridge). With arched ceilings and displays on how artists worked and what their studios were like during the baroque period, the Schwarzenberg interior is every bit as exuberant as the outside, and its hushed vibe might provide just the antidote to those tourist hordes outside. ✉ *Hradčanské nám. 2, Hradcany* ☎ *233–081–713* 🌐 *www.ngprague.cz* 🎫 *300 Kč* ⏲ *Closed Mon.* Ⓜ *Line A: Malostranská plus Tram No. 22.*

Šternberský palác (*Sternberg Palace*). The 18th-century Šternberský palác houses the National Gallery's collection of antiquities and paintings by European masters from the 14th to the 18th century. Holdings include impressive works by El Greco, Rubens, and Rembrandt. ✉ *Hradčanské nám. 15, Hradcany* ☎ *233–090–570* 🌐 *www.ngprague.cz* 🎫 *300 Kč* ⏲ *Closed Mon.* Ⓜ *Line A: Malostranská plus Tram No. 22.*

WORTH NOTING

Loreta (*Loreto Church*). The seductive lines of this church were a conscious move on the part of Counter-Reformation Jesuits in the 17th century, who wanted to build up the cult of Mary and attract Protestant Bohemians back to the fold. According to legend, angels had carried Mary's house from Nazareth and dropped it in a patch of laurel trees in Ancona, Italy. Known as Loreto (from the Latin for "laurel"), it immediately became a destination of pilgrimage. The Prague Loreto was one of many symbolic reenactments of this scene across Europe, and it worked: Pilgrims came in droves. The graceful façade, with its voluptuous tower, was built in 1720 by the ubiquitous Kilian Ignaz Dientzenhofer, the architect of the two St. Nicholas churches in Prague. ✉ *Loretánské nám. 7, Hradcany* ☎ *220–516–740* 🌐 *www.loreta.cz* 🎫 *150 Kč* Ⓜ *Malostranská plus Tram No. 22.*

Nový Svět. This picturesque, winding little alley, with façades from the 17th and 18th centuries, once housed Prague's poorest residents, but now many of the homes are used as artists' studios. The last house on the street, No. 1, was the home of the Danish-born astronomer Tycho

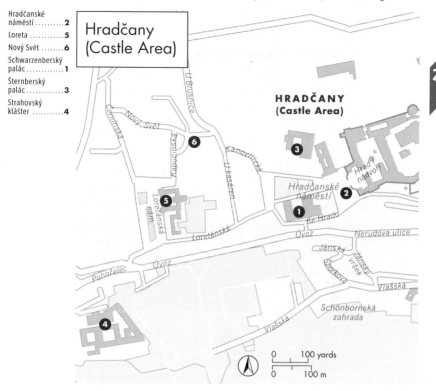

Hradčanské
náměstí 2
Loreta 5
Nový Svět 6
Schwarzenberský
palác 1
Šternberský
palác.............3
Strahovský
klášter 4

Hradčany
(Castle Area)

**HRADČANY
(Castle Area)**

2

Brahe. Supposedly Tycho was constantly disturbed during his nightly stargazing by the neighboring Loreto's church bells. He ended up complaining to his patron, Emperor Rudolf II, who instructed the Capuchin monks to finish their services before the first star appeared in the sky. ⊠ *Nový Svět, Hradcany* Ⓜ *Line A: Malostranská plus Tram No. 22.*

Strahovský klášter (*Strahov Monastery*). Founded by the Premonstratensian order in 1140, the monastery remained theirs until 1952, when the communists suppressed all religious orders and turned the entire complex into the **Památník národního písemnictví** (Museum of National Literature). The major building of interest is the **Strahov Library,** with its collection of early Czech manuscripts, the 10th-century Strahov New Testament, and the collected works of famed Danish astronomer Tycho Brahe. Also of note is the late-18th-century **Philosophical Hall.** Its ceilings are engulfed in a startling sky-blue fresco that depicts an unusual cast of characters, including Socrates' nagging wife Xanthippe; Greek astronomer Thales, with his trusty telescope; and a collection of Greek philosophers mingling with Descartes, Diderot, and Voltaire. ⊠ *Strahovské nádvoří 1, Hradcany* ☎ *233–107–704* ⊕ *www.strahovskyklaster.cz* ⊠ *80 Kč library* Ⓜ *Line A: Malostranská plus Tram No. 22 to Pohořelec.*

DID YOU KNOW?

The Loreto Church was built to symbolically reenact the legend of the Virgin Mary's house being carried by angels to Ancona, Italy.

2

PRAŽSKÝ HRAD (PRAGUE CASTLE)

Despite its monolithic presence, Prague Castle is not a single structure but a collection of structures dating from the 10th to the 20th centuries, all linked by internal courtyards. The most important are the cathedral, the Chrám svatého Víta, clearly visible soaring above the castle walls, and the Starý Královský palác, the official residence of kings and presidents and still the center of political power in the Czech Republic.

GETTING HERE AND AROUND

As with the neighboring environs, the best public transportation here is via Metro Line A to Malostranská and then continuing onward with Tram No. 22. Taxis work, too, of course, but they can be expensive. The Castle is compact and easily navigated. But be forewarned: the Castle, especially Chrám svatého Víta, teems with huge crowds practically year-round.

TIMING

The Castle is at its best in early morning and late evening, when it holds an air of mystery. (It's incomparably beautiful when it snows.) The cathedral deserves an hour—but budget more time, as the number of visitors allowed inside is limited and the lines can be long. Another hour should be spent in the Starý Královský palác, and you can easily spend an entire day taking in the museums, the views of the city, and the hidden nooks of the Castle.

VISITOR INFORMATION

Informační středisko (*Castle Information Office*). This is the place to come for entrance tickets, guided tours, audio guides with headphones, and tickets to cultural events held at the castle. You can wander around the castle grounds, including many of the gardens, for free, but to enter any of the historic buildings, including St. Vitus's Cathedral, requires a combined-entry ticket (valid for two days). There are two ticket options. The "Short Visit" (cheaper option) allows entry to St. Vitus's Cathedral, the Old Royal Palace, Golden Lane, St. George's Basilica, and Daliborka Tower. This will provide more than enough quality time in the castle. The more expensive "Long Visit" also includes entry to a permanent exhibition on the history of the castle called *The Story of Prague Castle* and to the Powder Tower. If you just want to walk through the castle grounds, note that the gates close at midnight from April through October and at 11 pm the rest of the year, and the gardens are open from April through October only. ✉ *Třetí nádvoří, across from entrance to St. Vitus's Cathedral, Pražský Hrad* ☎ *224–372–423* ⊕ *www.hrad.cz* 🎟 *Long visit 350 Kč, short visit 250 Kč, The Story of Prague Castle exhibit 140 Kč, Picture Gallery 100 Kč, Powder Tower 70 Kč, photo fee 50 Kč, audio guide 350 Kč (3 hrs)* Ⓜ *Line A: Malostranská plus Tram No. 22 to Pražský Hrad.*

TOP ATTRACTIONS

Bazilika svatého Jiří (*St. George's Basilica*). Inside, this church looks more or less as it did in the 12th century; it's the best-preserved Romanesque relic in the country. The effect is at once barnlike and peaceful, as the warm golden yellow of the stone walls and the small arched windows exude a sense of enduring harmony. Prince Vratislav I originally built it in the 10th century, though only the foundations remain from that time. The father of Prince Wenceslas (of Christmas carol fame) dedicated it to St. George (of dragon fame), a figure supposedly more agreeable to the still largely pagan people. The outside was remodeled during early baroque times, although the striking rusty-red color is in keeping with the look of the Romanesque edifice. The painted, house-shape tomb at the front of the church holds Vratislav's remains. Up the steps, in a chapel to the right, is the tomb Peter Parler designed for St. Ludmila, grandmother of St. Wenceslas. ✉ *Nám. U sv. Jiří, Pražský Hrad* ☎ *224–372–434* ⊕ *www.hrad.cz* 🎟 *Included in 2-day castle ticket (250 Kč–350 Kč)* Ⓜ *Line A: Malostranská plus Tram No. 22 to Pražský Hrad.*

Fodor's Choice
★

Chrám svatého Víta (*St. Vitus's Cathedral*). With its graceful, soaring towers, this Gothic cathedral—among the most beautiful in Europe—is the spiritual heart of Prague Castle and of the Czech Republic itself. The cathedral has a long and complicated history, beginning in the 10th century and continuing to its completion in 1929. Note that it's no longer free to enter the cathedral (entry is included in the combined ticket to see the main castle sights). It's perfectly okay just to wander around inside and gawk at the splendor, but you'll get much more out of the visit with the audio guide, which is available at the castle information center.

Once you enter the cathedral, pause to take in the vast but delicate beauty of the Gothic and neo-Gothic interior. Colorful light filters through the brilliant stained-glass windows. This western third of the structure, including the façade and the two towers you can see from outside, was not completed until 1929, following the initiative of the Union for the Completion of the Cathedral. Don't let the neo-Gothic

2

Pražský hrad (Prague Castle)

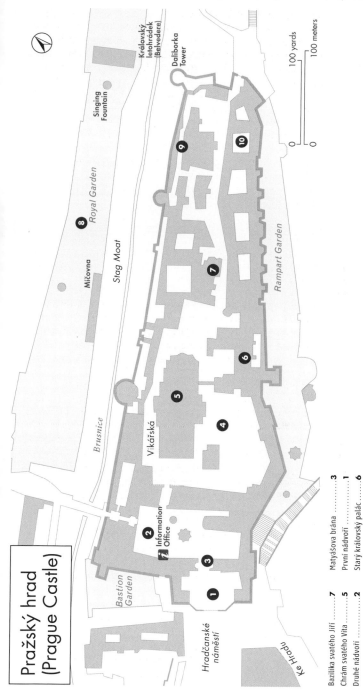

Bazilika svatého Jiří **7**
Chrám svatého Víta **5**
Druhé nádvoří **2**
Královská zahrada **8**
Lobkovický palác **10**

Matyášova brána **3**
První nádvoří **1**
Starý královský palác **6**
Třetí nádvoří **4**
Zlatá ulička **9**

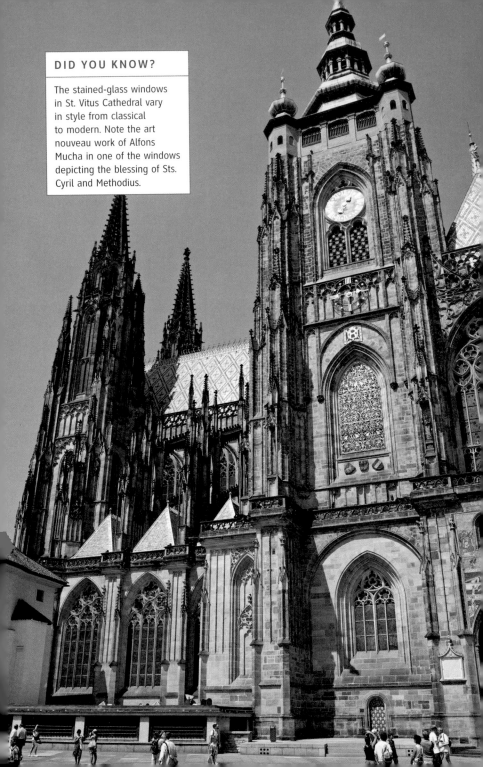

DID YOU KNOW?

The stained-glass windows in St. Vitus Cathedral vary in style from classical to modern. Note the art nouveau work of Alfons Mucha in one of the windows depicting the blessing of Sts. Cyril and Methodius.

illusion keep you from examining this new section. The six stained-glass windows to your left and right and the large rose window behind are modern masterpieces. Take a good look at the third window up on the left. The familiar art nouveau flamboyance, depicting the blessing of Sts. Cyril and Methodius (9th-century missionaries to the Slavs), is the work of Alfons Mucha, the Czech founder of the style. He achieved the subtle coloring by painting rather than staining the glass.

Walking halfway up the right-hand aisle, you will find the **Svatováclavská kaple** (Chapel of St. Wenceslas). With a tomb holding the saint's remains, walls covered in semiprecious stones, and paintings depicting the life of Wenceslas, this square chapel is the ancient core of the cathedral. Stylistically, it represents a high point of the dense, richly decorated—though rather gloomy—Gothic favored by Charles IV and his successors. Wenceslas (the "good king" of the Christmas carol) was a determined Christian in an era of widespread paganism. Around 925, as prince of Bohemia, he founded a rotunda church dedicated to St. Vitus on this site. But the prince's brother, Boleslav, was impatient to take power, and he ambushed and killed Wenceslas in 935 near a church at Stará Boleslav, northeast of Prague. Wenceslas was originally buried in that church, but so many miracles happened at his grave that he rapidly became a symbol of piety for the common people, something that greatly irritated the new Prince Boleslav. Boleslav was finally forced to honor his brother by reburying the body in the St. Vitus Rotunda. Shortly afterward, Wenceslas was canonized.

The rotunda was replaced by a Romanesque basilica in the late 11th century. Work began on the existing building in 1344. For the first few years the chief architect was the Frenchman Mathias d'Arras, but after his death in 1352 the work continued under the direction of 22-year-old German architect Peter Parler, who went on to build the Charles Bridge and many other Prague treasures.

The small door in the back of the chapel leads to the **Korunní komora** (Crown Chamber), the Bohemian crown jewels' repository. It remains locked with seven keys held by seven important people (including the president) and rarely opens to the public.

A little beyond the Chapel of St. Wenceslas on the same side, stairs lead down to the underground **royal crypt,** interesting primarily for the information it provides about the cathedral's history. As you descend the stairs, you can see parts of the old Romanesque basilica and portions of the foundations of the rotunda. Moving into the second room, you find a rather eclectic group of royal remains ensconced in sarcophagi dating from the 1930s. In the center is Charles IV, who died in 1378. Rudolf II, patron of Renaissance Prague, is entombed at the rear in his original tin coffin. To his right is Maria Amalia, the only child of Empress Maria Theresa to reside in Prague. Ascending the wooden steps back into the cathedral brings you to the white-marble **Kralovské mausoleum** (Royal Mausoleum), atop which lie stone statues of the first two Hapsburg kings to rule in Bohemia, Ferdinand I and Maximilian II, and another of Ferdinand's consort, Anne Jagiello.

The cathedral's **Kralovské oratorium** (Royal Oratory) was used by the kings and their families when attending mass. Built in 1493, the work represents a perfect example of late Gothic. It's laced on the outside with a stone network of gnarled branches, similar in pattern to the ceiling vaulting in the Královský palác. The oratory connects to the palace by an elevated covered walkway, which you can see from outside.

A few more steps toward the east end, you can't fail to catch sight of the ornate silver **sarcophagus of St. John of Nepomuk.** According to legend, when Nepomuk's body was exhumed in 1721 to be reinterred, the tongue was found to be still intact and pumping with blood. This strange tale served a highly political purpose: the Catholic Church and the Hapsburgs were seeking a new folk hero to replace the Protestant forerunner Jan Hus, whom they despised. The 14th-century priest Nepomuk, killed during a power struggle with King Václav IV, was sainted and reburied a few years later with great ceremony in a 3,700-pound silver tomb, replete with angels and cherubim; the tongue was enshrined in its own reliquary.

The eight chapels around the back of the cathedral are the work of the original architect, Mathias d'Arras. A number of old tombstones, including some badly worn grave markers of medieval royalty, can be seen within, amid furnishings from later periods. Opposite the wooden relief, depicting the Protestants' looting of the cathedral in 1619, is the **Valdštejnská kaple** (Wallenstein Chapel). Since the 19th century the chapel has housed the Gothic tombstones of its two architects, d'Arras and Peter Parler, who died in 1352 and 1399, respectively. If you look up to the balcony, you can just make out the busts of these two men, designed by Parler's workshop. The other busts around the triforium depict royalty and other VIPs of the time.

The Hussite wars in the 15th century put an end to the first phase of the cathedral's construction. During the short era of illusory peace before the Thirty Years' War, the massive south tower was completed, but lack of money quashed any idea of finishing the building, and the cathedral was closed in by a wall built across from the Chapel of St. Wenceslas. Not until the 20th century was the western side of the cathedral, with its two towers, completed in the spirit of Parler's conception.

A key element of the cathedral's teeming, rich exterior decoration is the **Last Judgment mosaic** above the ceremonial entrance, called the Golden Portal, on the south side. The use of mosaic is quite rare in countries north of the Alps; this work, constructed from 1 million glass and stone tesserae, dates to the 1370s. The once-clouded glass now sparkles again, thanks to many years of restoration funded by the Getty Conservation Institute. The central field shows Christ in glory, adored by Charles IV and his consort, Elizabeth of Pomerania, as well as several saints; the risen dead and attendant angels are on the left; and on the right the flames of Hell lick around the figure of Satan. ⊠ *Hrad III. nádvoří 2, Pražský Hrad* ☎ *224–372–434* ⊕ *www.katedralasvatehovita.cz* ⬛ *Included in 2-day castle ticket (250 Kč–350 Kč)* Ⓜ *Line A: Malostranská plus Tram No. 22 to Pražský Hrad.*

2

Druhé nádvoří (*Second Courtyard*). Except for the view of the spires of St. Vitus's Cathedral, the exterior courtyard offers little for the eye to feast on. Empress Maria Theresa's court architect, Nicolò Pacassi, received imperial approval to remake the castle in the 1760s, as it was badly damaged by Prussian shelling during the Seven Years' War in 1757. The Second Courtyard was the main victim of Pacassi's attempts at imparting classical grandeur to what had been a picturesque collection of Gothic and Renaissance styles. This courtyard also houses the rather gaudy **Kaple svatého Kříže** (Chapel of the Holy Cross), with decorations from the 18th and 19th centuries, which now serves as a souvenir and ticket stand.

Built in the late 16th and early 17th centuries, the Second Courtyard was originally part of a reconstruction program commissioned by Rudolf II. He amassed a large and famed collection of fine and decorative art, scientific instruments, philosophical and alchemical books, natural wonders, coins, and a hodgepodge of other treasures. The bulk of the collection was looted by the Swedes during the Thirty Years' War, removed to Vienna when the imperial capital returned there after Rudolf's death, or auctioned off during the 18th century. Artworks that survived the turmoil, for the most part acquired after Rudolf's time, are displayed in the **Obrazárna** (Picture Gallery) on the courtyard's left side as you face St. Vitus's. In rooms redecorated by castle architect Bořek Šípek, there are good Renaissance, mannerist, and baroque paintings that demonstrate the luxurious tastes of Rudolf's court. Across the passageway by the gallery entrance is the **Císařská konírna** (Imperial Stable), where temporary exhibitions are held. The passageway at the northern end of the courtyard forms the northern entrance to the castle, and leads out over a luxurious ravine known as the **Jelení příkop** (Stag Moat), which can be entered either here or at the lower end via the metal catwalk off Chotkova ulice, when it isn't closed for sporadic renovations. ⊠ *Obrazárna, Pražský Hrad* ☎ *224–372–434* ⊕ *www. hrad.cz* ⊠ *Courtyard free; Picture Gallery 150 Kč or 250 Kč–350 Kč as part of a 2-day ticket, free Mon. 4–6* Ⓜ *Line A: Malostranská plus Tram No. 22 to Pražský Hrad.*

Královská zahrada (*Royal Garden*). This peaceful swath of greenery affords lovely views of St. Vitus's Cathedral and the Castle's walls and bastions. Originally laid out in the 16th century, it endured devastation in war, neglect in times of peace, and many redesigns, reaching its present parklike form early in the 20th century. Luckily, its Renaissance treasures survived. One of these is the long, narrow **Míčovna** (Ball Game Hall), built by Bonifaz Wohlmut in 1568, its garden front completely covered by a dense tangle of allegorical *sgraffiti*.

The **Královský letohrádek** (Royal Summer Palace, also known as the Belvedere), at the garden's eastern end, deserves its unusual reputation as one of the most beautiful Renaissance structures north of the Alps. Italian architects began it; Wohlmut finished it off in the 1560s with a copper roof like an upturned boat's keel riding above the graceful arcades of the ground floor. During the 18th and 19th centuries military engineers tested artillery in the interior, which had already lost its rich furnishings to Swedish soldiers during their siege of the city in

Part of the Prague Castle complex, the Old Royal Palace has a splendid vaulted ceiling.

1648. The Renaissance-style *giardinetto* (little garden) adjoining the summer palace centers on another masterwork, the Italian-designed, Czech-produced Singing Fountain, which resonates from the sound of falling water. ⊠ *U Prašného mostu ulice and Mariánské hradby ulice near Chotkovy Park, Pražský Hrad* ☎ *224–372–434* ⊕ *www.hrad.cz* Ⓜ *Line A: Malostranská plus Tram No. 22 to Pražský Hrad.*

■ QUICK
BITES

Lobkowicz Palace Café. Break for a coffee, pastry, or even lunch and enjoy one of the loveliest views of the city from the outdoor terrace of the Lobkowicz Palace Café. The menu is a touch expensive, but full of delicious sandwiches, including ham and cheese, tuna, and smoked salmon, plus beverages and desserts. It's an enchanting place to while away an hour. ⊠ *Lobkovický palác, Jirska 3, Pražský Hrad* ☎ *233–356–978* ⊕ *www.lobkowicz.cz* Ⓜ *Line A: Malostranská plus Tram No. 22 to Pražský Hrad.*

Lobkovický palác (*Lobkowicz Palace*). Greatly benefiting from a recent renovation, this palace is a showcase for baroque and rococo styling. Exhibits trace the ancestry of the Lobkowicz family, who were great patrons of the arts in their heyday. (Beethoven was one of the artists who received their funding.) The audio tour adds a personal touch: it's narrated by William Lobwicz, the family scion who spearheaded the property's restitution and rehabilitation, and includes quite a few anecdotes about the family through the years. Although inside Prague Castle, this museum has a separate admission. ⊠ *Jiřská 3, Pražský Hrad* ☎ *233–312–925* ⊕ *www.lobkowicz.cz* ⊠ *300 Kč* Ⓜ *Line A: Malostranská plus Tram No. 22 to Pražský Hrad.*

Starý královský palác (*Old Royal Palace*). A jumble of styles and add-ons from different eras are gathered in this palace. The best way to grasp its size is from within the **Vladislavský sál** (Vladislav Hall), the largest secular Gothic interior space in Central Europe. Benedikt Ried completed the hall in 1493. (He was to late Bohemian Gothic what Peter Parler was to the earlier version.) The room imparts a sense of space and light, softened by the sensuous lines of the vaulted ceilings and brought to a dignified close by the simple oblong form of the early Renaissance windows. In its heyday, the hall held jousting tournaments, festive markets, banquets, and coronations. In more recent times, it has been used to inaugurate presidents, from the communist leader Klement Gottwald (in 1948) to modern-day leaders like Václav Havel and current president Miloš Zeman.

From the front of the hall, turn right into the rooms of the **Česká kancelář** (Bohemian Chancellery). This wing was built by Benedikt Ried only 10 years after the hall was completed, but it shows a much stronger Renaissance influence. Pass through the portal into the last chamber of the chancellery. In 1618 this room was the site of the second defenestration of Prague, an event that marked the beginning of the Bohemian rebellion and, ultimately, the Thirty Years' War throughout Europe. The square window used in this protest is on the left as you enter the room.

At the back of Vladislav Hall a staircase leads up to a gallery of the **Kaple všech svatých** (All Saints' Chapel). Little remains of Peter Parler's original work, but the church contains some fine works of art. The large room to the left of the staircase is the **Stará sněmovna** (council chamber), where the Bohemian nobles met with the king in a prototype parliament of sorts. The descent from Vladislav Hall toward what remains of the **Romanský palác** (Romanesque Palace) is by way of a wide, shallow set of steps. This **Jezdecké schody** (Riders' Staircase) was the entranceway for knights who came for the jousting tournaments. ⌧ *Hrad III. nádvoří, Pražský Hrad* ☎ *224–372–434* ⊕ *www.hrad.cz* 🎫 *Included in 2-day castle ticket (250 Kč–350 Kč)* Ⓜ *Line A: Malostranská plus Tram No. 22 to Pražský Hrad.*

Zlatá ulička (*Golden Lane*). A jumbled collection of tiny, ancient, brightly colored houses crouched under the fortification wall look remarkably like a set for *Snow White and the Seven Dwarfs*. Purportedly, these were the lodgings for an international group of alchemists whom Rudolf II brought to the court to produce gold. But the truth is a little less romantic: the houses were built during the 16th century for the castle guards. By the early 20th century Golden Lane had become the home of poor artists and writers. Franz Kafka, who lived at No. 22 in 1916 and 1917, described the house on first sight as "so small, so dirty, impossible to live in, and lacking everything necessary." But he soon came to love the place. As he wrote to his fiancée, "Life here is something special, to close out the world not just by shutting the door to a room or apartment but to the whole house, to step out into the snow of the silent lane." The lane now holds tiny stores selling books, music, and crafts, and has become so popular that an admission fee is charged. The houses are cute, but crowds can be uncomfortable, and the fact remains that you are paying money for the privilege of shopping in

DID YOU KNOW?

It used to be believed that the Golden Lane housed alchemists, but in actuality they were homes for castle guards and later for artists like Franz Kafka, who lived for a short time at No. 22.

jammed little stores. Within the walls above Golden Lane, a timber-roof corridor (enter between No. 23 and No. 24) is lined with replica suits of armor and weapons (some of them for sale), mock torture chambers, and the like. ⊠ *Zlatá ulička, Pražský Hrad* ☎ *224–372–434* ⊕ *www. hrad.cz* ▧ *Included in 2-day castle ticket (250 Kč–350 Kč)* Ⓜ *Line A: Malostranská plus Tram No. 22 to Pražský Hrad.*

WORTH NOTING

Matyášova brána (*Matthias Gate*). Built in 1614, this stone gate once stood alone in front of the moats and bridges that surrounded the castle. Under the Hapsburgs, the gate survived by being grafted as a relief onto the palace building. As you go through it, notice the ceremonial white-marble entrance halls on either side that lead up to the Czech president's reception rooms (which are only rarely open to the public). ⊠ *Pražský Hrad* ☎ *224–372–434* ⊕ *www.hrad.cz* Ⓜ *Line A: Malostranská plus Tram No. 22 to Pražský Hrad.*

První nádvoří (*First Courtyard*). The main entrance to Prague Castle from Hradčanské náměstí is certain to impress any first-time visitor. Going through the wrought-iron gate, guarded at ground level by colorful Czech soldiers and from above by the ferocious *Battling Titans* (a copy of Ignaz Platzer's original 18th-century work), you enter this courtyard, built on the site of old moats and gates that once separated the Castle from the surrounding buildings and thus protected the vulnerable western flank. The courtyard is one of the more recent additions to the Castle, designed by Maria Theresa's court architect, Nicolò Pacassi, in the 1760s. Today it forms part of the presidential office complex. Pacassi's reconstruction was intended to unify the eclectic collection of buildings that made up the Castle, but the effect of his work is somewhat flat. ■TIP→ Try to arrive on the hour to witness the changing of the guard; the fanfare peaks at noon with a special flag ceremony in the First Courtyard. ⊠ *První nádvoří, Pražský Hrad* ☎ *224–372–434* ⊕ *www. hrad.cz* Ⓜ *Line A: Malostranská plus Tram No. 22 to Pražský Hrad.*

Třetí nádvoří (*Third Courtyard*). The contrast between the cool, dark interior of St. Vitus's Cathedral and the brightly colored Pacassi façades of the Third Courtyard just outside is startling. Noted Slovenian architect Josip Plečnik created the courtyard's clean lines in the 1930s, but the modern look is a deception. Plečnik's paving was intended to cover an underground world of house foundations, streets, and walls dating to the 9th through 12th centuries and rediscovered when the cathedral was completed. (You can see a few archways through a grating in a wall of the cathedral.) Plečnik added a few features to catch the eye: a granite obelisk to commemorate the fallen of World War I, a black-marble pedestal for the Gothic statue of St. George (a copy of the National Gallery's original statue), an inconspicuous entrance to his Bull Staircase leading down to the south garden, and a peculiar golden ball topping the eagle fountain near the eastern end of the courtyard. ⊠ *Třetí nádvoří, Pražský Hrad* ☎ *224–372–434* ⊕ *www.hrad.cz* Ⓜ *Line A: Malostranská plus Tram No. 22 to Pražský Hrad.*

NOVÉ MĚSTO (NEW TOWN) AND VYŠEHRAD

To this day, Charles IV's building projects are tightly woven into the daily lives of Prague citizens. His most extensive scheme, Nové Město, or the New Town, is still such a lively, vibrant area you may hardly realize that its streets and squares were planned as far back as 1348. In other words, the area is about as "new" as the Charles Bridge.

NOVÉ MĚSTO (NEW TOWN)

Though Nové Město translates as "New Town," its origins go all the way back to the 14th century and Emperor Charles IV. As Prague outgrew its Old Town parameters, Charles IV extended the city's fortifications. A high wall surrounded the newly developed 2½-square-km (1½-square-mile) area south and east of the Old Town, tripling the walled territory on the Vltava's right bank. The wall extended south to link with the fortifications of the citadel called Vyšehrad.

But don't come here looking for Old Town charm. This part of the city was thoroughly rebuilt in the mid-19th century in the neoclassical and neo-Renaissance styles, and today forms the modern heart of the city, particularly around the two main squares: Václavské náměstí and Karlovo náměstí. The area is great for hotels and restaurants, but the number of traditional sights is relatively small with just a handful of important museums and churches.

GETTING HERE AND AROUND
The best Metro stops for this area are those at Karlovo náměstí (Line B), Muzeum (Lines A and C), and Můstek (Lines A and B).

TIMING
The New Town covers a large area and is best approached depending on what you want to see. Leave at least an hour or two to cover the areas around Václavské náměstí and Karlovo náměstí on foot, with another hour or two for the museums, churches, or parks you plan to visit.

TOP ATTRACTIONS

Karlovo náměstí (*Charles Square*). This square began life as a cattle market, a function chosen by Charles IV when he established the New Town in 1348. The horse market (now Wenceslas Square) quickly overtook it as a livestock-trading center, and an untidy collection of shacks accumulated here until the mid-1800s, when it became a green park named for its patron. Glassy, modern buildings clash with surrounding older architecture, but it's quite representative of Prague's past and present united in one spot. ⊠ *Bounded by Řeznická on the north, U Nemocnice on the south, Karlovo nám. on the west, and Vodičkova on the east, Nové Mesto* Ⓜ *Line B: Karlovo náměstí.*

THE SQUARE THAT'S ACTUALLY A ROAD

Václavské náměstí is a long, gently sloping boulevard rather than an actual square. More than Old Town Square, it's the commercial heart of Prague today much as it was a hundred years ago. At the end of November 1989, hundreds of thousands of Czechs gathered here to demand an end to the communist government. The image beamed to television sets around the world showed thousands of Czechs jangling their keys as a signal of protest: "Time to leave."

NEED A BREAK

Pivovarksy Dům. Parched from your circuit of the square? Walk up Ječná Street from Karlovo Náměstí to Lipová 15, where you'll find Pivovarksy Dům. They brew their own beers on the premises, including limited-edition flavors with coffee and banana, and pair them with Czech culinary staples like roast pork and dumplings or a bowl of goulash. ■ TIP→ Time your arrival outside of normal meal times, or you'll have to book in advance to get a table. ⊠ *Lipová 15, Nové Mesto* ☎ *296–216–666* ⊕ *www.pivovarsky-dum.com* Ⓜ *Line C: I.P. Pavlova or Line B: Karlovo náměstí.*

Mucha Museum. For decades it was almost impossible to find an Alfons Mucha original in his homeland, but in 1998 this private museum opened with nearly 100 works from this justly famous Czech artist's long career. Everything you expect to see from the man famed for his art nouveau style is here—the theater posters of actress Sarah Bernhardt, the eye-popping advertising posters, and the sinuous, intricate designs. Also exhibited are paintings, photographs taken in Mucha's studio (one shows Paul Gauguin playing the piano in his underwear), and even Czechoslovak banknotes designed by Mucha. ⊠ *Panská 7, 1 block off Wenceslas Sq., across from Palace Hotel, Nové Mesto* ☎ *224–216–415* ⊕ *www.mucha.cz* 🎫 *240 Kč* Ⓜ *Lines A & B: Můstek.*

Muzeum Antonína Dvořáka (*Antonín Dvořák Museum*). The stately red-and-yellow baroque villa housing this museum displays the 19th-century Czech composer's scores, photographs, viola, piano, and other memorabilia. The statues in the garden date to about 1735; the house is from 1720. Check the schedule for classical performances, as recitals are often held in the first floor of the two-story villa. ⊠ *Ke Karlovu 20, Nové Mesto* ☎ *224–918–013* ⊕ *www.nm.cz* 🎫 *50 Kč* ☽ *Closed Mon.* Ⓜ *Line C: I. P. Pavlova.*

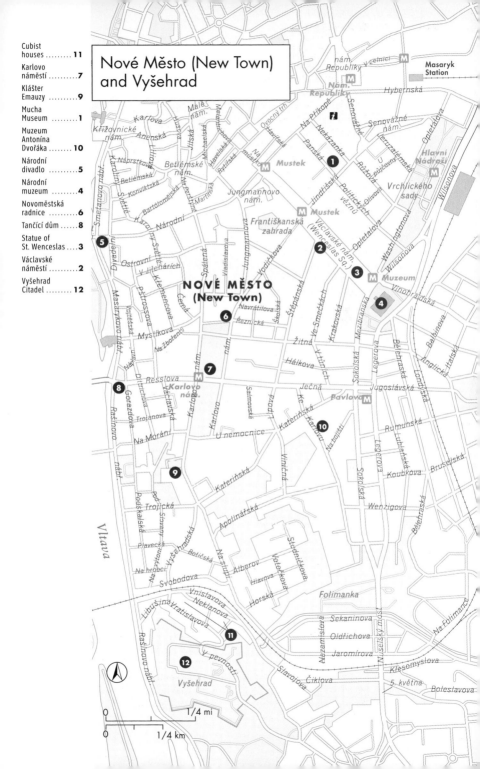

Cubist
houses 11
Karlovo
náměstí 7
Klášter
Emauzy 9
Mucha
Museum 1
Muzeum
Antonína
Dvořáka 10
Národní
divadlo 5
Národní
muzeum 4
Novoměstská
radnice 6
Tančící dům 8
Statue of
St. Wenceslas 3
Václavské
náměstí 2
Vyšehrad
Citadel 12

Nové Město (New Town) and Vyšehrad

The Dancing House earned the nickname "Fred and Ginger" for pairing a curving, feminine tower with a solid, straight one.

Národní divadlo (*National Theater*). Statues representing Drama and Opera rise above the riverfront side entrances to this theater, and two gigantic chariots flank figures of Apollo and the nine Muses above the main façade. The performance space lacks restraint as well: it's filled with gilding, voluptuous plaster figures, and plush upholstery. The idea for a Czech national theater began during the revolutionary decade of the 1840s. In a telling display of national pride, donations to fund the plan poured in from all over the country, from people of every socioeconomic stratum. The cornerstone was laid in 1868, and the "National Theater generation" who built the neo-Renaissance structure became the architectural and artistic establishment for decades to come. Its designer, Josef Zítek, was the leading neo-Renaissance architect in Bohemia. The nearly finished interior was gutted by a fire in 1881, and Zítek's onetime student Josef Schulz saw the reconstruction through to completion two years later. Today, it's still the country's leading dramatic stage. ■**TIP**➜ Guided tours in English (for groups only) can be arranged by phone or email in advance. ⊠ *Národní 2, Nové Mesto* ☎ *224–901–448 for box office* ⊕ *www.narodni-divadlo.cz* 🎫 *Tours 200 Kč* Ⓜ *Line A: Staroměstská.*

Fodor's Choice **Tančící dům** (*Dancing House*). This whimsical building, one of Prague's
★ most popular, came to life in 1996 as a team effort from architect Frank Gehry (of Guggenheim Bilbao fame) and his Croatian-Czech collaborator Vlado Milunic. A wasp-waisted glass-and-steel tower sways into the main columned structure as though they were a couple on the dance floor—the "Fred and Ginger" effect gave the building its nickname. It's notable for a Gehry piece as it's more grounded in the surrounding area

than his larger projects. ⚠ The building houses offices and isn't open to the general public. ✉ *Rašínovo nábř. 80, Nové Mesto.*

Václavské náměstí (*Wenceslas Square*). This "square"—more of a rectangle, actually—was first laid out by Charles IV in 1348, and began its existence as a horse market at the center of the New Town. Today, it functions as the commercial heart of the city center and is far brasher and more modern than the Old Town Square. Throughout much of Czech history, Wenceslas Square has served as the focal point for public demonstrations and celebrations. It was here in the heady days of November 1989 that some 500,000 people gathered to protest the policies of the then-communist regime. After a week of demonstrations, the government capitulated without a shot fired or the loss of a single life. After that, the first democratic government in 40 years (under playwright-president Václav Havel) was swept into office. This peaceful transfer of power is referred to as the Velvet Revolution. (The subsequent "Velvet Divorce" from Slovakia took effect in 1993.) ✉ *Václavské náměstí, Nové Mesto* Ⓜ *Line A: Muzeum; Lines A & B: Můstek.*

NEED A BREAK

Caffé Fresco. If you're worn out after the long uphill climb to the bluff, Café Fresco serves up Italian salads and panini, plus a revivifying set of espresso drinks. It's on the way to or from the Vyšehrad metro stop. And if your legs are really killing you, there's also a Thai massage studio next door. ✉ *Rezidence Vyšehrad, Lumírova 33, Vyšehrad* ☎ *234-724-230* ⊕ *www. caffe-fresco.com* Ⓜ *Line C: Vyšehrad.*

WORTH NOTING

Klášter Emauzy (*Emmaus Monastery*). Another of Charles IV's gifts to the city, the Benedictine monastery sits south of Karlovo náměstí. It's often called Na Slovanech (literally, "At the Slavs"), which refers to its purpose when it was established in 1347. The emperor invited Croatian monks here to celebrate mass in Old Slavonic, and thus cultivate religion among the Slavs in a city largely controlled by Germans. A faded but substantially complete cycle of biblical scenes by Charles's court artists lines the four cloister walls. The frescoes, and especially the abbey church, suffered heavy damage from a raid by Allied bombers on February 14, 1945; it's believed they may have mistaken Prague for Dresden, 121 km (75 miles) away. The church lost its spires, and the interior remained a blackened shell until a renovation was begun in 1998; the church reopened to the public in 2003. ✉ *Vyšehradská 49, cloister entrance on left at rear of church, Vyšehrad* ⊕ *www.emauzy.cz* 🎫 *50 Kč* Ⓜ *Line B: Karlovo náměstí.*

Národní muzeum (*National Museum*). Housed in a grandiose neo-Renaissance structure at the top of Wenceslas Square, the National Museum was built between 1885 to 1890 as a symbol of the Czech national revival. Indeed, the building's exterior is so impressive that invading Soviet soldiers in 1968 mistook it for parliament. The holdings are a cross between natural history and ethnography and include dinosaur bones, minerals, textiles, coins and many, many other things. In 2011, the museum closed until 2018 for a long-overdue renovation, though the annex next door at Vinohradská 1 continues to hold temporary exhibitions. ⊠ *Václavské nám. 68, Nové Mesto* ☎ *224–497–111* ⊕ *www. nm.cz* ◻ *Temporary exhibitions 100 Kč* Ⓜ *Lines A & C: Muzeum.*

Novoměstská radnice (*New Town Hall*). At the northern edge of Karlovo náměstí, the New Town Hall has a late-Gothic tower similar to that of the Old Town Hall, plus three tall Renaissance gables. The first defenestration in Prague occurred here on July 30, 1419, when a mob of townspeople, followers of the martyred religious reformer Jan Hus, hurled Catholic town councilors out the windows. Historical exhibitions and contemporary art shows are held regularly in the gallery, and you can climb the tower for a view of the New Town. As in Old Town, this town hall is a popular venue for weddings. ⊠ *Karlovo nám. 23, at Vodičkova, Nové Mesto* ☎ *224–948–229* ⊕ *www.nrpraha.cz* ◻ *50 Kč tower and exhibits on tower premises, gallery shows vary (not included in tower admission)* ⊘ *Closed Mon.*

Statue of St. Wenceslas. Josef Václav Myslbek's impressive equestrian representation of St. Wenceslas with other Czech patron saints around him has been a traditional meeting place for locals for years ("Let's meet at the horse," as the expression goes). In 1939, Czechs gathered here to oppose Hitler's annexation of Bohemia and Moravia. In 1969, student Jan Palach set himself on fire near here to protest the Soviet-led invasion of the country a year earlier. And in 1989, many thousands successfully gathered here and all along the square to demand the end of the communist government. ⊠ *Václavské nám., Nové Mesto* Ⓜ *Lines A & C: Muzeum.*

VYŠEHRAD

The high-top Vyšehrad Citadel once rivaled Prague Castle in size and importance, but much of the historic architecture was leveled in the Hussite wars of the 15th century. The area got a new lease on life in the 18th century as a military fortress, and the casements remain one of the leading attractions. There's also a grand neo-Gothic cathedral and the country's most important cemetery. For many Prague residents, though, a trip here means simply a chance to enjoy the fresh air and stunning views of Prague Castle in the distance.

GETTING HERE AND AROUND
Metro Line C (to Vyšehrad station) will get you closest to Vyšehrad Citadel (the High Castle), but even from here, the ruins are a good 15-minute walk away.

TIMING
Plan a whole day, as it takes about two hours to get here, and you'll want ample time to see the sights and relax on the grass—the castle grounds can easily absorb several hours. Vyšehrad is open every day, year-round, and the views are especially stunning on a day with clear skies.

Next to the Church of Sts. Peter and Paul lies the burial ground for several of the Czech Republic's most famous citizens.

TOP ATTRACTIONS

Cubist houses. Bordered to the north by Nové Město and to the south by Nusle, Vyšehrad is mostly visited for its citadel high above the river on a rocky outcropping. However, fans of 20th-century architecture—you know who you are—will find cubist gems between the area's river-front street and the homes that dot the hills on the other side. Prague's cubist architecture followed a great Czech tradition: embracing new ideas, while adapting them to existing artistic and social contexts to create something sui generis. Between 1912 and 1914 Josef Chochol (1880–1956) designed several of the city's dozen or so cubist projects. His apartment house at **Neklanova 30,** on the corner of Neklanova and Přemyslova, is a masterpiece in concrete. The pyramidal, kaleido-scopic window moldings and roof cornices make an expressive link to the baroque yet are wholly novel; the faceted corner balcony column, meanwhile, alludes to Gothic forerunners. On the same street, at **No. 2,** is another apartment house attributed to Chochol. Like the building at No. 30, it uses pyramidal shapes and a suggestion of Gothic columns. Nearby, Chochol's **villa,** on the embankment at Libušina 3, has an undulating effect, created by smoothly articulated forms. The wall and gate around the back of the house use triangular moldings and metal grating to create an effect of controlled energy. The **three-family house,** about 100 yards away from the villa at Rašínovo nábřeží 6–10, was completed slightly earlier, when Chochol's cubist style was still developing. Here the design is touched with baroque and neoclassical influence, with a mansard roof and end gables. ⊠ *Neklanova, Vyšehrad* Ⓜ *Line B: Karlovo náměstí.*

CLOSE UP

Prague's Plaques

The famous, the forgotten, and the victims. Throughout the center of town a large number of plaques and even busts are attached to the sides of buildings marking the famous and sometimes not-so-famous people who lived or worked there. Composer Frederick Chopin can be found across from Obecní dům (the Municipal House) on the side of the Czech National Bank. Scientists like Albert Einstein—who was friends with author Franz Kafka, according to a marker on Old Town Square—also turn up. Some Czech figures like composer Bedřich Smetana or painter Josef Manés might be recognizable, while many plaques commemorate totally obscure teachers, civic organizers, or members of the 19th-century national awakening.

One set of plaques stands out from the rest—those marking the victims of the Prague Uprising that took place May 5–8, 1945. These mark where Prague citizens who tried to battle the German army at the end of World War II were killed. Many plaques depict a hand with two upraised fingers and the phrase *věrni zůstaneme,* meaning "remain faithful." Foil-covered wreaths are still regularly hung underneath them.

The area around Wenceslas Square has several, including one on the side of the main Post Office on Jindřišská Street. Two plaques can even be found on the back of the plinth of the Jan Hus statue on Old Town Square.

Some of the more touching ones have black-and-white photographs of the victims, such as a marker for 23-year-old Viktorie Krupková, who was killed on Újezd near Říční Street, just across from Petřín.

The area around Czech Radio headquarters on Vinohradská Street in Vinohrady has many, as well as some plaques for victims of the 1968 Soviet-led invasion. Fighting for control of the radio station was fierce during the invasion.

Vyšehrad Citadel (*Vyšehrad Fortress*). Bedřich Smetana's symphonic poem *Vyšehrad* opens with four bardic harp chords that echo the legends surrounding this ancient fortress. Today the flat-top bluff stands over the right bank of the Vltava as a green, tree-dotted expanse showing few signs that splendid medieval monuments once made it a landmark to rival Prague Castle.

The Vyšehrad, or "High Castle," was constructed by Vratislav II (ruled 1061–92), a Přemyslid duke who became the first king of Bohemia. He made the fortified hilltop his capital. Under subsequent rulers it fell into disuse until the 14th century, when Charles IV transformed the site into an ensemble including palaces, the main church, battlements, and a massive gatehouse whose scant remains are on V Pevnosti ulice. By the 17th century royalty had long since departed, and most of the structures they built were crumbling. Vyšehrad was turned into a fortress.

Vyšehrad's place in the modern Czech imagination is largely thanks to the National Revivalists of the 19th century, particularly writer Alois Jirásek. Jirásek mined medieval chronicles for legends and facts to glorify the early Czechs, and that era of Czech history is very much in the popular consciousness today.

DID YOU KNOW?

The imposing architecture for the National Museum was created by Prague architect Josef Schulz. (And it's even more stunning at night.)

Traces of the citadel's distant past can be found at every turn, and are reflected even in the structure chosen for the visitor center, the remains of a Gothic stone fortification wall known as **Špička,** or Peak Gate, at the corner of V Pevnosti and U Podolského Sanatoria. Farther ahead is the sculpture-covered **Leopold Gate,** which stands next to brick walls enlarged during the 1742 occupation by the French. Out of the gate, a heavily restored **Romanesque rotunda,** built by Vratislav II in the 11th century, stands on the corner of K Rotundě and Soběslavova. It's considered the oldest fully intact Romanesque building in the city. Down Soběslavova are the excavated foundations and a few embossed floor tiles from the late-10th-century **Basilika svatého Vavřince** (St. Lawrence Basilica, closed to the public). The foundations, discovered in 1884 while workers were creating a cesspool, are in a baroque structure at Soběslavova 14. The remains are from one of the few early medieval buildings to have survived in the area and are worth a look. On the western side of Vyšehrad, part of the fortifications stand next to the surprisingly confined foundation mounds of a medieval palace overlooking a ruined watchtower called **Libuše's Bath,** which precariously juts out of a rocky outcropping over the river. A nearby plot of grass hosts a statue of Libuše and her consort Přemysl, one of four large, sculpted images of couples from Czech legend by J. V. Myslbek (1848–1922), the sculptor of the St. Wenceslas monument.

The military history of the fortress and the city is covered in a small exhibit inside the Cihelná brána (Brick Gate), but the real attraction is the **casemates,** a long, dark passageway within the walls that ends at a dank hall used to store several original, pollution-scarred Charles Bridge sculptures. A guided tour into the casemates and the statue storage room starts at the military history exhibit; it has a separate admission fee. ⊠ *V Pevnosti 5b, Vyšehrad* ☎ *241–410–247* ⊕ *www. praha-vysehrad.cz* ✍ *Grounds and cemetery free, casemates tour 60 Kč, Gothic cellar 50 Kč* Ⓜ *Line C: Vyšehrad.*

2

VINOHRADY AND ŽIŽKOV

Personalitywise, Vinohrady and Žižkov are a bit of an odd couple, as signified by their representative beverages: Vinohrady was once the wine-producing center of the city and has the mannered homes to match. Žižkov is known for its pubs and its boisterous beer scene.

VINOHRADY

From Riegrovy Park the eclectic apartment buildings and villas of the elegant residential neighborhood called Vinohrady extend eastward and southward. The pastel-tint formation of turn-of-the-20th-century houses—which not long ago were still crumbling after years of neglect—are now chockablock with upscale flats, slick offices, eternally packed restaurants, and all manner of shops. Much of the development lies on or near Vinohradská, the main street, which extends from the top of Wenceslas Square to a belt of enormous cemeteries about 3 km (2 miles) eastward. Yet the flavor of daily life persists: smoky old pubs still ply their trade on the quiet side streets; the stately theater, Divadlo na Vinohradech, keeps putting on excellent shows as it has for decades; and on the squares and in the parks nearly everyone still practices Prague's favorite form of outdoor exercise—walking the dog.

GETTING HERE AND AROUND

Vinohrady is best approached from Metro Line A. The neighborhood's main Metro stops are Muzeum, Náměstí Miru and Jiřího z Poděbrad.

TIMING

Here, as opposed to central Prague, you won't need to worry about timing your visit to avoid bands of roving tourists. Happily, this area is mostly occupied by local residents.

TOP ATTRACTIONS

Kostel Nejsvětějšího Srdce Páně (*Church of the Most Sacred Heart*). If you've had your fill of Romanesque, Gothic, and baroque, this church will give you a look at a startling modernist art deco edifice. Designed in 1927 by Slovenian architect Josip Plečnik (the same architect commissioned to update Prague Castle), the church resembles a luxury ocean liner more than a place of worship. The effect was purposeful, as during the 1920s and 1930s the avant-garde imitated mammoth objects of modern technology. Plečnik used many modern elements on the inside. You may be able to find someone at the back entrance of the church who will let you walk up the long ramp into the fascinating glass clock tower. It's hard to miss the structure, which looms as you exit the metro. ■ TIP➔ Note that entrance is only allowed 40 minutes before and after mass. ⊠ *Nám. Jiřího z Poděbrad, Vinohrady* ⊕ *srdcepane.cz* ☒ *Free* Ⓜ *Line A: Jiřího z Poděbrad.*

WORTH NOTING

Nový židovský hřbitov (*New Jewish Cemetery*). In this, the newest of the city's half-dozen Jewish burial grounds, you can find the modest **tombstone of Franz Kafka,** which seems grossly inadequate to Kafka's fame but oddly in proportion to his own modest sense of self. The cemetery is usually open, although guards sometimes inexplicably seal off the grounds. Men may be required to wear a yarmulke (you can buy one here if you need to). Turn right at the main cemetery gate and follow the wall for about 100 yards. Kafka's thin white tombstone lies at the front of section 21. City maps may label the cemetery "Židovské hřbitovy." ⊠ *Vinohradská at Jana Želivského, Vinohrady* ☎ *226–235–248* ⊕ *www.kehilaprag.cz* Ⓜ *Line A: Želivského.*

ŽIŽKOV

For Prague residents, Žižkov is synonymous with pubs. There are more places to knock back a Pilsner Urquell or a shot of Fernet Stock per square inch here than anywhere else in the city, giving it a kind of seedy reputation that it doesn't deserve. Nowadays the district is starting to recoup. Some of the city's coolest cafés, clubs, and trendy apartments have opened up here. There are still some—in fact, lots of—crumbling, run-down areas, but it's also one of the most interesting districts in the city for its nightlife and dining.

GETTING HERE AND AROUND

Žižkov is not directly served by any Metro line, though the Line A stop at Jiřího z Poděbrad will bring you within about 10 minutes' walking distance. By tram, you can reach the heart of Zizkov in 2–3 stops on No. 5, 9, or 26 departing from just north of the main train station, Hlavní nádraží.

TIMING

Here, as opposed to central Prague, you won't need to worry about timing your visit to avoid bands of roving tourists. There are few traditional sights and the area is almost entirely free of visitors.

TOP ATTRACTIONS

National Memorial on Vítkov Hill. Vítkov Hill, one of the highest points in the city, is topped by the largest equestrian statue in the world—a 16½-ton metal sculpture of one-eyed Hussite leader Jan Žižka on horseback. The 20th-century memorial was originally built to honor the war

2

Vinohrady and Žižkov

Kostel Nejsvětějšího
Srdce Páně 3

National Memorial on
Vítkov Hill 1

Nový židovský
hřbitov 4

Žižkov TV Tower 2

heroes of World War I, but was used for a time during the communist period (1953–62) to display the mummified body of the country's first communist leader, Klement Gottwald. Now, the building houses the National Museum's permanent exhibition of 20th-century Czech history, with moving displays on the founding of Czechoslovakia in 1918, the Nazi occupation in 1939, the communist coup d'état in 1948, the Warsaw Pact invasion in 1968, and finally the fall of communism in 1989. There's a great view over the city from the top of the building, and a fascinating exhibition downstairs on embalming and preserving Gottwald's body. ⊠ *U Památníku 1900, Žižkov* ☎ *222–781–676* ⊕ *www.nm.cz* ☜ *120 Kč* ☽ *Closed Mon.–Wed.* Ⓜ *Lines B & C: Florenc plus bus.*

WORTH NOTING

Žižkov TV Tower. Looking like a freakish, futuristic rocket ready to blast off, the Žižkov TV Tower is easily visible from around the city and perennially makes it onto Top 10 World's Ugliest Buildings lists. The upper-floor platform, reached by a high-speed elevator, gives a bird's-eye view of the numerous courtyards and apartment blocks that make up the city. There's also a bar, restaurant, and luxury hotel up there. Once back down on the ground, look up its 709-foot gray steel legs at the bronze statues of babies crawling on the structure, which were created by local provocateur artist David Černy. ⊠ *Mahlerovy sady 1, Žižkov* ⊕ *www.towerpark.cz* ☜ *200 Kč* Ⓜ *Line A: Jiřího z Poděbrad.*

LETNÁ, HOLEŠOVICE, AND TROJA

All three of these neighborhoods are up and coming, with new cultural and dining attractions popping up weekly. Come here to get away from the tourist masses and witness the rapid pace of the city's post–Velvet Revolution evolution.

LETNÁ

From above the Vltava's left bank, the large, grassy plateau called Letná gives you one of the classic views of the Old Town and the many bridges crossing the river. Beer gardens, tennis, and Frisbee attract people of all ages, while amateur soccer players emulate the professionals of Prague's top team, Sparta, who play in the stadium just across the road. The Technical Museum is also located near here.

GETTING HERE AND AROUND

On foot, get to Letná from the Old Town by walking north on Pařížská Street. Then cross the Čechův Bridge and climb the stairs. By Metro, take Line A to Hradčanská station and then nearly any tram (No. 1, 5, 25, or 26) heading east two stops to Letenské náměstí (Letná Square).

TIMING

Letná park is best enjoyed on a clear summer day, when the view of the bridges stretching out across the Vltava can be clearly seen, and photographed, in the distance. On the park's eastern end, approximately above Revoluční avenue, is a large beer garden, which is a wonderful spot to spend at least part of a warm evening.

TOP ATTRACTIONS

Letenské sady (*Letná Park*). Come to this large, shady park for an unforgettable view of Prague's bridges. From the enormous concrete pedestal at the center of the park—now occupied by a giant working metronome, which some say is marking time since the 1989 Velvet Revolution—the world's largest statue of Stalin once beckoned to citizens on the Old Town Square below. The statue was blown up in 1962, just seven years after it was completed. On sunny Sundays expats often meet up here to play ultimate Frisbee. In nice weather, there's a large and popular beer garden at the park's eastern end. Walk east along Milady Horákové Street after exiting the metro or take the tram. ✉ *Letná* Ⓜ *Line A: Hradčanská plus Tram No. 1, 25, or 26.*

WORTH NOTING

FAMILY **Národní technické muzeum** (*National Technical Museum*). This thoroughly renovated and kid-friendly museum is dedicated to the fun aspects of science, technology, and industry. There are full-sized steam locomotives, historic automobiles, and old aircraft on display. There are also engrossing exhibits on photograph and astronomy, and an active program of rotating temporary shows. ✉ *Kostelní 42, Letná* ☎ *220–399–111* ⊕ *www.ntm.cz* 💴 *170 Kč* ⊙ *Closed Mon.* Ⓜ *Line A: Hradčanská plus Tram No. 1, 5, 25, or 26 to Letenské náměstí.*

HOLEŠOVICE

The rapidly gentrifying neighborhood of Holešovice features many urban riches of its own, including perhaps the city's most underrated museum, Veletržní palace, which houses the National Gallery's permanent exhibition of modern art.

GETTING HERE AND AROUND

From Letná, 10 minutes of strolling will bring you to Holešovice's main square at Strossmayerovo náměstí. Just north along Dukelských hrdinů Street is Stromovka—a royal hunting preserve turned gracious park. By Metro, the closest stop to the area is Vltavská, on Line C.

TIMING

There are few tourists in this neck of the woods and little need to think about timing. Serious art fans could spend the better part of the day roaming the Veletržní palác's four big floors of exhibition space.

TOP ATTRACTIONS

Křížikova fontána (*Křížík's Fountain*). Originally built for the Jubilee Industrial Exhibition of 1891, this pressurized-water and colored-light show really comes into its own on summer nights just after sunset. Occasionally, live music accompanies the spectacle of lights, but more often recorded programs of film music, classics, or rock play over the illuminated dancing waters. Shows normally start on the hour at 8, 9, and 10 pm, but check the website for a current schedule. An interesting note: František Křížík, who built the fountain, was a famous inventor of his day and a friend of Thomas Edison. ✉ *Výstaviště, exhibition grounds, Holešovice* ☎ *723–665–694* ⊕ *www.krizikovafontana.cz* 💴 *230 Kč* Ⓜ *Line C: Nádraží Holešovice.*

Fodor's Choice **Veletržní palác** (*Trade Fair Palace*). The National Gallery's collection, *Art* ★ *of 19th, 20th, and 21st Centuries*, remains the keystone of the city's visual-arts scene that it has been since its opening in 1995. Touring the vast spaces of this 1920s functionalist exposition hall filled to the brim with quirky, stimulating, comprehensive modern and contemporary local art is the best way to see how Czechs surfed the forefront of the avant-garde wave until the cultural freeze following World War II. Also on display are works by Western European—mostly French—artists

Botanická
zahrada 1

Křížikova
fontána 4

Lapidárium 5

Letenské sady ... 8

Národní
technické
muzeum 7

Troyský zámek ... 3

Veletržní palác .. 6

Zoologická
zahrada
v Praze 2

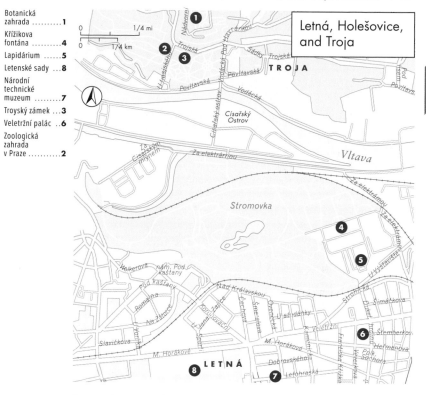

from Delacroix to the present—with paintings by Gauguin, Picasso, and Braque an unexpected bonus. Especially haunting are Jakub Schikanaeder's moody canvases and Arnost Hofbauer's hushed pilgrimage tableau (which eerily anticipates *Christina's World* by Andrew Wyeth). But painting is only the beginning—also occupying the many levels of the museum are collage, cubist sculpture, vintage gramophones, futuristic architectural models, art deco furnishings, and an exhaustive gathering of work from this new century, some of which is just as engrossing as the older stuff. Also, watch the papers and posters for information on traveling shows and temporary exhibits. ⊠ *Dukelských hrdinů 47, Holešovice* ☎ *224–301–122* ⊕ *www.ngprague.cz* 💷 *180 Kč* ✹ *Closed Mon.* Ⓜ *Line C: Vltavská.*

WORTH NOTING

Lapidárium. A fascinating display of 11th- to 19th-century sculptures rescued from torn-down buildings (or the vicissitudes of Prague's weather) is sheltered here. Original Charles Bridge statues can be found here, along with a towering bronze monument to Field Marshall Radetsky, a leader of the 19th-century Austrian army. Pieces of a marble fountain that once stood in Old Town Square now occupy most of one room. For horse lovers, there are several fine equestrian statues inside. ⊠ *Výstaviště 422, Holešovice* ☎ *702–013–372* ⊕ *www.nm.cz* 💷 *50 Kč* ✹ *Closed Mon. and Tues.* Ⓜ *Line C: Vltavská.*

TROJA

Troja is a remote, green district situated north of Holešovice on the bank of the Vltava. There are several attractions in this part of town, including the Prague City Gallery's branch at Troja Château, the Prague Botanical Gardens, and the zoo.

GETTING HERE AND AROUND
The easiest way to get here is to take Metro Line C to the stop Nádraží Holešovice and then Bus No. 112 from there.

TIMING
Given the time commitment to reaching Troja, you'll have to budget at least half a day (longer if you plan on taking in both the Botanical Gardens and the zoo). Try to plan your visit for a weekday, as both the gardens and zoo get big crowds on weekends.

TOP ATTRACTIONS
Botanická zahrada (*Botanical Gardens*). Not far from Prague Zoo, the public garden has a path that first takes you through a semidesert environment, then through a tunnel beneath a tropical lake and into a rain forest; you end up cooling off in a room devoted to plants found in tropical mountains. Sliding doors and computer-controlled climate systems help keep it all together. The impressive Fata Morgana, a snaking 429-foot greenhouse that simulates three different environments, has been drawing large crowds since it opened in 2004. ⊠ *Trojská 196, Troja* ☎ *234–148–111* ⊕ *www.botanicka.cz* ▧ *150 Kč* Ⓜ *Line C: Nádraží Holešovicé, then Bus No. 112.*

WORTH NOTING
Trojský zámek (*Troja Château*). Built in the late 17th century for the Czech nobleman Count Šternberg, this sprawling summer residence, modeled on a classical Italian villa, had the first French-style gardens in Bohemia. Inside, rich frescoes that took more than 20 years to complete depict the stories of emperors. Outside, a sweeping staircase is adorned with statues of the sons of Mother Earth. ■ **TIP→ The château is closed from early November through March.** ⊠ *U trojského zámku 1, Troja* ☎ *283–851–614* ⊕ *www.ghmp.cz* ▧ *120 Kč* ☉ *Closed Mon. and Nov.–Mar.* Ⓜ *Line C: Nádraží Holešovice, then Bus No. 112.*

FAMILY   **Zoologická zahrada v Praze** (*Prague Zoo*). Flora, fauna, and fresh air are the main things you can find in Prague's zoo. Hit hard by the floods in 2002 when some 134 animals perished, and again in 2013, when much of the zoo's grounds were inundated with water, Prague's zoo gets a periodic cleanup and offers a welcome break from the bustle of the city. Covering 160 acres on a slope overlooking the Vltava River, the zoo has thousands of animals representing 500 species. Take the chairlift for an outstanding view of the area. ⊠ *U trojského zámku 3, Troja* ☎ *296–112–30* ⊕ *www.zoopraha.cz* ▧ *200 Kč* Ⓜ *Line C: Nádraží Holešovice, then Bus No. 112.*

WHERE TO EAT

EATING AND DRINKING WELL IN PRAGUE

Traditional Czech food has developed over centuries and reflects the fresh fruits, vegetables, and animal products available locally from the land, lakes, and forests. The cuisine's relatively humble origins can be seen in soups, salads, and side dishes that feature abundant produce like cabbage, potatoes, cucumbers, beets, and onions.

Long Czech winters necessitated the development of preservation techniques like canning and smoking. The delicious soups, in particular, make a virtue of geography, combining items like sauerkraut, smoked meats, sausages, and potatoes, while often adding mushrooms and locally available herbs like dill, marjoram, and caraway seed.

Main courses frequently center on domestic meat and game. Pork is considered a delicacy, and appears on menus as roasts, tenderloins, and cutlets, pounded and fried into schnitzels. Whatever the form, rarely will you find it as flavorful and tender as it is here.

One unexpected treat is the appearance of fowl and forest game on menus, even in modest establishments. Duck is often given royal treatment, served with not one but two types of cabbage, a sliced apple, and, of course, those ubiquitous dumplings to soak up the juices.

Here are the classic dishes that you'll find on a typical Czech menu, divided by course.

STUDENÉ PŘEDKRMY (*STOO*-DEN-EH PR'ZHED-KR-MEE)

Menus typically begin with a section of cold appetizers. On a menu, this is usually a short list. In addition to ubiquitous foreign imports like sliced mozzarella and tomatoes or beef carpaccio, there may be some classically Czech choices as well, including *utopenec* (pickled pork sandwich), *tlačenka* (head cheese), and *šunkova rolka* (ham roll with horseradish cream).

Nakládaný Hermelín (*nah*-kla-den-ee). A favorite snack of cafés and pubs that consists of a small round of *hermelín* (a soft cheese closely resembling Camembert) pickled in oil, onions, and herbs and served with dark rye bread.

Utopenec (*oo*-toe-pen-etts). Literally translated as "drowned man," utopenec is uncooked pork sausage that has been pickled in vinegar. It's not only a common appetizer in Czech restaurants but a favorite beer-snack staple in pubs.

TEPLÉ PŘEDKRMY (*TEH*-PLEH PR'ZHED-KR-MEE)

These are warm appetizers and, depending of course on the type of establishment, may include old stalwarts like *topinka* (toasted or fried dark bread, rubbed with garlic cloves) or *ďabělské toasty* (devil's toasts).

Ďábelské toasty (*dya*-bel-skeh). A mixture of cooked ground beef, tomatoes, onions, and peppers served on fried or toasted white bread.

Domácí paštika (doh- *mah*-tsce pahsh-tee-kah). Homemade liver paté, usually served with some jelly and bread.

Klobása (kloh-*bah*-sa). A mainstay at the *občerstveni* (fast-food stand), this smoked sausage is also served in restaurants as an addition to certain types of guláš and soups or by itself.

POLÉVKY (POL-*EV*-KEE)

Czech meals nearly always start off with a soup of some kind.

Česnečka (*ches*-netch-kah). A Czech standby, this garlic soup is a thin—usually meatless—garlic-laced broth containing small pieces of potato, served with fried bread cubes.

Cibulačka (*tsi*-boo-latch-kah). A close relative of česnečka—though a little less potent—this onion soup is typically served with bread, and cheese is sprinkled on top. Unlike the French version, it's not made from meat broth, so it's usually quite light.

Kulajda (koo- *lie*-dah). This traditional creamy soup with fresh or dried forest mushrooms is flavored with wine vinegar, caraway, and dill.

Zelňačka (zell- *n'yatch*-kah). Cabbage is the main ingredient in this hearty soup whose flavor is accentuated by caraway and smoked pork or sausage. It can be a filling meal by itself when served in a small round loaf of bread.

Top left: *Česnečka*, a thin garlic soup; Top right: *Kulajda*, a traditional cream soup with mushrooms; Bottom right: *Šunkova rolka* (ham roll with horseradish cream)

HOTOVÁ JÍDLA (*HO*-TO-VAH *YEE'*DLA)
These are entrées that are premade and ready to be served. Listed here you can find the most traditional favorites *svíčková* (stewed beef) and goulash. If time is short, choose from this list.

Guláš (*goo*-losh). Less oily than its Hungarian counterpart, Czech goulash is cubes of beef or pork stewed and served in thin gravy. It's often served with *houskové knedlíky* (bread dumplings) and chopped onions on top.

Svíčková (*svitch*-koh-vah). A classic Czech combo that appears on menus around the country: sliced stewed beef served in a brown sauce, thickened with pureed root vegetables, and garnished with a dollop of whipping cream, cranberry sauce, and slice of lemon. It normally comes with *houskové knedlíky* (bread dumplings). It's often excellent, but the quality depends almost entirely on the cut of the beef.

Vepřo-knedlo-zelo (*veh*-pr'zho-*kne*'dlo-ze-lo). An affectionately shortened name for what's often considered to be the signature Czech dish (often served on one plate): roast pork, dumplings, and cabbage stewed with a bit of caraway.

JÍDLA NA OBJEDNÁVKU (*YEE'*DLA NA OB-YEH'D-NAHV-KOO)
This section of the menu lists main dishes that are cooked to order and nearly always includes a fried chicken cutlet (*kuřecí řízek*) or its pork equivalent (*vepřový řízek*), as well as beefsteak, prepared in various ways. Fancier places are likely to offer roast duck (*pečená kachna*), usually served with a mix of cabbage and both bread and potato dumplings.

Bramborák (*bram*-bohr-ahk). Available from a few fast-food stands around town as well as in restaurants, this large (6- to 8-inch) potato pancake is flavored with marjoram and deep-fried.

BEZMASÁ JÍDLA (BEZ- *MAH*-SAH YEED-LAH)
This section of the menu lists dishes that are prepared without meat (note that in some older, more traditional places you may still find pieces of smoked meat floating around). Listings can include *čočka* (stewed lentils), *smažený sýr* (fried cheese), and *rizoto se zeleninou* (risotto with vegetables).

Čočky (*choch*-kee). In this historic dish, green lentils are stewed with or without smoked meat (vegetarians beware). An egg and pickle are usually served with the meatless version.

Smažený sýr (*sma*-zhe-nee *see*'r). A post-war addition to the traditional Czech diet, this staple is literally translated as "fried cheese." A thick slab of an Edam-like cheese is breaded and deep fried, ideally giving it a crusty shell and a warm gooey interior. It's commonly served with tartar sauce—for spreading liberally on top—and fries.

PŘÍLOHY (PR'ZHEE-LO-HEE)
In classic Czech restaurants side orders aren't included with main courses, so look for them in this menu section. Regular dishes include *hranolky* (french fries), *Americké brambory* (literally, American potatoes; actually, fried potato wedges), *knedlíky* (sliced bread or potato dumplings), and *ryže* (rice). If in doubt about which side to try with which main, ask your server. In general, go with dumplings if the main comes in gravy, and with potatoes or rice for steaks and schnitzels.

MOUČNÍKY (MOE-OOCH- NIK-KEE)
The dessert section on any traditional Czech menu is not terribly long, but you might see *palačinky* (sweet pancakes), *zmrzlina* (ice cream), or *dort* (cake).

Palačinky (pala-*ching*-kee). Typically served with jam or ice cream inside and whipped cream on top, these pancakes

resemble crepes but are made with a thicker batter.

TREATS ON THE GO
If palačinky are not enough to keep your sweet tooth satisfied, there are still a few uniquely Czech treats around, which you can pick up at a grocery or convenience store. These are great as a snack or a little gift for someone back home.

Tatranka. Delicious wafer candy bars, covered with chocolate and wrapped in paper.

Kofola. This communist-era alternative to Coke from the 1960s tastes like a spicier Dr Pepper or a very sweet cough syrup.

Karlovarské oplatky. Crunchy, sweet, flat wafer cookies from Karlovy Vary that are filled with sugar or chocolate and about as big as a dinner plate.

Fidorka. Chocolate-coated wafers in coconut, peanut, and other flavors. Round, foil-wrapped, and about a quarter the width of a hockey puck.

Top left: *Smažený sýr,* or "fried cheese," is breaded and deep-fried, with a crusty shell and a warm interior; Top right: Fidorka, chocolate-coated wafers; Bottom right: *Palačinky,* filled pancakes with whipped cream on top

Updated by
Will Tizard

Prague generally gets high marks for architectural beauty and decidedly low marks for the quality of the food. But this is an unfair assessment based on impressions from the 1990s, when finding a decent meal really was something of a challenge. Since then, the global slow-food, fresh-food revolution has washed up onto the shores of Bohemia. Everywhere you look, serious restaurants are touting the freshness of their ingredients, and often claiming to source everything locally where possible. Some places are reviving classic Czech recipes that may be more than a century old, while others are liberally borrowing ideas and inspiration from cuisines around the world.

Part of the credit for this dining renaissance goes to the Ambiente chain of restaurants, which through its stable (including La Degustation, Lokál Dlouhááá, and Pizza Nuova) has greatly raised standards. And it's done wonders for the Czech national pride that excellent food is now easy to find. Other leading chefs have made their mark: Paul Day at Sansho, Roman Paulus at Alcron, and Jiří Nosek at Zdenek's Oyster Bar, among others. And Czechs have responded. A few years ago, it was a given the best restaurants were for visitors and businessmen. Now, many Czechs are discovering for themselves the pleasures of truly good food outside their kitchens.

International trends and fads, of course, have had an impact here, too. Every year seems to bring a new dining mania (and with it some great restaurants). The latest crazes for handcrafted burgers made from locally raised beef and for good Vietnamese cooking have brought a fresh crop of contenders. Past years have seen waves of sushi places, steak houses, and Thai noodle bars. We say, keep it coming.

Alas, what still needs an upgrade is service. English is widely spoken, but service can still be brusque or, worse, incompetent. Restaurateurs spend millions on the food, but don't put the same thought into training their staff. This will be surmounted in time, though, and in general the dining scene continues on the upswing.

Classic Czech fare is best sampled in a *hospoda,* or pub. These local joints have menus that usually include dishes for which Bohemian cuisine is justly (in)famous: pork and sauerkraut with bread dumplings; roast duck; beef in cream sauce; and, for the vegetarian, fried cheese. In recent years Czech brewers like Staropramen and Pilsner Urquell have opened chains of branded pubs (Potrefená Husa and Pilsner Urquell Original Restaurant, respectively). These chains are to the traditional pub what a new Swiss timepiece is to an old watch—light years ahead in terms of the quality. If you're looking to dip a toe into the waters of Czech cuisine, these pubs are an excellent place to begin.

3

PLANNER

RESERVATIONS
Through the week, reservations are not normally needed, but the situation changes on Friday and Saturday evenings. Likewise, in nice weather you'll always be better advised to phone ahead if you hope to get an outdoor seat. In our restaurant listings, we've noted places where reservations are absolutely essential to getting in the door.

WHAT TO WEAR
Casual dress is acceptable nearly everywhere, except in very nice or expensive restaurants. In restaurant listings dress is mentioned only when men are expected to wear a jacket or a jacket and tie, which is seldom the case.

SMOKING
The better restaurants have all but banned smoking indoors in response to customer demand (although technically the law allows for indoor smoking as long as the spaces are separated by a wall). Cheaper restaurants generally allow smoking, but only in segregated spaces. Pubs are a different animal altogether; a few are no-smoking, but the majority are not.

MEALTIMES
Most restaurants in Prague are open from 11 am to 11 pm. This closing time is very regular with traditional Czech restaurants and *hospody* (pubs); their kitchens usually shut down by 10 and sometimes earlier if it's a slow night. A small number of restaurants serve the late-night crowd, especially in the city center, but don't put off dinner too long, or you may have trouble finding an open kitchen. Mealtimes hold to the European standard. Lunch runs from noon until 2; dinner starts at 6 and runs until about 8 or 9. Czechs don't generally linger over meals, but you'll rarely feel any pressure from the staff to vacate your table.

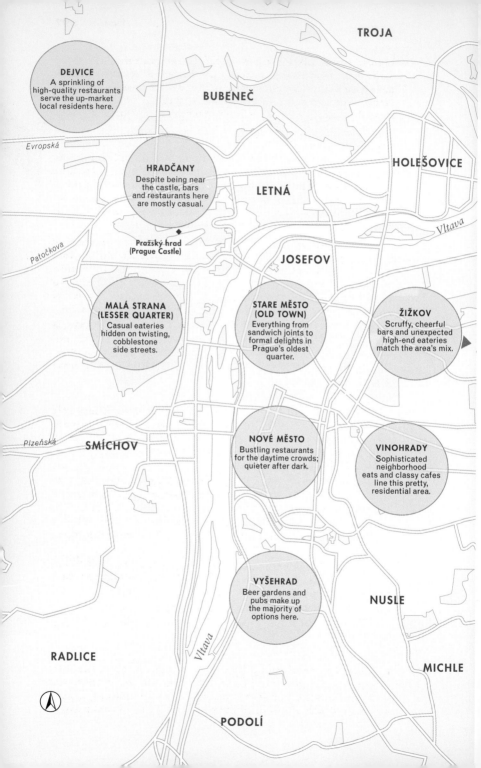

TROJA

DEJVICE
A sprinkling of high-quality restaurants serve the up-market local residents here.

BUBENEČ

Evropská

HRADČANY
Despite being near the castle, bars and restaurants here are mostly casual.

HOLEŠOVICE

LETNÁ

Vltava

Patočkova

Pražský hrad (Prague Castle)

JOSEFOV

MALÁ STRANA (LESSER QUARTER)
Casual eateries hidden on twisting, cobblestone side streets.

STARE MĚSTO (OLD TOWN)
Everything from sandwich joints to formal delights in Prague's oldest quarter.

ŽIŽKOV
Scruffy, cheerful bars and unexpected high-end eateries match the area's mix.

Plzeňská

SMÍCHOV

NOVÉ MĚSTO
Bustling restaurants for the daytime crowds; quieter after dark.

VINOHRADY
Sophisticated neighborhood eats and classy cafes line this pretty, residential area.

VYŠEHRAD
Beer gardens and pubs make up the majority of options here.

NUSLE

RADLICE

Vltava

MICHLE

PODOLÍ

MENUS

Most restaurants post menus outside. Prix-fixe meals are not popular in the evening, but many restaurants offer a *denní lístek* (daily menu) of three or four items that usually include a soup starter and a simple main course. If you want to try a traditional Czech meal, such as svíčková or guláš, you may find it's offered only at lunchtime in most restaurants outside of central Prague.

WINE

The Czech Republic produces its own wines; most of the better bottles come from southern Moravia in the area around Mikulov. Truth be told, many of these are not as good as varietals from traditional wine-growing countries in Europe, but every year brings a leap in improvement, and domestic vintages are slowly closing the gap. (And a few do hold their own in comparison.)

Most of the better restaurants will carry a few Czech labels on the wine list (usually at far lower prices), followed by long lists of French, Italian, and Spanish wines. Often the Czech wines will offer better value, though the waiter or sommelier will do his or her best to talk you into more expensive bottles. A few excellent restaurants, like Mozaika in Vinohrady, specialize in local wine and are good places to try them.

Bars and pubs also serve wine, but usually cheaper, barely drinkable versions of Czech grapes like Müller-Thurgau (white) and Frankovka (red). Some better Czech grapes to look out for include *Ryzlink* (Riesling) and Sauvignon Blanc (both white) and André or *Rulandské červené* (Pinot noir), both red.

PRICES

In better restaurants prices are slightly lower but generally comparable to what you would find in North America or Western Europe. In traditional Czech restaurants and hospody, especially outside the city center, price levels are much lower and can drop to a rock-bottom 90 Kč on the denní lístek.

Watch for a *couvert* (cover charge), which may appear in smaller print on a menu. Though a bit annoying, it's legitimate and is meant to cover bread, a caddy of condiments, and/or service. Remember that side orders usually have to be ordered separately, and will be tabulated accordingly. Taxes are included with all meal prices listed in the menu.

WHAT IT COSTS IN KORUNA				
	$	$$	$$$	$$$$
Restaurants	under 150 Kč	150 Kč–300 Kč	301 Kč–500 Kč	over 500 Kč

Prices are per person for a main course at dinner, or if dinner is not served, at lunch.

PAYING THE TAB

In a more traditional dining venue, such as a *restaurace* or hospoda, it's possible that the person you ordered from will not be the person who tallies your bill. In that case, you may hear your waiter say *kolega*, meaning a colleague will bring the bill. This situation is less likely in more modern establishments. In the bulk of low- and mid-price restaurants the waiter or bill person will tally your bill in front of you and stand by while you pull together the money to pay. If you want to do it the Czech way, quickly add on a suitable amount for a tip in your head, and say this new total when you hand over your money. If you need a bit of time, it's best to politely smile and say, "*Moment, prosím*" (One moment, please). Don't panic if you miss the moment; many people don't make the calculation quickly enough and just leave the money on the table. In the places frequented by tourists, particularly in the city center, the waiter (or a colleague) may expect this already and just leave the bill on the table for you.

TIPPING

Tipping in the Czech Republic has been based traditionally on rounding up the tab to a convenient number rather than calculating a percentage and adding it on, and in the hospody around the city (especially out of the tourist area) this is still how it's done. For example, paying 150 Kč on a bill of 137 Kč would be perfectly acceptable (though locals might stop at 140 Kč). At the better places, a 10% tip is common to recognize good food and service.

RESTAURANT REVIEWS

Listed alphabetically within neighborhoods.

STARÉ MĚSTO

Staré Město is where visitors spend most of their time and where most of the best (and worst) restaurants are found. Ironically, perhaps the worst place to have a meal is directly on Old Town Square. Sadly, pretty much all places here are tourist traps. Instead, try exploring the area around Dlouhá to the northeast of the square, which boasts lots of fine dining, wine bars, and new high-end Czech eateries. As for the other parts of Staré Město, it's probably a good area to stick closely to the recommendations in this book. If there's someone hustling for patrons outside, go elsewhere.

$$
BAKERY
✕ **Au Gourmand.** This sweet little café with tiled mosaic floors, globe lights, and a green pastry case provides an inviting spot for a lunch. It's similar to the neighboring Bakeshop Praha, but with a certain Gallic flair. Like its neighbor, it too has a few seats and a garden in the back, where you can enjoy a *salade niçoise* or a tomato-and-mozzarella sandwich. The fresh breads and good homemade ice cream elevate the offerings. $ *Average main: 150 Kč* ✉ *Dlouhá 10, Staré Mesto* ☎ *222–329–060* Ⓜ *Line A: Staroměstská* ⊕ *D1*.

$
BAKERY
✕ **Bakeshop Praha.** An American-style bakery and café counter, Bakeshop Praha sells familiar U.S. favorites, from avocado BLTs to entire pumpkin pies. Though it gets crowded during peak lunch hours, there is indoor seating, and the space, with penny-tiled floors and ceiling moldings, has a retro charm. But the takeaway sandwiches, giant cookies, and good coffee make it easy to grab and go. $ *Average main: 140 Kč*

BEST BETS FOR PRAGUE DINING

With thousands of restaurants to choose from, how will you decide where to eat? Fodor's writers and editors have selected their favorite restaurants by price, cuisine, and experience. Fodor's Choice properties represent the "best of the best" in every price category. You can also search by neighborhood for excellent eats. Or find specific details about a restaurant in the full reviews, listed alphabetically later in the chapter.

Fodor's Choice★

Aromi, $$$
Bio Zahrada, $
Cotto Crudo, $$$$
Cukrkávalimonáda, $$
La Finestra in Cucina, $$$
Lokál Dlouhááá, $$
Noi, $$
Sansho, $$$$
The Tavern, $$
U Modré kachničky, $$$
Zdenek's Oyster Bar, $$$$

By Price

$

Beas
Bio Zahrada
Pho Vietnam Tuan & Lan

$$

Café Savoy
Cukrkávalimonáda
Dish

Ichnusa Botega Bistro
Lemon Leaf
Lokál Dlouhááá
Noi
Pastacaffé
Pepe Nero Pizza & Pasta

$$$

Aromi
Hergetova Cihelna
La Finestra in Cucina
La Veranda
The Sushi Bar

$$$$

Alcron
La Degustation
Sansho
Spices Restaurant & Bar

By Cuisine

ASIAN

Noi, $$
Sansho, $$$$
The Sushi Bar, $$$
Yami, $$

Kampa Park, $$$$
Kavárna Slavia, $$

HIP HANGOUTS

Dish, $$
Ichnusa Botega Bistro, $$
Noi, $$
The Tavern, $$

HOTEL DINING

Alcron, $$$$
Le Grill, $$$$
Spices Restaurant & Bar, $$$$

OUTDOOR DINING

Bio Zahrada, $
Grosseto Marina, $$

OLD SCHOOL

Café Savoy, $$
Kampa Park, $$$$
Kavárna Slavia, $$

CLASSIC CZECH

Lokál Dlouhááá, $$
V Kolkovně, $$

HAUTE CZECH

La Degustation, $$$$
U Modré kachničky, $$$

FRENCH

Le Terroir, $$$$

SEAFOOD

Alcron, $$$$
The Sushi Bar, $$$
Zdenek's Oyster Bar, $$$$

By Experience

CHEAP EATS

Bakeshop Praha, $
Dish, $$
Lokál Dlouhááá, $$
The Tavern, $$

GREAT VIEWS

Grosseto Marina, $$
Hergetova Cihelna, $$$

✉ *Kozi 1, Staré Mesto* ☎ *222–316–823* 🌐 *www.bakeshop.cz* [M] *Line A: Staroměstská* ✣ *D1.*

$ VEGETARIAN 🍴 **Beas.** Right behind the soaring spires of Old Town's Týn cathedral, Beas offers inexpensive, Indian-style vegetarian and vegan food just a short walk from Old Town Square. Don't expect upscale service—you're going to bus your own table, but these dishes are worth the extra work. Great curries, *dhals* (stewed lentils), grilled flatbreads, fragrant basmati rice, rich grilled eggplant, and other vegetarian delights make you forget that nothing you're eating contains eggs, meat, or fish. Although meal prices are already low, the availability of free tap water, makes it even easier on the wallet. [$] *Average main: 80 Kč* ✉ *Týnská 19, Staré Mesto* ☎ *608–035–727* 🌐 *www.beas-dhaba.cz* 💳 *No credit cards* [M] *Line B: Nám. Republiky* ✣ *D1.*

$$$ ECLECTIC 🍴 **Brasserie mEating Point.** Ignore the silly name and you'll find a restaurant that's a cut above your typical hotel dining experience. Inside the King's Court hotel and looking out on Náměstí Republiky, mEating Point caters to international tastes. (The menu, which is written in English and Russian, should be a hint.) Terrace seating in mild weather trumps the interiors, where the decor suffers from too much flashiness: purple velvet chairs and a busy patterned carpet feel distracting. Nonetheless, the food hits the right notes, from crisp, tender calamari with a spicy tomato coulis to tuna and salmon tartare appetizers (not as common in Prague as in the States). The pastas here are also excellent, including a fresh tagliatelle with mushrooms and bacon. And if you want to stick to Czech standards, there are some clever spins on these as well, like duck with white cabbage. [$] *Average main: 350 Kč* ✉ *U Obecniho domu 3, Staré Mesto* ☎ *224–222–890* 🌐 *www.hotelkingscourt.cz* [M] *Line B: Náměstí Republiky* ✣ *E2.*

$$$$ ITALIAN Fodor's Choice ★ 🍴 **Cotto Crudo.** Having settled into its role as a leading light on Prague's culinary scene, the kitchen here dwells on crafting definitive Italian fare, overseen by chef Leonardo di Clemente. The comfortable Four Seasons restaurant and terrace graciously serves some of the finest Mediterranean cuisine in Prague, themed as cooked or raw, the latter in the form of a decadent mozarella bar and salami and prosciutto tower. Even fish, the bane of many a Czech restaurant kitchen, arrives here as intricately flavored sea bass with baked herb and salt crust. It pairs nicely with the hotel's own vibe, that of unquestioning luxury. Servers move seamlessly, the courses are expertly timed, and the sommelier eagerly suggests his recommendations. Despite the high prices and reverent treatment of the ingredients, the light, airy dining room is quite welcoming. And in a nod to the many family guests, there's a kids' menu, along with staff who love to pamper them. [$] *Average main: 501 Kč* ✉ *Four Seasons Prague, Veleslavinova 21, Staré Mesto* ☎ *221–426–880* 🌐 *www.cottocrudo.cz* ✍ *Reservations essential* [M] *Line A: Staroměstská* ✣ *A2.*

$$$ ITALIAN 🍴 **Divinis.** The austere decor—white walls and plank floors—at this wine-centric Italian restaurant on a quiet street near the Týn cathedral belies the quality and complexity of its food. Whether you stick to a simpler beetroot carpaccio with goat cheese or try something more complex like sliced octopus served in an orange vinaigrette, the dishes are skillfully prepared and attractively presented. Beef cheeks braised with

marsala and spinach or pork belly and lentils make excellent entrées, but if you're not up for a huge meal, opt for a pasta. The all-Italian wine list is one of the city's best. [$] *Average main: 500 Kč* ✉ *Týnská 21, Staré Mesto* ☎ *222–325–440* 🌐 *www.divinis.cz* ⏲ *Closed Sun.* ✍ *Reservations essential* [M] *Line A: Staroměstská* ✥ *D2.*

$$ ITALIAN 🍴 **Grosseto Marina.** You don't have to splurge at expensive places like Kampa Park for regal dining vistas over Charles Bridge or Prague Castle. For the price of a pizza or pasta, you can sit on the deck of this marina, anchored off the Vltava River. And on a warm summer evening, there's almost no nicer place in town to take in the cityscape. The quality of the food is surprisingly good, especially when the kitchen and the staff aren't too harried by the crowds. Understandably, you'll have to book well in advance to secure one of the coveted deck-top tables. [$] *Average main: 280 Kč* ✉ *Alšovo nábřeží 1, Staré Mesto* ☎ *222–316–744* 🌐 *www.grosseto.cz* ✍ *Reservations essential* [M] *Line A: Staroměstská* ✥ *A1.*

$$ CAFÉ 🍴 **Kavárna Obecní dům.** The magnificent art nouveau Municipal House has this ground-floor café that's every bit as opulent on the inside as the building is grand on the outside. Step through the doors and into another era—the first decade of the 20th century to be specific—when the practice of coffee drinking was given white-glove treatment. The food menu is on the light side, mostly sandwiches, salads, and cheese plates. As with other cafés in town, in addition to coffee, tea, and soft drinks, it's possible to order a glass of wine or beer. [$] *Average main: 200 Kč* ✉ *Nám. Republiky 5, Staré Mesto* ☎ *222–002–763* 🌐 *www.kavarnaod.cz* [M] *Line B: Náměstí Republiky* ✥ *E2.*

$$ CAFÉ 🍴 **Kavárna Slavia.** Easily the city's best-known café, Slavia serves good coffee, drinks, and light snacks, as well as the greatest hits of Czech cuisine: roast duck with potato dumplings and sauerkraut, beef guláš, and roast smoked pork with white cabbage and potato pancakes. Plus, the café offers rich views of the National Theater and Prague Castle. The spectacular location has a historic air that reaches back to the days of Viktor Oliva's painting *The Absinthe Drinker* (which hangs in the main room) through the 1970s and '80s when the late Václav Havel was a regular. [$] *Average main: 200 Kč* ✉ *Smetanovo nábř. 2, Staré Mesto* ☎ *224–218–493* 🌐 *www.cafeslavia.cz* [M] *Line A: Staroměstská* ✥ *A5.*

$$$ ITALIAN 🍴 **Kogo.** Long a favorite of American expats, this Italian mainstay in the Slovanský Dům shopping mall is of a far higher quality than the immediate surroundings suggest. The cavernous interior is frenzied with businessmen at lunch, who negotiate while wolfing down the well-done Italian standards. Fresh pastas (fettuccine with bacon and mushrooms, tagliatelle with a dollop of lamb ragout) are so firm they taste as if they've been in the water for mere seconds. The seafood case near the host's stand is a tip that fresh fish is another specialty here. Kogo's outdoor seating is covered, and open year-round. [$] *Average main: 400 Kč* ✉ *Na Příkopě 22, Staré Mesto* ☎ *221–451–258* 🌐 *www.kogo.cz* [M] *Line B: Náměstí Republiky* ✥ *E3.*

$$$$ ECLECTIC 🍴 **La Degustation.** One of Prague's three Michelin star holders is this elegant tasting room, where diners choose from one of two 8- to 10-course prix-fixe menus and sample artful delicacies over an extended evening. Dishes are divided by two thematic menus with courses expertly paired

Where to Eat in Prague

A   **B**   **C**   **D**

1

Pepe Nero Pizza and Pasta

La Veranda

V Kolkovně

La Degustation

Bakeshop Praha

Dlouhá

Široká

V kolkovně

Yami

Masná

Au Gourmand

Grosseto Marina

nám. Jana Palacha

STAROMĚSTSKÁ

Maitrea

Beas

Divinis

Tynská

Maiselova

Pařížská

Kaprova

2

Cotto Crudo

Velesla vínova

La Finestra in Cucina

Platnéřská

U radnice

STARÉ MĚSTO
(Old Town)

Staroměstské nám.

Štupartská

Celetná

Karlova

Krizovnická

Železná

Havlířská

Malé nám.

Melantrichova

Havelská

Na Příkopě

3

Hradčany and Malá Strana
see inset

Vltava

Liliová

Husova

Jilská

Le Terroir

Michalská

Náprstkova

Betlémské nám.

MUSTEK

Martinská

4

Betlémská

Konviktská

Bartolomějská

Na Perštýně

Jungmannovo nám.

Václavské náměstí
(Wenceslas Square)

0   250 yards
0   250 meters

Národní

Jungmannova

5

Kávarna Slavia

Burrito Loco

Spálená

NOVÉ MĚSTO
(New Town)

Vlaislavova

Vodičkova

Ostrovní

Jáma

6

Universal

Křemencova

Pštrossova

Ginger and Fred
The Globe Bookstore & Café
Lemon Leaf

Lazarská

Černá

Potrefená Husa

Pastacaffé

A   **B**   **C**   **D**

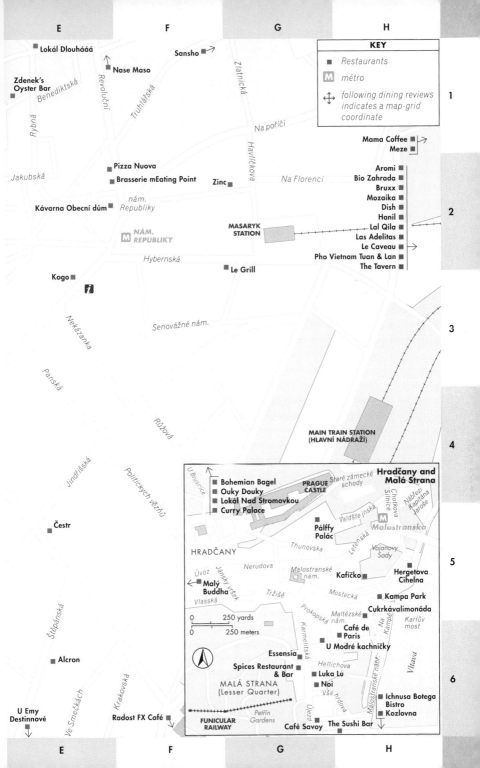

KEY

- ■ Restaurants
- Ⓜ *métro*
- ⬌ *following dining reviews indicates a map-grid coordinate*

Lokál Dlouháááá

Zdenek's Oyster Bar

Benediktská

Rybná

Revoluční

Nase Maso

Sansho ■➙

Zlatnická

Truhlářská

Jakubská

Pizza Nuova

Brasserie mEating Point

Zinc ■

nám. Republiky

Kávarna Obecní dům ■

Ⓜ NÁM. REPUBLIKY

Na poříčí

Havlíčkova

Na Florenci

Mama Coffee ■➙
Meze ■

Aromi ■
Bio Zahrada ■
Bruxx ■
Mozaika ■
Dish ■
Hanil ■
Lal Qila ■
Las Adelitas ■
Le Caveau ■➙
Pho Vietnam Tuan & Lan ■
The Tavern ■

MASARYK STATION

Hybernská

Le Grill ■

Kogo ■

🛈

Nekázanka

Senovážné nám.

Panská

Růžová

MAIN TRAIN STATION (HLAVNÍ NÁDRAŽÍ)

Jindřišská

U Brusnice

Bohemian Bagel ■
Ouky Douky ■
Lokál Nad Stromovkou ■
Curry Palace ■

PRAGUE CASTLE

Staré zámecké schody

Hradčany and Malá Strana

Chotkova Silnice

Nábřeží Kapitána Jaroše

Čestr ■

Pálffy Palác ■

Valdštejnská

Ⓜ Malostranská

HRADČANY

Thunovska

Letenská

Vojanovy Sady

Úvoz

Jánský vršek

Nerudova

Malostranské nám.

Kafíčko ■

Hergetova Cihelna ■

Štěpánská

Malý Buddha ■➙

Vlasská

Tržiště

Mostecká

Kampa Park ■

Cukrkávalimonáda ■

0   250 yards
0   250 meters

Prokopská

Maltézské nám.

Café de Paris ■

U Modré kachničky ■

Na Kampě

Karlův most

Alcron ■

Essensia ■

Spices Restaurant & Bar ■

Luka Lú ■

Hellichova

Noi ■

Karmelitská

Vše hrdova

Maltézské nábř.

Vltava

U Emy Destinnové ■➙

Ve Smečkách

Krakovská

Radost FX Café ■➙

FUNICULAR RAILWAY

Petřín Gardens

Újezd

Café Savoy ■➙

The Sushi Bar ■➙

Ichnusa Botega Bistro ■
Kozlovna ■

MALÁ STRANA (Lesser Quarter)

E   F   G   H

1   2   3   4   5   6

with wines. One menu focuses on classic local specialties, like smoked fish from the ponds of southern Bohemia, while the other consists of the master chef's inspirations, which may blend Continental cuisine with fantasy: think catfish, almonds, and celery root. Be sure to eat lightly beforehand, you'll need a full appetite to last through the multiple courses. One word of caution: fixed-price menus range in price from 2,200 Kč to 3,200 Kč, not including wine pairings. Dinner for two, with wine and tip, can easily climb into 10,000 Kč territory. But for many, the experience is worth every koruna. [$] *Average main: 1000 Kč* ✉ *Haštalská 18, Staré Mesto* ☎ *222–311–234* 🌐 *www.ladegustation.cz* ✍ *Reservations essential* [M] *Line A: Staroměstská* ✥ *D1.*

$$$ ITALIAN Fodor'sChoice ★ 🍴 **La Finestra in Cucina.** One of Prague's hottest tables, La Finestra is the meaty counterpart to its sister restaurant, Aromi, right down to the wooden tables and brick walls. Catering to local gourmands and bold-face names, this restaurant lives up to the hype. As at Aromi, waiters display an array of freshly caught fish that comprise the day's specials, but here they also do the same with meat, including dry-aged cuts flown in from Italy. Complementing this array of protein are fried chickpeas and fresh foccacia to nibble on and expertly crafted al dente pastas like oxtail agnolotti, and spaghetti with sea urchin. [$] *Average main: 500 Kč* ✉ *Platnéřská 13, Staré Mesto* ☎ *222–325–325* 🌐 *www.lafinestra.cz* ✍ *Reservations essential* [M] *Line A: Staroměstská* ✥ *B2.*

$$$ MODERN EUROPEAN 🍴 **La Veranda.** Aphrodisiac menus and seasonal specials are but two of the reasons to consider this elegant dining room and lounge near the Jewish Quarter. Another is the kitchen's love of unusual flavor combinations, sending out dishes like slowly braised lamb haunch with root vegetables, fresh pasta with lobster and tomato, and slow-roasted pork belly with spinach puree. Despite the quality of the cooking, La Veranda remains somewhat overlooked by visitors (though popular with locals), making a visit to this stylish, softly lighted room feel like you've been let in on a wonderful secret. They have a children's play area on Saturday. [$] *Average main: 450 Kč* ✉ *Elišky Krásnohorské 2, Staré Mesto* ☎ *224–814–733* 🌐 *www.laveranda.cz* ⏲ *Closed Sun.* ✍ *Reservations essential* [M] *Line A: Staroměstská* ✥ *C1.*

$$$$ FRENCH 🍴 **Le Terroir.** The finest wines available to humanity can be found here, along with inventive and occasionally playful dishes like frog legs with white asparagus and egg, or tuna sashimi with herring, papaya, and candied ginger. Don't forget the cheese course, as this restaurant has its own cheese room stocking rarities from France and Italy. But wine provides the real lure; bottles here start around $30 and head into the stratosphere, with the list separated into minute geographic distinctions. The clublike cellar is romantic and chic, but open-air dining on the patio is a must in spring and summer. [$] *Average main: 600 Kč* ✉ *Vejvodova 1, Staré Mesto* ☎ *222–220–260* 🌐 *www.leterroir.cz* ⏲ *Closed Sun. and Mon.* ✍ *Reservations essential* [M] *Lines A & B: Můstek* ✥ *C4.*

$$ CZECH Fodor'sChoice ★ 🍴 **Lokál Dlouhááá.** Sleek and relatively sophisticated, Lokál takes the Czech pub concept to a new level with fresh local ingredients, perfectly poured beers, and friendly, efficient service. It makes for an idealized version of a corner restaurant out of another era, right down to the stark white walls, waiters in vests, and bathrooms wallpapered with old

HUNTING FOR DUMPLINGS

The quality of Bohemian cooking declined precipitously during the communist period, and bad habits were hard to shake in the aftermath of the 1989 revolution. Consequently, Czech cuisine has gotten an undeserved bad rap. Thankfully, some restaurateurs have taken up the baton to right past wrongs, and if you know where to go, it's now possible to find excellent traditional cooking outside the home.

The Ambiente group, in particular, sees it as a priority to revive historic recipes and cooking techniques. This chain's flagship **La Degustation** (✉ *Haštalská 18* ☎ *222-311-234*) offers a multicourse tasting menu using recipes from the 19th century. It's a bit pricey at over 2,000 Kč a head, but if you want Czech at its best, this is where to dine. The chain also runs the cheaper **Lokál Dlouhááá tavern** (✉ *Dlouhá 33* ☎ *222-316-265*), and for much less money you can taste excellent renditions of pub staples like guláš and fried pork cutlets.

Brewpubs are another alternative for finding well-done domestic cooking. Good examples are the Pilsner Urquell chain, which runs **V Kolkovně** (✉ *V Kolkovně 8* ☎ *224-819-701*) in Old Town and **Kulat'ák** (✉ *Vítězné náměstí 12* ☎ *773-973-037*) in Dejvice. Here you'll find high standards for traditional Czech cuisine in a sleek environment with good service.

pinups and airplane posters. Many of the dishes have a modern twist: schnitzel is made from pork neck and served atop buttery whipped potatoes, while the Czech classic of svíčková is tangy and fresh (not often the case at most pubs). [$] *Average main: 150 Kč* ✉ *Dlouhá 33, Staré Mesto* ☎ *222-316-265* 🌐 *lokal-dlouha.ambi.cz* ✍ *Reservations essential* [M] *Line B: Náměstí Republiky* ✥ *E1.*

$$ VEGETARIAN 🍴 **Maitrea.** Vegetarians, you're in luck: the Czech Republic's best vegetarian restaurant just happens to be a five-minute walk from Old Town Square. Here, veg-food is not viewed as a radical departure from other cuisines; indeed, most of the dishes, like the chilis, burritos, and Czech classics svíčková and guláš, look and taste like the originals, only without the meat. The interior design is attractive but a bit space agey, with swoopy fabric light fixtures reminiscent of giant white mushrooms, which coincidentally turn up in many of the entrées. [$] *Average main: 150 Kč* ✉ *Týnská ulička 6, Staré Mesto* ☎ *221-711-631* 🌐 *www.restaurace-maitrea.cz* [M] *Line A: Staroměstská* ✥ *D1.*

$$ CZECH 🍴 **Nase Maso.** Butcher shops are serious business in the Czech Republic and many have barely changed for generations, at least in terms of offerings. This newly updated version, with friendlier service and a handy lunch counter, stocks dozens of sausage varieties, classic smoked meats, and delicate filets of pork and beef. Situated on a colorful street full of bars and boutiques, the shop makes for a handy refueling stop that offers an authentic taste of Bohemian tradition. [$] *Average main: 150 Kč* ✉ *Dlouha 39, Staré Mesto* ☎ *222-311-378* 🌐 *nasemaso.ambi.cz/en* 💳 *No credit cards* [M] *Náměstí Republiky* ✥ *E1.*

CAFÉ CULTURE

Prague has a rapidly evolving café culture, and finding a good cup of coffee here is now as easy as in any large city in Europe. Coffee standards took a beating under communism, but a clutch of new Italian- and American-inspired cafés has opened up. These are meshing with the older, traditional coffeehouses from the 19th and 20th centuries, and today's cafés run the gamut from the historic to the literary to the trendy. Most cafés are licensed to sell alcohol, and are open until at least 11 pm, some transforming into virtual bars by night. As a general rule, the old-fashioned-looking cafés serve traditional Czech snacks, such as marinated cheese, whereas those with splashy new façades carry a selection of more Western-style desserts, such as carrot cake and tiramisu.

$$
PIZZA
FAMILY
✕ **Pizza Nuova.** Turning out pies in true Neapolitan style, Pizza Nuova serves chewy pizzas that tend to get a bit soggy in the center—they're 100% authentic, if not the easiest to eat. The huge bilevel space, decked out in light and dark wood, also boasts a small outdoor eating area on Náměstí Republiky. During the day it fills with businessmen taking lunches and families with tots; at night the ambience turns downright swanky. All the pies come with authentic ingredients: San Marzano tomatoes, buffalo mozzarella, Grana Padano cheese. $ *Average main: 260 Kč* ✉ *Revoluční 1, Staré Mesto* ☎ *221–803–308* ⊕ *www.ambi.cz* ⚐ *Reservations essential* Ⓜ *Line B: Náměstí Republiky* ✛ *E2.*

$$
EASTERN
EUROPEAN
✕ **V Kolkovně.** For Czechs, this chainlet remains one of the most popular spots to take visitors for a taste of local cuisine without the stress of tourist rip-offs. And it's a solid choice. The wood-and-copper decor gives off an appropriate air of a brewery taproom, and you can wash down traditional meals—such as *svíčková* (beef tenderloin in cream sauce), roast duck, and fried pork cutlets, or upgrades of traditional food, such as turkey steak with Roquefort sauce and walnuts—with a mug of unpasteurized Pilsner Urquell. $ *Average main: 220 Kč* ✉ *V Kolkovně, V Kolkovně 8, Staré Mesto* ☎ *224–819–701* ⊕ *www. vkolkovne.cz* Ⓜ *Line A: Staroměstská* ✛ *C1.*

$$$
JAPANESE
✕ **Yami.** Yami is sushi without the pretension that often accompanies a sushi place in Prague, and while the prices have crept up in recent years, the sushi sets and rolls are still cheaper than much of the competition (without any compromise in quality). The "Ruby Roll," with tuna, butterfish, avocado, and cucumber, is a delight and makes for a filling main course. The soups and appetizers are excellent, too. Try to reserve in advance around mealtimes because this place can get crowded. $ *Average main: 320 Kč* ✉ *Masná 3, Staré Mesto* ☎ *222–312–756* ⊕ *www. yami.cz* Ⓜ *Line A: Starométská* ✛ *D1.*

$$$$
SEAFOOD
Fodor's Choice
★
✕ **Zdenek's Oyster Bar.** In the few short years since it's been open, Zdenek's Oyster Bar has established itself as the city's best seafood bar. Aside from the namesake oysters (more than a dozen different varieties), head chef Jiří Nosek has developed creative entrées around mussels, shrimp, crab, lobster, and various types of fish. The restaurant occupies a quiet corner in the middle of the Old Town. The interior is classy but

CLOSE UP

Good Food on the Go

There are plenty of bakeries and sandwich shops that offer nibbles to take away when guláš fatigue sets in. Among the best is **Bakeshop Praha** (✉ *Kozi 1* ☎ *222–316–823*), which sells everything from avocado BLTs to entire pies. Though it gets crowded during peak lunch hours, there is indoor seating if the street benches fill up. A bit closer to Old Town Square is **Au Gourmand** (✉ *Dlouhá 10* ☎ *222–329–060*), which has a certain Gallic flair. It, too, has a few seats, but there's a garden in the back where you can enjoy a *salade niçoise* or a tomato and mozzarella sandwich.

relaxed, and while the prices here can be high, you get what you pay for and there's never any pretension or attitude. $ *Average main: 600 Kč* ✉ *Malá Štupartská 5, Staré Mesto* ☎ *725–946–250* ⊕ *www.oysterbar. cz* ⟡ *Reservations essential* Ⓜ *Line A: Staroměstská* ✛ *E1.*

JOSEFOV

Josefov occupies a quiet corner of Old Town and it can get almost eerie at night. But there are a few good restaurants scattered in and around the neighborhood, and the setting can be magnificent. The stretch along Pařížská, which links the Old Town Square to the river, running due north, is lined with decent but expensive restaurants that cater to the customers dashing out of Louis Vuitton and Prada.

$$ ITALIAN ✕ **Pepe Nero Pizza & Pasta.** Whether Pepe Nero serves some of the best pizza in Prague is the source of constant debate among locals, but one thing is for sure: they have the city's best mozzarella. Tangy and creamy, the cheese is as authentic as can be. It tops the panoply of pizzas here, including pepperoni, mushroom, and red-pepper pies. For the carb-phobic, the mozzarella also appears in the Caprese and Vesuviana salads, both large enough for two, and several of the pasta dishes. The modern white interior bustles with Italians engaged in friendly banter with the staff—a sure sign of authenticity. $ *Average main: 230 Kč* ✉ *Bílkova 4, Josefov* ☎ *222–315–543* ⊕ *www.pepenero.cz* Ⓜ *Line A: Staroměstská* ✛ *C1.*

MALÁ STRANA

Malá Strana has come into its own as a dining scene of late. Overall, restaurants in the district tend to be less formal than in Old Town, though there are pockets of high-end dining near Charles Bridge and the embassies. For the most part, establishments here serve tourists and locals alike, which makes for some more consistent dining. The area around Maltézské náměstí has several wonderful restaurants, including

Mandarin Oriental's house restaurant. The eastern edge of Malá Strana along the Vltava River offers dining with amazing views, all for a price.

$$ FRENCH 🍴 **Café de Paris.** The twin stars of the show at this Gallic import are beef entrecôte and french fries. Café de Paris even makes its own "special sauce" (think béarnaise with a hint of mustard). If meat and *frites* are your fancy, waiters subsequently arrive bearing trays of them to serve at each diner's tableside. The look is classic French bistro, down to the old photographs and red banquettes lining the walls, which makes sense considering its location near the French Embassy. There are a few other things on the limited menu, like Caesar salad and a rotating option of soups, but there's little reason to stray from house specialties. [$] *Average main: 260 Kč ✉ Maltézské nám. 4, Malá Strana ☎ 603–160–718 🌐 www.cafedeparis.cz ✍ Reservations essential [M] Line A: Malostranská ✥ H6.*

$$ CAFÉ Fodor's Choice ★ 🍴 **Cukrkávalimonáda.** An excellent pit stop while exploring Malá Strana, this warm, inviting café and bakery serves freshly made soups, salads, sandwiches, and pasta dishes, making it a convenient oasis for lunch. Or just rest your feet with a coffee and a slice of pie or cake. The light-wood booths and exposed-beam ceilings give Cukrkávalimonáda a country-farmhouse feel. Lunchtime can be overcrowded, so try to book a spot in advance; at other times, you can normally find a seat. Note: the café closes daily at 7 pm. [$] *Average main: 180 Kč ✉ Lázeňská 7, Malá Strana ☎ 257–225–396 🌐 www.cukrkavalimonada.com 💳 No credit cards [M] Line A: Malostranská ✥ H5.*

$$$ ECLECTIC 🍴 **Hergetova Cihelna.** Between the attractive staff and sleek, minimalist interior, there's no shortage of glamour at Hergetova Cihelna. The most gorgeous thing, however, is the view of Charles Bridge from the expansive terrace. It makes Cihelna ideal for a leisurely lunch or a late-night cocktail—blankets are draped on the back of each chair if it gets chilly. The food represents a creative approach to Central European, Czech and French cuisine, from delectable guinea fowl to slow-baked pork cheeks or a healthy spelt wheat asparagus risotto. It's reliable fare—not exquisite, but then again, it's tough to compete with the vista. [$] *Average main: 500 Kč ✉ Cihelná 2b, Malá Strana ☎ 296–826–103 🌐 www.kampagroup.com [M] Line A: Malostranská ✥ H5.*

$$$ ITALIAN 🍴 **Ichnusa Botega Bistro.** On a side street between Malá Strana and Smíchov, the Ichnusa Botega Bistro evokes the island of Sardinia, with Mediterranean-blue accents, rustic wall decor, and plenty of seafood and wines from Italy's southern reaches. The owners are Sardinian so the experience is authentic overall. There's a printed menu, but the waiter will advise you on what's fresh and flavorful. For an appetizer, go for the big plate of fresh mozzarella or try the gorgeous prosciutto, cheese, and salami platter. For a main, the grilled fish can't be beat. [$] *Average main: 350 Kč ✉ Plaská 5, Malá Strana ☎ 605–375–012 🌐 www.ichnusabotegabistro.cz ⏲ Closed Sun. No lunch Sat. ✍ Reservations essential [M] Line A: Malostranská, then Tram No. 12, 20, or 22 to Újezd ✥ H6.*

$ CAFÉ 🍴 **Kafíčko.** The "Little Coffee" grinds freshly roasted beans from Brazil, Kenya, Colombia, and other renowned growing regions. Superlative strudel and small snacks in a peaceful setting make this a pleasant stop for refueling near Charles Bridge. [$] *Average main: 50 Kč* ✉ *Maltézské náměstí 15, Malá Strana* ☎ *724–151–795* 💳 *No credit cards* [M] *Line A: Malostranská* ✥ *H5.*

$$$$ EUROPEAN
🍴 **Kampa Park.** The zenith of riverside dining is offered at this legendary restaurant just off Charles Bridge, known almost as much for its chic decor and celebrity guests as it is for its elegant Continental cuisine and great wines—it's the kind of place where European royals and heads of state mingle with their head-of-studio counterparts from Hollywood. But the real star power arrives on the plate, with dishes like butter-poached lobster with avocado puree, or venison loin served with green lentils. The only drawback: the food and views command some of the highest prices in town. [$] *Average main: 800 Kč* ✉ *Na Kampě 8/b, Malá Strana* ☎ *257–532–685* 🌐 *www.kampagroup.com* ✍ *Reservations essential* [M] *Line A: Malostranská* ✥ *H5.*

3

$$ MEDITERRANEAN
🍴 **Luka Lu.** The decor is almost comically ominous—what's with the musical instruments and juxtaposed pictures of wolves and babies on the walls?—but the ambience is friendly at this pan-Balkan restaurant on a busy stretch of the Malá Strana. Their authentic kitchen cooks delicately spiced mincemeat sausages called *čevapčiči,* roasted lamb, and a "gourmet" *pljeskavice,* essentially an open-faced hamburger topped with bacon and cheese. Taking cues from Bosnian, Serb, and Macedonian cuisine, the menu branches out to cover the best of coasts and hill country, including caprese salad, salmon carpaccio, and an excellent selection of no-nonsense grilled fish plus hearty regional wines. [$] *Average main: 300 Kč* ✉ *Újezd 33, Malá Strana* ☎ *257–212–388* 🌐 *www.lukalu.cz* [M] *Line A: Malostranská* ✥ *G6.*

$$ THAI
Fodor's Choice ★
🍴 **Noi.** A lounge-y spot on a well-trafficked stretch of Újezd, Noi delivers on the promise of its Zen interior by cooking excellent Thai classics. Lithe staff are quick to accommodate their hip clientele at low tables surrounded by Buddha statues. And the kitchen excels at standards like a citrusy pad thai and addictive fried shrimp cakes. Curries, which run from tingly to tear-inducing hot, are cut by the creaminess of coconut milk and jasmine rice. There's an excellent selection of wines and special teas. [$] *Average main: 220 Kč* ✉ *Újezd 19, Malá Strana* ☎ *257–311–411* 🌐 *www.noirestaurant.cz* [M] *Line A: Malostranská* ✥ *G6.*

$$$ EUROPEAN
🍴 **Pálffy Palác.** Tucked inside an establishment that's literally palatial, age-old elegance and artful Continental cuisine combine on the second story of a baroque palazzo just below Prague Castle. A favorite for special occasions and affairs to remember, Pálffy is one of the few ancient locations in Prague to maintain a feel for the past without seeming stuffy, kitschy, or fake. Instead, it's all high ceilings, candle-light, and haute cuisine: grilled flank steak in mushroom ragout, roast duck, and braised shoulder of lamb. The overall effect is elegant yet lighthearted. [$] *Average main: 400 Kč* ✉ *Valdštejnská 14, Malá Strana* ☎ *257–530–522* 🌐 *www.palffy.cz* ✍ *Reservations essential* [M] *Line A: Malostranská* ✥ *G5.*

$$$$ ASIAN
🍴 **Spices Restaurant & Bar.** This newly updated space, with arched white-washed ceilings, terrace, lounge, and tasteful gold accents, just keeps improving, as you'd expect from a cuisine shrine inside the majorly chic Mandarin Oriental hotel. Head chef Jiří Stift has created a menu

DID YOU KNOW?

Malá Strana is considered to be a more casual dining spot when compared to the Old Town, and dining alfresco is common.

that cunningly focuses on exotic Asian dishes like Thai crab cakes and tandoori-baked swordfish, often sourced with fresh, local ingredients. With a menu ranging from the most alluring tastes of Southeast Asia to Korea, China and the subcontinent, Spices offers a tour-de-force for lovers of curries and seafood. $ *Average main: 600 Kč* ⊠ *Nebovidská 1, Malá Strana* ☏ *233–088–777* ⊕ *www.mandarinoriental.com* Ⓜ *Line A: Malostranská* ✛ *G6.*

$$$

JAPANESE

✕ **The Sushi Bar.** This narrow little room across the river from the National Theater is home to some of the city's best sushi, courtesy of the fish market next door. The selection is first-rate by Central European standards. Beyond sushi, the menu also includes a great seaweed salad and a rich vegetable stew. Though prices for individual maki pieces start relatively low, the bill can rise quickly, depending on how many you order. The space is tiny so try to reserve in advance. $ *Average main: 500 Kč* ⊠ *Zborovská 49, Malá Strana* ☏ *603–244–882* ⊕ *www.sushi. cz* Ⓜ *Line A: Malostranská* ✛ *H6.*

$$$

CZECH

Fodor'sChoice

★

✕ **U Modré kachničky.** This old-fashioned tavern puts on airs, but if you're looking for the perfect Czech venue for a special occasion, it's hard to beat the "Blue Duckling." Dusty portraits hanging on the walls and lavish curtains and table settings impart a certain slightly frilly 19th-century look. The menu, filled with succulent duck and game choices, brings things down to earth a notch. There's dining on two levels, but the upper floor's intimacy—with secluded tables in each nook and cranny and soft piano music wafting through the air—is preferable. $ *Average main: 500 Kč* ⊠ *Nebovidská 6, Malá Strana* ☏ *257–320–308* ⊕ *www.umodrekachnicky.cz* ⬧ *Reservations essential* Ⓜ *Line A: Malostranská* ✛ *G6.*

> **SCENIC SPOTS**
>
> Prague's best views belong to **Ginger & Fred,** on top of Frank Gehry's Dancing House (⊠ *Rašínovo nábř. 80* ☏ *221–984–160*). If you're visiting in the summer months, sit on the terrace. If the Charles Bridge is your ideal vista, try the terrace at **Hergetova Cihelna** (⊠ *Cihelná 2b* ☏ *296–826–103*). They keep blankets and heat lamps for when the nights get nippy.

HRADČANY

After Prague Castle and the few nearby attractions close down for the day, this area can feel a little lonely. There are no Metro stops here, and the climb up is a little too challenging to encourage foot traffic. You're unlikely to eat dinner up here. But for lunch, the steep stretch along Nerudova has several restaurants and cafés, as does the area around the Strahov Monastery.

$$

ASIAN

✕ **Malý Buddha.** Bamboo, wood, paper, incense—and the random creepy mask on the wall—are all part of the decor at this earthy hilltop hideaway near Prague Castle. Spring rolls, vegetable and mixed stir-fries, fish, and chicken dishes come in generous portions. The drink list is unusual, with ginseng wine, herbal drinks, and mystery shots of exotic alcoholic concoctions. This restaurant was one of the first in the city

HAUTE CZECH

Czech cuisine isn't limited to the simpler dishes you'll find at pubs; it can also go upscale and experimental. Aside from the aforementioned **La Degustation** (⇨ *see the "Hunting for Dumplings" box*), an excellent high-end Czech meal can be had at **U Modré kachničky** (✉ *Nebovidská 6* ☎ *257–320–308*) in Malá Strana. The specialty here, a restaurant whose name translates as the "Blue Duckling," is duck, naturally, and it's expertly prepared. **Čestr** (✉ *Legerová 75* ☎ *222–727–851*), a Czech-oriented steak house near the top of Wenceslas Square,

has resurrected long-dead Czech cattle-raising and butchering traditions going back hundreds of years. But don't be limited to restaurants that focus on Czech food; many high-end "Continental" restaurants will spotlight a local dish, too. Among the best of these is the aerie atop the Frank Gehry building known as Dancing House, **Ginger & Fred** (✉ *Jiráskovo náměstí 6* ☎ *221–984–160*), where a traditional love of game dishes is inspiringly reinterpreted in roast duck foie gras, while pork becomes caramelized, cured ham.

with a no-smoking policy—something still not universal in Prague—so the aromas are pure. It's as much about the atmosphere as the food here, which isn't complex but is cooked with heart. $ *Average main: 180 Kč* ✉ *Úvoz 46, Hradcany* ☎ *220–513–894* ⊕ *www.malybuddha.cz* ⊟ *No credit cards* ☾ *Closed Mon.* Ⓜ *Line A: Hradčanská* ✛ *F5.*

NOVÉ MĚSTO (NEW TOWN)

The sprawling area of the New Town, which surrounds the Old Town in a huge arc running from Karlovo náměstí in the south, through the Můstek area, and then on to Náměstí Republiky, holds hundreds of pubs and restaurants. There are clusters of good places to eat near all the quarter's main commercial centers, including Karlovo náměstí, the strip along Národní třída, Na příkopě, and Václavské náměstí (Wenceslas Square). Important Metro stations include Náměstí Republiky and Karlovo náměstí on Line B, Můstek on Lines A and B, Muzeum on Lines A and C, and Florenc on Line C.

$$$$
SEAFOOD
✗ **Alcron.** The Alcron restaurant, inside the Radisson Blu Hotel, offers the city's best seafood, bar none. Head chef Roman Paulus propelled the Alcron to a Michelin star two years in a row, and snagging one of 24 seats inside the intimate dining room can be a tricky but worthwhile feat. Highlights of the menu include filet of sea bass with tiger prawns, and sea scallops served with asparagus shoots. The non-nautical section of the menu is also excellent, with confit of rabbit leg and braised veal cheeks. Oversize reproductions of Tamara de Lempicka paintings adorn the walls of the small, elegant dining room. $ *Average main: 600 Kč* ✉ *Radisson Blu Alcron Hotel, Štěpánská 40, Nové Mesto* ☎ *222–820–410* ⊕ *www.alcron.cz* ☾ *Closed Sun.* ⚖ *Reservations essential* Ⓜ *Line A: Můstek* ✛ *E6.*

$
MEXICAN
✗ **Burrito Loco.** Authentic Mexican street food served 24 hours a day is a commodity Prague expats have dreamed of for years, and now, thanks

to local entrepreneur Glenn Spicker, it's a reality, with seven busy locations throughout the city. Classic tacos with crispy or soft shell and fillings of your choice, including fresh guacamole and an assortment of red or green hot sauces, draw customers of all stripes. Generous, spicy bean, beef or chicken burritos are more substantial and somehow complement Czech beer perfectly. [$] *Average main: 120 Kč* ✉ *Spalena 43, Nové Mesto* 🌐 *www.burritoloco.cz* 💳 *No credit cards* ✥ *C5.*

$$$ STEAKHOUSE 🍴 **Čestr.** The name, derived from a breed of spotted cow that was once bred in the Czech lands, is a nod to Čestr's mission: to revive long-forgotten cattle-raising and meat-preparation traditions. Not surprisingly, the meats are given loving treatment, and diners are offered a near-bewildering array of cuts (skirt, rump cap, top blade, flat, flap, filet mignon, among others). Leave it to the skillful waiters who can guide you through the menu. Pair your beef with fresh Pilsner Urquell beer on tap. The dining room, lit from above with blue-and-white patterned panels and surrounded in blond wood, gives a light quality to counter the substantial dishes. [$] *Average main: 320 Kč* ✉ *Legerová 75, Nové Mesto* ☎ *222–727–851* 🌐 *cestr.ambi.cz/en* ✍ *Reservations essential* [M] *Lines A & C: Muzeum* ✥ *E5.*

$$$$ FRENCH 🍴 **Ginger & Fred.** Serving Prague's most scenic meal, Ginger & Fred occupies the top floor of Frank Gehry's iconic Dancing House along the Vltava River. Run by the team behind the late, great Atelier restaurant, the food and service live up to the quality of the Castle views. The cuisine leans toward French, with entrées like roast duck foie gras with duck raviola and caramelized ham of Mangalica. Of course, diners pay a premium for the view, and the wine list, though extensive, suffers from extreme mark-up. Still, it's a great choice for a splurge. [$] *Average main: 675 Kč* ✉ *Rašínovo nábřeží 80, Nové Mesto* ☎ *221–984–160* 🌐 *www.ginger-fred-restaurant.cz* 🕓 *Closed Sun.* ✍ *Reservations essential* [M] *Line B: Karlovo Nám* ✥ *A6.*

$$ CAFÉ 🍴 **The Globe Bookstore & Café.** Prague's first English-language bookstore with a café draws both foreigners and Czechs for its large selection of novels, regional nonfiction, popular brunches, and memories of the go-go '90s. The recently upgraded menu includes an excellent burger, good salads, and more adventurous items like Thai curry. Head over in the evening for regular film and quiz nights, as well as occasional live music. [$] *Average main: 180 Kč* ✉ *Pštrossova 6, Nové Mesto* ☎ *224–934–203* 🌐 *www.globebookstore.cz* [M] *Line B: Karlovo Náměstí* ✥ *A6.*

$$ ECLECTIC 🍴 **Jáma.** American expatriates, Czech politicians, international consultants, and a constant crowd of students make this Czech-American hybrid pub feel like a place where everyone is welcome—especially when there's a big soccer game. Though just hanging out is of primary importance, the food is leagues ahead of most pubs of this type, with decent Tex-Mex dishes (hearty burritos, crisp nachos, and refreshing taco salads) mixing it up with Czech classics (roast beef with cream sauce, and hearty goulash) and international pub standards (big Caesar salads and juicy burgers). Lunchtime brings inexpensive three-course menus. [$] *Average main: 180 Kč* ✉ *V Jámě 7, Nové Mesto* ☎ *222–967–081* 🌐 *www.jamapub.cz* [M] *Lines A & B: Můstek* ✥ *B6.*

$$$$ EUROPEAN 🍴 **Le Grill.** Under the direction of head chef Ondřej Koráb, the main restaurant of the Grand Mark Hotel has established itself as one of the best restaurants in the country. Don't expect lots of innovation here, but dishes like trout with strawberries and quinoa or the American-style flap steak served with mashed potatoes are skillfully prepared and presented. Plush velvet chairs, recessed lighting, and neutral textiles make the atmosphere hushed and professional; it's ideal for business dinners. [$] *Average main: 600 Kč* ✉ *Hybernská 12, Nové Mesto* ☎ *226–226–126* 🌐 *www.themark.cz* [M] *Line B: Náměstí Republiky* ✥ *G2.*

$$ THAI 🍴 **Lemon Leaf.** Lemon Leaf serves a long list of Thai classics to an appreciative, dedicated clientele. Airy and luminous, with big pots of plants, tall windows, and funky lamps, this spot provides a solid alternative to European cuisine for lunch or dinner. Crunchy spring rolls and traditional Thai soups reeling with flavor are essential openers to one of the noodle dishes or spicy curries, but keep an eye on the little flame symbols in the menu that denote the hotness of dishes. [$] *Average main: 190 Kč* ✉ *Myslíkova 14, Nové Mesto* ☎ *224–919–056* 🌐 *www.lemon.cz* [M] *Line B: Karlovo Náměstí* ✥ *A6.*

$$ CAFÉ 🍴 **Pastacaffé.** Great coffees by the Tonino Lamborghini brand and fresh pastas turn this quiet New Town café into a small corner of Milan. Big, freshly cooked breakfasts start at 8 am on weekdays, while large salads, quick panini, *piadini,* and antipasti round out the menu the rest of the day. Plenty of light and fresh air from the large windows invite all-day loungers, but when the coffee kicks in, people get up and *go.* The cheap, simple dishes are expertly prepared. [$] *Average main: 170 Kč* ✉ *Vodičkova 8, Nové Mesto* ☎ *222–231–869* 🌐 *pastacaffe-vodickova.ambi.cz* [M] *Lines A & B: Můstek* ✥ *D6.*

$$ CZECH 🍴 **Potrefená Husa.** The "Wounded Goose" is a local chain of casual restaurants and sports bars owned by the Prague-based Staropramen brewery, and it's quite good at what it does: serving up bar staples and beer at a good value. This branch in Nové Město is one of several scattered throughout the city. The menus vary slightly from branch to branch, but all carry a similar mix of standards like chicken wings, grilled meats, soups, pastas, and salads. The decent quality to price ratio means they're always packed, especially on nights when there's an important hockey or soccer match. You'll usually find a full selection of Staropramen beers on tap, too. [$] *Average main: 220 Kč* ✉ *Resslova 1, Nové Mesto* ☎ *224–918–691* 🌐 *www.staropramen.cz* [M] *Line B: Karlovo Náměstí* ✥ *A6.*

$$ VEGETARIAN 🍴 **Radost FX Café.** Still going strong after more than 20 years, this popular vegetarian restaurant and café offers an eclectic assortment of salads, sandwiches, pizzas, and a smattering of Thai, Mexican, and American dishes, like the ever-popular Popeye "burger," made from spinach, hazelnuts, and cheese. There is dining in two rooms: a no-smoking café at the front and a more relaxed lounge at the back. The clientele vary throughout the day. Lunchtime brings in professionals from around the neighborhood, while evenings attract spillover from the dance club of the same name downstairs. [$] *Average main: 180 Kč* ✉ *Bělehradská 120, Nové Mesto* ☎ *224–254–776* 🌐 *www.radostfx.cz* 💳 *No credit cards* [M] *Line C: I.P. Pavlova* ✥ *F6.*

$$$$ ASIAN FUSION Fodor's Choice ★ 🍴 **Sansho.** When Sansho opened in 2011, it radically redefined the local dining scene. Head chef Paul Day introduced many novel concepts to Prague's foodies, like pairing a simple, unadorned interior with highly intricate Asian-fusion cuisine, leaving the full focus on the plate. The public was initially skeptical but once they gathered around the long, communal tables, they were won over by the quality of the cooking (not surprising, as Day learned his craft at London's Michelin-starred Nobu). Diners are encouraged to order a six-course tasting menu, featuring pork belly, lamb penang, and soft-shell crab among other delicacies. Desserts, especially the sticky toffee pudding, can reflect a little of the London background. [$] *Average main: 550 Kč* ✉ *Petrská 4, Nové Mesto* ☎ *222–317–425* 🌐 *www.sansho.cz* ⏲ *Closed Sun. and Mon.* ✍ *Reservations essential* [M] *Lines B & C: Florenc* ✥ *F1.*

3

$$$ ECLECTIC 🍴 **U Emy Destinnové.** An American cooking in the house where the celebrated Czech opera singer Ema Destinnová was born? Somehow chef Steven Trumpfheller pulls it off at this basement restaurant. The interior replicates a cozy living room, right down to the natty couches and chatty diners eating as though enjoying a Sunday supper at Mom's house. But the modern cooking is beyond mom's stove top—it's a hybrid of American and Continental influences, with entrées like a Black Angus N.Y. strip steak, Scottish salmon served in a lime-flavored artichoke puree, and veal medallions sautéed in a mushroom cream sauce. Enjoy live piano music on Wednesday and Thursday evenings. [$] *Average main: 380 Kč* ✉ *Kateřinská 7, Nové Mesto* ☎ *224–918–425* 🌐 *www.uemydestinnove.cz* ⏲ *Closed Sun.* [M] *Line A: Náměstí Míru* ✥ *E6.*

$$ EUROPEAN 🍴 **Universal.** Prices here have remained almost unchanged since it opened in the late 1990s, much to customers' delight. Universal is a Continental cornucopia of excellent salads, classically European main courses, titanic side orders of scalloped potatoes, luscious lemon tarts, and sweet profiteroles. An affordable midday menu makes it even more alluring at lunchtime, and the cheap house wine draws out after-dinner conversations. Reservations are advisable. [$] *Average main: 250 Kč* ✉ *V Jirchářích 6, Nové Mesto* ☎ *224–934–416* 🌐 *www.universalrestaurant.cz* [M] *Line B: Karlovo Náměstí* ✥ *B6.*

$$$$ EUROPEAN 🍴 **Zinc.** The story behind Zinc, the house restaurant of the Hilton Old Town hotel, is a comic case of culinary musical chairs. The site first held celeb-chef Gordon Ramsey's Maze restaurant, but after that shuttered, head chef Ari Munandar was quickly brought in from the Mandarin Oriental. The result? A successful mix of European and Asian flavors that's bringing in the crowds. Zinc may lack Ramsay's flair, but it's much more consistent, and for a Hilton, that's the sweet spot. Sink back into the dark banquettes under an open skylight and sample plates like Ceylon seafood curry and beef masala or a light barbecue pork-roll plate. [$] *Average main: 600 Kč* ✉ *V Celnici 7, Nové Mesto* ☎ *221–822–300* 🌐 *www.hiltonpragueoldtown.com* ✍ *Reservations essential* [M] *Line B: Náměstí Republiky* ✥ *G2.*

VINOHRADY AND ŽIŽKOV

VINOHRADY

Vinohrady is one of Prague's nicest residential areas and since the early 2000s has been home to many of the capital's best restaurants. The neighborhood has a couple of main hubs. Náměstí Miru and the Metro station of the same name are home to dozens of cafés and restaurants, with another clutch of great places to the immediate south along Americká. The area's second hub would be around the Jiřího z Poděbrad metro station, with fruitful hunting grounds for good lunch and dinner spots running west along Mánesova and south on Nitranská, both in the immediate area of the metro station.

$$$ ITALIAN Fodor's Choice ★

🍴 **Aromi.** Gracious, gregarious, and extremely confident, Aromi is easily among the top-tier of Italian restaurants in the city and proud of it. Classic pastas made in-house and fresh seafood shown off tableside are two of the crowd favorites, as are the superb salads and well-chosen Italian wines. With a new location offering alfresco dining, airy modernist interiors, and wine bottles on display, the restaurant imparts a Continental feel without being kitschy. Leave room for a post-dessert treat: Aromi stocks an exclusive list of rare grappas. The seasonal, multicourse tasting menus and excellent-value business lunches on weekdays are also a draw. [$] *Average main: 450 Kč* ✉ *Náměstí Míru 6, Vinohrady* ☎ *222–713–222* 🌐 *www.aromi.cz* [M] *Line A: Náměstí Míru* ✣ *H2.*

$ CAFÉ Fodor's Choice ★

🍴 **Bio Zahrada.** A cheerful little spot, this beautiful café and organic bakery, full of blond wood and clean white walls, has a relaxed, peaceful garden out back. Choose from a counter of delicious homemade baked goods, or opt for one of the daily luncheon specials (usually something simple but satisfying, like a rice curry or steamed vegetables). Or just come for a cup of coffee, easily the best in the area. [$] *Average main: 100 Kč* ✉ *Belgická 33, Vinohrady* ☎ *222–518–698* 🌐 *www.biozahrada.cz* 🕒 *Closed Sun.* [M] *Line A: Náměstí Miru* ✣ *H2.*

$$$ BELGIAN

🍴 **Bruxx.** Czech beer is facing increasing competition these days as younger Praguers set out to forge new traditions. Belgian ales, often tinged with fruit or nut flavors, served alongside kettles of mussels and golden frites with mayo sauce, are winning over not just locals but an upscale international clientele. With its high ceilings, dark paneling, and fleet-footed servers, Bruxx accommodates these new tastes. [$] *Average main: 350 Kč* ✉ *Namesti Miru 9, Vinohrady* ☎ *224–250–404* 🌐 *www.bruxx.cz* 💳 *No credit cards* ✣ *H2.*

$$ BURGER

🍴 **Dish.** In 2012, this bright new burger bar gave plenty of die-hard hamburger lovers reason to abandon their local fave and head to Vinohrady. The menu lists 11 burgers, including the house "Dish" burger with bacon and cheddar cheese and a one-of-a-kind cheeseburger named after the Czech city of Olomouc, known for its stinky cheese. Vegetarians are not forgotten, and veggie options include portobello mushrooms or eggplant-carrot puree patties as the base. The interior is warm, with exposed-brick walls, and an appealing terrace blossoms in mild weather. [$] *Average main: 170 Kč* ✉ *Římská 29, Vinohrady* ☎ *222–511–032* 🌐 *www.dish.cz* [M] *Lines A & C: Muzeum* ✣ *H2.*

$$
INDIAN
✕ **Lal Qila.** Vinohrady has several very good Indian restaurants, but this corner restaurant along one of the area's prettiest streets may just be the best. Those familiar with Indian cooking can expect all of the standard curries, tandoori dishes, samosas, naan, and other staples of Indian cuisine. The difference here is the level of cooking and the unwillingness to cut corners. The lamb dishes, for example, will have three or four good-size pieces of lamb. Another winning detail: the English-speaking waitstaff will go out of their way to please guests. $ *Average main: 260 Kč* ✉ *Italská 30, Vinohrady* ☎ *774–310–774* ⊕ *www.lalqila.cz* Ⓜ *Lines A & C: Muzeum* ✛ *H2.*

$$
MEXICAN
✕ **Las Adelitas.** The origins of Las Adelitas lie in Mexico City, where a group of friends dreamed of bringing authentic recipes from home to Central Europe. And the conclusion is the best Mexican food in Prague, found toward the end of Americká, about 10 minutes' walk south of Náměstí Miru. True to its roots, the restaurant is casual, welcoming, and ultrafriendly. But it's the food that keeps patrons coming. The hard- or soft-shell tacos, burritos, enchiladas, and tostadas are all freshly prepared, with a choice of red or green salsa or mole sauce. It also makes an affordable date night, as the tabletop candles lend the dining room a romantic feel. $ *Average main: 180 Kč* ✉ *Americká 8, Vinohrady* ☎ *222–542–031* ⊕ *www.lasadelitas.cz* ▭ *No credit cards* Ⓜ *Line A: Náměstí Miru* ✛ *H2.*

$$
ECLECTIC
✕ **Mozaika.** Located in a leafy residential neighborhood, Mozaika has remained popular by combining a light contemporary interior and sophisticated cooking with great service. Come here for grilled salmon blini or pork vindaloo with lentils. The burger menu, featuring the tangy Texas Smokey, is good but more expensive and not any better that other designer burger joints. The wine list blends well-chosen French and Italian bottles with the best domestic labels. Tables tend to be booked, so reservations are especially recommended. $ *Average main: 180 Kč* ✉ *Nitranská 13, Vinohrady* ☎ *224–253–011* ⊕ *www.mozaikaburger. cz* Ⓜ *Line A: Jiřího z Poděbrad* ✛ *H2.*

$
VIETNAMESE
✕ **Pho Vietnam Tuan & Lan.** In 2013, a surge of Vietnamese restaurants opened in Prague, but it was this cellar restaurant, not far from the I.P. Pavlova Metro station, that became a fast favorite. The spot is definitively no frills: order at the counter and then find a table; in a few minutes someone brings around your food. The most popular order remains *pho bo,* a flavorful tureen of noodles and sliced beef (or its chicken-flavored cousin *pho ga*), that you spice up at the table with a squeeze of lemon and shot of hot sauce. But the fresh spring rolls, *nem sai gon,* are a fresh and delicious accompaniment to the soup. $ *Average main: 140 Kč* ✉ *Anglická 15, Vinohrady* ☎ *775–465–678* ⊕ *photuanlan.com* Ⓜ *Line C: I.P. Pavlova* ✛ *H2.*

$$
BURGER
Fodor's Choice
★
✕ **The Tavern.** A hopping burger bar on the fringe of Riegrovy Sady park in Vinohrady, the Tavern arguably serves the city's best hamburgers and cheeseburgers. The restaurant began as the dream of an American couple to use classic American combinations, like bacon-cheddar or blue cheese and caramelized onion, and then re-create them with locally sourced beef and toppings. The result? It's been packed since the 2012 opening and shows no signs of slowing down. They also do

3

veggie burgers, along with American-style diner food, and pies, cocktails, and craft beers. **■ TIP→ Hours are irregular, so check the website before heading out here. Reservations only online, and only accepted for Thursday–Saturday nights. There's no phone and just seating for 12.** [$] *Average main: 160 Kč* ✉ *Chopinova 26, Vinohrady* 🌐 *www.thetavern.cz* ⏲ *Closed Sun. and Mon. No lunch Tues.* ✍ *Reservations essential* [M] *Line A: Jiřího z Poděbrad* ✥ *H2.*

ŽIŽKOV

Scruffy Žižkov is better known for its pubs and dives than for fine dining; nevertheless the southern part of the district abutting Vinohrady has some good cafés and restaurants. The best way to get here is to take the Metro to Jiřího z Poděbrad and walk north along Slavíkova.

$$$ SUSHI 🍴 **Hanil.** A nice counterpoint to heavier, meatier cuisine, Hanil serves decent sushi as well as Korean and other Asian dishes at affordable prices. The open, casual setting, accented with blond woods, attracts a largely local crowd of students and young professionals who appreciate the lack of pretension. Opt for the good-value sushi sets, or if you're feeling adventurous, try the *champong,* a spicy seafood and noodle dish, or the *ojingo bokum,* a soupy-looking squid stir-fry served on a hot plate. [$] *Average main: 400 Kč* ✉ *Slavíkova 24, Žižkov* ☎ *222–715–867* 🌐 *www.hanil.cz* [M] *Line A: Jiřího z Poděbrad* ✥ *H2.*

$ CAFÉ 🍴 **Le Caveau.** Beer quality is a sacred compact in Prague but wine didn't fare nearly as well under communism. Fortunately, a steady resurgence has produced not only excellent local vintages but demanding customers with sophisticated tastes. This comfortable local wine bar illustrates the trend with affordable Pinot by the glass, enjoyed by artsy patrons who settle into easy chairs and mismatched cafe seating to enjoy a glass or two along with filled croissants, light salads, and brownies. [$] *Average main: 140 Kč* ✉ *Namesti Jiriho z Podebrad 9, Žižkov* ☎ *775–294–864* 🌐 *www.broz-d.cz* 💳 *No credit cards* [M] *Line A: Jiřího z Poděbrad* ✥ *H2.*

SMÍCHOV

Smíchov is a former working-class neighborhood that got pulled into upscale territory in the late 1990s when several banks decided to locate their headquarters near the Anděl Metro station, the center of the neighborhood. The Anděl area has lots of great and cheap pubs and pizza joints. The northern part of the district, near Malá Strana, has a couple of excellent restaurants.

$$ EUROPEAN 🍴 **Café Savoy.** Stellar service and elegant meals of high quality at moderate prices are de rigueur here. This restored café, dating to the 19th century, serves everything from meal-size split-pea and cream-of-spinach soups to Wiener schnitzel, with huge salads complemented by fresh breads from the in-house bakery. The house cake, topped with marzipan, makes a properly sweet finish. If you're looking for eggs, Savoy's breakfasts are without question some of Prague's best. This is a great spot for weekend brunch, but book ahead. [$] *Average main: 240 Kč* ✉ *Vítězná 5, Smíchov* ☎ *257–311–562* 🌐 *www.cafesavoy.ambi.cz* ✍ *Reservations essential* [M] *Line A: Malostranská* ✥ *G6.*

$$ CZECH 🍴 **Kozlovna.** A rarity among the brewery-owned pubs in Prague, Kozlovna is affiliated with the smaller Velkopopovický Kozel beer. But aside from the animal horns outside the front door and the company's brews on tap, the branding is unobtrusive and the environment is friend and bustling. They serve huge portions of expertly made Czech classics at reasonable prices, and naturally everything goes great with beer: ribs, venison, and a sinus-clearing garlic soup are all superlative versions of the pub food you'll find elsewhere, without the intense premium you pay for a sleek environment and competent service. Just don't get too ambitious—sometimes the daily specials, especially anything that involves pasta, overreach. [$] *Average main: 180 Kč* ✉ *Lidická 20, Smíchov* ☎ *257–210–862* 🌐 *www.kozlovna.eu* 💳 *No credit cards* [M] *Line B: Anděl* ✥ *H6.*

3

LETNÁ, HOLEŠOVICE, AND TROJA

LETNÁ

This residential area north of the Old Town and across the river is not known for fine dining, but there are several decent places in the vicinity of Letenské náměstí that will do in a pinch. The neighborhood is popular with students, and prices here tend to be lower than in the center.

$$ INDIAN 🍴 **Curry Palace.** In a neighborhood across the river and north of the Old Town, behind Letná park, Curry Palace is a bit off the beaten path, but it's *the* place for Indian and Bangladeshi food. Try the excellent *rezela,* a specialty made with chicken or lamb spiced, from medium to very hot, with garlic-ginger paste and yogurt. You'll also find the usual mix of tandoori dishes and curries. This makes a perfect lunch or dinner stop after visiting the National Technical Museum. ■ **TIP→ From Hradčanská Metro station, take Tram No. 1, 25, or 26 to Letenské náměstí.** [$] *Average main: 250 Kč* ✉ *Jirečková 13, Letná* ☎ *775–146–252* 🌐 *www.currypalace.cz* [M] *Line A: Hradčanská* ✥ *F4.*

$$ CZECH 🍴 **Lokál Nad Stromovkou.** The same talented team behind Lokál Dlouhááá and Café Savoy refurbished this long-standing Czech pub near Stromovka Park in 2013. Not only did they add a fresh coat of paint to the walls, but they refreshed and reintroduced some traditional tavern classics like steak tartare served with toast, fresh trout in cumin butter, and roast leg of duck served with apple and red cabbage. The location is hard to find, so take a cab or map it out ahead of time. [$] *Average main: 190 Kč* ✉ *Nad Královskou oborou 31, Letná* ☎ *220–912–319* 🌐 *lokal-nadstromovkou.ambi.cz* [M] *Line A: Hradčanská, take Tram No. 1, 25, or 26 to Letenské náměstí* ✥ *F4.*

HOLEŠOVICE

This is a gentrifying, formerly scruffy area that with a couple of notable exceptions still lacks a destination restaurant. Still, if you happen to be staying in the area, there are plenty of low-cost pizzerias and pubs that serve food at an acceptable level of quality at prices that are much lower than in areas more popular with tourists.

$$ DINER 🍴 **Bohemia Bagel.** A lifeline to American breakfast when it opened in the '90s, today Bohemia Bagel remains popular with visitors and expats

looking for a taste of home. Offerings include the classic BLT and lox with cream cheese and capers, as well as eggs, pancakes, and a surprisingly good hamburger. This location pays homage to the classic diner format, with a popular weekend brunch and late hours that make up for its less-than-central location. [$] *Average main: 160 Kč* ✉ *Dukelských hrdinů 48, Holešovice* ☎ *220–806–541* 🌐 *www.bohemiabagel.cz* 💳 *No credit cards* [M] *Line C: Vltavská* ✥ *F4.*

$ CAFÉ 🍴 **Ouky Douky.** A Prague original, this combination Czech bookstore and coffeehouse draws a lively mix of students, intellectuals, and vagabonds from around the neighborhood. The coffee drinks are very good, as are the homemade daily soups and breakfast specials. The rest of the food is only so-so, but everyone is drawn to the convivial atmosphere. This was the first home of the Globe Bookstore and Café back in the 1990s. [$] *Average main: 140 Kč* ✉ *Janovského 14, Holešovice* ☎ *266–711–531* 🌐 *www.oukydouky.cz* [M] *Line C: Vltavská* ✥ *F4.*

KARLÍN

Though once a blighted testament to the fates of state-controlled industry, this area north and east of Old Town is these days in rebound, with tech companies, galleries, fashionable eateries, and a lively bustle.

$ BAKERY 🍴 **Mamacoffee.** Of the many new café options in this up-and-coming district, Mamacoffee leads the pack with fine brews of fair-trade java. Breakfast business is brisk, with excellent pastries to complement a creamy latte, but many customers linger throughout the afternoon over a well-brewed flat white. Hipster customers mingle with young moms and local business types, all drawn by the genial service and expert espresso making. [$] *Average main: 120 Kč* ✉ *Sokolovská 6, Karlín* ☎ *775–568–647* 🌐 *www.mamacoffee.cz* 🕒 *Closed weekends* 💳 *No credit cards* [M] *Křižíkova* ✥ *H1.*

$$$ MIDDLE EASTERN 🍴 **Meze.** Another leading light in the transformation of this corner of the city, this Middle Eastern specialist appeals to a new generation of Praguers with growing international tastes. Its classic falafel, baba ghanoush, and tzatziki platters make for healthy, light lunches and dinners. The service is on par with the city's new, modern standards for dining out. [$] *Average main: 320 Kč* ✉ *Karlinske namesti 6, Karlín* ☎ *223–000–665* 🌐 *www.mezerestaurant.cz* 🕒 *Closed weekends* 💳 *No credit cards* [M] *Line B: Křižíkova* ✥ *H1.*

WHERE TO STAY

Updated by
Jennifer Rigby

Prague is chock-full of charming places to stay. From beautifully restored monasteries to a capsule room at the top of the communist-era television tower, there's a remarkably wide range of choice for all budgets. Increased competition among hoteliers means that staff are almost invariably charming and knowledgeable, and speak excellent English.

The best areas to stay are the Old Town (Staré Město), the Lesser Quarter (Malá Strana), the Castle Area (Hradčany), and the New Town (Nové Město). The center of Prague is reasonably small, so staying outside of the center doesn't mean a massive slog to the castle. Neighborhoods like Smíchov, Žižkov, and Vinohrady are easily accessible by Prague's inexpensive, highly efficient metro and tram system.

Recent years have seen a drop in prices, even during high season (May–September). In winter rates can fall by a third or even half. The majority of hotels accept online bookings, so the best deals are found by searching a few months in advance of a trip and snapping up deals as soon as they're offered. It's best to book directly with the property.

Most hotels now offer free Wi-Fi and air-conditioning, and many of the high-end spots also offer extras, like complimentary afternoon tea, welcome drinks, or free airport transfers.

PLANNER

RESERVATIONS
During the peak season (May–October, excluding July and August) and over major holidays, reservations are a must; reserve 60 days in advance to stay in the hotel and room of your choice. For the remainder of the year, reserve 30 days in advance if possible. It's always a good idea to call or email to double-check your reservation before you come to avoid any hassles on arrival. Note that many hotel rooms use two single beds

WHERE SHOULD I STAY?

	NEIGHBORHOOD VIBE	PROS	CONS
Staré Město	The city's ancient center; tourists, nightlife, museums, and monuments.	Everything at your fingertips, including fantastic restaurants and Old Town Square.	Everyone else at your doorstep, visiting those very same things.
Malá Strana	With evocative, cobblestone alleys and Embassy Row, the Lesser Quarter is as authentic as Old Town but with fewer crowds.	Easy access to Old Town (just across the river); churches galore.	Hilly layout can mean a serious schlep to your hotel; not as hopping as Old Town come nightfall.
Hradčany	The neighborhood surrounding Prague Castle, this is a mix of gardens and historic buildings from every era.	Beautiful greenery; St. Vitus Cathedral and Prague Castle within walking distance.	Far from the action; fewer high-end eateries and far less street life.
Nové Město	The area near Wenceslas Square, "new" here means less than 700 years old.	Bustles with activity during the day; a short walk to Old Town; National Museum and lots of shopping.	Can get seedy after dark; lots of shopping but the architecture isn't as pretty as elsewhere.
Vinohrady	Leafy residential streets: think of it as Prague's Greenwich Village.	Quiet; filled with locals; charming restaurants and bars.	A Metro ride or walk to the center; not as tourist-friendly as other locales.
Smíchov	Just south of Malá Strana, Smíchov is a hodgepodge of sleek corporate towers standing amid rowdy, smoky pubs.	Lots of shopping thanks to the Novy Smíchov Mall; near the Staropramen brewery. Good Metro connections.	Not easy walking distance to Old Town; lacking in historical character.
Žižkov	Down the hill from Vinohrady, Žižkov is the edgy little brother to the more buttoned-up Vinohrady.	Great bars and music venues; a lively arts scene with the people to match.	A bit gritty and dirty; not walking distance to many other central locations.

4

pushed together; if you are counting on a proper double bed, ensure this with the reservations desk when booking your room.

FAMILY TRAVEL

Hotels in Prague are more family-friendly than ever before. The proliferation of high-end chains has helped mightily, as properties offer the same options they do on the other side of the Atlantic. Plus, there are plenty of options no matter where you stay. Suites at the Pachtuv Palace, for example, can be good value, and offer scads of space for little ones to run around in. (Don't worry, the chandeliers are quite high up.) The Four Seasons, meanwhile, provides amenities like bathrobes and coloring books on request; it also boasts a highly acclaimed restaurant that also has a children's menu. Most hotels in Prague will have cribs or extra beds for an additional fee, and can arrange babysitting services

given fair warning, but more complicated requests—say, a stroller—
might be harder to accommodate. Best to bring what you can ahead of
time; especially at the smaller, less expensive properties, options will be
more limited. Also, bear in mind that standard rooms in Prague tend to
be on the small side, and that if you're traveling with a child, a larger
room might be a wise decision if it's within your budget.

FACILITIES

In most cases, cable TV, breakfast, and some kind of Internet connection
are offered in hotels in all price ranges. Wi-Fi is the norm, though some
hotels may only offer a cable connection in the room (inconvenient if
you're carrying a smartphone or tablet). Wi-Fi networks can sometimes
be spotty in the more inexpensive hotels, and may only work in the
lobby or other public areas, although that is improving. Hotels at $$
and $$$ ranges usually have restaurants, cafés, room service, private
baths, and hair dryers. At $$$$ hotels, you can expect luxury ameni-
ties like robes, a sauna, steam bath, pool, concierge, and babysitting.
Perversely, at $$$$ places, however, you might find yourself paying
extra for the buffet breakfast.

PRICES

Many hotels in Prague go by a three-season system: the lowest rates are
charged from November through mid-March, excluding Christmas and
New Year's, when high-season rates are charged; the middle season is
July and August; the high season, from the end of March through June
and again from mid-August through the end of October, brings the
highest rates. Easter sees higher-than-high-season rates, and some hotels
increase the prices for other holidays and trade fairs. Always ask first.

WHAT IT COSTS IN KORUNA			
$	**$$**	**$$$**	**$$$$**
Hotels under 2,200 Kč	2,200 Kč–4,000 Kč	4,001 Kč–6,500 Kč	over 6,500 Kč

Prices in the reviews are the lowest cost of a standard double room in high season.

USING THE MAP

Throughout the chapter, you'll see mapping symbols and coordinates
(✛ F2) after property names or reviews. To locate the property on a
map, turn to the Where to Stay map. The letter and number following
the symbol are the property's coordinates on the map grid.

STAR RATINGS

A word to star-rating aficionados: unlike many other countries, the
Czech Republic doesn't have an official rating system, so hotels rate
themselves. They invariably toss on a star or two more than they actually merit.

HOTEL REVIEWS

Listed alphabetically by neighborhood. Hotel reviews have been shortened. For full information, visit Fodors.com.

STARÉ MĚSTO (OLD TOWN)

Staré Město, Prague's Old Town, is a highly desirable neighborhood in which to stay. The mix of baroque and Gothic buildings provides a storybook feeling. Hotels here are of the old-made-new variety. Don't be surprised to be standing in a hotel lobby that was originally built in the 17th century but looks and smells like a fresh coat of plaster and paint was added a month ago. Trendy restaurants, hip cafés, superior clubs, and the city's best clothing boutiques are all in this area.

4

$$$ HOTEL **Buddha Bar Hotel.** The concept here is "Chinoiserie-meets-art-nouveau," as best as we can tell, meshing the hotel's original 100-year-old structure with Asian script and Buddhas throughout. **Pros:** stylish design; Mecca for club-going hipsters. **Cons:** room rates can go up fast if booked late; rooms seem dark. [$] *Rooms from: 5500 Kč* ✉ *Jakubská 8, Staré Mesto* ☎ *221–776–300* 🌐 *www.buddhabarhotelprague.com* 🛏 *38 rooms* 🍴 *Some meals* [M] *Line C: Nám. Republiy* ✥ *G3.*

$$ HOTEL **Design Hotel Jewel Prague.** A friendly jewel-themed hotel that's close to all the Old Town action, the staff here go the extra mile, from the little afternoon tea cakes brought to your room to the bedtime story cards distributed in the evening. **Pros:** cute touches; bright, individual rooms; free Wi-Fi and laptop rental. **Cons:** buffet breakfast could be fresher; some street noise. [$] *Rooms from: 3200 Kč* ✉ *Rytířská 3, Staré Mesto* ☎ *224–211–699* 🌐 *hoteljewelprague.com* 🛏 *10 rooms* 🍴 *No meals* [M] *Lines A & B: Můstek* ✥ *F4.*

$$$$ HOTEL Fodor's Choice ★ **Emblem Hotel Prague.** Rivaling the best design hotels in capital cities around the world, this unique retreat goes toe to toe with many of the city's grande dame hotels; it's smart, fresh, and funky, with a modern art deco theme created by a host of top-notch designers. **Pros:** major design chops; good restaurant; private club for guests. **Cons:** rooms are a little impersonal; rooftop spa is small. [$] *Rooms from: 8100 Kč* ✉ *Platnéřská 19, Staré Mesto* ☎ *226–202–500* 🌐 *emblemprague.com* 🛏 *59 rooms* 🍴 *No meals* [M] *Line A: Staroměstská* ✥ *F3.*

$$$$ HOTEL **Four Seasons Hotel Prague.** Though it has plenty of competition at the top end of the market, the Four Seasons luxury chain is keeping up, with renovations to the modern wing of the hotel (there are three buildings in all; the modern structure is joined by existing buildings from the 18th and 19th centuries), outfitting rooms with flat-screen TVs, Eames desk chairs, a herringbone-patterned carpet and more. **Pros:** sumptuous beds; incredible views. **Cons:** pricey breakfast; conservative styling. [$] *Rooms from: 15000 Kč* ✉ *Veleslavinova 2a, Staré Mesto* ☎ *221–427–000* 🌐 *www.fourseasons.com/prague* 🛏 *157 rooms* 🍴 *No meals* [M] *Line A: Staroměstská* ✥ *E3.*

$$$ HOTEL **Grand Hotel Bohemia.** This art nouveau *palais* dominates a picturesque corner near the Prašná brána (Powder Tower) and Náměstí Republiky. **Pros:** city-center location; fascinating history. **Cons:** a few nickel-and-dime charges (breakfast costs extra in cheaper rooms); pricier than

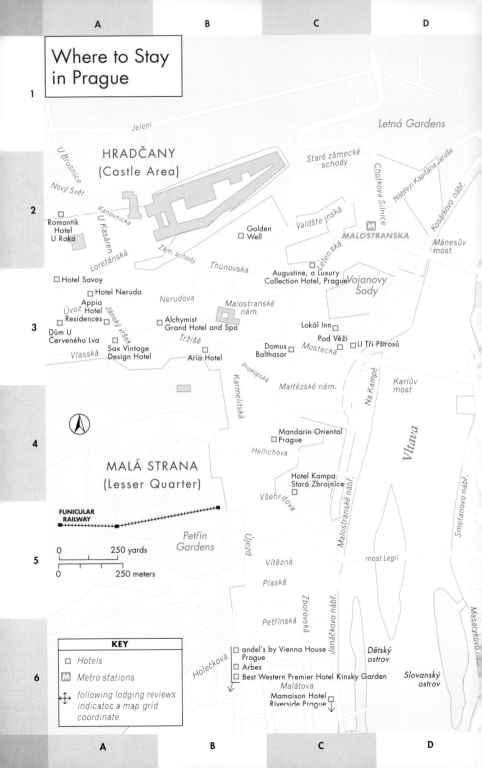

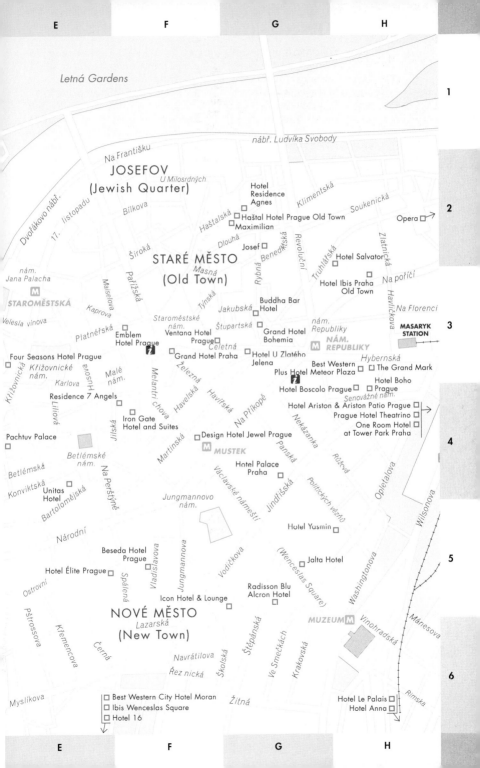

comparable hotels in the area. [$] *Rooms from: 5400 Kč* ✉ *Králodvorská 4, Staré Mesto* ☎ *234–608–111* 🌐 *www.grandhotelbohemia.cz* 🛏 *73 rooms, 5 suites* 🍴 *Breakfast* [M] *Line B: Nám. Republiky* ✥ *G3.*

$$ HOTEL 🏨 **Grand Hotel Praha.** The main selling point here is the amazing location (practically on top of one of Prague's most famous sights, the astronomical clock) but this has its downside: with the wonderful views comes a big a tourist scrum from the moment you venture outside. **Pros:** can't get closer to the astronomical clock unless you sleep in its tower; good price for location. **Cons:** high density of tourists outside; could do with decor update. [$] *Rooms from: 3200 Kč* ✉ *Staroměstské náměstí 481/22, Staré Mesto* ☎ *221–632–556* 🌐 *www.grandhotelpraha.cz* 🛏 *38 rooms* 🍴 *Breakfast* 💳 *No credit cards* [M] *Line A: Staroměstská* ✥ *F3.*

$$ HOTEL Fodor's Choice ★ 🏨 **Haštal Hotel Prague Old Town.** A brilliantly priced, family-run hotel located in a quiet spot just a few minutes from Old Town Square. **Pros:** great location on a quiet street; very clean rooms; free Wi-Fi in rooms. **Cons:** breakfast room can get busy; folksy feel might not appeal to everyone. [$] *Rooms from: 2500 Kč* ✉ *Haštalská 16, Staré Mesto* ☎ *222–314–335* 🌐 *www.hotelhastalprague.com* 🛏 *31 rooms* 🍴 *Breakfast* [M] *Line A: Staroměstská* ✥ *G2.*

$$ HOTEL Fodor's Choice ★ 🏨 **Hotel Residence Agnes.** This gorgeous hotel, with a chic courtyard and atrium, is tucked away on a quiet alley in Old Town and is a haven from the hustle and bustle of Prague. **Pros:** homey feel; helpful staff. **Cons:** rooms sell out quickly. [$] *Rooms from: 4000 Kč* ✉ *Haštalská 19, Staré Mesto* ☎ *222–312–417* 🌐 *www.residenceagnes.cz* 🛏 *22 rooms* 🍴 *Breakfast* [M] *Line B: Nám. Republiky* ✥ *G2.*

$ HOTEL 🏨 **Hotel U Zlatého Jelena.** Authentically austere, what U Zlatého Jelena lacks in personality and amenities it makes up for with a killer location off Old Town Square. **Pros:** excellent location; large rooms. **Cons:** no air-conditioning; street noise in non-courtyard rooms. [$] *Rooms from: 1700 Kč* ✉ *Celetná 11, Staré Mesto* ☎ *257–531–925* 🌐 *www.goldendeer.cz* 🛏 *19 rooms* 🍴 *Breakfast* [M] *Line A: Staroměstská* ✥ *G3.*

$$ HOTEL 🏨 **Iron Gate Hotel and Suites.** If you're looking for history, the Iron Gate has it in spades—the original building dates to the 14th century, and the architectural details are fascinating (ask to see a room with painted ceiling beams). **Pros:** historical; each room is unique; located on a gorgeous cobblestone street. **Cons:** hard beds; mediocre breakfast. [$] *Rooms from: 3100 Kč* ✉ *Michalská 19, Staré Mesto* ☎ *225–777–777* 🌐 *www.irongatehotel.com* 🛏 *43 rooms* 🍴 *Breakfast* [M] *Line A: Staroměstská* ✥ *F4.*

$$ HOTEL 🏨 **Josef.** Cool, clean, white lines dominate the decor of this ultra-hip modern boutique hotel designed by London-based Czech architect Eva Jiricna. **Pros:** large patio for breakfast in the courtyard; just a few minutes' walk from Old Town Square; great breakfast and on-site bakery. **Cons:** the minimalist design might not be for everyone; glass dividers in some bathrooms give no privacy. [$] *Rooms from: 3600 Kč* ✉ *Rybná 20, Staré Mesto* ☎ *221–700–111* 🌐 *www.hoteljosef.com* 🛏 *109 rooms* 🍴 *Breakfast* [M] *Line B: Nám. Republiky* ✥ *G2.*

$$ HOTEL 🏨 **Maximilian.** A beautifully designed hotel in the heart of Old Town is tasteful fusion of light, airy modernism. **Pros:** lovely design; great breakfast spread; excellent online-booking discounts. **Cons:** upper-floor

rooms could use more light; no in-house restaurant. Ⓢ *Rooms from: 3600 Kč* ✉ *Haštalská 14, Staré Mesto* ☎ *225-303-111* ⊕ *www.maximilianhotel.com* ↪ *71 rooms* ⦿ *Breakfast* Ⓜ *Line A: Staroměstská* ✛ *G2.*

$$$
HOTEL
Fodor's Choice
★
🏨 **Pachtuv Palace.** Made from four structures—a baroque palace, two medieval houses, and a neoclassical building from 1836—the Pachtuv Palace can't be matched for authenticity. **Pros:** friendly service; giant rooms. **Cons:** some street noise; staff can be disorganized at times. Ⓢ *Rooms from: 5700 Kč* ✉ *Karolíny Světlé 34, Staré Mesto* ☎ *234-705-111* ⊕ *www.pachtuvpalace.com* ↪ *48 rooms* ⦿ *Breakfast* Ⓜ *Line A: Staroměstská* ✛ *E4.*

$$$
HOTEL
🏨 **Residence 7 Angels.** In a residence that originally dates to 1411, this hotel offers a great location not far from Old Town Square's Astronomical Clock. **Pros:** spacious rooms, some with frescoes; good breakfast. **Cons:** rooms can be difficult to get to, especially for those with disabilities; spotty Wi-Fi. Ⓢ *Rooms from: 5000 Kč* ✉ *Jilská 20, Staré Mesto* ☎ *224-234-381* ⊕ *www.residence7angels.cz* ↪ *10 rooms* ⦿ *Breakfast* Ⓜ *Line A: Můstek* ✛ *F4.*

$$$
HOTEL
🏨 **Unitas House.** The rooms in this former convent once served as interrogation cells for the communist secret police and the late president Václav Havel was once even a guest here. **Pros:** clean rooms; great location on a quiet street. **Cons:** simple decor is uninspiring for the price. Ⓢ *Rooms from: 5400 Kč* ✉ *Bartolomějská 9, Staré Mesto* ☎ *224-230-533* ⊕ *www.unitas.cz* ↪ *22 rooms* ⦿ *Breakfast* Ⓜ *Line B: Národní třída* ✛ *E4.*

$$$
HOTEL
🏨 **Ventana Hotel Prague.** Surprisingly quiet considering its location just steps from Old Town Square, the Ventana delivers old-school style and charm in spades. **Pros:** calm and cozy retreat; good location; staff have old-school charm. **Cons:** pricey; rooms vary in wow-factor, so check them out carefully. Ⓢ *Rooms from: 5400 Kč* ✉ *Celetná 7, Staré Mesto* ☎ *221-776-600* ⊕ *www.ventana-hotel.net* ↪ *29 rooms* ⦿ *Breakfast* Ⓜ *Lines A & B: Můstek* ✛ *F3.*

MALÁ STRANA (LESSER QUARTER)

With a bewitching storybook suite of baroque palaces and Renaissance facades, the Lesser Quarter—at the other end of the Charles Bridge from the Old Town—is the darling of Prague. Mostly a quiet area, removed from the bustle across the river, it also has some good traditional restaurants and pubs. Malá Strana provides an excellent location for visiting Prague Castle just up the hill, but may not be the best choice for people with mobility problems. Other cons: car access on the narrow cobblestone streets is restricted, parking is difficult, and you'll spend a lot of your time walking on the Charles Bridge to get to the Old Town.

$$$$
HOTEL
Fodor's Choice
★
🏨 **Alchymist Grand Hotel and Spa.** A baroque fever-dream of Prague masterminded by an Italian developer, the Alchymist doesn't go the understated route. **Pros:** unique design; high-quality spa. **Cons:** steep uphill walk from the tram; loud A/C. Ⓢ *Rooms from: 6700 Kč* ✉ *Tržiště 19, Malá Strana* ☎ *257-286-011* ⊕ *www.alchymisthotel.com* ↪ *46 rooms* ⦿ *Breakfast* Ⓜ *Line A: Malostranská* ✛ *B3.*

4

$$$ HOTEL

🏨 **Appia Hotel Residences.** A stylish hotel comprised of rooms and apartments, in a slightly off-the-beaten-track location in Malá Strana. **Pros:** lovely courtyard and 12th-century hall; quiet and stylish. **Cons:** too quiet for some; staff professional but not warm. [$] *Rooms from: 4000 Kč* ✉ *Šporkova 3/322, Malá Strana* ☎ *257–215–819* 🌐 *www.appiaresidencesprague.cz* 🛏 *21 rooms* 🍴 *Breakfast* [M] *Line A: Malostranská* ✥ *A3.*

$$$$ HOTEL

🏨 **Aria Hotel.** This property kicked off Prague's luxury hotel boom in the early 2000s and still holds up well against the competition. **Pros:** gorgeous gardens make for a quiet escape; excellent restaurant and breakfast; Apple televisions in all rooms, along with killer sound systems. **Cons:** proximity to the embassy can lead to tiresome security checks; some of the suites are small and might be better labeled as standard rooms. [$] *Rooms from: 6700 Kč* ✉ *Tržiště 9, Malá Strana* ☎ *225–334–111* 🌐 *www.ariahotel.net* 🛏 *51 rooms* 🍴 *Breakfast* [M] *Line A: Malostranská* ✥ *B3.*

$$$$ HOTEL Fodor's Choice ★

🏨 **Augustine, a Luxury Collection Hotel, Prague.** There's plenty of competition in Prague's high-end hotel market, but the Augustine—now part of Starwood's Luxury Collection—has vaulted to the top. **Pros:** impeccable service; clever design; impressive spa. **Cons:** breakfast not always included; noisy wood floors. [$] *Rooms from: 9000 Kč* ✉ *Letenská 12, Malá Strana* ☎ *266–112–233* 🌐 *www.augustinehotel.com* 🛏 *101 rooms* 🍴 *No meals* [M] *Line A: Malostranská* ✥ *C2.*

$$ HOTEL

🏨 **Domus Balthasar.** This chic retreat is hidden in plain sight on one of the busiest streets in Prague, the road up from Charles Bridge in Malá Strana. **Pros:** reasonably priced; modern decor and good Wi-Fi; friendly service from hip staff. **Cons:** very busy street; no lift; ceilings in attractive loft rooms too low for anyone over 6 feet. [$] *Rooms from: 2200 Kč* ✉ *Mostecká 5, Malá Strana* ☎ *257–199–499* 🌐 *www.domus-balthasar.cz* 🛏 *8 rooms* 🍴 *No meals* [M] *Line A: Malostranská* ✥ *C3.*

$$ B&B/INN

🏨 **Dům U Červeného Lva** (*House at the Red Lion*). An intimate, immaculately kept baroque building dating to the 15th century, this hotel is right on the main thoroughfare in the Lesser Quarter, a five-minute walk from Prague Castle's front gates. **Pros:** intimate rooms; beautiful location not far from Prague Castle. **Cons:** no elevator; no air-conditioning; no reception desk in the hotel. [$] *Rooms from: 3200 Kč* ✉ *Nerudova 41, Malá Strana* ☎ *257–533–832* 🌐 *www.hotelredlion.cz* 🛏 *6 rooms* 🍴 *Breakfast* [M] *Line A: Malostranská* ✥ *A3.*

$$$$ HOTEL Fodor's Choice ★

🏨 **Golden Well.** Consistently rated one of Prague's best boutique hotels, the Golden Well is hidden away at the top of a narrow side street in Malá Strana. **Pros:** great views at fantastic restaurant; friendly service; spacious rooms. **Cons:** outlet shortage; far from the subway and tram stop. [$] *Rooms from: 6700 Kč* ✉ *U Zlate Studne 4, Malá Strana* ☎ *257–011–213* 🌐 *www.goldenwell.cz* 🛏 *19 rooms* 🍴 *No meals* [M] *Line A: Malostranská* ✥ *B2.*

$$ HOTEL

🏨 **Hotel Kampa Stará Zbrojnice.** The secluded and picturesque location of this historic inn that once served as an armory is the main selling point here. **Pros:** location is gorgeously positioned by Kampa Park; live music at breakfast. **Cons:** the breakfasts could use more variety; uninspiring room decor and thin pillows. [$] *Rooms from: 3000 Kč* ✉ *Všehrdova 16, Malá Strana* ☎ *272–114–444* 🌐 *www.sivekhotels.com/en/hotel-kampa-stara-zbrojnice* 🛏 *84 rooms* 🍴 *Breakfast* [M] *Line A: Malostranská* ✥ *C4.*

$$ HOTEL
🏨 **Hotel Neruda.** Built in 1348, this landmark—now a flashy boutique hotel with major design chops—is where the author Jan Neruda and his mother lived in 1860. **Pros:** designer rooms have lots of character; historic location. **Cons:** design can impinge on the livability of the hotel; no nearby metro and an uphill walk from the nearest tram stop. [$] *Rooms from: 3000 Kč* ✉ *Nerudova 44, Malá Strana* ☎ *257–535–557* 🌐 *www.designhotelneruda.com* 🛏 *42 rooms* 🍴 *Breakfast* [M] *Line A: Malostranská* ⊕ *A3.*

$$ B&B/INN Fodor's Choice ★
🏨 **Lokál Inn.** The funky 18th-century Lokál Inn offers an unbeatable combination of location, ambience, and convenience. **Pros:** central location; historic surroundings; modern amenities. **Cons:** rooms get a bit of noise from restaurant at night. [$] *Rooms from: 3200 Kč* ✉ *Míšeňská 12, Malá Strana* ☎ *257–014–800* 🌐 *www.lokalinn.cz* 🛏 *14 rooms* 🍴 *Some meals* [M] *Line A: Malostranská* ⊕ *C3.*

$$$$ HOTEL Fodor's Choice ★
🏨 **Mandarin Oriental Prague.** Architects wisely chose to retain many of the Dominican monastery's original flourishes when it was restored, creating a peaceful, inspired backdrop for the Mandarin Oriental's luxurious offerings. **Pros:** historic building; lovely setting; attentive, personalized service; luxurious beds. **Cons:** some rooms are small; Wi-Fi and breakfast can cost extra depending on your reservation. [$] *Rooms from: 9000 Kč* ✉ *Nebovidská 1, Malá Strana* ☎ *233–088–888* 🌐 *www.mandarinoriental.com/prague* 🛏 *99 rooms* 🍴 *No meals* [M] *Line A: Malostranská* ⊕ *C4.*

$$ HOTEL
🏨 **Pod Věží.** The family-friendly Pod Věží is perched on the end of the famous Charles Bridge, so close you even get a free ticket to the tower if you stay here. **Pros:** almost on Charles Bridge itself; friendly staff; nice touches like daily gifts for guests; large rooms. **Cons:** can be loud. [$] *Rooms from: 3800 Kč* ✉ *Mostecká 58/2, Malá Strana* ☎ *257–532–041* 🌐 *www.podvezi.com* 🛏 *12 rooms plus 16 rooms in adjacent building* 🍴 *Breakfast* [M] *Line A: Malostranská* ⊕ *C3.*

$$ HOTEL
🏨 **Sax Vintage Design Hotel.** This bold, bright, and affordable hotel was was favored by former Secretary of State Madeleine Albright (there's a framed letter of thanks on the wall). **Pros:** good price and free happy hour; hotel sits on a quiet street; friendly staff. **Cons:** this might be too much for those with more conservative tastes; for those in Prague for the nightlife, this side of the river might be less than ideal. [$] *Rooms from: 2400 Kč* ✉ *Jánský vršek 3, Malá Strana* ☎ *257–531–268* 🌐 *www.hotelsax.cz* 🛏 *22 rooms* 🍴 *Breakfast* [M] *Line A: Malostranská* ⊕ *A3.*

$$ HOTEL
🏨 **U Tří Pštrosů.** This historic inn has taken a couple of licks—first it was flooded, then burned to the ground, and then rebuilt, only to be taken by the communists, and finally restituted to the family owners. **Pros:** location, location, location. **Cons:** small rooms up top; could be too much in the thick of it for some. [$] *Rooms from: 2900 Kč* ✉ *Dražického nám. 12, Malá Strana* ☎ *777–876–667* 🌐 *www.utripstrosu.cz* 🛏 *18 rooms* 🍴 *Breakfast* [M] *Line A: Malostranská* ⊕ *C3.*

HRADČANY

For some, Prague Castle is the romantic capital in this city. Though it is a hectic spot during the day with a lot of foot traffic, it is quiet and even spacious in the evening; the starlit castle grounds open onto hilly parks perfect for long strolls while drinking in a breathtaking panoramic view of the city.

$$$ HOTEL **Hotel Savoy.** A modest yellow Jugendstil façade conceals one of the city's most luxurious small hotels. **Pros:** peaceful location above it all; shiny new lobby bar; meeting facilities. **Cons:** long (uphill) walk home, as it's away from the center; pricey. [$] *Rooms from: 5500 Kč* ✉ *Keplerova 6, Hradcany* ☎ *224–302–430* 🌐 *www.hotelsavoyprague.com* 🛏 *61 rooms* 🍴 *Breakfast* [M] *Line A: Malostranská* ✣ *A3.*

$$ HOTEL **Romantik Hotel U Raka.** With the quaint look of a woodsman's cottage from a bedtime story, this private guesthouse has a quiet location on the ancient, winding street of Nový Svět, just behind the Loreto Church and a 10-minute walk from Prague Castle. **Pros:** near Prague Castle, but secluded for those who truly want to get away; in-room fireplaces in some rooms. **Cons:** tiny size makes rooms hard to come by; cramped breakfast area; no Metro station nearby. [$] *Rooms from: 2800 Kč* ✉ *Černínská 10, Hradcany* ☎ *220–511–100* 🌐 *www.hoteluraka.cz* 🛏 *6 rooms* 🍴 *Breakfast* [M] *Line A: Malostranská* ✣ *A2.*

NOVÉ MĚSTO (NEW TOWN)

Not exactly "new," this district dates back to the 14th century, and includes bustling Wenceslas Square. New Town isn't as clean and architecturally fragile as Old Town, but what it loses in baroque curls it makes up for in good location at slightly cheaper prices.

$$ HOTEL **Beseda Hotel Prague.** Large, white, airy, and located inside an attractive, 19th-century building that used to be a municipal meeting hall; it's based in an interesting part of New Town which manages to be both quiet and close to a lot of nightlife. **Pros:** light, airy lounge area; good deals in off-season; good conference facilities. **Cons:** less touristy location may not appeal to everyone; spotty service; no restaurant. [$] *Rooms from: 2800 Kč* ✉ *Vladislavova 1477/20, Nové Mesto* ☎ *222–500–222* 🌐 *www.hotelbesedaprague.com* 🛏 *136 rooms* 🍴 *Breakfast* 💳 *No credit cards* [M] *Line B: Národní třída* ✣ *F5.*

$ HOTEL **Best Western City Hotel Moran.** This renovated 19th-century town house is a comfortable choice for those who want consistency in the quality of their accommodations. **Pros:** free Wi-Fi throughout hotel; comfortable beds in spacious rooms. **Cons:** rooms facing the tram street can be noisy for lighter sleepers; a bit of a hike to Old Town Square. [$] *Rooms from: 1600 Kč* ✉ *Na Moráni 15, Nové Mesto* ☎ *224–915–208* 🌐 *bestwestern-city-moran.hotel-rn.com* 🛏 *57 rooms* 🍴 *Breakfast* [M] *Line B: Karlovo nám* ✣ *E6.*

$$ HOTEL **Best Western Plus Hotel Meteor Plaza.** Though this hotel shares a street with the fancy-pants Grand Mark, and also occupies a baroque town palace, it's a step down in terms of atmosphere and quality (at an admittedly lower price). **Pros:** just a few steps from the Municipal House and five minutes on foot from downtown; friendly staff. **Cons:** interior not very inspiring; breakfast room can fill up quickly; tiny lift. [$] *Rooms from: 3000 Kč* ✉ *Hybernská 6, Nové Mesto* ☎ *224–192–559,* 🌐 *www.hotel-meteor.cz* 🛏 *88 rooms* 🍴 *Breakfast* [M] *Line B: Nám. Republiky* ✣ *H3.*

$$$$ HOTEL 🏨 **The Grand Mark.** This shiny new hotel—steps from Náměstí Republiky—brings a high level of service and attention to detail to a still-scruffy part of the center. **Pros:** big, beautiful garden at the back; excellent service; great bathrooms. **Cons:** only a small gym (but guests receive passes to use a nearby fitness club); the street is not especially attractive. [$] *Rooms from: 6800 Kč* ✉ *Hybernská 12, Nové Mesto* ☎ *226–226–111* 🌐 *www.grandmark.cz* 🛏 *75 rooms* 🍴 *No meals* [M] *Line B: Nám. Republiky* ✣ *H3.*

$$ HOTEL 🏨 **Hotel Boho Prague.** This isn't the flowing hippie boho vibe that the name implies: Hotel Boho is chic, sleek, cool, and located on a fairly uninspiring but quiet street not far from bustling Náměstí Republiky. **Pros:** trendy long bar; good spa. **Cons:** a little impersonal; located on an uninspiring street. [$] *Rooms from: 4000 Kč* ✉ *Senovázná 1254/4, Nové Mesto* ☎ *234–622–600* 🌐 *www.hotelbohoprague.com* 🛏 *57 rooms* 🍴 *No meals* 💳 *No credit cards* [M] *Line B: Náměstí Republiky* ✣ *H4.*

$$$ HOTEL 🏨 **Hotel Boscolo Prague.** Dripping with glamour, this mammoth 19th-century neoclassical palace is part of the Marriott Hotel's high-end Autograph Collection. **Pros:** luxurious feel; cushy linens. **Cons:** sometimes rude staff; expensive breakfast not always included in the room rate. [$] *Rooms from: 5400 Kč* ✉ *Senovážné nám. 13, Nové Mesto* ☎ *224–593–000* 🌐 *prague.boscolohotels.com* 🛏 *152 rooms* 🍴 *No meals* [M] *Line B: Nám. Republiky* ✣ *H4.*

$ HOTEL 🏨 **Hotel Élite Prague.** A 14th-century Gothic façade and many poetic architectural details have been preserved in this hotel, thanks to an extensive renovation. **Pros:** nice historic feel; close to the National Theater. **Cons:** the neighborhood can get overrun with partiers at night. [$] *Rooms from: 2100 Kč* ✉ *Ostrovní 32, Nové Mesto* ☎ *224–932–250* 🌐 *www.hotelelite.cz* 🛏 *78 rooms* 🍴 *Breakfast* [M] *Line B: Karlovo náměstí* ✣ *E5.*

$ HOTEL 🏨 **Hotel Ibis Praha Old Town.** Walk into this hotel and you may think you've entered the 1960s. **Pros:** within easy walking distance of Old Town Square; good value for money; swimming pool. **Cons:** expensive buffet breakfast (297 Kč per person); the enormity of the hotel detracts from any intimacy; no restaurant. [$] *Rooms from: 1900 Kč* ✉ *Na Poříčí 5, Nové Mesto* ☎ *266–000–999* 🌐 *www.ibis.com/gb/hotel-5477-ibis-praha old-town/index.shtml* 🛏 *271 rooms* 🍴 *Breakfast* [M] *Line B: Nám. Republiky* ✣ *H3.*

$$ HOTEL 🏨 **Hotel Palace Praha.** Perched on a busy corner in the city center, this pistachio-green art nouveau building trumpets its Victorian origins. **Pros:** helpful and knowledgeable staff; great location; good deals to be had. **Cons:** a little faded; gilded style not for everyone. [$] *Rooms from: 3200 Kč* ✉ *Panská 12, Nové Mesto* ☎ *224–093–111* 🌐 *www.palacehotel.cz* 🛏 *124 rooms* 🍴 *Breakfast* [M] *Line A: Můstek* ✣ *G4.*

$$ HOTEL 🏨 **Hotel Salvator.** This efficiently run establishment just outside the Old Town offers more comforts than most in its class, including flat-screen TVs and minibars in some rooms. **Pros:** lovely restaurant and courtyard; in-house tourist office. **Cons:** courtyard-facing rooms can be noisy at mealtimes; bland room decor. [$] *Rooms from: 2400 Kč* ✉ *Truhlářská 10, Nové Mesto* ☎ *222–312–234* 🌐 *www.salvator.cz* 🛏 *39 rooms* 🍴 *Some meals* [M] *Line B: Nám. Republiky* ✣ *H2.*

4

$ HOTEL
🏨 **Hotel Yasmin.** A sprightly presence on an imperious street (think communist-era blocks), the Yasmin offers modern design at good prices. **Pros:** close to Wenceslas Square; good breakfast spread; free access to sauna and gym. **Cons:** bland rooms; slow, overworked elevator. [$] *Rooms from: 1800 Kč* ✉ *Politických vězňů 12, Nové Mesto* ☎ *234–100–100* 🌐 *www.hotel-yasmin.cz* 🛏 *196 rooms* 🍴 *Breakfast* [M] *Line A: Můstek* ✥ *H5.*

$ HOTEL
🏨 **Ibis Wenceslas Square.** The price and the location make this brand hotel a reasonable pick for the price. **Pros:** comfortable beds; air-conditioning. **Cons:** very little nightlife in the area; except for corner locations, rooms are rather small; price does not include breakfast, which is an additional charge. [$] *Rooms from: 1800 Kč* ✉ *Kateřinská 36, Nové Mesto* ☎ *222–865–777* 🌐 *www.ibis.com/gb/hotel-3195-ibis-praha-wenceslas-square/index.shtml* 🛏 *181 rooms* 🍴 *No meals* [M] *Line C: I.P. Pavlova* ✥ *E6.*

$$ HOTEL
Fodor's Choice ★
🏨 **Icon Hotel & Lounge.** From the fashionable staff to its plush, all-natural bedding, this hotel is dressed to impress. **Pros:** youthful, exuberant staff; all-day breakfast spread; good Metro and tram connections. **Cons:** small spa; busy, urban location will not appeal to everyone. [$] *Rooms from: 4000 Kč* ✉ *V jámě 6, Nové Mesto* ☎ *221–634–100* 🌐 *www.icon-hotel.eu* 🛏 *31 rooms* 🍴 *Breakfast* [M] *Lines A & B: Můstek* ✥ *G5.*

$$ HOTEL
🏨 **Jalta Hotel.** The Jalta is arguably the smartest, most interesting hotel on central Wenceslas Square, with a historically protected façade that dates to the 1950s in the style of socialist realist. **Pros:** underground nuclear shelter below the hotel to check out; attractive rooms; friendly staff. **Cons:** may be too close to the action for some; the cheaper rooms are small. [$] *Rooms from: 4000 Kč* ✉ *Václavské nám. 45, Nové Mesto* ☎ *222–822–111* 🌐 *www.hoteljalta.com* 🛏 *94 rooms* 🍴 *Breakfast* [M] *Lines A & C: Muzeum* ✥ *G5.*

$$ HOTEL
🏨 **Opera.** This hotel is clean, well managed, and a decent value, but won't appeal to everyone because of the uninspiring location just beside the busy "Magistrale," the main highway that cuts through the center of the city. **Pros:** clean rooms; large bathrooms; nice but small sauna and whirlpool. **Cons:** some top-floor rooms have an obstructed view; it's a 15-minute walk to Old Town Square. [$] *Rooms from: 3200 Kč* ✉ *Těšnov 13, Nové Mesto* ☎ *222–315–609* 🌐 *www.hotel-opera.cz* 🛏 *67 rooms* 🍴 *Breakfast* [M] *Line C: Florenc* ✥ *H2.*

$$ HOTEL
🏨 **Radisson Blu Alcron Hotel.** Opened in 1932, the Alcron was one of Prague's first luxury hotels; a major renovation of the building in 1998 modernized the look but restored the art deco building and the crystal chandeliers. **Pros:** good price considering location and style; helpful staff; excellent restaurant. **Cons:** rooms vary in size; conservatively styled rooms compared with the public spaces. [$] *Rooms from: 3500 Kč* ✉ *Štěpánská 40, Nové Mesto* ☎ *222–820–000* 🌐 *www.radissonblu.com/en/hotel-prague* 🛏 *204 rooms* 🍴 *Breakfast* [M] *Line A: Můstek* ✥ *G5.*

VINOHRADY

Literally translated as "vineyards," which this area was many centuries ago, you can still find vestiges of grapevines in parks like Havlíčkovy sady. Today it's home to some of the city's wealthiest residents, as seen in the splendid town houses and handsome squares. For visitors, the wealth means excellent restaurants and pleasant tree-lined streets, perfect for meandering after an exhausting day in the center.

$ HOTEL

Hotel Anna. The bright neoclassical façade and art nouveau details have been lovingly restored on this 19th-century building on a quiet residential street. **Pros:** staff are helpful, with an excellent command of English; Wi-Fi included; pets are welcome. **Cons:** some guests find walls to be thin; though peaceful, the neighborhood is outside the city center; air-conditioning costs extra. [$] *Rooms from: 1600 Kč* ✉ *Budečská 17, Vinohrady* ☎ *222–513–111* 🌐 *www.hotelanna.cz* 🛏 *24 rooms* 🍴 *Breakfast* [M] *Line A: Nám. Míru* ✥ *H6.*

$$ HOTEL
Fodor's Choice ★

Hotel Le Palais. This venerable 19th-century mansion served as the home and shop of Prague's main butcher (one of the front rooms was even used to produce and sell sausage until 1991). **Pros:** gorgeous hotel; helpful, courteous staff. **Cons:** nice neighborhood but requires public transit to get anywhere; small beds in basic rooms. [$] *Rooms from: 3600 Kč* ✉ *U Zvonařky 1, Vinohrady* ☎ *234–634–111* 🌐 *www.lepalaishotel.eu* 🛏 *72 rooms* 🍴 *Breakfast* [M] *Line C: I.P. Pavlova* ✥ *H6.*

$$ HOTEL

Hotel 16. A popular, family-run hotel in leafy Vinohrady, rooms here are comfy and the welcome from the staff is genuine. **Pros:** friendly welcome; good breakfast; convenient trams to Old Town. **Cons:** homey decor might not be too all tastes; long walk to Old Town. [$] *Rooms from: 2700 Kč* ✉ *Kateřinská 16, Vinohrady* ☎ *224–920–636* 🌐 *www.hotel16.cz* 🛏 *14 rooms* 🍴 *Breakfast* [M] *Line C: I.P. Pavlova* ✥ *E6.*

ŽIŽKOV

Although Prague is a safe city where anyone can amble about alone, this is one of its seedier parts—a bit grittier and louder than other sections. That said, it's also a great neighborhood for extroverts who like student bars, music clubs, and hangouts where a fashion parade of people with piercings, tattoos, dreadlocks, or a dog—and sometimes all of the above—come to socialize. Being an eclectic and punk hood, it may come as little surprise that Žižkov is a popular spot for students or backpackers to stay at a hostel.

$$ HOTEL

Hotel Ariston & Ariston Patio Prague. This hotel is best used as a fallback; it's clean and the staff are proud of the property, but the explosion of floral prints, aged televisions, and tired carpeting doesn't make for a destination property. **Pros:** spacious rooms; spotlessly clean. **Cons:** very little nightlife in the area; rooms facing the street receive some cling-clangy tram noise. [$] *Rooms from: 2200 Kč* ✉ *Seifertova 65, Žižkov* ☎ *222–782–517* 🌐 *www.hotelaristonpatioprague.cz* 🛏 *62 rooms* 🍴 *Breakfast* [M] *Line C: Hlavní nádraží* ✥ *H4.*

$$$$ HOTEL
Fodor's Choice ★

One Room Hotel at Tower Park Praha. Perhaps the most unique hotel in Prague, a night in this luxuriously decked-out capsule-room at the top of the communist-era TV tower is quite an experience. **Pros:** unforgettable location; amazing views. **Cons:** Gritty Žižkov is an unlikely place for such glamour. [$] *Rooms from: 15000 Kč* ✉ *Tower Park Prague, Mahlerovy sady 1, Žižkov* ☎ *210–320–085* 🌐 *towerpark.cz* 🛏 *1 room* 🍴 *Breakfast* [M] *Line A: Jiřího z Poděbrad* ✥ *H4.*

$ 📺 **Prague Hotel Theatrino.** This colorful, art nouveau hotel is big on char-
HOTEL acter, but short on real luxury, making it a decent budget choice if you're
for looking for something original. **Pros:** good breakfast; rooms have
individual style; close to lots of bars and nightlife. **Cons:** long walk to
the center; no A/C (save for the fifth floor). $ *Rooms from: 1600 Kč*
✉ *Bořivojova 53, Žižkov* ☎ *227–031–894* ⊕ *www.hoteltheatrino.cz*
↝ *73 rooms* 🍽 *Breakfast* Ⓜ *Line C: Hlavní nádraží* ✛ *H4.*

SMÍCHOV

Smíchov means "mixed neighborhood." When the city had walls, the
neighborhood was on the outside, and all manner of people could live
there. Although it's still a colorful, working-class area, lots of new
construction has made it a shopping and entertainment hub as well,
with good views of and relatively easy access—via tram, Metro, or on
foot—to the city's historical center and its new riverside drinking and
eating hangout, Náplavka.

$ 📺 **andel's by Vienna House Prague.** Right next to one of the city's best
HOTEL shopping malls, this simple, modernist property is where many of the
young, up-and-coming British trendsetters stay. **Pros:** great water pressure in showers; wide choice of foods for breakfast; convenient Metro
connection to the center. **Cons:** a business hotel, so the breakfast room
can be busy in the morning; mall area is long on shopping but a bit
short on personality. $ *Rooms from: 1500 Kč* ✉ *Stroupežnického 21,
Smíchov* ☎ *296–889–688* ⊕ *andelsbyviennahouseprague.h-rez.com*
↝ *239 rooms* 🍽 *Breakfast* Ⓜ *Line B: Anděl* ✛ *B6.*

$$ 📺 **Arbes.** For those travelers who like to stay in more "local" spots, this
HOTEL is for you. **Pros:** rooms are airy; convenient to public transportation
(both tram and Metro). **Cons:** still a walk to Old Town; rooms are
clean but not especially interesting. $ *Rooms from: 2700 Kč* ✉ *Viktora
Huga 3, Smíchov* ☎ *251–116–555* ⊕ *www.hotelarbes.cz* ↝ *27 rooms*
🍽 *Breakfast* Ⓜ *Line B: Anděl* ✛ *B6.*

$ 📺 **Best Western Premier Hotel Kinsky Garden.** You could walk the mile from
HOTEL this hotel to Prague Castle entirely on the tree-lined paths of Petřín, the
hilly park that starts across the street. **Pros:** great location for runners,
as Petřín hill is right across the street; near a tram stop; free Wi-Fi in
rooms. **Cons:** at least a 15-minute walk to the Charles Bridge; uphill
walk from the nearest tram stop. $ *Rooms from: 1800 Kč* ✉ *Holečkova
7, Smíchov* ☎ *257–311–173* ⊕ *www.hotelkinskygarden.cz* ↝ *62 rooms*
🍽 *Breakfast* Ⓜ *Line B: Anděl* ✛ *B6.*

$$$ 📺 **Mamaison Hotel Riverside Prague.** True to its name, the Riverside is situ-
HOTEL ated right above the Vltava across from Frank Gehry's Dancing House.
Pros: clever design; incredible views. **Cons:** no gym; interior rooms are
dark. $ *Rooms from: 6000 Kč* ✉ *Janáčkovo nabř. 15, Smíchov* ☎ *225–
994–611* ⊕ *www.mamaisonriverside.com* ↝ *97 rooms* 🍽 *Breakfast*
Ⓜ *Line B: Anděl* ✛ *C6.*

5

PERFORMING
ARTS

Updated by
Jennifer Rigby

There's an old saying in the Czech Republic which goes, "Co Čech, to muzikant" (Every Czech is a musician). That might be stretching it a bit, but as visitors to Prague quickly realize, culture and performing arts are right at the heart of this beautiful city and its residents.

Music constantly drifts across the cobbled streets in Old Town; theater shows pop up in parks in the balmy summer months; and the calendar is chockablock with world-beating film festivals. And the best part? The affordable ticket prices. It's almost criminal to come to this city and not take in a performance, from opera to ballet, when they are so accessible.

Prague's musical history is a rich and varied one, from hometown composers like Antonín Dvořák or Bedřich Smetana to expats like Mozart, whose *Don Giovanni* made its debut here in 1787 and is still performed regularly. You can also catch the work of more modern Czech composers like Bohuslav Martinů, or even Vladimir Franz, the head-to-toe tattooed composer who gave more seasoned politicians a run for their money in recent presidential elections.

There's something particularly lovely about the regular classical music performances that take place in ancient churches dotted around the city too, but do follow the recommendations to ensure you're getting the best of the bunch.

And it's not all classical. The avant-garde is alive and kicking in the Czech capital, from its youthful theater troupes, some of which perform in English, to a recent crop of thoughtful filmmakers. Interesting modern dance performances also sit alongside more traditional forms. Both the National Theater and State Opera have their own ballet companies staging a mix of classic and contemporary pieces.

Even if you aren't normally a culture vulture, consider taking in a performance while you are in town. The shows are world-class and many of the concert halls are jaw-droppingly gorgeous. Note: big theaters and concert halls go dark in July and August; luckily there are festivals aplenty to keep the "magic" of art alive in Prague year-round.

PLANNER

WHERE TO GET TICKETS

Booking online before you arrive will make everything cheaper. Try the venues themselves or the ticket agencies below. Alternatively, the concierge at your hotel may be able to reserve tickets for you. You can also go directly to the theater box office a few days in advance or immediately before a performance. If you are interested in seeing a specific festival, like Prague Spring, definitely purchase tickets in advance directly from the organizer or one of these listed agencies.

Bohemia Ticket International. The oldest ticket agency in Prague specializes in classical, jazz, opera, and ballet. ⊠ *Na Příkopě 16, Nové Mesto* ☎ *224–215–031* ⊕ *www.bohemiaticket.cz.*

Sazka Ticket. This is the exclusive seller of tickets to events at O2 Arena, which hosts big concerts and sports events. You can buy tickets online or at newsagents and tobacco shops throughout town. The O2 Arena box office is usually only open on the day of the event, so purchasing your tickets there is not recommended. ⊠ *Politických vězňů 15, Nové Mesto* ☎ *224–091–435* ⊕ *www.sazkaticket.cz.*

Ticketportal. Tickets for big gigs, venues, festivals, and theaters are available through this agency, which shares its head office location with Sazka. You can purchase tickets online or at various outlets including hotels, Metro stations, tourist offices, and the venues themselves, such as Divadlo Hybernia. On rare occasions, Ticketportal has the exclusive rights to a show. ⊠ *Politických vězňů 15, Nové Mesto* ☎ *221–419–420 for Divadlo Hybernia branch, 224–224–461 for Můstek Metro station branch* ⊕ *www.ticketportal.cz.*

Ticketpro. This is the main outlet for tickets to all shows and clubs, especially stadium concerts, with several branches across the city (and country). There's pop, rock, and theater options on the website, as well as a special kid's events section. Ticketpro also has an easy search engine that allows you to search what's going on by date. ⊠ *Václavské nám. 38, Nové Mesto* ☎ *234–704–204* ⊕ *www.ticketpro.cz.*

Ticketstream. This big ticket agency offers tickets for a mixture of events, and has lots of locations across the city center, including some shared branches with Bohemia Ticket. ⊠ *Na Příkopě 16, Nové Mesto* ☎ *224–263–049* ⊕ *www.ticketstream.cz.*

WHAT TO WEAR

When getting dressed for a night of culture, take your cue from the city locals. You'll note that it is still common for people to dress up for performances, especially at the larger, traditional venues. Most women will be in cocktail dresses, and most men will don at least a shirt and tie (if not a full suit).

CONCERTS TO AVOID

Experiencing classical music in a church setting can be an amazing experience. Unfortunately in Prague, standards vary widely for church concerts. Low-quality shows are advertised in Old Town Square and Malá Strana and rely on non-repeat tourist patrons to stay in business.

CLOSE UP

Mozart in Prague

Considering that Wolfgang Amadeus Mozart visited Prague only four times, it's impressive how indelible his mark on the city is. On his first trip, in early 1787, he visited Count Thun and his wife. They lived in what is now the British Embassy in Malá Strana, and Mozart stayed at an inn on Celetná Street. During this trip he conducted his *Prague Symphony* and a day later, on January 20, a performance of his opera *The Marriage of Figaro*, which had a more successful run in Prague than in Vienna. One legend from this time has the host of a party inviting him an hour before all the other guests and making him compose new dances for the evening.

His second trip is the most famous. The maestro came to visit composer F.X. Dušek and his new wife, opera singer Josephine, in 1787 at their rural villa, Bertramka (although he also kept rooms at the Uhelný třída Inn). After several missed deadlines, he conducted the world premiere of *Don Giovanni* on October 29 at Stavovské divadlo. He tried out a number of church organs in his spare time.

His third visit was just a pass-through, but the fourth and final trip came just months before he died in 1791. He promised to write a new opera to mark the coronation of Leopold II as king of Bohemia. Unfortunately, *La Clemenza di Tito*, which premiered at the Stavovské divadlo on September 6, was written quickly, and was not as well received as *Don Giovanni*. Once news of his death on December 5 reached Prague, his friends staged a memorial service that ended with church bells ringing all over town.

To avoid disappointment, choose bigger, better-known churches, and make sure the performance features a professional chamber group.

CLASSICAL MUSIC

Considering the Czech people's love of classical music, it will come as no surprise to read that music is often ringing in the streets throughout the city. Pausing near the Charles Bridge to catch a particularly beguiling string quartet is one of Prague's great pleasures. But it's also worth it to seek out the professionals that perform in historic venues, from massive concert halls to baroque churches. Pick one of the better chamber ensembles (we've listed some here), as the programs are usually more adventurous and you're likely to hear little-known composers. Or get tickets to see a professional orchestra; the program may not take many risks, but you're practically guaranteed an evening of virtuoso playing, and often international guest musicians will take the stage. Steer clear of lesser-known ensembles or venues that cater to tourists, which can be subpar.

Collegium Marianum. One of the most well-respected ensembles in town, Collegium Marianum is your best bet if looking to explore baroque music. They often revive seldom-heard works from archives and perform them on period instruments. Performances are usually organized around a historical or geographical theme. ⊠ *Vodičkova 700/32, Staré*

DID YOU KNOW?

Classical music has deep roots in Prague, and compared to other European cities, performances are very inexpensive (if not free!).

Mesto ☎224–229–462 ⊕ *www.collegiummarianum.cz* Ⓜ *Line A: Staroměstská.*

Czech National Symphony Orchestra. This major full-size orchestra plays most often at the Rudolfinum. The orchestra has attracted some well-known guest conductors, and performs classical, jazz, and some film scores. ☎267–215–388 ⊕ *www.cnso.cz.*

Czech Philharmonic. Antonín Dvořák conducted the orchestra's first performance back in 1896. Guest conductors have included Gustav Mahler and Leonard Bernstein. Since 1990 there has been a rapid turnover in chief conductors, but the performances have been of consistently high quality. Most programs include some works by Czech composers. ✉ *Rudolfinum, nám. Jana Palacha, Staré Mesto* ☎227–059–249 ⊕ *www.ceskafilharmonie.cz* Ⓜ *Line A: Staroměstská.*

Nostitz Quartet. Named after a famous 18th-century patron of the arts, this ensemble has won a few prestigious awards. They give excellent performances of works by Mozart and Czech composers, and are one of the better groups to appear in various church concerts around town. The group does not have a website but you can track them down through their Facebook page. ⊕ *www.facebook.com/nostitzquartet.*

PKF - Prague Philharmonia. Founded in 1994, this orchestra is youthful and forward-thinking in more ways than one, boasting a chief conductor (Jakub Hrůša) who was born in 1981 as well as a program which aims to send listeners home with, as they put it, a new "joie de vivre." Their work ranges from classic and romantic to contemporary composers and a children's concert series. The group play regularly, including at the Rudolfinum and Prague Castle. ☎224–267–644 ⊕ *www.pkf.cz.*

Prague Chamber Orchestra without Conductor. Famous for playing often (but not always) without a conductor, this ensemble covers the classics up through 20th-century composers. Usually they play about four concerts a year in the Rudolfinum. ☎274–772–697 ⊕ *www.pko.cz.*

Fodor's Choice ★ **Prague Symphony Orchestra** *(FOK).* The group's nickname stands for Film-Opera-Koncert. They started in 1934, but it wasn't until 1952 that they became the official city orchestra. In the 1930s they did music for many Czech films, although they don't do much opera and film anymore. The ensemble tours extensively and has a large back catalog of recordings. Programs tend to be quite diverse, from Beethoven to Bruckner. They also offer public rehearsals for a mere 100 Kč. ✉ *Obecní dům, Nám. Republiky 5, Staré Mesto* ☎222–002–336 ⊕ *www.fok.cz* Ⓜ *Line B: Nám. Republiky.*

Wihan Quartet. Many quartets borrow names from composers, but few choose the name of a musician: Wihan was a cellist who knew Dvořák. The quartet has won numerous awards since it started in 1985, and has participated in international broadcasts. Most of their sets include at least one Czech composer. ⊕ *www.wihanquartet.co.uk.*

CHURCH CONCERTS

Church concerts have become a staple of the Prague classical music scene. The concerts help churches to raise money and also give visitors more of an opportunity to hear classical music, often in an opulent setting. Banners or signs at the churches announce when there's a concert. Listings can also be found in English on the website ⊕ *www.pis.cz.*

■ TIP➜ Many churches aren't heated; ask before buying your ticket and dress appropriately.

Barokní knihovní sál (*Baroque Library Hall*). Beautiful 18th-century frescoes and colorful stuccowork in a monastery library hall make for one of the more charming concert halls in a city with no shortage of charming concert halls. This is usually a good bet for a quality performance, as it is effectively home to the Collegium Marianum ensemble. ⊠ *Melantrichova 971/19, Staré Mesto* ☎ *224–229–462* ⊕ *www.tynskaskola. cz* Ⓜ *Line A: Staroměstská.*

Bazilika sv. Jakuba (*Basilica of St. James*). This is an excellent venue for organ concerts thanks to the church's organ, which was finished in 1709 and restored in the early 1980s to its original tone structure. All those years later, it's still one of the best in town. ⊠ *Malá Štupartská 6, Staré Mesto* ☎ *604–208–490* ⊕ *www.auditeorganum.cz/organ.html* Ⓜ *Line A: Staroměstská.*

Bazilika sv. Jiří (*Basilica of St. George*). Listen to small ensembles playing well-known Vivaldi and other classical "greatest hits" in a Romanesque setting. Located in Prague Castle, the building—or parts of it at least—dates to the 11th century, and holds the tombs of some very early princes. ⊠ *Nám. U sv. Jiří, Pražský Hrad* ☎ *224–372–434* ⊕ *www. kulturanahrade.cz* Ⓜ *Line A: Hradčandská.*

Chrám sv. Mikuláše (*Church of St. Nicholas, Staré Město*). The impressive chandelier inside this baroque landmark was a gift from the Russian czar. Private companies rent out the church for concerts by professional ensembles and visiting amateur choirs and orchestras. The quality and prices vary, but the location—right on the edge of Old Town Square—always delivers, as does the beauty of the church's interior. ⊠ *Staroměstské nám., Staré Mesto* ☎ *224–190–990* ⊕ *www.svmikulas. cz* Ⓜ *Line A: Staroměstská.*

Fodor'sChoice
★ **Kostel sv. Mikuláše** (*Church of St. Nicholas, Malá Strana*). Ballroom scenes in the movie *Van Helsing* used the interior of this beautiful baroque church, probably the most famous of its kind in Prague. The building's dome was one of the last works finished by architect Kilian Ignatz Dientzenhofer before his death in 1751, and a memorial service to Mozart was held here after his death. Local ensembles play concerts of popular classics here throughout the year. ⊠ *Malostranské nám., Malá Strana* ☎ *257–534–215* ⊕ *www.stnicholas.cz* Ⓜ *Line A: Malostranská.*

Kostel sv. Šimona a Judy (*Church of Sts. Simon and Jude*). This decommissioned church with a restored organ and frescoes is used by the Prague Symphony Orchestra for chamber concerts and recitals and it's also a popular venue for music festivals. The baroque altar is actually an elaborate painting on the wall. ✉ *Dušní ulice, Josefov* ☎ *222–002–336* ⊕ *www.fok.cz/koncertni-jednatelstvi* Ⓜ *Line A: Staroměstská.*

Fodor's Choice   **Zrcadlová kaple Klementina** (*Mirrored Chapel of the Klementinum*). Now
★   part of the National Library, this ornate little chapel in the middle of the
Klementinum complex is worth a peek. Concerts are held almost daily
and the music features the usual suspects—Mozart, Bach, and Vivaldi.
Different concert companies program the space; signs nearby usually
have the day's schedule. ✉ *Marianské nám., Staré Mesto* ☎ *221–663–
331* ⊕ *www.nkp.cz* Ⓜ *Line A: Staroměstská.*

FILM

Hollywood descended on Prague en masse in the early 1990s, using its
beauty as a stand-in for nearly every conceivable European city from
Paris to Amsterdam. And it helped that Prague was far more affordable than any of those Western European capitals. It's still common
to run into a film crew on the streets, although it's less likely to be a
blockbuster now. Movie watchers, however, are more easily found.
Multiplexes are the dominant force, and locals fill them regularly. For
something indie, foreign, or Czech with subtitles, head to Prague's
many independent and well-run art cinemas, which seem to have a
different festival almost every week. Most films are shown in their
original-language versions, but it pays to check. If a film was made in
the United States or Britain, the chances are good that it will be shown
with Czech subtitles rather than dubbed (the exception being cartoons).
Film titles, however, are usually translated into Czech. Movies in the
original language are normally indicated as *českými titulky* (with Czech
subtitles). Prague's English-language websites carry film reviews and
full timetables.

■**TIP➜** You can reserve tickets in advance at all movie theaters and
multiplexes. Also note: unlike movie tickets in the U.S., your ticket often
has an assigned seat number.

Aero. Film junkies make the trek to this out-of-the-way gem of a theater
knowing it's worth the trip. The tiny cinema is hidden in the middle of
a residential block, and keeps an ambitious schedule of two or three
different films a day: festivals, retrospectives, oldies but goodies (think
Scarface and *The Big Lebowski*) plus feature films with English subtitles. Czech translations are done through headphones. Visiting guests
have included Terry Gilliam, Godfrey Reggio, and Paul Morrisey. The
theater also has an outdoor beer garden in the summer months and a
lively indoor bar year-round. ✉ *Biskupcova 31, Žižkov* ☎ *608–330–088*
⊕ *www.kinoaero.cz* Ⓜ *Line A: Želivského.*

Bio Oko. Bargain ticket prices, live music before the films, and a schedule
that offers greater variety and more "big name" films are just a few reasons to check out this theater outside the city center. New international
releases as well as Czech films (sometimes with subtitles) and festival
series give Oko a varied lineup. There's a refurbished bar and café
here outfitted with Wi-Fi, and it even offers a video streaming service.

✉ *Františka Křížka 15, Holešovice* ☎ *608–330–088* ⊕ *www.biooko. net* Ⓜ *Line C: Vltavská.*

Cinema City Nový Smíchov. Cinema City Nový Smíchov feels like your usual multiplex until you try the "4DX" experience, which involves moving seats and special effects in your seat like fog and lightning. Located in the Nový Smíchov shopping center, the cinema is an experience for all five senses. ✉ *Nový Smíchov, Obchodní centrum Nový Smíchov, Smíchov* ☎ *255–742–021* ⊕ *www.cinemacity.cz/en/novysmichov* Ⓜ *Line B: Anděl.*

Cinema City Slovanský dům. This is pretty much the only multiplex in the center of town that runs about 10 movies at once, mostly the latest Hollywood films in English (with Czech subtitles). It occasionally runs Czech films with English subtitles. ✉ *Na Příkopé 22, Nové Mesto* ☎ *255–742–021* ⊕ *www.cinemacity.cz/en/slovanskydum* Ⓜ *Line B: Nám. Republiky.*

Institut Français de Prague. Bonjour! What do we have here? A little bit of Paris in Prague, that's what. Hidden in the basement of the French Institute is a full-size movie theater; most of the programming consists of recent French films as well as classics, also in French. Some of the films have English subtitles, and the admission fee is usually nominal (80 Kč). They also host an annual French Film Festival in November. No food or drinks allowed (but on the ground floor there's an excellent café). "Serious" film watching only. ✉ *Štěpanská 35, Nové Mesto* ☎ *221–401–011* ⊕ *www.ifp.cz* Ⓜ *Lines A & B: Můstek.*

Fodor's Choice ★ **Lucerna.** Easily the city's handsomest old movie palace, this art nouveau venue was designed by former President Václav Havel's grandfather and built in 1916. It's a great place to recapture the romance and glamour of film. Grab a drink at the bar, where there is sometimes a live piano player, even if the interior could do with a little more love. Watch out for the upside-down horse sculpture, plus rider, in the passage outside—it's a sly echo of one on the square, which has the Czech Republic's patron saint, St. Wenceslas, the right way up. ✉ *Vodičkova 36, Nové Mesto* ☎ *224–216–973* ⊕ *www.lucerna.cz* Ⓜ *Lines A & B: Můstek.*

Světozor. Prague's central art-house cinema has a great location near the Lucerna shopping passage and an excellent selection of offbeat American films, classic European cinema, and the best of new Czech films. Many films are subtitled in English and the theater even has its own brand of beer. ✉ *Vodičkova 41, Nové Mesto* ☎ *224–946–824* ⊕ *www. kinosvetozor.cz* Ⓜ *Lines A & B: Můstek.*

PERFORMANCE ARTS CENTERS AND MAJOR VENUES

Divadlo Kolowrat. Home to the much-loved Prague Shakespeare Company, which stages the Bard's works in English, this small venue in a repurposed palace also houses The Swan Theater Club, a bar and restaurant heavily populated by Czech actors and celeb-types. Get your tickets in person at the box office or online. ✉ *Ovocný trh 6, Staré*

CLOSE UP

5 Czech Films to Check Out

Journey to the Beginning of Time (Cesta do pravěku) (1955; dir. Karel Zeman). A luminary figure in the development of special effects, Zeman made this film nearly 40 years before *Jurassic Park*, which is a truly remarkable feat. The story centers on the journey that four young boys undertake on a river through time; it gives life to the pictures and bones we find in museums. Some tremendous set pieces will take your breath away.

Happy End (1967; dir. Oldřich Lipský). Not even 70 minutes long, this film is as unconventional as it is impressive. Opening with a title card that reads "The End," the film builds on its backwardness as it moves in linear fashion from its main character's death to birth. Your expectation of progress in the opposite direction will have you shaking with mirth even as you appreciate moments of visual poetry.

The Fireman's Ball (Hoří, má panenko) (1967; dir. Miloš Forman). Made on a shoestring budget shortly before the Soviet invasion in August 1968, Forman's film has rightly been called one of the country's most important films. This very thinly veiled critique of authoritarianism is presented with a flair for comedy and a high level of entertainment, and it remains an intelligent allegory that some may say is still relevant today.

The Ear (Ucho) (1970; dir. Karel Kachyňa). This film's screenwriter was a communist activist in his youth, which caused the film to be banned upon its release and not screened in public until the Velvet Revolution. It takes place during a single evening at the house of Ludvik, a high-level civil servant, who becomes convinced his house has been bugged. The atmosphere is electric, as recurring flashbacks to a party earlier in the evening—shot from Ludvik's perspective—effortlessly reel the viewer in.

Jára Cimrman Lying, Sleeping (Jára Cimrman ležící, spící) (1983; dir. Ladislav Smoljak). This comedy takes a look at the life of the most famous Czech who never lived. The film is bookended by scenes in the present, when museum visitors are told about all of the incredible events that have occurred in the character's life; in 2005 Jára Cimrman was voted the most important Czech in history in a national poll.

Mesto ☏ *778–058–333 for Swan Theater Club* ⊕ *www.pragueshakespeare.com/venues* Ⓜ *Lines A & B: Můstek.*

Kongresové centrum Praha (*Congress Center*). Somehow, this former Palace of Culture, built in 1981, has never found a place in people's hearts. The large, functionalist, multipurpose building has several performance spaces that can seat thousands, but overall it has a very sterile feel. Plays—usually musicals—and special events come here. As the largest venue in the city, it also hosts the majority of conferences. ✉ *5 kvetna 65, Nusle* ☏ *261–171–111* ⊕ *www.kcp.cz* Ⓜ *Line C: Vyšehrad.*

Lichtenštejnský palác (*Lichtenstein Palace*). Home to the Czech music academy (HAMU), this baroque palace from the 1790s has the large Martinů Hall for professional concerts and a smaller gallery occasionally used for student recitals. The pleasant courtyard sometimes has

Opera performances draw large crowds at the Národní divadlo (National Theater).

music in the summer months. ⊠ *Malostranské nám. 13, Malá Strana* ☎ *257–534–206* Ⓜ *Line A: Malostranská.*

Meet Factory. If you want to take the pulse of Prague's contemporary arts scene, get yourself down to Meet Factory. It can be a little tricky to find (look out for the building with car sculptures driving vertically up it, across the train tracks), but it's worth it for the variety of cool art, theater, dance, and music performances that take place in this interesting and unusual space. ⊠ *Ke Sklárně 3213/15, Smíchov* ☎ *251–551–796* ⊕ *meetfactory.cz* Ⓜ *Line B: Smíchovské nádraží.*

Fodor's Choice
★ **Národní divadlo** (*National Theater*). This is the main stage in the Czech Republic for drama, dance, and opera. The interior, with its ornate and etched ceilings, is worth the visit alone. Most of the theater performances are in Czech, but some operas have English supertitles, and ballet is an international language—right? Book the opera online ahead of time for fantastic discounts; you'll get to see top-quality performances in sumptuous surroundings at a snip of the price you could pay in other European capitals. Stavovské divadlo and Kolowrat are also part of the National Theater system. ⊠ *Národní 2, Nové Mesto* ☎ *224–901–448* ⊕ *www.narodni-divadlo.cz* Ⓜ *Line B: Národní třída.*

O2 Arena. Formerly the Sazka Arena (tickets are still sold through Sazka Ticket), this indoor sports venue often hosts big-time rock and pop acts, like Justin Bieber and The Cure. It's also the current home of local ice hockey legends, Sparta Praha. The security level is very high, and almost airportlike. A small nail file or pocket scissors can delay your entrance. ⊠ *Českomoravská čp. 2345/17, Vysocany* ☎ *266–771–000* ⊕ *www. o2arena.cz* Ⓜ *Line B: Českomoravská.*

Obecní dům (*Municipal House*). The main concert hall, a true art nouveau gem named after composer Bedřich Smetana, is home to the Prague Symphony Orchestra and many music festivals. A few smaller halls, all named for famous figures, host chamber concerts. Tours of the building are also offered. It's well worth a visit, even if you only pop your head in. ⊠ *Nám. Republiky 5, Staré Mesto* ☎ *222–002–101* ⊕ *www. obecnidum.cz* Ⓜ *Line B: Nám. Republiky.*

Fodor's Choice

★

Rudolfinum. Austrian Crown Prince Rudolf lent his name to this neo-Renaissance concert space and exhibition gallery built in 1884; it's only been open to the public since 1992. The large concert hall, named for Antonín Dvořák, who conducted here, hosts concerts by the Czech Philharmonic. The smaller Josef Suk Hall, on the opposite side of the building, is used for chamber concerts. Rival theaters may have richer interiors, but the acoustics here are excellent (and the exterior is also pretty fancy). ⊠ *Alšovo nábřeží 12, Staré Mesto* ☎ *227–059–227* ⊕ *www.rudolfinum.cz* Ⓜ *Line A: Staroměstská.*

Fodor's Choice

★

Stavovské divadlo (*Estates Theater*). It's impossible to visit Prague without knowing that Mozart conducted the world premiere of *Don Giovanni* on this stage way back in 1787. Fittingly, the interior was used for scenes in Miloš Forman's movie *Amadeus*. It's stylish and refined without being distracting. This is a branch of the National Theater, and high-quality productions of Mozart are usually in the repertoire together with other classic operas, plays, and the occasional smaller ballet. ⊠ *Ovocný trh 6, Nové Mesto* ☎ *224–901–448* ⊕ *www.narodni-divadlo.cz/en/estates-theatre* Ⓜ *Lines A & B: Můstek.*

Velký sál, Lucerna (*Great Hall, Lucerna*). Part of the fascinating Lucerna complex, the Velký sál is a beautiful art nouveau ballroom with a big main floor and some loges. It hosts medium-size rock and pop bands in wonderful historic surroundings. Everyone from Ray Charles to Maurice Chevalier has played here, so soak up the history as you sway to the beat. ⊠ *Štěpánská 61, Nové Mesto* ☎ *224–225–440* ⊕ *www.lucerna.cz* Ⓜ *Lines A & B: Můstek.*

PUPPET SHOWS AND BLACK-LIGHT THEATER

Black-light theater, a form of nonverbal theater—melding live acting, mime, video, and stage trickery—made a global splash when Czechoslovakia introduced it at Expo '58. Some black-light shows have been running for thousands of performances. Tickets can be pricey compared with other art options in town, and it is an acquired taste, but kids often love it. Puppetry also has a long tradition, but most of the shows are dialogue-intensive and aimed at a young audience.

All Colours Theater. Since 1993 this small theater has been presenting a small repertoire of nonverbal shows. *Faust* is their main performance, although they occasionally revive other works. Some legends claim that the real Faust lived in Prague, which gives the show some local significance. The interior feels a little tired. ⊠ *Rytířská 31, Staré Mesto* ☎ *224–186–114* ⊕ *www.blacktheatre.cz* Ⓜ *Lines A & B: Můstek.*

If you find yourself taken with the marionettes for sale in Prague, take in a performance at one of the puppet shows and watch them come to life.

Divadlo Image. This is the new home of a dance, pantomime, and black-light company that has a repertoire of long-running classics of the genre and a "best of" show, which children will appreciate. ✉ *Národní 25, Josefov* ☎ *732–156–343* ⊕ *www.imagetheatre.cz* Ⓜ *Line A: Staroměstská.*

Divadlo Ta Fantastika. A black-light show called *Aspects of Alice,* based loosely on *Alice in Wonderland,* has run here almost daily for more than 2,000 performances. The theater was established in Florida in 1981, and moved to Prague after the Velvet Revolution. It's been running at its current address, a minor baroque palace, since 1993. ■**TIP➔** It's one of the best black-light options. ✉ *Karlova 8, Staré Mesto* ☎ *222–221–366* ⊕ *www.tafantastika.cz* Ⓜ *Line A: Staroměstská.*

Křižíkova fontána. Pressurized water and colored lights keep pace with recorded music that ranges from recent film scores to a tribute to Rihanna, and selections of classical music. It's an odd mix, but it's fun. Live acts, such as ballerinas, actors, and full orchestras, share the stage on occasion. Tickets are available at the venue. ✉ *Výstaviště, Holešovice* ☎ *723–665–694* ⊕ *www.krizikovafontana.cz* Ⓜ *Line C: Nádraží Holešovice.*

FAMILY **Národní divadlo marionet** (*The National Marionette Theater*). This puppet company has been presenting Mozart's *Don Giovanni* with string puppets set to recorded music sung in Italian since 1991. The opera is slightly tongue-in-cheek, and Mozart himself makes a guest appearance. A new production of *The Magic Flute,* in German, is occasionally performed as well. ✉ *Žatecká 1, Staré Mesto* ☎ *224–819–322* ⊕ *www.mozart.cz* Ⓜ *Line A: Staroměstská.*

DID YOU KNOW?

Black-light theater, like this performance by the Wow Show (⊕ *www.wow-show. com*), was introduced in Czechoslovakia in 1958 at the World Expo. Performers use tinted makeup illuminated with a black light to create dramatic images and optical illusions.

Fodor's Choice Nová Scéná (*The New Stage*). The cool glass-block façade of the Nová
★ scena, which opened in 1983, stands out among the ornate 19th-century buildings in the area. Black-light theater company Laterna Magika (which takes its name from the original black-light presentation at Expo '58) perform here, and the rest of the program schedule is handled through the Národní divadlo. Contemporary dance pieces and other language-free performances dominate the calendar. ⊠ *Národní 4, Nové Mesto* ☎ *224–901–111* ⊕ *www.novascena.cz* Ⓜ *Line B: Národní třída.*

THEATER AND DANCE

Theater and dance in Prague is where the modern arts scene really comes alive. Inventive young companies sadly often perform only in Czech, but there are good English options too. A variety of dance companies bring the theatrical experience to visitors without the language barrier.

Divadlo Alfred ve dvoře. Most of the programming for this small, out-of-the-way theater is physical, nonverbal theater and dance, along with some music. It's a great place to see cutting-edge, unconventional productions; each year has a different theme. It's also home to Motus, a not-for-profit organization, set up by young local artists, producers, and presenters to promote and produce interesting and inventive new art. ⊠ *Fr. Křížka 36, Bubenec* ☎ *233–376–985* ⊕ *www.alfredvedvore. cz* Ⓜ *Line C: Vltavská.*

Fodor's Choice **Divadlo Archa** (*Archa Theater*). Funky, contemporary, and underground,
★ Archa is the main venue for modern theater, dance, and avant-garde music. Some visiting troupes perform in English, and other shows are designated as English-friendly in the program. The centrally located theater opened in 1994, and is often referred to as the Alternative National Theater. ⊠ *Na Poříčí 26, Nové Mesto* ☎ *221–716–333* ⊕ *www.archatheatre.cz* Ⓜ *Line B: Nám. Republiky.*

Divadlo Ponec. A former cylinder factory, then a movie theater, this neoclassical building was renovated into a modern dance venue in 2001. The house presents a lot of premieres, and is the main "dance" theater in town. Several dance festivals are based here. ⊠ *Husitská 24/a, Žižkov* ☎ *224–721–531* ⊕ *www.divadloponec.cz* Ⓜ *Lines B & C: Florenc.*

Švandovo divadlo. If you want to join the theater-loving masses and there's nothing on in English, Švandovo is your best bet. Plays—a rotating mix ranging from Shakespeare to Ibsen to contemporary showings—are subtitled above the stage in English. The theater also serves as a major venue for the Prague Pride festival. ■**TIP→** Sit in the balcony, on the right side, facing the stage for the best view. ⊠ *Štefánikova 57, Smíchov* ☎ *257–318–666* ⊕ *www.svandovodivadlo.cz* Ⓜ *Line B: Anděl.*

NIGHTLIFE

PRAGUE'S BEER CULTURE

If there's one thing people associate with the Czech Republic, it's beer. And with good reason: the Czechs brew some of the world's best lagers. Whether it's the water, Czech hops, or simply that pilsner was invented here is up for debate, but the golden liquid is central to Czech culture.

Accordingly, don't be surprised to see beer consumed in all manner of social situations, from construction workers cracking a can with their breakfast roll to high-schoolers meeting for some suds after class. It's simply central to most of the country's interactions; the Czechs drink more beer per capita than any other nation in the world. More than that, however, the Czechs take pride in the quality of their beer, so even if it's not normally your thing, don't be afraid to try a pint during a visit here.

A RARE BREW

Only a select few restaurants and pubs serve unpasteurized beer, called *tankové pivo*. You'll see it advertised prominently on the menu outside. The breweries bring it only to pubs they select, picking those that move a high volume of beer and adhere to their strict standards. The beer is kept in pressurized tanks and pumped in fresh by trucks weekly. The benefit? Unpasteurized beers retain their "spicy" characteristics from the Czech hops, yielding a more complex set of tastes than the beers that are exported.

A PUB PRIMER

A *pivnice* is a Czech beer hall named after *pivo,* or beer. Expect a range of beer, usually drunk in high quantities along with simple snacks. And one Czech phrase you'll learn very quickly here is "*pivo, prosím,*" or "beer, please."

ETIQUETTE

Don't be intimidated by Prague pubs: they're happy to host you and show off their wares, so to speak. Ordering a beer is quite easy: Ask for a pivo when the waiter comes by (it may take a minute or two, but they'll get to you). Though most pubs serve beers from a single brewer, you might have options between a 10- or 12-degree quaff; if you're not sure and just ask for a beer, you'll probably end up with the lighter 10-degree stuff. If you don't want another round, when the waiter comes by and asks, say "Ne, dekuju" (No, thanks).

As for the check itself (which will get tallied around 10:30 or 11 pm on weeknights and later on weekends if you don't finish first), it's a strip of paper on the table. Each mark on the paper represents a beer that you've had. The waiter will count them up and tell you how much you owe—though do try and keep your own count, and be mindful how much the beers cost if you want to be absolutely sure not to get overcharged.

A small tip is the norm here, essentially rounding up to the nearest large number

(usually coming to a few extra dollars) and handing it to your server, or another server who will come by with a money pouch to handle the transaction. There's no need to tip an additional 15% unless you think you've received exceptional service.

PRAGUE'S MUST-TASTE

Czech beers are rightfully famous for their quality. While it's easy to find beers from big brewers like Staropramen or Gambrinus on tap most anywhere, more and more pubs are utilizing a "fourth pipe" (or tap) to showcase a local, independent brew that you might not have seen before. Here are a few to keep an eye out for:

Bernard Lager: This Bohemian pilsner stands up well to the famous Pilsner Urquell thanks to its intense hoppiness.

Opat Kvasničák Nefiltrovaný: A tasty, unfiltered brew with sweet and sour notes.

Kozel dark: A winner at the World Beer Awards, Kozel makes this dark beer as well as more traditional lagers.

U Medvídku X-33: Available only at the famed traditional pub of the same name, the X-33 sounds like a secret government project, but is actually one of the stronger beers in the country, at 12% alcohol.

6

Updated by
Jennifer Rigby

Prague is a city that takes its liquid refreshment, and its after-dark entertainment, seriously. The beer is rightfully world-famous and beer gardens are a dream, a new trend for cocktail bars has taken the city by storm, and music and dancing options are plentiful.

Plus, with such a small city center, you'll rarely have to travel far to find the best bars and clubs. In fact, one of the great pleasures of Prague is wandering around Old Town and just popping into any of the bars that take your fancy (and that don't look hideously overpriced). ■ **TIP→ Go for the back streets, and don't pay much more than 50 Kč for a beer.** Another Prague perk is the relaxed hours. In the past, bars used to close down by 10 pm or so, but now Czechs have taken cheerfully to all-nighters spent discussing philosophy in smoky dives, listening to jazz in cavernous underground clubs, or dancing on tables in avant-garde clubs.

Many of the best nightlife spots combine international pizzazz with a bit of Czech eccentricity—think beers delivered by a miniature railway or a cocktail bar where absinthe is a major component in most of the menu options.

Prague is also a very musical city, which is reflected in its nightlife. A lot of the clubs also host live music performances, and the atmospheric jazz clubs offer great shows almost every night of the week.

Clubbers have plenty of options too, although anyone looking for the cutting edge of cool is unlikely to find it in Prague, because having a good time is much more important. There's an increasingly visible gay scene, too.

For those who want to look beyond the bar, there are evening cruises on the Vltava that show off the city's gorgeous waterfront, which is beauti-fully lit as the sun sets. In recent years, a thriving scene on Náplavka (a riverside walkway in Nové Mesto) has sprung up, offering cheap and cheerful pop-up pubs right alongside the water, often accompanied by food and fashion markets. And if we're talking alfresco drinking,

DID YOU KNOW?

Prague offers the rare opportunity to try unpasteurized beer, which can only be served fresh, not bottled.

Prague's beer gardens, comprising no-frills benches and brews in its beautiful parks, are a must-visit in summer.

And while Prague isn't Monte Carlo, gambling is legal, and there is a range of establishments from exclusive high-end casinos to all-night herna bars with slot machines and video-game terminals. Most gamers say the top venues lack ambience and only the brave try the nonstop herna bars.

PLANNER

HOURS

Pubs used to close by 10 pm in the communist era, but Prague has since embraced all-night opening with vigor. It's not unusual to see pubs open until 4 or 5 in the morning, and the streets can buzz until almost as late. On the other hand, some old-fashioned pubs still do close fairly early, and it's best to check for live music venues, as noise restrictions can mean the show's over by 10 pm; this doesn't apply to underground jazz bars.

STAG PARTIES AND SAFETY

Stag parties used to be the curse of the city's nightlife scene for anyone looking for a quiet and pleasant evening with a few friends. There are still a few groups out and about on any given night in matching tacky outfits singing songs on the street, but just a fraction of what it used to be. Many of the pubs that used to cater to them have shifted their focus to better service and quality food in an attempt to make up for the loss of stag business, which is good news for the average visitor and downtown resident.

In an effort to control street rowdiness associated with stag parties in the touristy center, Prague adopted a ban on street drinking in certain main areas, but it does not apply to restaurants with sidewalk seating or beer gardens in parks.

A word of caution about adult entertainment: thanks to the former popularity of Prague as a stag destination, several dance and strip clubs have sprung up on the side streets at the upper end of Wenceslas Square. With the downturn in stag parties, many of the establishments have become quite aggressive in attracting clients, and have people on nearby streets offering to show passersby a place for a "good time."

Although these places are legal, they aren't always safe or cheap. Some establishments charge large sums of money for every quarter-hour you stay or have other hidden fees; others simply charge outrageous fees for drinks. Around these areas, be sure to watch your wallet. Professional thieves frequent the same areas and target those who have had too much to drink.

STARÉ MĚSTO

Prague's historical heart is also the heart of its nightlife. It's packed with jazz bars, old pubs, and high-end cocktail bars.

BARS AND PUBS

Bonvivant's. The cocktail maker's cocktail bar of choice in Prague, Bonvivant's has a nostalgic feel and an eccentric owner who is clearly passionate about his drinks. Upmarket but not pricey, this is a perfect place for for an adventure in mixology and some tasty tapas in a refined setting. There are some amusing house rules. ⊠ *Bartolomějská 305, Staré Mesto* ☎ *775–331–862* ⊕ *www.facebook.com/bonvivantsctc* Ⓜ *Line B: Národní třída.*

Hemingway Bar. Absinthe is all over Prague, and if you want to dabble in the green fairy's magic, there are worse places than the sophisticated cocktail bar Hemingway, which is named after the man himself. You won't find any flaming absinthe here, but you will find a range of interesting cocktails, alongside Champagne and 200 varieties of rum—all of which were the famous writer's drinks of choice. ⊠ *Kařolíny Světlé 26, Staré Mesto* ☎ *773–974–764* ⊕ *www.hemingwaybar.cz/bar-prague* Ⓜ *Lines A & B: Můstek.*

Kristian Marco (river bar). As you walk by in summer, you'll be drawn in by the gentle guitar playing of the resident musician, or the smell of the barbecue, or the hum of conversation and clink of glasses. The beer is more expensive than some other bars, and the food can be pricey, but you pay for the location, right on the water's edge near the National Theater, with the castle looming over you on the other side of the river. ⊠ *Smetanovo nábřeží 198/1, Staré Mesto* ☎ *No phone* ☯ *Closed Nov.–Apr.* Ⓜ *Lines A & B: Můstek.*

Fodor'sChoice
★
Lokál. This modern take on a traditional Czech pub has been an absolute hit with locals and in-the-know visitors since it opened in 2009, so it's worth making a reservation at peak times. The beer comes from sleek silver tanks, there's some interesting stuff on the walls, and you sit on long, dark wooden benches as your waiter delivers seemingly endless foaming mugs of the amber nectar. There's also a good selection of Czech food as well as *slivovice* (fiery plum brandy) for the daring—the walnut one is particularly good. ⊠ *Dlouhá 33, Staré Mesto* ☎ *222–316–265* ⊕ *lokal.ambi.cz* Ⓜ *Line B: Náměstí Republiky.*

Prague Beer Museum. With 30 Czech craft beers on tap, this is the place to go in Old Town if you're hunting for an unusual brew in a fun environment. The owners scoured the countryside for their beers, and one is apparently only available as long as a friend of the brewer doesn't break up with his girlfriend (he delivers the beer on the way to visiting her in Prague). There's a second location in Vinohrady. ⊠ *Dlouhá 46, Staré Mesto* ☎ *732–330–912* ⊕ *www.praguebeermuseum.cz* Ⓜ *Line B: Náměstí Republiky.*

Fodor'sChoice
★
U Medvídků. A former brewery dating as far back as the 15th century, U Medvídků now serves draft Budvar shipped directly from České Budějovice, as well as its own super-strong beer X Beer 33, which is

6

brewed on-site. It's perhaps the most authentic of the city center Czech pubs, which also means that it's often pretty busy, and service can be correspondingly slow. However, it's also big enough that you've got a good chance of finding a seat. The interior, including the taps, have a turn-of-the-20th-century feel. Occasionally, the bar offers exclusive Budvar brews available only at this location. There's a hotel on-site, too. ✉ *Na Perštýně 7, Staré Mesto* ☎ *224–211–916* ⊕ *www.umedvidku. cz* Ⓜ *Line B: Národní třída.*

Fodor's Choice **U Zlatého Tygra.** The last of the old, smoky, surly pubs in the Old Town, ★ the "Golden Tiger" is famous for being one of the best Prague pubs for Pilsner Urquell. It's also renowned as a former hangout of one of the country's best-known and beloved writers, Bohumil Hrabal, who died in 1997, as well as Velvet Revolution hero and then president, Václav Havel. Reservations are not accepted; one option is to show up when the pub opens at 3 pm, with the rest of the early birds, and settle in for the rest of the night. You won't be disappointed. ✉ *Husova 17, Staré Mesto* ☎ *222–221–111* ⊕ *www.uzlatehotygra.cz* Ⓜ *Line A: Staroměstská.*

CLUBS

Harley's. Sometimes Harley's can be a bit intense. It's quite small and can get absolutely boiling hot, so if the crowds are heaving, give it a miss. However, if you're in the right mood and get onto the dance floor early enough, it can be lots of fun. The music veers from chart hits to cheesy tunes and then back to rock. Look out for the motorbikes, which are strapped to the walls and ceiling. ✉ *Dlouhá 18, Staré Mesto* ☎ *602–419–111* ⊕ *www.harleys.cz* Ⓜ *Line A: Staroměstská.*

Karlovy Lázně. Inside a former bathhouse next to the Charles Bridge, this club claims to be the biggest in central Europe. We're not sure about that, but it is pretty big, with five levels of music ranging from house to soul and even old-school disco (and sometimes a bit of Czech and international cheesiness). Lines can be long on weekends. Recently the venue introduced an all-inclusive VIP area that can be booked by small groups. Bear in mind this is a bit of a meat market and the crowd is pretty young and touristy. ✉ *Smetanovo nábř. 198, Staré Mesto* ☎ *739–054–641* ⊕ *www.karlovylazne.cz* Ⓜ *Line A: Staroměstská.*

M1 Lounge. A sleek club on a side street in Old Town, M1 Lounge has been known to host movie stars in town for a shoot as well as Prague's local party crowd. Despite its proximity to a lot of the big sights, it somehow manages to feel a little bit exclusive; that is, until the dance music comes on and everyone takes to the floor the same as in any old place. Check the website to find out what music will be offered, as it changes every night of the week. ✉ *Masná 1, Staré Mesto* ☎ *227–195–235* ⊕ *www.m1lounge.com* Ⓜ *Line A: Staroměstská.*

GAY AND LESBIAN

Friends. This (appropriately named) friendly bar in Old Town serves reasonably priced beer—and Western-priced mixed drinks—in a roomy cellar space. There's plenty of seating most weeknights, but it does get busy on weekends. It opens at 6 pm, videos play every night, happy hour starts at 9, and a DJ spins after 10 on weekends, luring people onto a small dance floor—try karaoke on Tuesday. There's no cover. ✉ *Bartolomějská 11, Staré Mesto* ☎ *734–304–183* ⊕ *www.friendsprague.cz* Ⓜ *Lines A & B: Můstek.*

JAZZ CLUBS

Fodor's Choice ★ **AghaRTA.** Bearing the name of an old Miles Davis album, this small but charming vaulted basement is home base for many local jazz acts. The management also runs a jazz record label and sells their CDs at the club's store. The historic place can't handle big acts, so the club's ongoing jazz festival often puts name acts into Lucerna Music Bar. Music starts around 9 pm, but come an hour earlier to get a seat. ✉ *Železná 16, Staré Mesto* ☎ *222–511–858* ⊕ *www.agharta.cz* Ⓜ *Lines A & C: Můstek.*

Ungelt. Hidden in the side streets behind Old Town Square, this basement has been around since the 15th century and has been a cozy club with good music since 2000. The house bands are decent, and play jazz, blues, or fusion, depending on the night. Its central location means there's mainly an international crowd, but you can still see some classic Czech sights—a sleeping dachshund perched on a bar stool, unaware of and unimpressed by the stage acts, for example. ✉ *Týn 2, Staré Mesto* ☎ *224–895–748* ⊕ *www.jazzungelt.cz* Ⓜ *Line A: Staroměstská.*

ROCK AND LIVE MUSIC CLUBS

Roxy. Part nightclub, part performance space, the Roxy doubles as a residence for DJs and as a popular venue for electronica and touring cult bands. The large former theater has a comfortable, lived-in feel that borders on warehouse chic. All exits from the club are final, and patrons are encouraged not to hang around the area. Upstairs, the NoD space has all manner of bizarre acts. Monday is free. ✉ *Dlouhá 33, Staré Mesto* ☎ *602–691–015* ⊕ *www.roxy.cz* Ⓜ *Line B: Nám. Republiky.*

JOSEFOV

Josefov specializes in the stylish cocktail crowd, plus it's the place to catch the boat for most of the evening cruises. This end of Old Town also has the best shopping, and you'll rarely run into stag parties.

BARS AND PUBS

Fodor's Choice ★ **L'Fleur.** One of a gaggle of swanky cocktail bars that have recently taken Prague by storm, L'Fleur mixes it with the best of them, blending old-school elegance and classic cocktails with local flavors (try the Georgie Shrub for a hit of traditional Czech spirit, Becherovka). ✉ *V Kolkovně 920/5, Josefov* ☎ *734–255–665* ⊕ *www.lfleur.cz* Ⓜ *Line A: Staroměstská.*

6

Tretter's. The lost elegance of the 1930s, with clean lines on dark wood, is re-created in a bar that serves Manhattans, martinis, and other classic cocktails, sometimes with live jazz in the background. This was a trendsetter in Prague when it first opened for classic cocktails, and it remains a great joint for a sophisticated tipple. ⊠ *V Kolkovně 3, Josefov* ☎ *224–811–165* ⊕ *www.tretters.cz* Ⓜ *Line A: Staroměstská.*

U Rudolfina. Some people claim that the way the beer is tapped here makes it the best in town, which probably explains the constant crowds. This was one of the first places in the world to offer unpasteurized beer from tanks, rather than kegs. And the place still retains its old-fashioned charm, making it one of the best authentic Czech pubs in a heavily touristed area. Groups should make reservations—a free table is rare. ⊠ *Křížovnická 10, Josefov* ☎ *210–320–853* ⊕ *www.urudolfina. cz* Ⓜ *Line A: Staroměstská.*

Fodor's Choice **Zlatá Praha (InterContinental Prague hotel).** On the roof of this distinctly
★ uninspiring building is a bar with wonderful city views. The 9th-floor Zlatá Praha restaurant and bar has an outdoor rooftop terrace that perfect for an evening glass of Bohemia Sekt (Czech sparkling wine) while soaking up gorgeous views. ⊠ *Pařížská 30, Josefov* ☎ *296–631–111* ⊕ *www.icprague.com/dining/zlata-praha* Ⓜ *Line A: Staroměstská.*

EVENING BOAT TRIPS

Boat Party Prague. Join the floating party with a young international crowd for drinking and dancing on an outside deck or inside dance floor. A pre-party kicks off at 8:30, the boat sets sail at 11. The DJ spins pop and dance hits and the ticket includes booze and free entry to a nearby club at 1 am. Party reps sell tickets under the astronomical clock in Old Town Square. ⊠ *Dvořákovo nábřeží, Josefov* ☎ *608–543–364* ⊕ *boatpartyprague.com* 🖃 *380 Kč–730 Kč* Ⓜ *Line B: Nám. Republiky.*

Dinner Cruise with Music. This "dinner cruise" often degenerates into a sing-along once the beer kicks in, so be prepared for boisterous merriment. The boat is heated, and this cruise runs in both winter and summer. The relatively early departure hour (7 pm) means you can catch the sunset in summertime, and than dine by candlelight, which is lovely. Entry price includes a buffet dinner and welcome drink, but no additional beverages. ⊠ *Dvořákovo nábřeží, under Čechův most, Josefov* ☎ *742-202-505* ⊕ *www.evd.cz* 🖃 *970 Kč* Ⓜ *Line A: Staroměstská.*

Jazzboat. Jazz, food, drinks, floating down the Vltava, and spectacular views of Prague—if you're a jazz fan (or a fan of river cruises), it doesn't get much better than this. The Jazzboat sails throughout the year; but blankets are provided during the summer if it gets chilly for those sitting outside. ■TIP➜ **Be punctual, as the boat sails at 8:30 pm on the dot.** ⊠ *Usually takes off from Pier 5, under Čechův most, Josefov* ☎ *731-183-180* ⊕ *www.jazzboat.cz* 🖃 *690 Kč* Ⓜ *Line A: Staroměstská.*

U Bukanýra. The name works out to "At the Buccaneer," but the logo bears more than a passing resemblance to Humphrey Bogart in *The African Queen*. This anchored "house-boat music bar" gives you the feeling of being on the river without having to commit to a three-hour tour. Besides a few life preservers, the nautical theme isn't taken too far. Beware that the boat sometimes does change its "permanent" location. ✉ *Nábř. L. Svobody, under the Štefánikův bridge, Josefov* ☎ *777–221–705* ⊕ *www.bukanyr.cz* Ⓜ *Line A: Staroměstská.*

MALÁ STRANA

A mix of tourist traps and authentic late-night haunts, Malá Strana is a beguiling place to drink, in the shadow of Prague Castle.

BARS AND PUBS

Bluelight bar. Despite its location just off the main drag up from Charles Bridge, the Bluelight bar manages to remain a laid-back, smoky haunt for some dedicated late-night drinking. The rock walls of the cave-like space are covered in graffiti, and the clientele is a mixed bag, but somehow it works. This is the perfect destination for a nightcap—just don't blame us if you're still ensconced hours later. ✉ *Josefská 42/1, Malá Strana* ☎ *257–533–126* ⊕ *www.bluelightbar.cz* Ⓜ *Line A: Malostranská.*

Olympia. A hot spot from the 1930s returned to its former glory provides a somewhat romanticized but enjoyable take on a Czech pub. Part of the Kolkovna chain that has locations around the city, Olympia appeals to visitors and locals alike who like the special unpasteurized Pilsner Urquell. There's also a great a menu of Czech classics to help soak up all that delicious beer. Try the schnitzel or the steak tartare. ✉ *Vitežná 7, Malá Strana* ☎ *251–511–080* ⊕ *www.kolkovna.cz* Ⓜ *Line A: Malostranská.*

U Hrocha. Probably the most authentic and atmospheric old boozer in the touristy Castle Area, this traditional Czech pub is just below Prague castle. U Hrocha (The Hippo) is nothing fancy (think wooden benches, smoke, and stone walls) but the Pilsner is delicious, and soon you'll feel right at home. The waiters can seem surly, but we don't think they mean it. ✉ *Thunovská 10, Malá Strana* ☎ *257–533–389* ⊕ *www.facebook.com/U-Hrocha-54902101598* Ⓜ *Line A: Malostranská.*

JAZZ CLUBS

U Malého Glena. Commonly known as "Little Glen," patrons are willing to cram in to hear solid house jazz and blues bands, as well as a few visiting acts. Get there early to stake out a seat near the stage; the tunnel-shape vault can be crowded but that only adds to the atmosphere. Upstairs they serve food until midnight. ✉ *Karmelitská 23, Malá Strana* ☎ *257–531–717* ⊕ *www.malyglen.cz* Ⓜ *Line A: Malostranská.*

ROCK AND LIVE MUSIC CLUBS

Malostranská Beseda. Once the town hall, then a mecca for writers and artists, it's now a three-story music and theater club. Every level of this attractive building has something different going on—there's an art gallery under the roof, a "video café," a live music bar, a restaurant, a café, and a basement beer pub. ■ **TIP**➜ **The live acts are mostly popular Czech bands.** ✉ *Malostranské nám. 21, Malá Strana* ☎ *257–409–112* ⊕ *www.malostranska-beseda.cz* Ⓜ *Line A: Malostranská.*

HRADČANY

Head up the castle hill to quaff beers that were brewed in a 13th-century monastery.

BARS AND PUBS

Fodor'sChoice **Klášterní pivovar Strahov.** The first references to this gorgeous hilltop
★ brewery inside a monastery are from the turn of the 14th century, and while we don't think the monks still actually make the beer, the tasty Pivo Sv. Norbert (Beer St. Norbert) is brewed on the spot. There's a decent food menu and outdoor seating. ✉ *Strahovské nádvoří 301, Hradcany* ☎ *233–353–155* ⊕ *www.klasterni-pivovar.cz* Ⓜ *Line A: Malostranská.*

NOVÉ MĚSTO

Some areas of the neighborhood, particularly around Wenceslas Square, are still dealing with the aftereffects of the stag-party craze, but others have embraced funky, alternative evening offerings.

BARS AND PUBS

Gin and Tonic Club. With 6,400 combinations, this stylish gin palace offers everything from a perfect traditional tipple with ice and a slice to a G&T with sun-dried tomatoes or even bacon. Small plates complement the gin-heavy menu and there's a gorgeous little candlelit garden for mild nights. ✉ *Navrátilova 11, Nové Mesto* ☎ *777–669–557* ⊕ *www.gintonicclub.com* Ⓜ *Lines A & B: Můstek.*

Jáma (*The Hollow*). An outdoor beer garden hidden from passersby on the street provides a refuge from the noisy downtown crowds. The indoor bar is decorated with old rock-and-roll posters. Beer and hard cider on tap go with Mexican food and some pretty good burgers. Internet access is available here for a reasonable price, and Wi-Fi access is free. ✉ *V Jámě 7, Nové Mesto* ☎ *222–967–081* ⊕ *www.jamapub.cz* Ⓜ *Lines A & B: Můstek.*

Fodor'sChoice **Náplavka.** The riverside promenade near the Dancing House building
★ comes alive in the summer months when around a dozen pop-up pubs open up and serve a variety of local brews throughout the day. The pop-ups are everything from tents, small chambers in the walls of the walkway, to punters perched on garden furniture or picnic tables. Further along are fashion and food markets, occasionally floating on boats on the Vltava itself. Everything closes down in the height of winter, in January and February. ✉ *Náplavka, Nové Mesto* Ⓜ *Line B: Karlovo nám.*

Fodor's Choice
★
Pivovarský dům. This brewpub, which opened in 1998, may be short on history, but it makes up for that with outstanding beer. The dark, light, and seasonal microbrew beers are stellar. (Fermenting beer can be viewed through a window.) The food is good, but a slight letdown when compared with the drinks, which include sour cherry beer and even a Champagne beer for the more adventurous. Take heed: there is often a line to get in. ⊠ *Lípová 15, Nové Mesto* ☏ *296–216–666* ⊕ *www. pivovarskydum.com* Ⓜ *Lines A & B: Můstek.*

U Fleků. The oldest brewpub in Europe—open since 1499—makes a tasty, if overpriced, dark beer. But the steady stream of tours means it can be hard to find a seat (in the evenings, at least); they serve around 2,000 pints of it every day. A brewery museum (phone for reservations) opened in 1999, and cabaret shows have been added to the entertainment. ⚠ **Beware of waiters putting unordered shots of liquor on your table.** If you don't insist they remove them right away, they'll be on your bill, and service can be indifferent to rude. But the raucous, beer-swilling, mug-clinking bonhomie makes up for that. ⊠ *Křemencova 11, Nové Mesto* ☏ *224–934–019* ⊕ *www.ufleku.cz* Ⓜ *Line B: Karlovo nám.*

Vinárna U Sudu. Although Prague is beer territory, this pays homage to that other camp: wine. A mazelike, multilevel cellar forms the large wine bar in a baroque building. Make note of where your travelling companions are or you might never find them again—the interior is that cavernous. But, this also makes for a cozy drinking hole in the cold winter months. ∎**TIP➜** This is usually one of the first places during the year to crack open burčák, tasty new wine served shortly after harvest. ⊠ *Vodičkova 10, Nové Mesto* ☏ *222–232–207* ⊕ *www.usudu. cz* Ⓜ *Line B: Karlovo nám.*

FAMILY
Fodor's Choice
★
Výtopna. Located on the very touristy Wenceslas Square, the drinks here are delivered by miniature train. It's gimmicky but great fun when the drinks pull up to the table. ⊠ *Václavské náměstí 56, Nové Mesto* ☏ *725–190–646* ⊕ *vytopna.cz* Ⓜ *Line C: Muzeum.*

Vzorkovna. Currently the holder of the unofficial title of Prague's most alternative city-center pub, Vzorkovna operates a confusing chip system for payment (you get the change back at the end of the night, but don't lose the chip, they'll charge you). It's an acquired taste, with a rough pop-up feel of bars in metropolises like London or New York, plus that uniquely Prague junkyard vibe, with dusty floors, and a giant dog wandering around. The beers on tap are from the award-winning Únětický Pivovar brewery, and reasonably priced for such a centrally located bar. ⊠ *Národní 339/11, Nové Mesto* ☏ *No phone* Ⓜ *Line B: Národní třída.*

CASINOS

Casino Ambassador. One of the first casinos to open in the 1990s, the Casino Ambassador remains one of the big daddies of Prague's gambling scene. Games include American roulette, blackjack, poker, and pontoon, plus free refreshments for players. Nongamblers can play beginner slots, a practice session where you don't gamble with money. ⊠ *Hotel Ambassador, Václavské náměstí 7, Nové Mesto* ☏ *224–193–681* ⊕ *www.vipcasinoprague.com* Ⓜ *Lines A & B: Můstek.*

CLUBS

Duplex. Effectively an international super club in the center of Prague, Duplex is the go-to spot for international DJs playing in the Czech Republic, like David Guetta, as well as the top local acts. Because of the location and the aggressive marketing at street level, the crowd is heavy with tourists and prices are above the norm. But the sheer size of the club—a multilevel penthouse with great views from the terrace—keeps things interesting and bearable. ✉ *Václavské nám. 21, Nové Mesto* ☎ *732–221–111* ⊕ *www.duplex.cz* Ⓜ *Lines A & B: Můstek.*

Nebe. Sometimes all you want is some guaranteed good pop tunes, a friendly vibe, and a packed dance floor. If that's what you're after, Nebe will never let you down. Plus there's no cover charge. There are a couple of branches, but this slightly hidden one on Křemencova is the best of the bunch. ✉ *Křemencova, Nové Mesto* ☎ *608–644–784* ⊕ *www.nebepraha.cz* Ⓜ *Line B: Můstek.*

Radost FX. A clubbing institution dating from the early '90s, this place still draws a loyal following. The dance floor can be a little cramped, but other rooms offer lots of seats and couches for hanging out. Those with two left feet can chill upstairs with a drink or eat food until late in the vegetarian restaurant. ✉ *Bělehradská 120, Nové Mesto* ☎ *603–193–711* ⊕ *www.radostfx.cz* Ⓜ *Line C: I.P. Pavlova.*

GAY AND LESBIAN

JampaDampa. One of the city's few lesbian clubs has a karaoke night and an occasional drag king show. The bilevel space, including a vaulted basement, is a little less flashy than most other clubs. Drinks are quite reasonably priced, considering it is close to Wenceslas Square. ✉ *V Tůních 10, Nové Mesto* ☎ *704–718–530* ⊕ *www.jampadampa.cz.*

JAZZ CLUBS

Reduta. This is where President Bill Clinton jammed with Czech President Václav Havel in 1994, and lots of pictures of that night are still hanging around the joint. Reduta was one of the bigger clubs in the 1960s and '70s, and still feels a little like a dated museum of those glory days. The coat-check person can be pretty aggressive, which is another throwback to the pre-1989 era, but the jazz is worth any aggravation. ✉ *Národní 20, Nové Mesto* ☎ *224–933–487* ⊕ *www.redutajazzclub.cz* Ⓜ *Line B: Národní třída.*

ROCK AND LIVE MUSIC CLUBS

Fodor's Choice ★ **Lucerna Music Bar.** Rock bands on the comeback trail, touring bluesmen, plus Beatles and Rolling Stones cover bands make up the live schedule. Another big draw are the nights—usually Saturday—of 1980s or '90s music videos. The nostalgia-fest will have you dancing your socks off until the wee small hours, alongside what feels like half of Prague and much of the rest of Europe as well. It's good fun. ✉ *Vodičkova 36, Nové Mesto* ☎ *224–217–108* ⊕ *www.musicbar.cz* Ⓜ *Lines A & B: Můstek.*

RedRoom. A welcoming scene, good acoustics, and a great open mic night make this little spot a cozy choice for hearing some quality live rock acts in Prague. ⊠ *Myslíkova 283/28, Nové Mesto* ☎ *602–429–989* ⊕ *redroom.cz* Ⓜ *Line B: Národní třída.*

VINOHRADY

A beautiful district much loved by expats, Vinohrady has a great local scene of trendy bars and clubs, as well as laid-back traditional pubs.

BARS AND PUBS

Parlament. Located a short walk beyond Wenceslas Square, Parlament is a modern take on a traditional Czech boozer, with everything that implies: tasty food, great beer (they serve Staropramen), and good times. ⊠ *Korunní 1, Vinohrady* ☎ *224–250–403* ⊕ *www.vinohradskyparlament.cz.*

Fodor'sChoice ★ **Prosekárna.** A chic little spot in a Vinohrady side street, Prosekárna is crammed with hundreds of varieties of prosecco. Make reservations but do leave time to explore this beautiful neighborhood. ⊠ *Slezská 48, Vinohrady* ☎ *775–565–813* ⊕ *www.prosekarna.cz* Ⓜ *Line A: Jiřího z Poděbrad.*

Fodor'sChoice ★ **Riegrovy Sady.** Forget everything you ever knew about "beer gardens." This is the real deal. Benches, beer, sausages, and big screens for sporting events, all perched on top of the hill in one of Prague's loveliest city parks. Watch out, though—you can easily spend the day here without even noticing that you're in a park. It's a particularly lovely spot at sunset, with great views over the city. ⊠ *Riegrovy sady, Vinohrady* Ⓜ *Line A: Nám. Jiřího z Poděbrad.*

CLUBS

Retro. With a location just a bit out of the center, this fun club provides an escape from the hassle of downtown. The street-level part is a pleasant functionalist-style café with outdoor seating, and the lower level houses a club with a big dance floor. The name is a bit misleading. There are some '80s nights, but the bulk of the schedule is hip-hop and other more contemporary sounds. ⊠ *Francouzská 4, Vinohrady* ☎ *222–510–592* ⊕ *www.retropraha.cz* Ⓜ *Line A: Nám. Míru.*

GAY AND LESBIAN

On Club. It claims to be the largest gay club in Prague, and with three floors that's probably right. There's a disco, several bars, and other attractions for a male crowd. Catch dancing every night, special parties on weekends, and the occasional fashion show at the aptly named "He" club. ⊠ *Vinohradská 40, Vinohrady* ☎ *No phone* ⊕ *www.onclub.cz.*

Fodor'sChoice ★ **The Saints.** This small British-owned pub and cocktail bar is centrally located near several other gay and gay-friendly establishments in Vinohrady. The owners also run a gay-friendly travel and

6

accommodations service. ⊠ *Polská 32, Vinohrady* ☎ *222–250–326* ⊕ *www.praguesaints.cz* Ⓜ *Line C: Nám. Míru.*

Termix. Borderline claustrophobic on weekends, this club has precious little standing room—especially with the decorative automobile sticking out of the bar wall. The music themes vary from night to night. It's closed Monday and Tuesday. Note: The street-level door is easy to miss. ⊠ *Třebízského 4a, Vinohrady* ☎ *222–710–462* ⊕ *www.club-termix.cz* Ⓜ *Line C: Nám. Míru.*

ŽIŽKOV

This edgy neighborhood offers a lot to the discerning, thirsty traveler who ventures out of the city center. Apparently it has the densest cluster of pubs in the world, so if you end up here, it's best to try out the random places that catch your eye.

BARS AND PUBS

Vlkova 26. The cool kids hang out at this out-of-the-way Žižkov basement bar to drink and chat late into the night. It's cozy, with dim lights, candles, wooden benches, and the bare brick walls. There are DJs and theme music nights when everyone gets up to dance. ⊠ *Vlkova 699/26, Žižkov* Ⓜ *Line A: Nám. Jiřího z Poděbrad.*

Fodor's Choice ★ **Žižkov Television Tower.** Once just a slightly weird communist landmark, the TV tower now houses a swanky cocktail bar, restaurant, and one hotel room, all inside the capsules clinging to its main structure. The bar attracts a well-heeled European crowd, with it's great views at sunset in particular, inventive drinks, and great service. The plush booths, the retro '70s-style decor, and unusual location make for a sophisticated treat. Artist David Černý's huge baby sculptures crawling up the tower are reason enough to visit. ⊠ *Mahlerovy sady 1, Žižkov* ☎ *210–320–081* ⊕ *towerpark.cz* Ⓜ *Line A: Nám. Jiřího z Poděbrad.*

ROCK AND LIVE MUSIC CLUBS

Fodor's Choice ★ **Palác Akropolis.** Housed in a funky art deco–esque building a little out of the city center, this is the city's best live music club. When shows are sold out, though, this place can be pretty packed. The main room closes at 10 pm due to noise concerns. DJs play in the two side bars until much later, though. ⊠ *Kubelíkova 27, Žižkov* ☎ *299–330–913* ⊕ *www.palacakropolis.cz* Ⓜ *Line A: Nám. Jiřího z Poděbrad.*

SMÍCHOV

The highlight of this area has to be the home of Staropramen, the attractive brewery that's been sitting proudly on the river, brewing beer since 1869.

BARS AND PUBS

Pivovary Staropramen (*Staropramen Brewery*). The slogan for this place could be, "For beer, go directly to the source." *Staropramen* means "old source," and it's definitely one of the most ubiquitous beers in the city. The brewery tour is fairly diverting, but it's the in-house bar that really draws the crowds with incredibly fresh, ice-cold beers, which are brewed on-site. ■ TIP➜ The brewery runs a chain of Potrefená Husa restaurants, with classic Czech food and beer, across the country as well. ✉ *Nádražní 84, Smíchov* ☎ *257–191–111* ⊕ *www.pivovary-staropramen.cz* Ⓜ *Line B: Anděl.*

JAZZ CLUBS

Fodor's Choice ★ **Jazz Dock.** If you missed your boat tour, don't despair. You can still hear notes and beats wafting aross the water while supping a cocktail in a decadent manner. This extremely cool, glass-enclosed nightclub and jazz bar that's built on a dock, offers a view of the passing boat traffic and lit-up landmark buildings like the National Theater. Inside are a 30-foot-long bar and two concerts per night. ✉ *Janáčkovo nábř. 2, Smíchov* ☎ *774–058–838* ⊕ *www.jazzdock.cz* Ⓜ *Line A: Anděl.*

ROCK AND LIVE MUSIC CLUBS

Futurum. Slightly out of the city center, the decor at this stalwart club could be described as odd, but cool. Think 1950s sci-fi crossed with art deco, and you're on the right track. It's a fun, pretty casual night out though. Video parties draw the crowds, but there are some live performances too, usually from punk or goth bands, or DJs playing electronic music. ✉ *Zborovská 7, Smíchov* ☎ *257–328–571* ⊕ *futurum.musicbar.cz* Ⓜ *Line B: Anděl.*

Fodor's Choice ★ **Meet Factory.** This spot is almost too cool for school. Established more than a decade ago by leading Czech modern artist David Černý as a place for cultural and artistic collaboration, the space houses a gallery, concert hall, and theater—there's so much to do it'll make your head spin. It really is a brilliant place for live music from all genres, but there's often up-and-coming rock and electronica from local and international bands. To get here, cross over the railway tracks on a little bridge and keep an eye out for the car sculptures driving up the side of the building. ✉ *Ke Sklárně 3213/15, Smíchov* ☎ *251–551–796* ⊕ *meetfactory.cz* Ⓜ *Line B: Smíchovské nádraží, then Tram No. 12, 14, or 20.*

6

LETNÁ, HOLEŠOVICE, AND TROJA

There's a mixed nightlife bag outside the city center, but there are also some really cool beer gardens and clubs. Take the opportunity to really get under the skin of Prague and check them out.

BARS AND PUBS

Fodor'sChoice **Letenské Sady.** You can pay a lot for a pint and great views in Prague, or
★ you could go to this cunningly located beer garden at the top of Letná Park and pay hardly anything for cold, crisp pints while you gaze over the river and the breathtaking rooftops of Staré Město. It's a truly great beer garden, even if its other facilities (food choices, toilets) are a little basic. ⊠ *Letenské Sady, Letná* Ⓜ *Line A: Malostranská.*

CLUBS

Cross Club. It's a bit of a trip out of the city center (although it's only about 10 minutes on a night tram), but if you're a fan of alternative culture and really memorable nights, it's worth it. The club is a mixture of many different things: otherworldly metal sculptures; floors and floors of different music, including lots of drums and bass; interesting artistic happenings, such as poetry readings, theater shows, film screenings, author readings, and an afternoon kids' theater; and a gorgeous garden lit in a variety of bright colors. But, it all comes together for a great night out, if not one for the fainthearted. Its closing hours are listed as "??" which should give you some idea of its general ethos. ⊠ *Plynární 1096/23, Holešovice* ☎ *No phone* ⊕ *www.crossclub.cz/cs* Ⓜ *Line C: Nádraží Holešovice.*

SaSaZu. A restaurant and nightclub and music venue in a warehouse in the middle of a market isn't really the place you'd expect to draw Prague's high-heeled glitterati, but SaSaZu often does. The restaurant serves delicious and inventive pan-Asian fusion cuisine, and the club can be a lot of fun too, as long as it's not a quiet night, because the vast space—which can house 2,500—can feel a little empty. It usually plays chart hits and has hosted a wide range of big international acts such as Ke$ha, Lily Allen, Tiësto, Public Enemy, and Busta Rhymes. ⊠ *Bubenské nábřeží 306, Holešovice* ☎ *778–054–054* ⊕ *www.sasazu. com* Ⓜ *Line C: Vltavská.*

Fodor'sChoice **Stalin parties.** This free, open-air party at the top of Letná Park on Friday
★ and Saturday nights is the hottest ticket in town. The bar and DJs are located right next to the huge Metronome monument, which marks the spot that once housed the world's largest statue of Stalin. Chill vibes, a young, international crowd, and great views over the sparkling city lights make this a cool option on warm nights. Beer is for sale, but queues can be long—good thing bringing a can of your own is acceptable. Currently only open in summer, and overseen by an art collective who also run a container bar in Malá Strana. ⊠ *Letenské sady, Letná* ☎ *No phone* ⊕ *cont.ainall.cz/stalin* Ⓜ *Line A: Malostranská.*

SHOPPING

Updated by
Jennifer Rigby

Shopping in Prague still feels like an adventure. Around one corner, you'll find a crumbling shop front and a glimpse of a stooped jeweler hard at work restoring an ancient pocket watch. Around the next, a cutting-edge design boutique selling witty Czech-made home accessories.

In recent years Czech fashion and design has come of age. While it's no Paris, there's a funky, even punky, edge to many of the clothes and objects on offer that will stand out anywhere in the world.

But traditional pleasures still abound. Endearing traditional crafts are available on every cobblestoned street. Each region of the Czech Republic has its own specialty, and many are represented in Prague. Intricate, world-renowned hand-blown glassware, wooden toys and carvings, ceramic dishes, and delicate lace all make perfect "I got it in Prague" gifts. The Czechs are also masterful herbalists, and put plants to good use in fragrant soaps and bath products made on local farms.

That said, every city has its kitsch, and Prague is no different. Marionettes have been a favorite Czech handicraft and storytelling vehicle since the late 18th century, and they are ubiquitous here. The trick is avoiding mass-produced versions at tourist kiosks and getting your hands on the real puppet deal.

There are plenty of real deals in the city's antique shops, art galleries and *antikvariats*—secondhand book and print stores. Some are vast, dusty caverns, some look like an elderly aunty has tipped out her entire attic willy-nilly, while still others are pristine, prissy, and pricey. Either way the unpredictable jumbles of merchandise offer a fun day of flea market–like spelunking—you may pick through communist-era buttons in one shop and find cubist office chairs or ancient Czech manuscripts in the next.

If you like your souvenirs to sparkle, garnet peddlers abound. But take heed: all that glitters isn't garnet—many are not the real deal. True Czech garnets are intensely dark red. Also known as pyrope or Bohemian garnet, these precious stones have been mined here for centuries. Tight clusters of garnets are found on antique pieces, while modern baubles are often sleeker and set in gold or silver. Stick to our recommended shops for quality gems, and inquire about the setting—if a low-priced bauble seems too good to be true, it could be set in low-quality pot metal.

The international jet set isn't forgotten either. If you crave big luxury labels, the aptly named Paris Street (aka Pařížská ulice) will give you your dose of runway glam. Do not expect any steals here, although they are available elsewhere in the city's impressive selection of European chain stores.

Most of Prague's shops are open from 10 am until 6 or 7 pm, and malls tend to stay open until 9 or 10 pm.

If shopkeepers in Prague seem aloof, don't be dissuaded—try greeting them with a friendly "*dobrý den*" when entering a store, and you may be surprised by their warmth.

PLANNER

V.A.T. KNOW-HOW
For those living outside the European Community, you can claim back the V.A.T on your purchases. When shopping, ask for a V.A.T. refund form, and find out whether the merchant gives refunds (not all stores are required to do so). Have the form stamped by customs officials when you leave the country and drop it off at the refund-service counter to receive 21% back on all your purchases (15% back on books or food from grocery stores). ⇨ *See the Travel Smart chapter for more information.*

MAJOR SHOPPING AREAS
Dlouhá. One of the coolest streets in central Prague, Dlouhá extends off Old Town Square but is worlds away from the tourist hordes. Half the delight is the architecture, and the other half is finding hip, seemingly hidden boutiques that specialize in Czech fashion and design. ⊠ *Dlouhá, Staré Mesto.*

Na Příkopě. Overflowing with popular chains like Zara and H&M, Na Příkopě feels like a major shopping street you'd find in any European capital. In the shadow of Prašná brána—one of the original city gates—it is perhaps more picturesque than most, but be warned: it can be crowded. ⊠ *Na Příkopě, Nové Mesto.*

Pařížská ulice. Feeling swanky? Get yourself down to tree-lined Pařížská ulice, which hosts all the big international designers from Dior to Prada. Even the air smells expensive here. ⊠ *Pařížská ulice, Staré Mesto.*

Václavské náměstí. This historic boulevard is now full of international chains and hawkers. Extending from the National Museum to Na Příkopě, Václavské náměstí has an energy level on a par with Times Square. Prague's megabookstore and two British department stores are all crammed in. ⊠ *Václavské náměstí, Nové Mesto.*

Christmas markets in Prague show off the regional handicrafts.

STREET MARKETS

Fodor's Choice ★ **Christmas Market.** December is arguably the prettiest time of year to visit Prague, thanks to the Christmas Market in the city's main squares. From the beginning of December (just before St. Nicholas' Day), wooden booths sell Czech handicrafts, piping-hot snacks, and spicy mulled wine. Performances by choirs and musical ensembles are held in Old Town Square throughout the month, all in the glow of the towering spruce tree. ■TIP➔ There's also a similar market around Easter. ⊠ *Staroměstské náměstí, Staré Mesto.*

Sapa - Little Hanoi. It's a bit of a trip from the city center, but it's worth it for fans of Vietnamese culture and cuisine. Little Hanoi in Prague feels just like the real thing—thousands of Vietnamese people came over during communist times and have made the place, or at least this corner of it, their home. You'll find traditional crafts woven from willow branches such as baskets and some cut-price clothes, but the real draw is the atmosphere and the food—try some great dishes or buy ingredients to re-create your favorite dishes. To get here, take Bus No. 113 from the Kačerov Metro stop or Bus No. 198 from the Smíchovské Nádraží bus station to Sídliště Písnice. ⊠ *Libušská 319/126* ⊕ *www.sapa-praha.cz.*

STARÉ MĚSTO

A jumble of funky boutiques, bookshops, antiques stores, jewelry dens, and souvenir shops converge in what is arguably Prague's prettiest district.

ANTIQUES

Art Deco Galerie. The quintessential vintage shop just off Old Town Square is pleasantly cluttered with art deco–era sculptures and furnishings. Those with eclectic style will love the intricate brooches, turban-style headbands, and silk scarves here. ⊠ *Michalská 21, Staré Mesto* ☎ *224-223-076* ⊕ *www.artdeco-galerie-mili.com* Ⓜ *Lines A & B: Můstek.*

Fodor'sChoice
★ **Bric a Brac.** If you like the sensation of unearthing your treasure, this wonderfully cluttered antiques store is the ticket. About the size of a closet, this shop uses every nook to display a mix of Communist-era badges, tin "Pilsner Urquell" signs, charming old typewriters, and more. Memorable gifts can be found among the clutter—that colorful Czech tobacco tin could make a great jewelry box. Ask the friendly English-speaking shopkeeper for tips. ⊠ *Týnská 7, Staré Mesto* ☎ *222-326-484* Ⓜ *Line A: Staroměstská.*

Dorotheum. Central Europe's answer to Sotheby's, this world-renowned auction house was founded in Austria in the early 1700s, and set up shop in Prague in 1992. It's a serious antiques haunt for serious collectors, so prices are quite steep and items are appropriately opulent. The decorative dishes and sculptures, 19th-century paintings, ornate furniture, jewelry, and watches are worthy investments. ⊠ *Ovocný trh 2, Staré Mesto* ☎ *224-222-001* ⊕ *www.dorotheum.cz* ⊗ *Closed Sun.* Ⓜ *Lines A & B: Můstek.*

Starožitnosti Ungelt. Tucked away beneath an archway behind Týn Church, this elegant shop features a selection of art nouveau and art deco items. Beautiful and unusual glass vases from Czech designers sit alongside furniture, glittering brooches, and delicate porcelain butterflies. ⊠ *Týn 1, Staré Mesto* ☎ *224-895-454* ⊕ *www.antiqueungelt.cz* Ⓜ *Line A: Staroměstská.*

TOP BUYS IN PRAGUE

- Maps of Prague's art deco and cubist architecture from Kubista

- Organic body products, made with Czech produce and herbs, from Manufaktura

- A unique Bohemian crystal vase from Preciosa

- A linden-wood marionette from Truhlar Marionety

- An innovative Czech-designed jacket from Space

- A rock-and-roll postcard from Music Antiquariat

ART GALLERIES

Galerie NoD. Above the Roxy music club on Dlouhá street, this gallery space is filled with youthful energy. Exhibits feature edgy work by up-and-coming artists focusing on anything from puppets to photography. The gallery also hosts experimental theater, music, and comedy nights, and touts an adjacent bar and café sprinkled with twentysomethings on laptops. ⊠ *Dlouhá 33, Staré Mesto* ☎ *733-307-600* ⊕ *nod.roxy.cz* Ⓜ *Line B: Nám. Republiky.*

7

Galerie Peithner-Lichtenfels. Jam-packed with paintings and drawings, this gallery is overseen by an approachable owner perched behind a cluttered desk. Among the wares are works by both famous and lesser-known Czech artists. A glass-covered table near the front of the store is crowded with small original drawings. ⊠ *Michalská 12, Staré Mesto* ☏ *224–227–680* ⊕ *www.gplc.cz* Ⓜ *Line A: Staroměstská.*

Galerie UBK. Specializing in postwar surrealism, this airy gallery features work from many of the leading Czech artists present and past, including globally significant painter Josef Šíma. If artwork prices are too many koruny for your comfort, a good alternative is picking up a book on the artist's exhibition, also for sale here. ⊠ *Betlémské nám. 8, Staré Mesto* ☏ *605–260–635* ⊕ *www.galerieubetlemskekaple.cz* Ⓜ *Line B: Národní třída.*

BEAUTY

Botanicus. Organic body and bath products here, like "Lettuce and Olive Oil" soap, are crafted from fresh fruits, vegetables, and herbs on a rural Czech farm. Inside the spacious and fragrant store there are myriad other all-natural products that make charming gifts for those back home, including tempting chutneys and condiments. ⊠ *Týnsky Dvůr 3, Staré Mesto* ☏ *234–767–446* ⊕ *www.botanicus.cz* Ⓜ *Line B: Nám. Republiky.*

Guerlain. The Prague branch of this international makeup chain is rather fancy. Set in an imposing building in the heart of the Old Town, the sales assistants look fierce but are friendly, and will gladly guide you through the cosmetics and perfumes on offer in the calming white surrounds of the store. You can also book a fragrance consultation with a perfume expert, or even spa treatments at L'institut, the on-site spa. ⊠ *Dlouhá 16, Staré Mesto* ☏ *227–195–330* ⊕ *www.guerlain.cz* Ⓜ *Line A: Staroměstská.*

Ingredients. An extremely swanky beauty boutique run by two Czechs, with Sisley Boudoir, the on-site aromatherapy and treatment center. Rare perfumes, skin-care products, and candles are displayed amid contemporary art. ⊠ *Jáchymova 2, Staré Mesto* ☏ *224–239–477* ⊕ *www. ingredients-store.cz* Ⓜ *Line A: Staroměstská.*

Kosmetické delikatesy Madeleine. Like a perfume delicatessen, this lovely shop has flowers in the window and perfumes lining the walls; it's a calming presence near Old Town Square. The friendly staff will help you choose the scent that suits you best. ⊠ *Dlouhá 10, Staré Mesto* ☏ *721–536–566* ⊕ *www.madeleine.cz* Ⓜ *Line A: Staroměstská.*

Fodor's Choice ★ **Manufaktura.** Established in 1991 in a bid to preserve traditional Czech and Moravian crafts, Manufaktura is now a thriving business with branches across the country. At this centrally located outpost, home-spa products like bath salts and creams are arranged in a pleasant, folksy manner, as are cosmetics made with Czech beer—yes, beer. Other branches, like the one in Malá Strana on Zlatá ulička u Daliborky 7, sell wooden toys and other items. ⊠ *Celetná 12, Staré Mesto* ☏ *601–310–608* ⊕ *www.manufaktura.cz* Ⓜ *Line B: Staroměstská.*

BOOKS AND PRINTS

Galerie Antikvariat Ztichlá klika. Rare books, old books, new books, art—this place is cavernous, but it has something for everyone. It's partly underground too, which only adds to the appeal. Be warned: you might lose hours browsing the shelves and shelves of books and walls of photographs and paintings, all of which are for sale. Be sure to take a moment to appreciate the quirky signage as well—the shop is also known as the "blue tiger," for reasons that will become obvious. It's only open Tuesday–Friday 1–7 pm. ⊠ *Betlémská 10-14, Staré Mesto* ☎ *222-222-079* ⊕ *www.ztichlaklika.cz* Ⓜ *Line B: Národní třída.*

CHILDREN'S CLOTHING

FAMILY **Benetton.** The preppy line downsizes its colorful polo shirts and crewneck sweaters for little 'uns, adding a few sequins and cartoon character prints for fun, inside this small shop on the hectic fringe of Old Town Square. The huge Na Příkopě store has children's clothes downstairs and a really rather fancy sweeping staircase in the center of the shop. ⊠ *Železna 1, Staré Mesto* ☎ *731–413–522* ⊕ *www.benetton.com* Ⓜ *Lines A & B: Můstek.*

CLOTHING

Alice Abraham. Inside her eye-catching boutique, this Czech designer with an eye for the dramatic shows off her wares. Clearly fond of animal prints, glitz, and daring cuts, Abraham is unafraid of pushing the fashion envelope, and her styles are anything but demure. ⊠ *Vězeňská 3, Staré Mesto* ☎ *224–815–511* ⊕ *www.aliceabraham.com* Ⓜ *Line A: Staroměstská.*

Anne Fontaine. This store is effectively Paris in Prague—a French designer, understated French decor, and rails of blouses dripping with that "je ne sais quoi" of French elegance. The blouses—the designer's signature item—are all in black or white, but come in different styles and shapes, from sleek to sheer. Anne Fontaine shares shop space with Petrusse, a richly-patterned shawl, blanket, and scarf designer. ⊠ *Masna 12, Staré Mesto* ☎ *602–662–594* ⊕ *www.annefontaine.cz* Ⓜ *Lines A & B: Můstek.*

Beata Rajska. The shop is imposing, and the sales assistants are positively forbidding, but don't let that deter you, because the clothes are worth it. Many of the pieces would make fantastic special occasion outfits, so it's not surprising to learn that the shop dressed contestants for the Miss Czech Republic, Miss Europe, and Miss World pageants throughout the early 2000s, and now offers custom tailoring. If nothing else, it's fun to try a few items on and think, "Someday..." ⊠ *Dlouhá 3, Staré Mesto* ☎ *222–314–174* ⊕ *www.beatarajska.com* Ⓜ *Line B: Staroměstská.*

Bohème. The understated clothes and decor here tend toward creamy tones, muted grays, and warm browns. Czech designer Hana Stocklassa's garments are classics with unexpected elements—modern takes on knitwear or a shirt with a collar that's cut like a paper chain. Trying things on is a pleasure beneath the golden lighting from round overhead lamps. ✉ *Dušní 8, Staré Mesto* 🕿 *224–813–840* ⊕ *www.boheme. cz* Ⓜ *Line B: Nám. Republiky.*

Coco Boutique. The window display at this vintage store is always entertaining—think sequin ball gown and a jauntily placed bowler hat on the same mannequin. In fact, the shop window might be all you see as the opening hours are idiosyncratic at best. But, if you do happen across Coco when it's open,

POP-UP PRAGUE

The fad for "pop-up" shops has not passed Prague by—so make sure to explore if you see a promising-looking, hastily scrawled sign in Old Town. Half the fun is getting lost down the alleyways and making your own discoveries anyway.

you're in for a secondhand treasure-trove treat (including some vintage designer pieces). ✉ *Michalská 15, Staré Mesto* Ⓜ *Line B: Staroměstská.*

Fodor'sChoice **Czech Labels And Friends.** It's clear that the Czech and Slovak design-
★ ers whose clothes line the shelves at this bright boutique don't take themselves too seriously. Each piece has an element of surprise—from eye-popping colors to classic shapes that hide unexpected materials, or a T-shirt with the slogan "Me? Normal? Never." You'll like wearing these unique designs as much as the designers seem to have enjoyed making them. ✉ *Železná 12, Staré Mesto* 🕿 *778–000–715* ⊕ *www.locallabels. cz/en/content/2-contact* Ⓜ *Line B: Staroměstská.*

Diesel. Tough jeans, slinky dresses, and edgy accessories by the Italian label occupy two floors of this glitzy store. If your pristine wardrobe needs a few gritty updates and you've got some spare pennies, anything here will do the trick. ✉ *Pařížská 28, Staré Mesto* 🕿 *222–317–647* Ⓜ *Lines A & B: Můstek.*

DNB. Inside her chic studio close to the river, Czech designer Denisa Nova shows off carelessly sexy clothing that is both wearable and luxurious. Slouchy denim, extra-long silk T-shirts, and an occasional pop of color (think purple jumpsuits) seal the effortless deal. ✉ *Naprstkova 4, Staré Mesto* 🕿 *603–876–860* ⊕ *www.denisanova.cz* Ⓜ *Line B: Národní třída.*

Dusni3. From Vivienne Westwood to Mellow Yellow shoes, this modern white store offering premium womenswear brands in sleek surroundings is *the* place to find high-end international street style. ✉ *Dušní 3, Staré Mesto* 🕿 *234–095–870* ⊕ *www.dusni3.cz* Ⓜ *Line B: Staroměstská.*

Ermenegildo Zegna. Men in the market for finely tailored suits (made-to-measure services are available) and posh basics like zip-front jackets and smart trainers, will relish the atmosphere at this international store. Signature colognes scent the store, which also sells stylish aviator and round-frame sunglasses to complete the man-about-town look. ✉ *U Prašné brány 3, Staré Mesto* 🕿 *224–810–018* ⊕ *www.zegna.com* Ⓜ *Line B: Nám. Republiky.*

Hugo Boss. For modern menswear, whether formal or casual, the German designer's gorgeously tailored pieces are unmatched. This store, stretching grandly around a Pařižská street corner, also stocks a fine selection of luggage and accessories. ✉ *Pařížská 19, Staré Mesto* 🕿 *222–327–260* ⊕ *www.hugoboss.com* Ⓜ *Line A: Staroměstská.*

Kenzo. This Franco-Japanese fashion house makes clothing with a relaxed, bohemian feel. Nothing is too constricting or finished, particularly the billowy dresses and tops in lightweight fabrics, printed with smudgy tribal and floral patterns. Menswear is lighthearted and casual. Even the formal suits feature loose-fitting pants and long cardigans. ⊠ *Náměstí Republiky 5, Staré Mesto* ☎ *222–002–302* ⊕ *www.kenzo. com* Ⓜ *Line B: Nám. Republiky.*

Klára Nademlýnská. If there's one word that describes this boutique—just off Old Town Square—and the wares within, it's funky. Catering to carefree hipsters, this Czech designer excels in the little details—unusual draping, fun animal prints, an unexpected horse necklace—which make each item unique and original. ⊠ *Dlouhá 3, Staré Mesto* ☎ *224–818– 769* ⊕ *www.klaranademlynska.cz* Ⓜ *Line B: Nám. Republiky.*

La Sartoria. Big, luxurious rugs, Frank Sinatra playing in the background, the set of whiskey glasses in the window, and the dartboard. Oh, right: there are clothes, too, such as beautifully tailored suits and jackets perfect for a weekend in the country. ⊠ *Hastalska 9, Staré Mesto* ☎ *606–788–878* ⊕ *www.lasartoria.cz* Ⓜ *Line A: Staroměstská.*

Fodor's Choice ★ **Leeda.** This artistic-minded shop is chic, original, and just a little bit mad. Stocked with genuine and original Czech designs, items range from painted dresses to billowing silk skirts. The designers collaborate with graphic designers, photographers, and musicians, which makes the little store feel all the more like a great embodiment of Czech design. ⊠ *Bartolomějská 1, Staré Mesto* ☎ *775–601–185* ⊕ *www.leeda.cz* Ⓜ *Line B: Národní třída.*

Navarila. Now in two inviting Old Town locations, Czech designer Martina Nevarilova offers a great line of relaxed and cozy knitwear, often in bold colors or stripes. The shops are worth a look if you're feeling the chill of the Prague winter or if you're on the hunt for a classy and unique cover-up for other occasions. The other store location is at Haštalska 8/939. ⊠ *Elišky Krásnohorske 4/11, Staré Mesto* ☎ *271–742–091* ⊕ *www.navarila.cz* Ⓜ *Line B: Národní třída.*

Onvi & Onavi. Boasting various urbane brands and occupying several residences on a posh street, Onvi & Onavi is great fun to browse in. From Luisa Cerano's soft knits and chic coats to Jacob Cohen's handmade jeans, always with that extra decorative detail, there are plenty of options to tempt you to part with your koruny. ⊠ *U Prašné brány 1, Staré Mesto* ☎ *222–002–313* ⊕ *www.onvi.cz* Ⓜ *Line B: Nám. Republiky.*

Parazit Fashion Store. A cool, graffiti-chic space which champions Czech and Slovak fashion students and young designers, making limited-edition clothes, accessories, and gifts. The owners take their fashion seriously, adopting their motto from Nicholas Cage's character in the David Lynch film *Wild At Heart*: "This snakeskin jacket represents a symbol of my individuality, and a belief in personal freedom." ⊠ *Karlova 25, Staré Mesto* ☎ *731–171–517* ⊕ *www.parazit.cz* Ⓜ *Line B: Staroměstská.*

Report's. High quality and prices to match sum up this shop's selection of sleek Italian suits and country club–ready weekend wear. Crystal chandeliers illuminate display cases of crisp button-up shirts and silk ties,

7

many in bright colors that add pop to those dashing suits. Touches of humor can be found in the fun pieces, like the blue suede shoes—Elvis-inspired perhaps? ✉ *Žatecká 55, Staré Mesto* ☎ *224–813–948* ⊕ *www. reports.cz* Ⓜ *Line B: Nám. Republiky.*

Šatna. This funky little shop specializes in vintage and secondhand finds. If you can face a bit of rummaging, think extremely promising attic with cut-price pieces for men and women from designers like Ralph Lauren, as well as more random bits and pieces. The store also stocks interesting jewelry, including earrings made of headphones and scissors. ✉ *Konviktská 13, Staré Mesto* Ⓜ *Line B: Staroměstská.*

Space Praga. One of the coolest shops in Prague, Space is usually teeming with funky young Czech women on the lookout for something new and different. The garments are beautiful one-offs, from the flowing skirts to the patterned bras; browsing the racks makes you feel like you're looking through somebody's wonderful closet. There's a branch for children around the corner (on Kozi), too. ✉ *Vězeňská 6, Staré Mesto* ☎ *725–100–317* Ⓜ *Line A: Staroměstská.*

Timoure et Group. Led by two Czech designers, this label churns out sleek, minimalist career and casual wear like wrap dresses and trenches. The flagship Prague store is relaxed and welcoming, with elegant T-shirts neatly displayed. ✉ *V kolkovné 6, Staré Mesto* ☎ *222–327–358* ⊕ *www. timoure.cz* Ⓜ *Line A: Staroměstská.*

Versace. Perched on a pretty corner of U Prašné brány within view of the sprawling Hotel Paris, this shop has all the trappings you'd expect from Versace. Window displays feature neon touches and mannequins in loud prints. Inside, marble floors and ornate paisley curtains complete the opulent scene. ✉ *U Prašné brány 3, Staré Mesto* ☎ *224–810–016* Ⓜ *Line B: Nám. Republiky.*

FOOD AND WINE

Absintherie. Absinthe is everywhere in Prague. It's a bit of a tourist cliché, but even if you aren't a fan of the "green fairy," it can be a fun gift for folks back home. This shop is the real deal for the fiery spirit—try a wee nip at the bar while you're there if you're brave enough! There's also an on-site museum with old advertisement posters, bottles, and absinthe spoons. ✉ *Jilská 7, Staré Mesto* ☎ *224–251–999* ⊕ *www.absintherie. cz* Ⓜ *Line A: Staroměstská.*

Fodor'sChoice   **Masna na Kozím plácku.** This food shop on a quiet stretch of Kozí is
★   like walking into a bygone era before supermarkets took over the high street. Think the best bread, meat, and cheese shop from the 18th century that you can possibly imagine, and you've just described this place. Shelves groan with fresh produce, the air is full of delicious smells, and friendly staff are ready to help tease your taste buds. *Dobrou chut'!* (That's Czech for "Bon appétit!") ✉ *Kozí 9, Staré Mesto* ☎ *255–795–404* ⊕ *www.masnanakozimplacku.cz* Ⓜ *Line B: Staroměstská.*

Monarch. There's been a bit of a wine boom in the Czech Republic in recent years, as international customers are finally waking up to the country's superb local producers. This discreet Spanish-themed wine bar and shop is a great place to enjoy a glass of wine and plate of tapas before shopping for a bottle or two of the wines you've sampled to take home. There's also a vast selection of international vintages. ⊠ *Na Perštýně 15, Staré Mesto* ☎ *224–239–602* ⊕ *www.monarch.cz* Ⓜ *Lines A & B: Můstek.*

GLASS

FodorśChoice
★ **Artěl.** This American company, led by designer Karen Feldman, merges modern style with traditional Czech techniques, using mouth-blown molten crystal and hand-painted glassware, for instance. Items are so painstakingly crafted that they're bound to become family heirlooms, but all are far from prim. They also make handbags to order and have a couple of other shops around town. ⊠ *Celetná 29, entrance on Rybna, Staré Mesto* ☎ *224–815–085* ⊕ *www.artelglass.com* Ⓜ *Line B: Nám. Republiky.*

Material. The light dancing on the incredibly eye-catching glassware in this elegant boutique makes it almost impossible to walk on by. But the unusual jewelry, stunning brightly-colored chandeliers, and an array of beads and Bohemia crystal will make you want to stay and shop. The prices are not for the fainthearted, but the pieces are worth it if you want to bring home something truly original. ⊠ *Tyn 1 - Ungelt, Staré Mesto* ☎ *608–664–766* ⊕ *www.i-material.com* Ⓜ *Line A: Staroměstská.*

Preciosa. A genuine Czech glass success story, Preciosa has its headquarters just outisde Prague and is now a global manufacturer, melting 40 tons of glass every day. In this sparkling shop just by Old Town Square, you can buy the chandeliers, glass sculptures, and jewelry the company is famous for. ⊠ *Jáchymova 26/2, Staré Mesto* ☎ *488–118–106* ⊕ *www.preciosa.com* Ⓜ *Line A: Staroměstská.*

St.Vol. Part art gallery, part shop, this is probably the funkiest interpretation in the city of the Czech tradition of making beautiful glassware. This fact hasn't escaped the international community or some of the Czech Republic's most famous citizens, including late President Havel, who called on designer Borek Spirek's talents for the restorations of Prague Castle. Whether or not the unusual, extravagant items here suit your taste, a visit to the shop, complete with gold pillars, is unlikely to be forgotten. ⊠ *Valentinská 11, Staré Mesto* ☎ *224–814–099* ⊕ *www.stvol.eu* Ⓜ *Line A: Staroměstská.*

HOME DECOR

Art Shop Prague. In this store, the city's famous Astronomical Clock is old news. The walls are lined with numerous new clock designs from a number of different Czech designers. Some are ceramic and some just totally wacky—from melting timepieces to a clock made out of a baseball glove. ⊠ *Malá Štupartská 5, Staré Mesto* ☎ *222–313–108* ⊕ *www.artshopprague.cz* Ⓜ *Line A: Staroměstská.*

FodorśChoice
★ **Kubista.** On the ground floor of the stunning House at the Black Madonna, this gorgeous museum shop brings original and replica cubist and art deco pieces into the real world. Marvel at angular

black-and-white vases by Vlastislav Hofman, and let your eyes linger on the lines of a 1930s tubular armchair. Maps of Prague's art deco, cubist, and modern architecture are also sold here. ✉ *Ovocný trh 19, Staré Mesto* ☎ *224–236–378* ⊕ *www.kubista.cz* ⊗ *Closed Mon.* Ⓜ *Line B: Nám. Republiky.*

Modernista. Innovation is revered at this store inside the Municipal House, a magnet for fans of cubist and modernist furniture and decor. Originals, reproductions, and work by new Czech designers are available, making it nearly impossible to leave without something distinctive—a streamlined steel liquor cabinet or a cool cubist vase, perhaps. There are other branches in Vinohrady and at the Rudolfinum; this store focuses on ceramics and porcelain. ✉ *Náměstí Republiky 5, Staré Mesto* ☎ *222–002–102* ⊕ *www.modernista.cz* Ⓜ *Line B: Nám. Republiky.*

Nobis Life. Want to make over your home? This is interior design of the "whole kitchen" rather than the "one attractive vase" variety, so you won't be able to fit it all into your suitcase, but the sleek store could help unleash your creative potential and provide some inspiration in the form of classic and modern styles. ✉ *Dlouhá 32, Staré Mesto* ☎ *222–212–859* ⊕ *www.nobis.cz* Ⓜ *Line B: Náměstí Republiky.*

Qubus Design. Tucked away on a narrow stretch of Rámová, this great homewares shop is made even better by its friendly staff, who might just offer you a cup of coffee. The lure of what's for sale is really the draw here though—a fetching pair of gold ceramic Wellington boots, as well as funky home accessories from nonconformist Czech designers, such as some sleek glass shelves bisected by a floor lamp, cabinet, and vase. ✉ *Rámová 3, Staré Mesto* ☎ *222–313–151* ⊕ *www.qubus.cz* Ⓜ *Line B: Nám. Republiky.*

JEWELRY AND ACCESSORIES

Česky Granát. This shop's friendly staff are eager to answer any questions about their stock of gorgeous garnets and amber jewelry. Delicate necklaces and dangling earrings may set you back up to $500, but some pieces in the gleaming selection of charms and rings cost only one-tenth as much. ✉ *Celetná 4, Staré Mesto* ☎ *224–228–281* Ⓜ *Lines A & B: Můstek.*

Coccinelle Accessories. Soft leather and shades of rose and blue abound in this expensive-looking Italian handbag store. Window displays coordinate bags and wallets and bureau drawers are stuffed with soft, floral-patterned scarves to finish the look. ✉ *U Obecního domu 2, Staré Mesto* ☎ *222–002–340* ⊕ *www.coccinelle.cz* Ⓜ *Line B: Nám. Republiky.*

Granát Turnov. This store is part of the Granát Co-op, the world's most prolific producer of Bohemian garnet jewelry. The elegant Dlouhá branch has two separate rooms. Gold and silver jewelry, including an especially nice selection of brooches, is to the right. Pricier diamond-clad pieces are to the left. ✉ *Dlouhá 30, Staré Mesto* ☎ *222–315–612* ⊕ *www.granat.eu* Ⓜ *Line B: Nám. Republiky.*

Halada. This classy German jewelry company supplys trinkets by carefully chosen brands. Stunning pearls in different shades, as well as gold, silver, and platinum pieces are fixtures. The branch on Pařížská offers the most varied selection, while the serene shop on Na Příkopě focuses on pearls. ✉ *Pařížská 7, Staré Mesto* ☎ *222–311–868* ⊕ *www.halada.cz* Ⓜ *Line A: Staroměstská.*

Hermès. Those iconic silk scarves that embody Parisian chic can be found here arranged in perfect rows in a glass display case among other equestrian-inspired accessories. Racks of gem-color silk ties are on display upstairs, but it's the lush leather goods on the first floor that are the main attraction. ✉ *Pařížská 12, Staré Mesto* ☎ *224–817–545* ⊕ *www.hermes.com* Ⓜ *Line A: Staroměstská.*

Louis Vuitton. Bling watches and well-heeled patrons abound at this luxurious boutique on the corner of Pařížská and Siroka. Here you'll find a fleet of scarves, luggage, and of course, bags, all bearing the famous "LV" logo. ✉ *Pařížská 3, Staré Mesto* ☎ *224–812–774* ⊕ *www.louis-vuitton.com* Ⓜ *Line A: Staroměstská.*

Swarovksi Bohemia. There's no avoiding the allure of this brand's crystal, and the store itself is an attractive complement, outfitted with some spectacular crystal pillars. Pick up a playful key-ring charm or glittering bauble at relatively affordable prices. It's worth spending some time reveling in the window-filled space, as shoppers outside point excitedly at the displays. ✉ *Celetná 7, Staré Mesto* ☎ *222–315–585* ⊕ *www.swarovski.com* Ⓜ *Lines A & B: Můstek.*

Zlatnictví Miloslav Ráž. The real treat at this old-school jewelry store is getting a glimpse of the jeweler at work—he may even give you a wave if you're lucky. The store has a variety of items including rings and other jewels, some of which are displayed in the window, but you can also create your own unique piece with a designer. It can be expensive, but you're getting handcrafted items with real gems, after all. ✉ *V kolkovně 8, Staré Mesto* ☎ *603–440–874* ⊕ *www.zlatnictviraz.cz* Ⓜ *Line A: Staroměstská.*

MARKETS

Havelská. Havelská is a charming open-air market, centrally located in Staré Město, featuring touristy kitsch, seasonal trinkets, and handmade jewelry alongside fresh fruits and vegetables. The market is open daily. ✉ *Havelská, Staré Mesto* Ⓜ *Lines A & B: Můstek.*

MUSIC

Music Antiquariat. CDs, books, and records are lovingly curated at this music shop tucked behind Old Town Square. The owner lived in West Berlin where his friend, an autograph hunter, snapped celebrities in their heyday. Now the negatives and pictures decorate the store, alongside old rock-and-roll photographs and postcards that are for sale. It's a delightful throwback to a pre-digital music era. ✉ *Týnská ulička 8, Staré Mesto* ☎ *222–317–231* ⊕ *www.musicantiquariat.cz* ☾ *Closed Sun.* Ⓜ *Line B: Staroměstská.*

SHOES

Beltissimo. The bright green shop frontage can be a little off-putting but you should not judge this book by its cover. The shop stocks high-end labels for men and women—quirky and sophisticated heels by Marc Jacobs, and comfortable Camper trainers—alongside its own brand. ⊠ *U Prašné brány 1, Staré Mesto* ☎ *222–315–803* ⊕ *www.beltissimo. eu* Ⓜ *Line B: Nám. Republiky.*

Rimowa. This branch of the German luggage brand is almost a museum to its wares, with suitcases and bags displayed on plinths like artworks. The hard-backed cases in an array of colors are destined for the holiday wardrobes of the well-heeled, no doubt already purchased just down the street at one of Pařížská's many world-class designer stores. ⊠ *Pařížská 26, Staré Mesto* ☎ *777–997–886* ⊕ *www.rimowa.de* Ⓜ *Line B: Staroměstská.*

SHOPPING MALLS AND DEPARTMENT STORES

Kotva. A warrenlike hexagonal layout makes this Czech department store feel more adventurous than most. Across the tram tracks from the massive Palladium, it houses the standard clothing and household goods shops as well as electronics, beauty products, and luggage, and also offers a health and wellness center and even a salt cave. ⊠ *Nám. Republiky 8, Staré Mesto* ☎ *224–801–111* ⊕ *www.od-kotva.cz* Ⓜ *Line B: Nám. Republiky.*

Palladium. This gigantic mall draws hordes of shoppers to its four floors, one of which is all bars and restaurants serving everything from sushi to Indian food. Amid the gangs of teenagers and 200 shops, including U.K. favorite Top Shop and a two-floor H&M, keep in mind that this historic building served as the city's army barracks in the 19th century. ⊠ *Nám. Republiky 1, Staré Mesto* ☎ *225–770–250* ⊕ *www.palladiumpraha.cz* Ⓜ *Line B: Nám. Republiky.*

SPORTING GOODS

Hudy Sport. The two floors here overflow with hiking, camping, and rock-climbing equipment from top brands like North Face. This store is also a good place to pick up a backpack, laptop bag, or water bottle. Look for end-of-season sale bins. ⊠ *Na Perštýně 14, Staré Mesto* ☎ *224–218–600* ⊕ *www.hudy.cz/praha.perstyn* Ⓜ *Line B: Nám. Republiky.*

TOYS

FAMILY **Pohádka.** You'll be drawn in by the amazing window display, which features anything and everything from puppets climbing trees to wooden airplanes. However, you'll stay to be a part of the sheer joy that bursts out of this two-floor toy shop. Packed with attractive wooden toys, stuffed animals, puzzles, and games, it harks back to a more innocent age. There's also a good selection of marionettes if you have your heart set on taking one home. ⊠ *Celetná 32, Staré Mesto* ☎ *224–239–469* ⊕ *www.czechtoys.cz* Ⓜ *Line B: Nám. Republiky.*

MALÁ STRANA

There are plenty of souvenir shops just off Charles Bridge, but explore the other streets for more unusual options.

BOOKS AND PRINTS

Shakespeare & Sons. The cozy Malá Strana store boasts two floors of books, mostly in English, and displays work by local and international artists. Bookworms will be intoxicated by the sheer choice and reverent attitude to the tomes; this is a real old-school bookshop. Everyone else can soak up the expat atmosphere and pretend that they too never have to leave the Golden City. ✉ *U Lužického semináře 10, Malá Strana* ☎ *257–531–894* ⊕ *www.shakes.cz* Ⓜ *Line A: Malostranská.*

CAMERAS

Analogue. A photography and camera-lover's paradise, Analogue offers a knowledgeable staff passionate about analog photography, Lomography cameras (the trend for which apparently began in Prague in 1991), Polaroids, and more. There's a public darkroom, exhibitions, and a lab, and you can also get passport photos done here (the U.S. Embassy is just down the road). ✉ *Vlašská 357/10, Malá Strana* ☎ *603–530–035* ⊕ *www.analogue.cz* Ⓜ *Line A: Malostranská.*

HOME DECOR

Cihelna Concept Store. Attractively located by the river, this design concept shop near the gorgeous Hergetova Cihelna restaurant profiles the best in Czech design in a clean, unfussy space, from funky chairs to inventive lighting. ✉ *Cihelna 2b, Malá Strana* ☎ *257–317–318* ⊕ *www.cihelnaprague.com* Ⓜ *Line A: Malostranská.*

Slavica Polish Pottery. A nice change from the same old tourist shops, this authentic Polish pottery offers beautiful, bright, traditional homeware. They will also ship your hand-decorated gifts back home (at an additional cost) if you have run out of space in your suitcase—or if you don't trust yourself or your airline with breakable souvenirs. ✉ *Vlašská 631/11A, Malá Strana* ☎ *732–181–104* ⊕ *www.slavicapottery.com* Ⓜ *Line A: Malostranská.*

JEWELRY AND ACCESSORIES

Antique Újezd. This dimly lit antiques shop fills bureau drawers with vintage accessories and trinkets, as well as a selection of dainty 1930s pocketbooks, clutches, and bejeweled coin purses. There are also glass cases housing a pricey supply of diamonds, pearls, and gems, as well as a selection of paintings, furniture and the odd cat porcelain piece. ✉ *Újezd 37, Malá Strana* ☎ *257–217–177* ⊕ *www.antiqueujezd.cz* Ⓜ *Line A: Malostranská.*

7

DID YOU KNOW?

Many of the city's stores and boutiques are housed in stunning old buildings, so don't forget to look up and enjoy the architectural detail that Prague is so famous for.

MARIONETTES

Marionety. A fresh wooded scent greets visitors to this pleasant puppet shop on steep Nerudova Street. Discover an array of linden-wood marionettes, including classic characters like Tinkerbell and Charlie Chaplin, eerily reptilian wizards, and princesses in pink. Artist biographies are found alongside a few displays, and plaster puppets—cheaper but not quite as charming—are also on offer. ⊠ *Nerudova 51, Malá Strana* 🕾 *774–418–236* ⊕ *www.loutky.cz* Ⓜ *Line A: Malostranská.*

Fodor's Choice **Truhlář Marionety.** Among Prague's many marionette peddlers, this shop
★ below the Charles Bridge stands out for its selection of unadorned linden-wood marionettes handmade by local and regional artisans. There's also a quirky stock of decorative wooden toys, such as rocking horses and giant mermaids, fit for a lucky child's bedroom. ⊠ *U Lužického semináře 5, Malá Strana* 🕾 *602–689–918* ⊕ *www.marionety. com* Ⓜ *Line A: Malostranská.*

HRADČANY

It's all about the views in the Castle Area, but while you're checking out the views, check out the traditional craft shops as well.

TOYS

FAMILY **Hračky (Rocking Horse Toy Shop).** Take a trip back in time to when toys were made from wood and model cars were cherished. Everything about this store will make you smile, from the friendly owner's greeting to the stock of cheerful wind-up music boxes and animal figurines. Look closely at those wood-carved rocking horses and three-headed dragons—many items are handmade by Czech craftsmen. The shop even sells kits with colored pencils and pastels for budding young artists. ⊠ *Loretánské nám. 3, Hradcany* 🕾 *603–515–745* Ⓜ *Line A: Hradčanská.*

NOVÉ MĚSTO

Prague's New Town (or Nové Město) is home to all the big department stores and international brands, which are located in two main shopping areas—Václavské náměstí and Na Příkopě. But don't miss the various covered arcades or "passages" around the city, because they are home to a few interesting boutiques as well as nail bars and wine shops.

ANTIQUES

JHB Starožitnosti. This shop has beautiful art deco and art nouveau diamond rings, porcelain and brass decorative objects, and furniture. But the company's specialty is clocks from the 18th- and 19th centuries hailing from Austria, the Czech Republic, France, and Germany. Antique pocket watches featured in the window displays also draw longing stares from knowing collectors and passing tourists alike. ⊠ *Panská 1, Nové Mesto* 🕾 *222–245–836* ⊕ *www.jhbantique.cz* Ⓜ *Lines A & B: Můstek.*

Merchants along the Charles Bridge have to apply for special permits to sell their wares along this high-traffic area. Only original handicrafts are selected.

BEAUTY

Sephora. The makeup mainstay remains a dependable source for high-quality cosmetics and skin-care products from international brands. This location is not overwhelmingly large, like some of the chain's other stores, so you should have no trouble finding your favorite Clinique moisturizer or Dior mascara. ⊠ *Václavské náměstí 19, Nové Mesto* ☎ *234–656–100* ⊕ *www.sephora.cz* Ⓜ *Lines A & B: Můstek.*

BOOKS AND PRINTS

Antikvariát Karel Křenek. Despite the extensive collection of antique maps, prints, and engravings dating from the 16th century, this shop is refreshingly bright and clean. Among the shop's treasures: beautiful Japanese woodblocks and a well-known map depicting Asia as the winged horse Pegasus. The shop also mounts and frames works on request. ⊠ *Národní 18, Nové Mesto* ☎ *222–314–734* ⊕ *www.karelkrenek.com* Ⓜ *Line B: Národní třída.*

Globe Bookstore & Coffeehouse. A fine place to peruse the shelves of English-language titles, this friendly store leads to a café down the hall, where lattes, laptops, and expats are de rigueur. If you're hoping to attend English-language literary, film, or arts events while in Prague, check out the wall of fliers near the front desk. ⊠ *Pštrossova 6, Nové Mesto* ☎ *224–934–203* ⊕ *www.globebookstore.cz* Ⓜ *Line B: Národní třída.*

Kiwi Travel Bookshop. With more than 17,000 items in stock (including those featured on the online store), you'll find English-language travel guides, useful local maps, books about travel, and even a few globes scattered around the premises—but in keeping with the adventurous spirit, you might need to hunt them down a bit. Sales associates are quite helpful, and most speak some English. ⊠ *Jungmannova 23, Nové Mesto* ☎ *224–948–455* ⊕ *www.mapykiwi.cz* Ⓜ *Line B: Národní třída.*

Fodor's Choice **Mucha Museum shop.** The perfect place for your art nouveau or Alfons
★ Mucha fix (the world-famous Czech artist who made his name painting Sarah Bernhardt in fin de siècle Paris), this charming shop is located in a museum dedicated to the artist. You'll find posters, postcards, calendars, glass, jewelry, scarves, books, lamps, and more, all with the signature Mucha motifs. ⊠ *Kaunický palác, Panská 7, Nové Mesto* ☎ *224–216–415* ⊕ *www.mucha.cz* Ⓜ *Lines A & B: Můstek.*

Neoluxor Bookstore. With its four floors, music section, and coffee shop, this bookstore is the biggest in the Czech Republic, reminiscent of major American chains and known as "the palace." Only a small area in the basement is set aside for English-language books, but the store is an excellent source for maps of the Czech Republic and other European cities and countries, and has some travel guidebooks in English. ⊠ *Václavské nám. 41, Nové Mesto* ☎ *296–110–384* ⊕ *www.neoluxor. cz* Ⓜ *Line A: Muzeum.*

CLOTHING

Ivana Follová. Ivana Follová's little boutique at the top of Wenceslas Square shows off her wares in enticing style—think a chic, green space in central Prague. The designer specializes in silk, which she dyes in bold patterns and shapes into gauzy, graffitied garments, from wedding dresses to coats. She also stocks distinctive accessories like chunky costume jewelry by other Czech designers. ⊠ *Mezibranská 9, Nové Mesto* ☎ *222–211–357* ⊕ *www.ivanafollova.cz* Ⓜ *Lines A & B: Muzeum.*

Mango. The latest trends are presented with a refined touch by this Spanish brand, which mixes flirty dresses with sophisticated structured jackets and classic leather satchels. The size of the store will make your jaw drop—it could very well host rock concerts—and there's even a moving walkway to get you to the back of the shop. ⊠ *Na Příkopě 8, Nové Mesto* ☎ *224–218–884* ⊕ *www.mango.com* Ⓜ *Lines A & B: Můstek.*

Marks & Spencer. The Czech flagship location of the popular British department store is housed inside the historic Melantrich building on Wenceslas Square. Reasonably priced essentials, from clothes to accessories, can be found here as well British specialty food items. ■TIP➔ Glance upwards as you head in to the shop—during the Velvet Revolution in 1989, Václav Havel addressed the crowds from the building's balcony. ⊠ *Václavské nám. 36, Nové Mesto* ☎ *224–237–503* ⊕ *www.marks-and-spencer.cz* Ⓜ *Lines A & B: Můstek.*

Pietro Filipi. Taking its inspiration from the elegance and quality of Italian couture, this Czech brand makes timeless clothing for style-conscious professionals. Classic styles, bright colors, and quality design and materials are the watchwords here. ⊠ *Národní 31, Nové Mesto* ☎ *222–365–239* ⊕ *www.pietro-filipi.com* Ⓜ *Line B: Národní třída.*

The Room. The Room stocks creative European brands for fashion-conscious men, from cool Chinese-French Three Animals to Alex Monhart's swanky Czech-made black backpacks. ⊠ *Školská 7, Nové Mesto* ☎ *222–967–770* ⊕ *www.basmatee.cz* ☾ *Closed Sun.* Ⓜ *Lines A & B: Můstek.*

FOOD AND WINE

Cellarius. Try out acclaimed Moravian wines, or pick up a select imported bottle at one of two locations: in the lovely, historic Lucerna Passage, or at the Budecska Street store, which also features a wine cellar and garden restaurant. Both stores offer tastings. ⊠ *Lucerna Passage, Stepanska 61, Nové Mesto* ☎ *224–210–979* ⊕ *www.cellarius.cz* Ⓜ *Lines A & B: Můstek.*

GLASS

Moser. Elegant glass stemware and decorative bowls and candlesticks are hand-blown or -cut, and gorgeous enough to outfit the dining tables of Europe's aristocratic elite. This historic Czech company, established in Karlovy Vary in 1857, maintains two Prague locations. Both stores are breathtaking, boasting chandeliers, tea sets, and porcelain figurines on multiple floors, in addition to all that graceful glass. ⊠ *Na Příkopě 12, Nové Mesto* ☎ *224–211–293* ⊕ *www.moser-glass.com* Ⓜ *Line B: Nám. Republiky.*

JEWELRY AND ACCESSORIES

Belda Shop. This jewelry shop feels more like a gallery than a shop, with its statement pieces gleaming in the light. But don't be put off; it's a family-run business and the staff are friendly. The carefully curated sculptures and accessories are typified by an amazing use of metal and precious stone. ⊠ *Mikulandská 10, Nové Mesto* ☎ *224–933–052* ⊕ *www.belda.cz* ☾ *Closed weekends* Ⓜ *Line B: Národní třída.*

MUSIC

Bontonland Megastore. This behemoth of a music store is situated underground, somewhere between the Metro station and the street, giving it an intriguing cavelike atmosphere. This is the best place to purchase Czech music and films, and there is a limited supply of English-language media, too. ⊠ *Palác Koruna, Václavské nám. 1, Nové Mesto* ☎ *601–309–183* ⊕ *www.bontonland.cz* Ⓜ *Lines A & B: Můstek.*

SHOES

Baťa. Shoes, glorious shoes! Five floors of them, to be exact, are housed in this shoe giant that has locations around the world but got its start right here in what is now the Czech Republic. A well-planned layout makes the massive selection in the country's largest shoe shop less overwhelming, but shoe junkies could spend days browsing the rows of sandals, sneakers, and even boat shoes. ■ TIP→ There's a clearance section on the top floor for bargain hunters. ⊠ *Václavské nám. 6, Nové Mesto* ☎ *221-088-478* ⊕ *www.bata.cz* Ⓜ *Lines A & B: Můstek.*

SPORTING GOODS

Adidas. The iconic three stripes, the emblems of the brand, are discreetly displayed all over this unusually spacious concept store on a crowded stretch of Na Příkopě. Sneakers, funky T-shirts, and other sports gear fill the bright space drawing European tourists inside. ⊠ *Na Příkopě 12, Nové Mesto* ☎ *224-210-160* ⊕ *www.adidas.cz* Ⓜ *Lines A & B: Můstek.*

Intersport. This enormous megastore inside Galerie Myslbek supplies gear for every sport under the sun. Less mainstream pursuits like roller hockey and rock climbing are covered, but you'll also see basic necessities for runners and tennis players. There is a selection of backpacks for day trips or lengthy hikes, which could come in handy for excursions outside Prague. ⊠ *Na Příkopě 21, Nové Mesto* ☎ *221-088-097* ⊕ *www.intersport.cz* Ⓜ *Lines A & B: Můstek.*

Nike. Relentless pop music pulses through the shop's dizzying array of athletic wear. Zip-front jackets complete with the famous Swoosh logo, neon tennis outfits, and even "Nike Prague" T-shirts can be yours if you have the patience to deal with crowds of teenagers. A wall of casual shoes and athletic footwear is all the way in the back of the store, where you can also customize your sneakers—a staff member will take you through the process, but note that customized sneakers are not completed the same day you order them. ⊠ *Na Příkopě 22, Nové Mesto* ☎ *221-451-181* ⊕ *www.nikeprague.cz* Ⓜ *Line B: Náměstí Republiky.*

TOYS

FAMILY **Sparkys.** This is Prague's preeminent toy store, with goodies for babies, toddlers, and older children. Let the little ones run wild among three floors of Lego, puzzles, and games. Sparkys also stocks an adorable array of stuffed animals, including Krtek, the cute Czech cartoon character whose popularity spread across the communist world in the second half of the 20th century. ⊠ *Havířská 2, Nové Mesto* ☎ *224-239-309* ⊕ *www.sparkys.cz* Ⓜ *Line B: Nám. Republiky.*

SHOPPING MALLS AND DEPARTMENT STORES

Debenhams. If you need an extra pair of socks or a seasonal item, like a beach towel, this U.K. department store is a dependable choice. Relatively affordable selections of clothes and accessories for men and women are current but not overly trendy. The upstairs coffee bar has free Wi-Fi access. ✉ *Václavské nám. 21, Nové Mesto* ☎ *221–015–026* ⊕ *www.debenhams.cz* Ⓜ *Lines A & B: Můstek.*

Fodor's Choice ★ **Náplavka.** Every Saturday sees the hipster riverside hangout of Náplavka transformed into a farmers' market selling staples like potatoes and apples as well as more artisanal products like traditional Czech dumplings and honey wine, smoked meats, and tortellini. ✉ *Náplavka, Nové Mesto* ⊕ *www.farmarsketrziste.cz* ⊙ *Closed Jan.* Ⓜ *Line B: Karlovo Náměstí.*

Slovanský dům. A bit classier than the average mall, this collection of shops is flanked by a shady courtyard and features a few decent restaurants. Stores include big names like Armani and Calvin Klein, but it's the chic little boutiques, like Danish fashion brand Micha, that set this mall apart. There's also a movie theater showing new releases, sometimes in English. ✉ *Na Příkopě 22, Nové Mesto* ☎ *604–904–081* ⊕ *www.slovanskydum.com* Ⓜ *Line B: Nám. Republiky.*

Tesco (My Narodni). A one-stop wonder, this U.K. supermarket outpost in the My Narodni development stocks clothing for the whole family, plus home goods, cosmetics, English-language magazines, and a full basement floor of groceries. It's a mecca for tourists, expats, and Czechs alike, and those in the know head up to the top floor for the pleasant rooftop bar during the summer. ✉ *Národní třída 26, Nové Mesto* ☎ *222–815–111* ⊕ *itesco.cz/prodejny/obchody-tesco/my-narodni* Ⓜ *Line B: Národní třída.*

VINOHRADY

This beautiful, European neighborhood is less touristy, but there are still some interesting boutiques if you're prepared to go a little further afield.

CLOTHING

Pour Pour. Can't bear the thought of leaving Prague without something completely unique? Stop by this little shop filled with eclectic creations—from underwear to funny diaries—by young, up-and-coming Czech designers. With a rotating collection, the shop is all about originality, and unexpected fashions and finds will remind you that getting dressed can be an adventure. ✉ *Vinohradská 74, Vinohrady* ⊕ *www.facebook.com/pourpourshop* ⊙ *Closed weekends* Ⓜ *Line A: Jiřího z Poděbrad.*

Prague Thrift Store. Prague's got good game when it comes to thrift and retro stores, and this emporium in Vinohrady is one of the oldest and best. Moreover, a percentage of the profits go to charity. ✉ *Šumavská 29, Vinohrady* ☎ *608–623–339* ⊕ *www.thriftshop.cz* Ⓜ *Line A: Jiřího z Poděbrad.*

7

ŽIŽKOV

This rough-and-tumble area is more famous for its pubs, but if you're in the area, check out some of the cool new galleries and boutiques.

ART GALLERIES

Bliss Farm Gallery. Bliss Farm is quintessential Žižkov cool. An "open art studio space" and shop, the place is packed with paintings, silkscreen printed T-shirts, and even stuffed animals, as well as all sorts of other interesting bits and bobs. The products are handmade by local artists, and often recycled. ⊠ *Čajkovského 1716/22, Žižkov* ☎ *775-031-487* ⊕ *www.blissfarm.cz* ⊙ *Closed Sun.* Ⓜ *Line A: Jiřího z Poděbrad.*

SMÍCHOV

This area offers a reasonable range of modern shops and international brands, as well as Nový Smíchov, the big daddy of shopping centers.

MUSIC STORES

Dům Hudebnich Nastroju. Prague is a musical city, and if you're inspired by your surroundings you should check out this store near the Novy Smichov shopping center, which stocks everything from brass instruments to bongos. Follow the sounds of an oboe, flute, or double bass if you're lost. ⊠ *Štefánikova 19, Smíchov* ☎ *224-213-996* ⊕ *www.hnkliment.cz* Ⓜ *Line B: Anděl.*

SHOES

Humanic. From bright flip-flops to spiky stilettos, with some high-tops on the side, this affordable Austrian chain has all the latest trends in shoes. Located next to Nový Smíchov, it's basically Prague's version of DSW, where you can try shoes on without having to wait for sales help. ⊠ *OC Nový Smíchov, Plzenská 8, Smíchov* ☎ *257-289-490* ⊕ *www.humanic.net* Ⓜ *Line B: Anděl.*

SHOPPING MALLS AND DEPARTMENT STORES

Nový Smíchov. This bright and airy mall is manageably sized, with a convenient mix of shops and an indoor playground. Zara, H&M, Levi's, Clinique, and a two-floor Tesco are in the mix. There's also a cinema and a nice park with good views of the city behind the mall. ⊠ *Plzeňská 8, Smíchov* ☎ *251-101-061* ⊕ *www.novysmichov.eu* Ⓜ *Line B: Anděl.*

8

DAY TRIPS FROM PRAGUE

DAY TRIPS
FROM PRAGUE

TOP REASONS
TO GO

★ **Visit spooky Sedlec:**
The Kostnice outside of
Kutná Hora is a mesmer-
izing church decorated
with human bones.

★ **Find a storybook
come to life:** A true medieval castle—babbling
brook and all—can be
found in Karlštejn.

★ **Take a historic tour:**
The home of Archduke
Franz Ferdinand, whose
assassination started
World War I, is remark-
ably well preserved in
Konopiště; look for the
bear living in the moat.

★ **Pay remembrance to the
past:** In Terezín, a baroque
fortress turned into a concentration camp is both
powerful and chilling.

★ **Sample the wine:** It's
not all about beer. Try
the locally produced
wine at pretty Mělník.

1 **Kutná Hora.** From the
downright macabre to the
simply lovely; in Kutná Hora
you can see a church of
bones, a majestic cathedral,
and an attractive Czech town.

2 **Karlštejn.** The quickest
castle excursion from Prague
can get mobbed but ticks all

the European fairy-tale castle
boxes you could ask for.

3 **Křivoklát.** Take yourself
back in time at this evocative castle, complete with a
torture-chamber tour.

4 **Mělník.** A lovely town,
a lazy river, and a glass of
delicious local wine. What
more could you ask for?

GETTING ORIENTED

Prague is undeniably a showstopper. But to really experience the Czech Republic, you've got to get out of the city, and luckily it's an easy feat. A plethora of sights surround the capital city, whether you're looking for something medieval, majestic, or even macabre. In a couple of hours or less you'll have forgotten the cramped city and be lost in the rolling countryside or admiring the glorious castles and cathedrals.

Prague's public transport system can deliver you to any of these destinations any day of the week, and some can even be reached by boat in summer. Car rentals are simple to set up. Or make it easy on yourself and book a day tour. Any way you choose, a side trip into Bohemia is a worthy addition to any Prague itinerary.

5 Český Šternberk. Go way out of Prague and be impressed by this massive castle perched over the river.

6 Konopiště Castle. With a moat of bears, a hall of horns, and an untamed park, the surroundings of this castle really deliver.

7 Lidice. This village is a haunting memorial to the horrors of World War II.

8 Terezín. A trip to this city is emotional and educational—a glimpse into a former WWII Jewish ghetto and concentration camp.

Updated by
Jennifer Rigby

As the saying goes, the world is a book, and those who don't travel read only one page. The same applies to visitors who come to the Czech Republic but visit only Prague. Don't get us wrong: it's a great page to read, but if you want the whole story, you need to get out of the capital and embrace the adventures beyond.

You can stay overnight or for a whole weekend, but it's not essential; there's plenty to do with just a few hours set aside. The UNESCO-listed Kutná Hora is worth a visit, especially to experience the bone church, one of the most memorable, and strangely beautiful, attractions close to Prague. The surrounding town is charming too and offers plenty of options if you do plan an overnight.

There's more charm to be found in the myriad castles which dot the landscape around Prague. Karlštejn is a typical fairy-tale château atop a mountain; Křivoklát is secluded and quiet; and Konopiště is the hunting lodge of the doomed Archduke Franz Ferdinand. All the castles offer great hiking opportunities, but if hiking is your thing, it's worth going further afield to the breathtaking Pravčická Brána, or rock bridge, where you can roam through the forest, or take a guided boat ride through gorges. If you want to sample some Czech wine, Mělník has vineyards aplenty. There are more sobering—in every sense—sights around as well, such as Lidice and Terezín, two sites that resonate with the horrors of World War II.

Traveling may not come as easy as in Prague—fewer tourist facilities, fewer English speakers, and fewer nightlife and entertainment options. But the trade-off will be more bang for your buck and a genuine feel for the country and its people, plus a real sense of adventure.

PLANNING

WHEN TO GO

Many of the Czech Republic's castles and monuments are closed November through March. Some, especially those closer to Prague, stay open year-round, although with shortened hours. The busiest time for a visit is June through August; April and October will be less crowded. When school is in session, expect school groups during the week.

GETTING HERE

In general, buses are faster and cheaper, while trains are easier to navigate and a bit more comfortable. Bus drivers don't typically announce the stops, so when boarding, ask the driver to let you know when you should get off. If you are planning a trip, it's worth it to know your options ahead of time; visit ⊕ *www.idos.cz* for an online timetable (an English version is available). If you are taking a bus from Florenc, go to the station a day or two before your trip and purchase your tickets. People with tickets board first, and you'll get an assigned seat (and not have to stand). The ticket will be printed with the platform number. There's a computer in the Florenc station where you can check bus times as well.

GUIDED TOURS FROM PRAGUE

Guided bus tours are available from several companies for Karlštejn, Konopiště, Kutná Hora, Český Šternberk, and Terezín. The ease of booking and traveling (compared with figuring out the train and bus schedules or renting a car) are often worth the time constraints and extra cost. Wittmann Tours specializes in tours to Terezín as well as to Jewish sites all over the country. If you are looking for something more specialized, Avantgarde Prague offers tailor-made tours.

Avantgarde Prague. A well-established tour company, offering group and private tours that include a visit to a nuclear bunker, a focus on World War II in Prague, and hour-long drives through Prague in vintage cars (driver included). This is a good option for the time-poor, as tours can be speedy. ⊠ *Jáchymova 3, Staré Mesto* ☎ *226–235–080* ⊕ *www. avantgarde-prague.com.*

FAMILY **Biko Adventures Prague.** Biko offers a gentle and family-friendly full-day tour by bike through small villages (with stops for beer and baked goods) to Karlštejn castle (35 km [22 miles] away). Other options include a ride along the Vltava riverbank to a microbrewery or a bike tour through huge blocks of flats ending in a lush national park. ⊠ *Vratislavova 58/3, Vyšehrad* ☎ *733–750–990* ⊕ *www.bikoadventures.com.*

Premiant City Tour. Knowledgeable guides and a wide range of day-trips, many of which can also be taken privately. Book at easy-to-find booths on Na Příkopě. ⊠ *Na Příkopě 12 and 23, Nové Mesto* ☎ *606–600–123* ⊕ *www.premiant.cz.*

Wittmann Tours. Interesting and informative trips from the first company to offer tours focusing exclusively on the former Jewish ghetto of Terezín. ⊠ *Novotného lávka 5, Staré Mesto* ☎ *222–252–472, 739–571– 003 for last-minute reservations* ⊕ *www.wittmann-tours.com.*

RESTAURANTS AND HOTELS

In general, food and lodging should be cheaper than in Prague, but some restaurants, especially those close to the center or near a tourist attraction, can be just as pricey. You won't find the same range of options either, and be prepared for fewer English speakers—but people will probably be friendlier than in the big city, and, anyway, that's all part of the adventure

Hotel reviews have been shortened. For full information, visit Fodors. com.

WHAT IT COSTS IN KORUNA			
$	$$	$$$	$$$$
Restaurants	under 150 Kč	150 Kč–300 Kč	301 Kč–500 Kč	over 500 Kč
Hotels	under 3,500 Kč	3,500 Kč–5,000 Kč	5,001 Kč–7,000 Kč	over 7,000 Kč

Restaurant prices are the average cost of a main course at dinner or, if dinner is not served, at lunch. Hotel prices are the lowest cost of a standard double room in high season.

KUTNÁ HORA

70 km (44 miles) east of Prague.

Kutná Hora is a UNESCO World Heritage Site, and the town proudly boasts of its "ten centuries of architecture" that run the gamut from Gothic to cubism. The town is worth a visit any time, but really gets going around the beginning of April when the Awakening Kutná Hora festival is celebrated, which marks the beginning of the tourist season. Historic peddlers, dancers, and fencers celebrate the city's silver-mining history at the Royal Silvering Festival held every June. There are also some traditional Czech eateries; a great silver-mining museum; and the stunning Cathedral of St. Barbara, which dates from 1388.

Nearby, Sedlec Ossuary, or the "Bone Church," is one of the Czech Republic's most famous sights. The small chapel is decorated floor to ceiling with human bones. The shapes, chandeliers, and sculptures are strangely, hauntingly beautiful, adding up to a breathtaking and morbid memento mori.

GETTING HERE

Both buses and trains make the short trip to Kutná Hora, but the train is a better bet. A train ticket will cost about 100 Kč, and you will most likely be dropped off at the Kutná Hora main station, which is in the suburb of Sedlec, about 2 km (1¼ miles) away. (About half the trains are direct; half involve a change in Kolín.) If you are given a ticket that says *město* (city), that means you'll be going to the train station in town. However, since you are in Sedlec anyway, take advantage of the fact and walk about 10 minutes (signs point the way and there's a map in the station) to the bone church. You can then walk into town—about 25 minutes. It's an easy straight shot, but not the most scenic. Buses

Kutná Hora

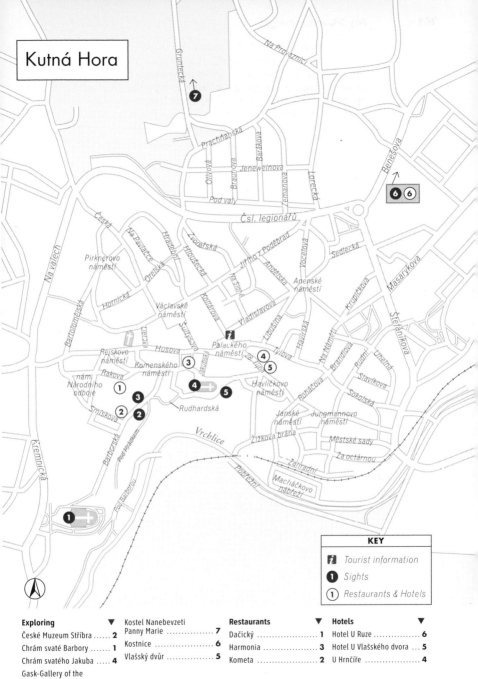

KEY

🛈	*Tourist information*
❶	*Sights*
①	*Restaurants & Hotels*

Exploring ▼
České Muzeum Stříbra 2
Chrám svaté Barbory 1
Chrám svatého Jakuba 4
Gask-Gallery of the
Central Bohemian
Region 3

Kostel Nanebevzeti
Panny Marie 7
Kostnice 6
Vlašský dvůr 5

Restaurants ▼
Dačický 1
Harmonia 3
Kometa 2

Hotels ▼
Hotel U Ruze 6
Hotel U Vlašského dvora ... 5
U Hrnčíře 4

leave from either Prague's Florenc main station or Černý Most on the outskirts of town, off the Metro Line B (yellow). Direct ones are not frequent; the ride takes about 20 minutes longer than the train, and the cost is about 100 Kč. By car, follow Vinohradská třída west out onto the E65, then take the D11 to Route 38 into Kutná Hora. The drive takes about an hour.

Visitor Information Info-Centre Kutná Hora. ⊠ *Palackého nám. 377* ☎ *327–512–378* ⊕ *www.kutnahora.cz.*

EXPLORING

FAMILY **České Muzeum Stříbra** (*Czech Museum of Silver*). A silver mine is a little more romantic than a run-of-the-mill coal mine, and this silver museum combines all manner of period mining and minting equipment with the real deal: the chance to tour a medieval silver mine. It's fun, but if you're claustrophobic it's worth noting that the tunnel is a bit tight, and you're underground for about 30 minutes. The city boasted some of the deepest mines in the world back in the 16th century, and the trek nowadays will probably make you glad you weren't a miner. Tours start every half-hour; last admission is 90 minutes before closing. ⊠ *Barborská ul. 28* ☎ *327–512–159* ⊕ *www.cms-kh.cz* 🎫 *70 Kč–140 Kč, 20 Kč for foreign-language explanation* ⊗ *Closed Dec.–Feb., and Mon. in Nov. The mine can shut down in bad weather.*

Fodor's Choice **Chrám svaté Barbory** (*St. Barbara's Cathedral*). Getting to this beautiful
★ cathedral is nearly as pleasurable as a visit to the Gothic church itself. It's about a 10-minute walk from the main Palackého náměstí along a road lined with baroque statues, from which you can gaze at the surrounding countryside and watch the massive shape of the cathedral come closer. From afar, the church resembles a grand circus tent more than a religious center. As the jewel in Kutná Hora's crown, it's a high point of Gothic style, although through the centuries there have been alterations and improvements. St. Barbara's was started in the late 1300s; it drew on the talents of the Peter Parler workshop as well as two luminaries of the late 15th century, Matyáš Rejsek and Benedikt Ried. Upon entering, look up. The soaring ceiling is one of the church's most impressive features it was added in 1558, and replaced and restored in the late 1800s. If you walk to the western façade, you'll see a lovely view over the town and the visibly leaning tower of St. James's Church. Do explore the whole of the church—gazing down at the splendor below from the elevated sections is particularly lovely. St. Barbara is the patron saint of miners, and glimpses of this profession can be seen throughout the interior, including Gothic frescoes of angels carrying shields with mining symbols. There's also a special Mintner's Chapel, which holds a statue of a miner, a novelty for its time. ⊠ *Barborská ul.* ☎ *327–515–796* ⊕ *www.khfarnost.cz* 🎫 *85 Kč* ⊗ .

Chrám svatého Jakuba (*St. James's Church*). If you've already been to St. Barbara's, you'll have seen the tilting tower of this church next to the old mint. It doesn't keep normal operating hours, but go ahead and try the door anyway. It was originally built in the Gothic style, but a massive baroque transformation occurred in the 17th and 18th centuries;

The looming St. Barbara's Cathedral is a tribute to Kutná Hora's miners.

the onion dome was added in 1737. The baroque paintings on the wall are Czech masterpieces. ⊠ *Havlíčkovo nám.*

Galerie Středočeského kraje (*GASK - Gallery of the Central Bohemian Region*). Opposite the parade of Gothic statues leading you down into town sits this massive gallery housed inside a former Jesuit college. Long, long open corridors and a reverential vibe make this an ideal space to display art. A series of rotating collections, both historic and contemporary, come through these floors. The gallery's permanent exhibition collection is displayed not by date order, but instead based on the "diverse spectrum of a person's emotional and mental life." Don't miss the gift shop with its collection of arty books and avant-garde handbags. The shelving alone is a work of art. ⊠ *Barborská ul. 53–24* ☎ *725–377–433* ⊕ *www.gask.cz* ⊠ *80–200 Kč* ⊘ *Closed Mon.*

Kostel Nanebevzetí Panny Marie (*Church of the Assumption of the Virgin*). The Church of the Assumption of the Virgin, across the street from the ossuary at the former Sedlec Monastery, exemplifies the work of Giovanni Santini (1667–1723). A master of expressive line and delicate proportion, this one-of-a-kind architect fathered a bravura hybrid of Gothic and baroque. ⊠ *Vítězná, Sedlec* ☎ *326–551–049* ⊕ *www.kutna-hora.net/chram-panny-marie.php* ⊠ *30 Kč.*

Fodor's Choice ★ **Kostnice** (*ossuary*). This is the reason many people outside the Czech Republic have heard of, and make the trip to, Kutná Hora. Forget all that beautiful baroque architecture and descend into the darkness with some bones. Bones from about 40,000 people have been lovingly arranged in the Kaple Všech svatých (All Saints Chapel), more commonly called the Bone Church. Built in the 16th century, this

DID YOU KNOW?

Morbid, marvelous, or both?
The ossuary outside Kutná
Hora uses thousands of
ancient bones for decorative
purposes creating chalices,
chandeliers, and even this
family coat of arms.

church forced the movement of a nearby graveyard. Monks from the nearby Sedlec Monastery decided to use the displaced cemetery bones to decorate the church with beautiful, weird, and haunting results. ■ **TIP→ Check out the chandelier as it's made with every bone in the human body. It's downright spooky.** ✉ *Zámecká 127, Sedlec* ☎ *326–551–049* 🌐 *www.kostnice.cz* 🎟 *90 Kč, 110 Kč for ossuary and church.*

Vlašský dvůr (*Italian Court*). Coins were first minted here in 1300, made by Italian artisans brought in from Florence—hence the mint's odd name. The Italian Court was where the Prague groschen, one of the most widely circulated coins of the Middle Ages, was minted until 1726. There's a **coin museum,** where you can see the small, silvery groschen being struck and buy replicas. ✉ *Havlíčkovo nám. 552* ☎ *327–512–873* 🌐 *www.vlassky-dvur.cz* 🎟 *85 Kč.*

WHERE TO EAT

$$ CZECH Fodor's Choice ★ 🍴 **Dačický.** A medieval tavern feel and big plates of Czech food make Dačický a warm, authentic experience. The yellow walls decorated with cartoon-style murals, long, shared wooden tables, and the massive chandelier also add to the ambience. Try the pork knee and the beer sampler, but don't expect to be able to move for a couple of hours, because the portions are huge and the beer is plentiful. [$] *Average main: 200 Kč* ✉ *Rakova 8* ☎ *603–434–367* 🌐 *www.dacicky.com.*

$$ CZECH 🍴 **Harmonia.** A charming spot just off Komenského náměstí near St. James's, Harmonia serves good food at good prices. The small back patio is relatively secluded and the perfect place for an espresso and quiet conversation. Food, like chicken cutlets and steaks, is simple and hearty. ■ **TIP→ It's also no-smoking, which is rare in this part of the world.** [$] *Average main: 150 Kč* ✉ *Husova 104* ☎ *327–512–275* 🌐 *www.restauranthармonia.cz.*

$$ CZECH 🍴 **Kometa.** Heading toward, or coming back from St. Barbara's, plan a coffee break on the beautiful Kometa terrace under the shade of a huge tree and looking over the Jesuit College. The food is acceptable, offering Czech staples, but it's more of an atmospheric stop. [$] *Average main: 150 Kč* ✉ *Barborská 29* ☎ *327–515–515* 🌐 *www.restaurantkometa.cz.*

WHERE TO STAY

$ HOTEL 🏨 **Hotel U Ruze.** Just steps from the Sedlec Ossuary, this small, friendly hotel has a pleasant garden and attached restaurant, and secure parking. **Pros:** close to Bone Church; friendly welcome; clean, airy rooms. **Cons:** away from main Kutná Hora sights. [$] *Rooms from: 1800 Kč* ✉ *Zámecká 52* ☎ *327–314–692* 🌐 *www.ruzehotel.com* 🛏 *11 rooms* 🍽 *Breakfast.*

$ HOTEL 🏨 **Hotel U Vlašského dvora.** Lovely views from this hotel make it a nice option for an overnight stay in Kutná Hora. **Pros:** good views; nice breakfast; free Wi-Fi. **Cons:** lots of steps; the lack of A/C make the rooms hot in summer. [$] *Rooms from: 1600 Kč* ✉ *Ulice 28. října 511* ☎ *327–514–618* 🌐 *www.vlasskydvur.cz* 🛏 *10 rooms* 🍽 *Breakfast.*

$ B&B/INN 🏨 **U Hrnčíře.** If you are looking for a more rustic stay, head over to U Hrnčíře, where you will find basic decor but a good restaurant and a view of St. James's Church. **Pros:** old picturesque building; good restaurant. **Cons:** steep stairs and no elevator. [$] *Rooms from: 800 Kč* ✉ *Barborská 24* ☎ *603–511–322* 🌐 *www.hoteluhrncire.cz* 🛏 *5 rooms* 🍴 *Breakfast.*

KARLŠTEJN

29 km (18 miles) southwest of Prague.

If you've only a few hours to spend outside of Prague, going to Karlštejn is an easy and delightful day trip. The town itself seems to exist mainly to support visitors to the castle, so if you are looking for some Czech authenticity this probably isn't the one to choose. But for castle lovers and nature lovers, it's a lovely outing.

GETTING HERE

There's no bus service to Karlštejn from Prague, but it's a quick, simple, and scenic train journey (50 Kč) from the main station. Many trains leave every day from Hlavní nádraží—look on the schedule for trains heading to Beroun. When you arrive at the Karlštejn station, exit the station, turn right, and walk back along the small lane parallel to the railway tracks to find the town. Follow the signs reading "Hrad." After a few minutes, cross a bridge over the river, and turn right onto the main road, which resembles a small highway (the absence of a pedestrian sidewalk doesn't bother the locals). Be wary of traffic, but continue for another two or three minutes until you reach a road going up the hill to your left. This is the main road up to the village and castle.

A visit to Karlštejn can also be combined with a challenging 13-km (8-mile) hike through beautiful forests and along a small wooded waterfall from Beroun. Get off at the Beroun station, walk toward town and make a right just before an underpass. Follow the red-marked trail through the hills and dales, passing through the tiny village of Svatý Jan before arriving in Karlštejn—just above the village—about three hours later. Don't set out without water, good shoes, and, above all, a decent local hiking map available at the visitor's center.

By car from Prague, take Highway 4—on the western side of the Vltava—to the edge of the city, then go right on Highway 115, southwest through Radotín. Take the Karlštejn exit, which puts you on Highway 116, and after a few more minutes you end up beside the Berounka River. You can find a large parking lot at the bottom of the hill below Karlštejn. No vehicles are allowed on the road up to the castle.

Visitor Information Karlštejn Information Center. ✉ *Nad parkovištěm 334, above parking lot* ☎ *311–681–370* 🌐 *www.karlstejnsko.cz.*

TIMING

December is actually a good time to come here, as the city hosts a number of Christmas concerts on weekends and there are usually fewer crowds than in summer. In September a wine festival is held, complete with tastings, craft booths, artistic displays, and a visit from Charles IV himself (sort of).

EXPLORING

Fodor's Choice ★ **Karlštejn castle.** If it's a picture-book European castle you're after, look no further. Perched atop a wooded hillside, Karlštejn comes complete with battlements, turrets, and towers. Once Charles IV's summer palace, Karlštejn was originally built to hold and guard the crown jewels (which were moved to Prague Castle's St. Vitus's Cathedral in 1619). There is a fairly strenuous hike up to the castle—lined with souvenir stands and overpriced snack bars—but it's worth the journey. Once you've reached the top, take time to walk the ramparts and drink in the panorama of the village and countryside below. There's a slightly bewildering list of different interior tours, but the pick of the bunch is tour number two, which includes the castle's greatest treasure, the Chapel of the Holy Cross, which once held the crown jewels. Tours of the chapel are limited (and more expensive than the other tour route), so you must book in advance. There's an exterior tour, too, if it's a sunny day, or you can poke your head around the exterior courtyards at no cost. Because of its proximity to Prague, it is the most-visited site outside of the Czech capital, so be prepared for crowds, especially in the high summer months. Email for tour reservations. ✉ *Karlštejn 18* ☎ *311–681–617 for castle info and advance bookings* ✉ *rezervace@hradkarlstejn.cz* 🌐 *www.hradkarlstejn.cz* 🎟 *Tour 1: 270 Kč; Tour 2: 330 Kč; Tour 3: view from the great tower, 100 Kč; Tour 4: 40 Kč to walk walls behind the 3rd gate without a guide* 🕒 *Closed Jan. 9–Feb. 3, and Mon. Sept.–June. Chapel closed Nov.–Apr. Tour 3 May–Sept. only.*

WHERE TO EAT AND STAY

$$ CZECH 🍴 **Restaurace a Penzion Pod dračí skálou.** This traditional hunting lodge–style restaurant is the most rustic and fun of Karlštejn's eateries. To find it, follow the main road uphill out of the village about a third of a mile from town. If you've visited the castle, take the path to your left when you leave; or if walking from Beroun, you'll pass by before reaching the Castle. The portions of pork, chicken, beef, and game are generous for the price. A small terrace is popular with cyclists in nice weather. [$] *Average main: 200 Kč* ✉ *Karlštejn 130* ☎ *311–681–177* 🌐 *www.poddraciskalou.eu.*

$$ CZECH 🍴 **U Janů.** The best of the many touristy restaurants in the town proper, this spot is just on the upper edge of the village, not far from where the castle path starts. It also offers a nice big terrace with slight views of the castle. Decent Czech-style food, including some game and fish options, is offered on the menu. The pension can also be a comfortable place to stay if you feel like being outside of Prague for a night but close to the action at Karlštejn. [$] *Average main: 150 Kč* ✉ *Karlštejn 28* ☎ *725–805–965* 🌐 *www.ujanukarlstejn.cz.*

$ HOTEL 🏨 **Hotel Karlštejn.** The newest and best proper hotel in town, the Karlštejn offers 11 modern but pared-down rooms. **Pros:** inexpensive, clean, modern rooms for the area; sauna and whirlpool. **Cons:** no elevator. [$] *Rooms from: 2000 Kč* ✉ *Pod hradem 7* ☎ *222–539–539* 🌐 *www.hotel-karlstejn.cz* 🛏 *11 rooms* 🍽 *Breakfast.*

8

KŘIVOKLÁT

43 km (27 miles) west of Prague.
One of the most evocative castles in the country, Křivoklát is the real deal. A brisk walk up the hill to the top feels like a trip back in time as you leave the trappings of modern life behind.

GETTING HERE

A train is the best, and prettiest, way to reach Křivoklát. Trains depart from Hlavní nádraží, and a change in Beroun is required. The scenic ride will take about 1½ hours and cost around 100 Kč. Trains aren't all that regular, so check your return options before setting off.

A PAGAN SPRING

Spirits swing to life in Křivoklát on April 30, when many Czech villages celebrate something called Čarodejnice. Roughly translated as "witch-burning"—a pagan-rooted festival to ward off the winter spirit and welcome the bounty of spring—it turns Křivoklát into a gleeful scene of Slavic festivities and mock Celtic battles. Hundreds of Czechs from all over come to enjoy the music, merriment, and cheap wine into the wee hours.

If you're driving, the fastest way to Křivoklát is to follow Route 6 from Prague toward Karlovy Vary and after Jeneč turn onto Route 201 via Unhošte to Křivoklát. The trip is about an hour. For a beautiful drive (and an extra 15 minutes) take the E50 Highway from Prague toward Plzeň, then exit at Křivoklát to Route 116. Follow this highway, which goes along a river before veering up into the hills, to Route 201, which winds back south toward Křivoklát. Parking is just beneath the castle.

Visitor Information Křivoklát Tourist Information. ⊠ *Dr. M. Tyrš 93* 📞 *313-558-981* ⊕ *www.mestys-krivoklat.cz.*

TIMING

In summer you'll see cyclists zooming around the region and locals visiting the castle in swarms. In the beginning of December, Křivoklát holds an Advent fair, complete with musicians, performances, and lots of crafts.

EXPLORING

Fodor'sChoice **Křivoklát.** A man dressed as a monk asleep in the corner; children practic-
★ ing archery; traditional craftsmen offering their wares—close your eyes in Křivoklát's strangely atmospheric courtyard and you can easily imagine the scene with hunters clattering back atop their horses. Because the castle is a little farther from Prague, it's much less crowded and more authentic, so you can let your imagination run wild as you wander the walls and gaze out on the surrounding forest and the Berounka River winding lazily by below. The evocative name helps as well, even if it's a little hard to pronounce (it means "twisted branches" in Czech). There also aren't many signs, which helps with the feeling that you are having an adventure. You'll meet a lot of locals, rather than tourists, enjoying the castle, mainly because it's a national favorite thanks to its many

romantic references in Czech literature. The river area is also popular with hikers and cyclists.

Křivoklát began life as a humble hunting lodge back in the 12th century. Greater things were to come, thanks to King Wenceslas I, who commissioned the first castle here. Future inhabitants expanded and beautified the place, including Charles IV and his son, Wenceslas IV. A number of fires significantly damaged the buildings, and toward the end of the 16th century it lost its importance and fell into disrepair. Following the Thirty Years' War, the Schwarzenbergs took over and revived it. It's been in state hands since 1929.

A walk around the castle walls is one of the most enjoyable reasons to visit. Take a tour and you'll pass through the Great Hall (one of the largest Gothic halls in Central Europe, second only to one in Prague Castle) plus another hall, both loaded with Gothic paintings and sculpture; a beautiful chapel (another highlight of the interior tour), the castle library, a castle prison complete with torture instruments, and lots of hunting trophies. It's truly one of the more interesting castle tours around. One-hour tours are offered regularly in Czech, and tours in English must be requested in advance. If you didn't plan ahead, sitting in the courtyard and nursing a beer from the hilltop pub is also enjoyable. ✉ *Křivoklát 47* ☎ *313–558–440 for castle info and tour reservations* 🌐 *www.krivoklat.cz* 🎫 *Gothic palace tour 200 Kč; castle tour 240 Kč; castle walls tour 80 Kč* 🕓 *Closed Dec.–Mar. (except festivals; check website for details), and Mon. Sept.–June.*

8

WHERE TO EAT

$$ CZECH 🍴 **U Jelena.** The pleasant riverside setting and the hearty hunting theme—as well as proximity to the castle itself—are the main draws here, but the food, from the familiar *svíčková* (slices of beef loin in cream sauce) to more elaborate dishes like venison steak with Cumberland sauce, is also worthwhile. If you'd like to stay overnight, there are a few rooms upstairs, outfitted simply but with a cozy feeling thanks to wooden furnishings and pleasant lighting. Most have good views of the woodsy surroundings, and there's a lovely terrace that overlooks the river as well. [$] *Average main: 250 Kč* ✉ *Hradní 53* ☎ *313–558–529* 🌐 *www.ujelena.eu.*

MĚLNÍK

About 40 km (23 miles) north of Prague.

This pretty town is the closest place to Prague to go for homegrown Czech wine. It's home to rolling countryside, the ubiquitous castle, and the meeting of two sleepy rivers.

GETTING HERE

The only direct route to Mělník is by bus. The bus takes about 45 minutes and departs from Nádraží Holešovice on Metro Line C (red). It should cost around 50 Kč, and you can buy tickets from the driver. You'll be dropped off at the bottom of the hill, and it's a signposted short walk up to the town center, where you'll find the sights, including the square and castle. If you're coming by car, take Highway 9 from Prague's northern tip, which heads all the way to Mělník. Park on the small streets just off the main square (head in the direction of the towers to find it).

In the summer an all-day boat trip along the Vltava River is a lovely option. Check out Prague Steamboat Company's website for sailing times.

Boat Travel Prague Steamboat Company. ⊠ *Rašínovo nábřeží, Staré Mesto* ☎ *224–931–013* ⊕ *www.praguesteamboats.com.*

Visitor Information Mělník Tourist Information. ⊠ *Legionářů 51* ☎ *315–627–503* ⊕ *www.mekuc.cz/misto/informacni-centrum.*

EXPLORING

Zámek. The town's castle may be petite but it hovers grandly over the confluence of the Labe (Elbe) River and two arms of the Vltava. The view here is stunning, and the sunny hillsides are covered with vineyards. Indeed, the town is known best for its special Ludmila wines made from these grapes. As the locals tell it, Emperor Charles IV was responsible for bringing wine production to the area. Having a good eye for favorable growing conditions, he encouraged vintners from Burgundy to come here and plant their vines. Every autumn, usually in late September, Mělník celebrates what is likely the region's best Vinobraní, an autumn festival held when barrels of young, still fermenting wine, called *burčak* are tapped. If you happen to come at this time, look for the rare red-wine version.

The courtyard's three dominant architectural styles jump out at you, reflecting alterations to the castle over the years. On the north side, note the typical arcaded Renaissance balconies, decorated with *sgraffiti*. To the west, a Gothic touch is still easy to make out. The southern wing is clearly baroque (although also decorated with arcades). Inside the castle at the back you can find a *vinárna* (wine room) with decent food and excellent views overlooking the rivers. On the other side is a **museum** of paintings, furniture, and porcelain belonging to the old aristocratic Lobkowicz clan, which has recovered quite a few castles and estates from the state. For day-tripping wine-lovers, tour the wine cellars under the castle and book a wine tasting. ⊠ *Zámek Mělník* ☎ *315–622–121* ⊕ *www.lobkowicz-melnik.cz* 🎫 *Castle 110 Kč, wine cellar tour 50 Kč (up to 360 Kč with wine tasting).*

WHERE TO EAT AND STAY

$$
CZECH
✕ **Zámecká Restaurace.** You'll find the best place to eat—and the best view—in town right in the castle. The terrace looks out on the vineyards, river, and fields beyond, which is the perfect spot to dine on a sunny day. The restaurant offers a daily menu of Czech classics as well as a tasty fondue option. Sipping a glass of Ludmila wine and taking in the astonishing scenery is a treat at a very reasonable price. The castle also boasts a café and wine bar. $ *Average main: 250 Kč* ⊠ *Mělník*

Castle, Svatováclavská 19/16 ☎ *317–070–150* 🌐 *www.lobkowicz-melnik.cz/zamecka-restaurace* ⏲ *Closed Sun. Nov.–Mar.*

$ B&B/INN 🏨 **Pension Hana.** Most of the better accommodations options in the town are on the outskirts, but this small home with a garden is a 10-minute walk from the center. **Pros:** public swimming pool nearby; cyclist-friendly. **Cons:** could be a little basic for the refined visitor. [$] *Rooms from: 900 Kč* ✉ *Fügnerova 714* ☎ *603–512–485* 🌐 *www.penzion-melnik.cz* 🛏 *10 rooms* 🍴 *Breakfast.*

ČESKÝ ŠTERNBERK

48 km (30 miles) southeast of Prague.

A real-deal Czech castle, complete with descendants of its 13th-century founders still living inside. Český Šternberk may not be the easiest day trip from Prague, but for history, atmosphere, and authenticity, it's hard to beat.

GETTING HERE

Both trains and buses go daily to Český Šternberk, but it's not the easiest trip. (If you are willing to do an arranged tour with a company, that's certainly the simplest way to arrive.) Buses depart from Prague's southernmost bus station, Roztyly, which is about 15 minutes by metro from the city center on Metro Line C (red). There's an information office outside the Metro station, and the bus platforms stretch to your left and down the hill. Purchase tickets (about 65 Kč) directly from the driver, and be prepared to change buses, usually in Benešov.

Trains leave from Hlavní nádraží and stop in many small towns on the way; you will have to change trains in Čerčany, about one hour out of Prague. Though the train ride is about 20 minutes longer than the trip by bus, it's a bit more scenic and easier to figure out. The trip takes about two hours. In summer you may be lucky enough to score a ride on an old-fashioned steam train. Ask at the main station for the *parní vlak* (steam train). If you're driving, take the D1 highway out of Prague (the main highway to Brno) and take the turnoff to Český Šternberk, following Route 111 to the castle, which perches over the highway. The drive takes just under an hour.

VISITOR INFORMATION

A small tourist office is below the castle near the main parking lot and can help to prebook castle tours. Their hours are quite haphazard, but there's not much reason to need them.

TIMING

In winter, late autumn, and early spring the castle is either closed or has restricted hours. Summers see the most tourists, so May and September are your calmest bets. There's a falconer display most summer days and a historical festival held every October that features "live" characters from the castle's history.

KONOPIŠTĚ CASTLE

45 km (27 miles) southeast of Prague.

Bears, hunting trophies, and history are found at the country residence of the doomed Archduke Franz Ferdinand, whose 1914 assassination ignited World War I and changed the course of modern history.

GETTING HERE

For being so close, Konopiště can feel a little remote. Buses leave mainly from the Roztyly metro station, on Line C (red line), and occasionally from the main Florenc bus station. The trip will take about an hour, and requires a change in Benešov to the Konopiště stop. Tickets cost around 50 Kč. Alternatively, you can follow the signs from the bus station and walk about 2½ km (1½ miles). Trains leave from the main train station; they also take about an hour and cost 70 Kč. The same walk will be required. Or you can take a taxi. By car, take the D1 highway southwest toward Brno, and exit following the signs to Benešov. Signs on this road lead you to Konopiště.

Visitor Information Konopiště Tourist Information. ✉ *Malé nám. 1700, Benešov* ☎ *317–726–004 for main tourist office in Benešov.*

EXPLORING

Zámek Konopiště (*Konopiště Castle*). Set in a huge, beautiful park, Konopiště Castle dates to the 14th century and is best known as the hunting lodge of the ill-fated Archduke Franz Ferdinand, whose assassination sparked World War I. He no doubt had a whale of a time hunting in the grounds before he met his untimely end, and now visitors can wander the forests, gaze at the lake, and even watch plays in summer, as well as musing on the Archduke's global significance. In a suitably historic touch, there's also bear who lives in the castle moat; he's a bit shy so you might not see him.

The castle itself is also worth a look, with a carefully preserved interior including many original furnishings from Ferdinand's time. The rooms reflect his incredible opulence as well as his fondness for hunting—there are animal trophies and weapons everywhere. For a properly immersive experience, you can even stay inside the castle walls at a little pension.

Getting to the castle usually involves a 1/3-mile walk through the woods. It can only be seen on a guided tour; book in advance for an English-speaking guide. If one isn't available, ask for an English text to accompany the tour. An atmospheric night tour is also offered. ✉ *Zámek Konopiště, Benešov* ☎ *317–721–366* ⊕ *www.zamek-konopiste.cz* 🎟 *Tours 240 Kč* ⊙ *Closed Mon., weekdays in Nov., and Dec.–Mar.*

WHERE TO STAY

$ 📷 **Pension Konopiště.** Konopiště is near enough to Prague that you don't
B&B/INN   really need to stay overnight, but if you fancy a night in the countryside, this pension inside the castle walls and attached to a motorcycle museum

Česky Šternberk or the "Star on the Hill" lives up to its name.

is a lovely option. **Pros:** great location; individual approach. **Cons:** no restaurant. $ *Rooms from: 1900 Kč* ✉ *Konopiště 30, Benešov* ☎ *317–702–658* ⊕ *www.penzion-konopiste.cz* ➨ *6 apartments* ⦿ *Breakfast.*

LIDICE

18 km (11 miles) northwest of Prague.

No more than a speck on the map to the northwest of Prague, this tiny village became a part of the tragic history of World War II. Adolf Hitler ordered Lidice to be razed to the ground as a lesson to the Czechs and a representation of what would happen to anyone who opposed his rule. The act was a retaliation for the assassination of the Nazi leader Reinhard Heydrich by Czech patriots. On the night of June 9, 1942, a Gestapo unit entered Lidice. The entire adult male population were shot, nearly 200 men; about the same number of women were sent to the Ravensbrück concentration camp. The children were either sent to Germany to be "Aryanized" or accompanied the women to the death camp. By June 10 the entire village was completely wiped out.

The name Lidice soon became an example around the world of what the Nazis were capable of. A group of English miners from Birmingham took up the cause and formed "Lidice Must Live," an initiative to build a new village of Lidice. The city is adjacent to the memorial, which is an amazing and beautiful site, albeit one that is usually visited only by school groups. For most tourists, and even Czechs, heartbreaking Lidice still doesn't seem to be on the map. If you are driving and plan to go to Terezín, make Lidice a short stop on your way.

GETTING HERE

It's a shame that an important memorial so close to Prague can be a bit tricky to reach by public transportation, although it's a quick trip once you are on board. There's no train service to Lidice, but there is a regular bus service from Zličín, at the end of the Metro Line B (yellow)—the same place you can get the airport bus. You can also get bus A56, Prague-Kladno, from stop no. 3 above the Metro station Nádraží Veleslavín (Line A). Before getting on the bus, ask the driver if he stops in Lidice. Tickets (30 Kč) are purchased directly from the driver; ask him to let you know when the stop comes up. The trip should take about 20 minutes, and when all goes well, you'll be let off at an intersection across from the memorial itself.

By car, Lidice is an easy 30-minute journey. From the Dejvice area, follow Evropská třída out of Prague past the airport, then continue west on D7 until you see the well-marked memorial, with a parking lot, beside the highway. If you're driving, it's ideal to combine this with a trip to Terezín, about 30 km (18 miles) farther along in the same direction from Prague.

EXPLORING

Lidice Memorial. There is an eerie silence at Lidice. The lovely green rolling hills, small pond, babbling brook, and groves of trees are typical of the Czech countryside; but somehow the events that happened here remain in the air. It's incredibly moving to walk around the empty area, constantly reminding yourself that within living memory, this was a thriving village before the Nazis effectively erased it from the map. You'll first enter the colonnade that houses a small museum. Inside, you're introduced, through photographs, to the original inhabitants of the city. German documentation from the time describes the horror of the mass murder in a disturbingly straightforward fashion. The staff doesn't speak much English, but they can play a short film in English on request. The grounds of the memorial are free to wander. You can buy a map inside the museum for 10 Kč or book a guide to escort you around the entire area for 500 Kč. Heading straight from the museum you'll encounter a vast rose garden. At the opposite end of the garden from the memorial is a rose map with a history of the garden and detailing which roses are planted where and why. For example, the west portion of the garden is planted with light-color roses to honor the children. Heading straight down the hill from the museum, at the end of the terrace, you'll come to a round building called In Memoriam. Here, rotating thematic exhibitions are presented. Signs point out what used to be at that particular location, and you'll find the remains of a few foundations, such as a church and a school, scattered about. Be sure to walk over toward the Children's War Victims Memorial. This life-size sculpture of the 82 children gassed by the Nazis is haunting in its detail, particularly the delicate facial expressions. On the opposite side of the path is a stark cross, which marks the place where the men were executed. You can continue walking to the end of the field to see the former location of the town's cemetery. ✉ Ul. 10 června 1942 ☎ 312-253-088 ⊕ www.lidice-memorial.cz 💶 90 Kč, 500 Kč guided tour (in English).

TEREZÍN

48 km (30 miles) northwest of Prague.
Just the word Terezín (Theresienstadt in German) immediately recalls the horrors of the Jewish Holocaust for Czechs. Originally built as a military city in the 18th century, Nazis quickly saw its potential, and removed the 7,000 original inhabitants to turn the city into a Jewish ghetto, and the fortress into a prison. Terezín was the main Nazi concentration camp in Bohemia; but it wasn't designed as a death camp, even though in the end more than 38,000 people died in either the ghetto or prison. The city was supposed to be a "model" Jewish settlement, part of a humane façade the Nazis presented to the Red Cross in 1944.

GETTING HERE
There's no train service directly to Terezín. Several buses leave the Nádraží Holešovice station daily, and weekends offer a bit more choice. The trip lasts almost an hour. To get a good overview of the city, ask the driver for a ticket to Terezín bioveta, the stop just outside the town proper, closer to the **Malá Pevnost** (Small Fortress). Starting here and taking the guided tour (included in the ticket price; make an advance reservation online) will give you a good overview of not only the main prison camp but also the ghetto itself.

If you're driving, take the E55 north out of Prague (this is the main highway going to Dresden and Berlin) and head toward Lovosice. You can either take Exit 35 at Doksany and follow the country road straight to Terezín or continue to Lovosice, and from there turn right; the road leads directly into Terezín. There's a large parking lot next to the Malá Pevnost. The trip takes about 50 minutes. To visit Střekov, follow the road signs from Terezín to Litoměřice, then take Highway 261 to Ústí nad Labem.

Visitor Information **Litoměřice Tourist Information.** ⊠ *Mírové nám. 16, Litomerice* ☎ *416–916–440* ⊕ *www.litomerice.cz.* **Terezín Tourist Information.** ⊠ *Nám. ČSA 179* ☎ *775–711–881* ⊕ *www.terezin.cz.*

EXPLORING

Magdeburg Barracks. The city's second museum is the Magdeburg Barracks. Under the Nazis, the building was primarily used for administration offices, but it's been reconstructed into an education facility. There's an excellent re-creation of how a former dormitory would have looked, plus exhibits detailing the arts in Terezín. Inspiring displays show how people in the ghetto continued to hold literary, musical, theatrical and artistic happenings. ⊠ *Tyrsova 204* ☎ *416–782–225* ⊕ *www.pamatnik-terezin.cz* 🕮 *1 unit 175 Kč, all units 215 Kč.*

Museum of the Terezín Ghetto. Told in words and pictures, the town's horrific story is depicted at the Museum of the Terezín Ghetto, just off the central park in town. A short documentary is also shown in many languages. Tell the staff that you speak English; they'll let you roam the building and flag you down when the next English-language video is being shown. ⊠ *Komenského ul.* ☏ *416–782–225* ⊕ *www.pamatnik-terezin.cz* ▣*1 unit 175 Kč; all units 215 Kč.*

Fodor'sChoice **Terezín Memorial** (*Památník Terezín*). The most powerful aspect of Ter-
★ ezín is that you don't need much imagination to visualize how it looked
under Nazi rule. When it was a Jewish ghetto, more than 59,000 people
were crammed into this camp. Terezín was actually an exception among
the many Nazi concentration camps in Central Europe. The Germans,
for a time, used it as a model city in order to deflect international criti-
cism of Nazi policy toward the Jews. In the early years of the war—
until as late as 1944—detainees had a semblance of a normal life, with
limited self-rule, schools, a theater, even a library. (Pictures drawn by
the children at Terezín are on display in Prague's Jewish Museum.)
These areas can be experienced in more detail through exhibitions in
the Magdeburg Barracks. As the Nazi war effort soured, the conditions
for the people in Terezín worsened. Transports to Auschwitz and other
death camps were increased to several times a week, and eventually
87,000 Jews were murdered in this way. Another 35,000 died from
starvation or disease.

The enormity of Terezín's role in history is difficult to grasp at first, but
the Památník Terezín (Terezín Memorial) encompasses all the existing
buildings that are open to the public and has produced an excellent
guide to direct you around the city. Buildings include the Magdeburg
Barracks, where the Jewish Council of Elders met, and the Jewish cemetery's crematorium just outside the town walls.

The **Malá Pevnost** (Small Fortress) functioned as a jail, mainly for
political prisoners and others resisting the German occupation, holding them in abject conditions. Around 30,000 prisoners came through
here during the war. A tour through the fortress is chilling; you'll first
visit the administrative area, where new prisoners were brought, and
then glimpse their cells; crudely furnished with stone floors and long
wooden beds. Not much has been done to spruce up the place for visitors, leaving the original atmosphere intact. As a military prison, 150
people could be held in the cells; under the Nazis, it was typical to have
1,500 prisoners held in the same space. There was no gas chamber here;
but the appalling hygienic conditions led to many deaths, and about
300 prisoners were executed. Many of the juxtapositions are deeply
cruel, such as the swimming pools for guards and their families, which
prisoners would pass on their way to their execution.

Those who did not die in detention were shipped off to other concentration camps. Above the entrance to the main courtyard stands the
horribly false motto "Arbeit macht Frei" (Work Brings Freedom). At
the far end of the fortress, opposite the main entrance, is the special
wing built by the Nazis when space became tight. These windowless
cells display a brutal captivity. ⊠ *Principova alej 304* ☏ *416–782–225*
⊕ *www.pamatnik-terezin.cz* ▣*1 unit 175 Kč, all units 215 Kč* ☉ *Crematorium closed Sat.*

The gate of Terezín had the cruel and horribly false sign, "Work Brings Freedom" above the entrance.

Pravčická Brána. The largest natural rock bridge in Europe, Pravčická Brána is the symbol of the beautiful countryside known as Czech Switzerland, which sits on the border with Germany. It's a bit of a hike from Prague, but if you plan ahead, it's the perfect day trip. Take the train to Děčín, which takes just over 90 minutes, followed by the local bus to Hřensko, the nearest village, which takes another 30 or so minutes. The driver, or the tourists getting off, will let you know where the best stop is for the bridge. From there, it's a lovely and atmospheric walk up through the forest to reach the rock formation, which comes complete with a museum and restaurant called The Falcon's Nest—supplies are brought in via pulley. This being the Czech Republic, there's also a pub where you can order fine beer in the shadow of the bridge itself. For 75 Kč, you can scramble around nearby rock formations, which have a similarly alien appeal, for a better vantage point. A series of gentle, well-marked hikes on pretty forest trails and mossy gorges will take you a circular route back, ending up in Hřensko. The highlight of these trails is being punted along the river—when the paths run out—in a precarious boat with a ferryman who tells you (in German and Czech and hand gestures) how the rocks over your head look like different animals and monsters. Each boat trip costs around 50 Kč.

If you want to see a bit of real Czech magic, head for Pravčická Brána. It's a schlep from Prague, but it can be done in a day with some forward-planning.. ⊠ *Pravčická Brána, Hrensko* ☎ *412–554–286 for local tourist information* ⊕ *www.pbrana.cz* ☉ *Closes early (around 4 pm) in winter.*

WHERE TO EAT

Terezín has very little in the way of services for visitors. There are a couple of depressing haunts, serving mostly inedible pub standards from menus run off on mimeograph machines. Duck out of town to nearby Litoměřice down the road about 2 km (1 mile). Buses run regularly from the main square, and it's barely a five-minute ride. After the heavy atmosphere of Terezín, it's refreshing to walk down the tree-lined main street between colorful buildings bustling with shops and people.

$$ CZECH 🍴 **Radniční Sklípek.** This spot is local favorite, and it's easy to see why. Here the setting, a Gothic cellar with arched ceilings, is as pleasant as the food. The menu is heavy on Czech specialties and game, and service is attentive. If you're an oenophile, ask to see their historic wine cellars, or just order a bottle from the extensive wine list that includes regional Czech and French varieties. There are occasional wine-tasting events too. [$] *Average main: 200 Kč* ✉ *Peace Square, Mírové nám. 21, Litomerice* ☎ *731–422–013* 🌐 *www.radnicni-sklipek.cz.*

SOUTHERN
BOHEMIA

WELCOME TO SOUTHERN BOHEMIA

TOP REASONS TO GO

★ **Sense the enchantment:** Feel like a storybook character strolling through Český Krumlov.

★ **Loop around the streets:** Get lost among the tiny streets of Tábor.

★ **Take the bike lane to lunch:** Bike around and eat the fresh carp caught from the fishponds of Třeboň.

★ **Go for baroque:** Experience rustic baroque with a visit to the 19th-century living-museum village of Holašovice.

★ **Sip the suds:** Drink the local brew in České Budějovice, Český Krumlov, or Třeboň.

1 Český Krumlov. A fanciful city with a stunning castle and gardens: Český Krumlov is *the* must-see in Southern Bohemia.

2 Tábor. With streets designed to thwart invading armies, Tábor will lose you in its beauty and friendliness.

3 Písek. Strung along the river, the city with the oldest Gothic bridge in the country is also home to some great museums.

4 Třeboň. The spas of Southern Bohemia can be found in Třeboň. Peat-moss bath, anyone?

GETTING ORIENTED

Southern Bohemia is one of the most popular regions in the Czech Republic. Chock-full of castles and pretty cities with well-preserved squares, it's a favorite weekend getaway for many Prague locals. Well-marked hiking and biking trails encourage lots of sporty times, and it's easy for visitors to take part, since even some of the train stations rent bicycles. The towns themselves are active, too, and many hold a variety of festivals throughout the year. Being so close to Prague, several of these cities can be done in a day trip; but to get a true flavor of the town and its inhabitants, it's worth your time to stay over or spend a couple of days jumping between a few of the outer areas. The attractiveness of the landscape combined with cultural pursuits makes Southern Bohemia an amazing place to explore.

9

5 Jindřichův Hradec.
Authentic and attractive, Jindřichův Hradec is the perfect example of a true Southern Bohemian town: interesting castle, beautiful architecture, and real people.

6 Hluboká nad Vltavou.
A castle to die for. The fairy-tale hulk of turreted white can be seen for miles around.

7 České Budějovice.
Southern Bohemia's largest city, with a beautiful medieval square and lots of outdoor activities.

Updated by
Raymond
Johnston

Southern Bohemia calls itself the "pearl of the Czech Republic," and it's not just a clever nickname. The richness and beauty of this corner of the country bordering Germany and Austria are undisputable.

The natural landscape is lovely—soft rolling hills crisscrossed with rivers and dotted with ponds mark most of the territory—and the Šumava Mountains to the southwest are a popular ski destination. Coming from Prague, you'll cross the border somewhere north of Tábor, while heading east the indiscernible crossing to Moravia comes near to Telč. Forestry and fishing make up most of the area's important industry, with tourism and beer brewing more fun runners-up.

The history of the cities is intertwined with many an aristocratic name. The Hapsburgs, Rosenbergs, and Schwarzenbergs all had a large influence on the region, and their nobility is reflected in the area's many castles and beautifully preserved historic squares. The 15th century saw the territory wrapped up in the religious wars sparked by Jan Hus, whose reformist ways angered the Catholic Church and eventually led to his martyrdom. Evidence of the Hussite Wars in the mid-1400s is visible in Tábor.

Český Krumlov is the one must-see destination and often the only stop for visitors, which means huge crowds on summer weekends. The castle here rivals any monument in Prague.

PLANNING

WHEN TO GO

Southern Bohemia is a nature lover's paradise, and in nice weather it seems that the whole country heads here for cycling and hiking trips. Most of the main attractions are closed November through March, as well as Monday year-round, so winter will be quiet, but no less lovely in its snowy way. Many towns will host weekend Christmas markets, so December is a particularly pretty time. Note: roads get congested with weekenders on Friday and Sunday.

GETTING HERE

Trains normally depart from the Hlavní nádraží main station while buses leave from either the main Florenc station or the southern Roztyly station, accessible from a Metro stop on Line C (red). When exploring your transport options, look into private bus lines like RegioJet (also called Student Agency but its services are not just for students). They offer more direct routes, plus free hot drinks and videos onboard. Tickets must be purchased ahead of time; they have a window at the Florenc station.

GUIDED TOURS TO SOUTHERN BOHEMIA

Guided bus tours are available from several companies covering several of the destinations in Southern Bohemia. Most need to be booked at least a day in advance. These are only two of many organizers.

Čedok. The country's original tour operator offers a variety of longer trips through the region. Experiences include Český Krumlov, a spa visit in Třeboň, and combinations of other cities and even regions. ⊕ *www.cedok.com.*

Martin Tours. Information can be found at their booths at Staroměstské náměstí (Old Town Square), náměstí Republiky (Republic Square), Václavské náměstí (Wenceslas Square), and other locations in Prague. Southern Bohemia itineraries can include overnight stays or 10-hour excursions. Destinations include České Budějovice, Hluboká, and Český Krumlov. ⊕ *www.martintour.cz.*

RESTAURANTS AND HOTELS

Outside of Prague, prices for food and hotels are lower, but service—especially in functional English—sometimes lags behind. With Austria so close, you are much more likely to find German-language menus in restaurants and German-speaking staff in both restaurants and hotels. *Hotel reviews have been shortened. For full information, visit Fodors. com.*

WHAT IT COSTS IN KORUNA			
$	$$	$$$	$$$$
Restaurants	under 150 Kč	150 Kč–350 Kč	351 Kč–500 Kč	over 500 Kč
Hotels	under 2,200 Kč	2,200 Kč–4,000 Kč	4,001 Kč–6,500 Kč	over 6,500 Kč

Restaurant prices are the average cost of a main course at dinner, or if dinner is not served, at lunch. Hotel prices are the lowest cost of a standard double room in high season.

ČESKÝ KRUMLOV

48 km (29 miles) southwest of Třeboň; 186 km (112 miles) south of Prague.

It's rare that a place not only lives up to its hype but exceeds it. Český Krumlov, the official residence of the Rožmberk family for some 300 years, is such a place. It's the only must-see in Southern Bohemia, with a storybook landscape so perfect it resembles a movie set. Hordes of other tourists pass through, but if you stay overnight you can experience the city after the tour buses have departed, and in the evening when quiet descends, the town is twice as spellbinding.

Český Krumlov's lovely looks can be put down to a castle and a river. Krumlov castle is one of the most gorgeous in the country; perched on a hill watching over its quaint village with the Vltava River doing its picturesque winding best. The castle area offers plenty of sightseeing, and the extensive gardens are worth an hour or two. Down in the town, the medieval streets are beyond charming.

As in the rest of Southern Bohemia, outdoor activities are plentiful here. Check with the local tourist information office about places to rent bikes or rafts, or pick up an area hiking map.

GETTING HERE

A direct bus to Český Krumlov leaves Prague from both the Florenc and the Na Knížecí stations. The trip lasts a hair under three hours, and costs 215 Kč. There's no direct train; with a change at České Budějovice, a train trip clocks in at more than three hours and costs around 190 Kč. Note that the train station is a 20-minute hike from the main square, while the bus station is much closer. Your best choice would be to purchase a bus ticket at least a day or two before travel; Český Krumlov is a popular destination.

Car travel from Prague is fairly straightforward and takes three hours. Simply follow the directions to České Budějovice, and once there follow the signs to Český Krumlov. When you arrive in Český Krumlov you'll be confronted by a confusing array of public parking areas, with no indication of how close the parking lot is to the Old Town. One safe bet is to use Parking Lot No. 2, which if you follow the tiny lanes as far as they go, will bring you to just behind the town brewery, and an easy 10-minute walk from the main square.

VISITOR INFORMATION

Český Krumlov's tourist information office is on the main square. Well-versed and extremely helpful, the staff can assist you in everything from what to see to where to go. They can recommend restaurants and hotels as well as book tickets and assist with bus and train schedules, or even boat and bike travel.

The Vltava travel agency is a solid bet if you're considering outdoor activities. They'll rent boats and bikes as well as arrange excursions.

Information Český Krumlov Tourist Information. ⊠ *Nám. Svornosti 2* 🕾 *380–704–622* ⊕ *www.ckrumlov.cz.* **Vltava.** ⊠ *Hradební 60* 🕾 *380–711–988* ⊕ *www.ckvltava.cz.*

TIMING

Wintertime can be lonely in Český Krumlov, and most of the sites are closed, including the castle. On the flip side, avoid weekends in the summer; hordes of tourists, both Czech and German, flood the streets. Also, midday when the tour buses arrive can be a bit overwhelming. The city holds a Renaissance festival called the Five-Petaled Rose Celebration every June; an Early Music Festival and an International Music Festival in July; an Autumn Fair at the end of September; and a number of holiday events in December.

EXPLORING

TOP ATTRACTIONS

Egon Schiele Center. A large and rambling former brewery now showcases the work of Schiele along with other modern and contemporary Czech and European artists. The Renaissance building, built in three phases in the early 1600s, is a wonder, with soaring ceilings in some places and wooden-beamed rooms in others. Schiele often painted landscapes of Český Krumlov from the castle's bridge. The museum does close unexpectedly on occasion in winter, but is one of the only sites in town normally open year-round. ✉ *Široká 71* ☎ *380–704–011* ⊕ *www. schieleartcentrum.cz* ✑ *160 Kč.*

FAMILY

Fodor's Choice

★

Hrad Krumlov (*Krumlov Castle*). Like any good protective fortress, the castle is visible from a distance, but you may wonder how to get there. From the main square, take Radniční Street across the river and head up the staircase on your left from Latrán Street. (Alternatively, you can continue on Latrán and enter via the main gateway, also on your left.) You'll first come across the oldest part of the castle, a round 13th-century **tower** renovated in the 16th century to look something like a minaret, with its delicately arcaded Renaissance balcony. Part of the old border fortifications, the tower guarded Bohemian frontiers from the threat of Austrian incursion. It's now repainted with an educated guess of its Renaissance appearance, since the original designs have long been lost. From dungeon to bells, its inner secrets can be seen climbing the interior staircase. Go ahead and climb to the top; you'll be rewarded with a view of the castle grounds and across the countryside.

9

Next up is the moat, fearlessly protected by a pair of brown bears—truthfully not really much help in defending the castle; their moods range from playful to lethargic. But bears have been residents of this moat since 1707. In season, the castle rooms are open to the public. Crossing the bridge, you enter the second courtyard, which contains the ticket office. The Route 1 tour will parade you past the castle chapel, baroque suite, and Renaissance rooms. The highlights here are the 18th-century frescoes in the delightful **Maškarní Sál** (Masquerade Hall). Route 2 takes you through the portrait gallery and the seigneurial apartments of the Schwarzenbergs, who owned the castle until the Gestapo seized it in 1940. (The castle became state property in 1947.) In summer you can visit the Lapidarium, which includes statues removed from the castle for protection, and the dungeon.

A succession of owners all had the same thing in mind: upgrade the castle a bit more opulently than before. Vilém von Rožmberk oversaw a major refurbishment of the castle, adding buildings, heightening the tower, and adding rich decorations—generally making the place suitable for one of the grandest Bohemians of the day. The castle passed out of the Rožmberks' hands, however, when Vilém's brother and last of the line, the dissolute Petr Vok, sold both castle and town to Emperor

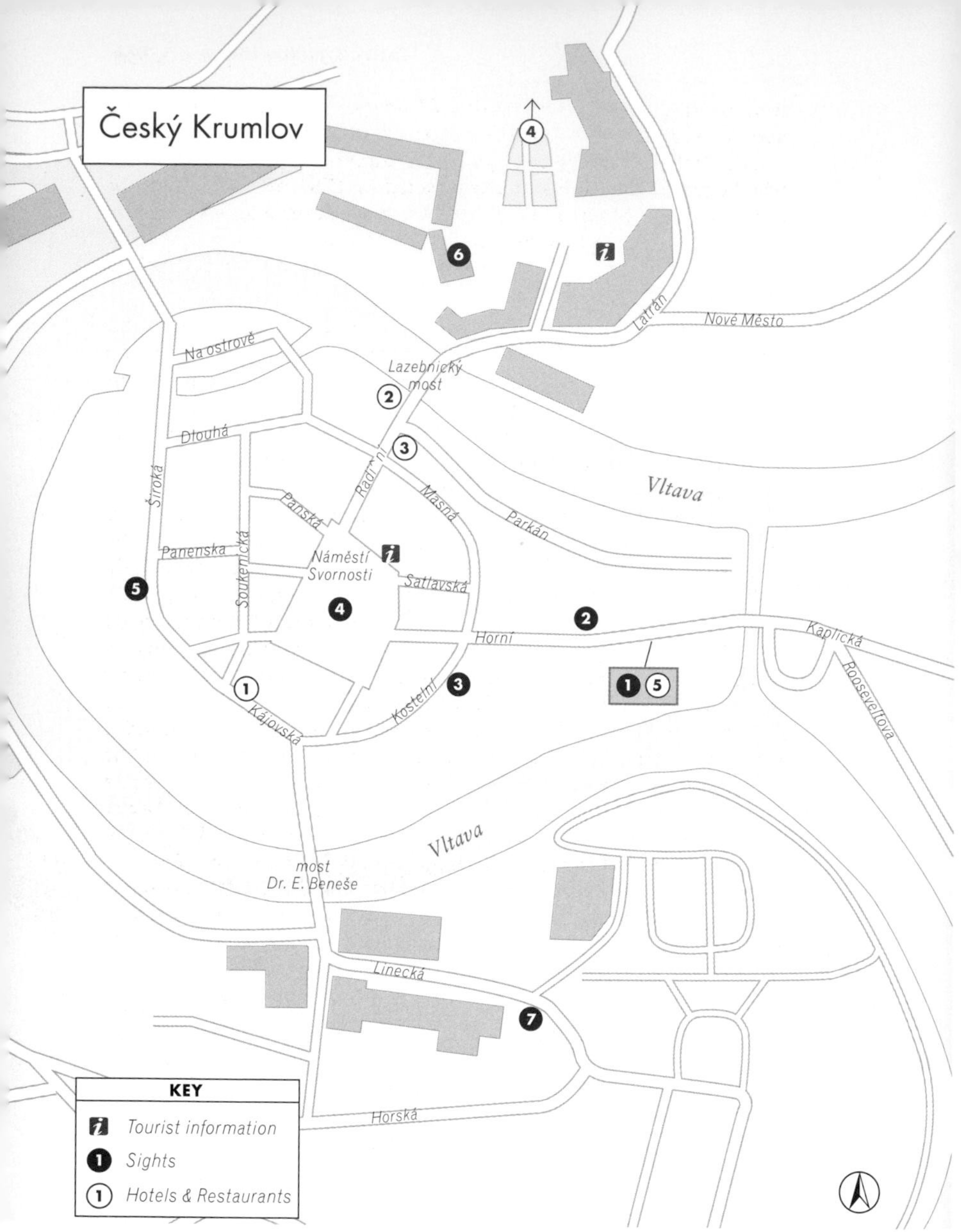

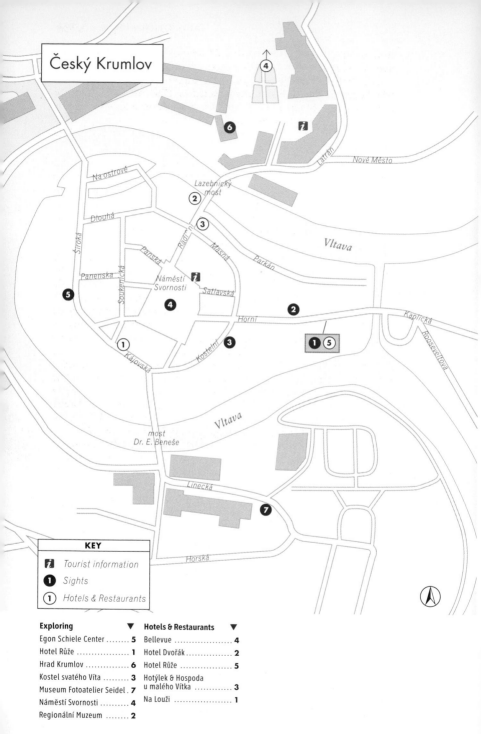

Český Krumlov
Na ostrově
Lazebnický most
Dlouhá
Široká
Radniční
Panská
Masná
Parkán
Vltava
Panenska
Soukenická
Náměstí Svornosti
Satlavská
Horní
Kaplická
Roosevelova
Kostelní
Kájovská
Latrán
Nové Město
Vltava
most Dr. E. Beneše
Linecká
Horská
KEY
Tourist information
Sights
Hotels & Restaurants

Exploring ▼

Egon Schiele Center **5**
Hotel Růže **1**
Hrad Krumlov **6**
Kostel svatého Víta **3**
Museum Fotoatelier Seidel . **7**
Náměstí Svornosti **4**
Regionální Muzeum **2**

Hotels & Restaurants ▼

Bellevue **4**
Hotel Dvořák **2**
Hotel Růže **5**
Hotýlek & Hospoda u malého Vítka **3**
Na Louži **1**

Rudolf II in 1602 to pay off his debts. Under the succeeding Eggenbergs and Schwarzenbergs the castle continued to be transformed into an opulent palace. The Eggenbergs' prime addition was a **theater**, which was begun in the 1680s and completed in 1766 by Josef Adam of Schwarzenberg. Much of the theater and its accoutrements—sets, props, costumes, stage machinery—survive intact as a rare working display of period stagecraft. Theater buffs will appreciate a tour, and tickets should be reserved in advance.

Continuing along outside, the third courtyard bears some beautiful Renaissance frescoes, while the fourth contains the Upper Castle, whose rooms can be visited on the tours. From here you'll arrive at a wonderfully romantic elevated passageway with spectacular views of the huddled houses of the Old Town. The Austrian expressionist painter Egon Schiele often stayed in Český Krumlov in the early 1900s, and liked to paint this particular view over the river; he titled his Krumlov series *Dead City*. The middle level here is the **most Na plášti** (Cloaked Bridge), a massive construction spanning a deep ravine. Below the passageway are three levels of high arches, looking like a particularly elaborate Roman viaduct. At the end of the passageway you come to the theater, then to the nicely appointed **castle garden** dating from the 17th century. A cascade fountain, groomed walking paths, flower-beds, and manicured lawns are a restful delight. The famed open-air **Revolving Theater** is here, as is the **Musical Pavilion**. If you continue walking away from the castle, the park grows a bit wilder and quieter. Unlike the castle, the courtyards and passageways are open to the public year-round. ⊠ *Zámek 59* ☎ *380–704–711* ⊕ *www.castle.ckrumlov.cz* 🎫 *Castle tours (in English): 250 Kč Route I, 240 Kč Route II. Theater tour (in English) 300 Kč. Tower 50 Kč, castle museum 100 Kč, garden free. Combination discounts available. Included on Český Krumlov Card* ☉ *Castle museum and tower closed Mon. Nov.–Mar.; no castle tours Mon. Apr.–Oct.; theater closed Nov.–mid-May; garden closed Nov.–Mar.*

WORTH NOTING

Hotel Růže. Gorgeous *sgraffiti* façades decorate this former Jesuit school, now the Hotel Růže. Abundant Renaissance flourishes point to the fact that the city used to be on the Bavarian-Italian trade route. Be sure to visit the parking area (really!); the view is perfect. ⊠ *Horní 154* ⊕ *ruze. hotel.cz.*

Kostel svatého Víta (*St. Vitus's Church*). This neo-Gothic church with its octagonal tower provides a nice contrast with the castle's older tower across the river. Step inside to see the elaborate baptismal font and frescoes. Much reconstruction took place in the 17th and 18th centuries; however, the Gothic entrance portal dates to 1410. ⊠ *Kostelní ul.* ⊕ *www.farnostck.bcb.cz.*

Museum Fotoatelier Seidel (*Seidel Photographic Studio Museum*). Head across the other side of the river from the castle and explore a more lived-in side of the city. This refurbished home used to belong to photographer Josef Seidel, and is now a museum dedicated to his work and the history of photography. The exhibit is a fascinating mix of home

9

DID YOU KNOW?

The picturesque historic center of Česky Krumlov has been a UNESCO World Heritage Site since 1992.

and workplace, with period furnishings plus photographic studio. The building itself is lovely, and includes a picturesque garden, and photography lovers will enjoy the historic camera collection plus samples of Seidel's work. ✉ *Linecká 272* ☎ *380–712–354* 🌐 *www.seidel.cz* 🎫 *100 Kč plus 30 Kč to take photographs; discount with Český Krumlov Card* 🕒 *Closed Mon. Jan.–Mar.*

Náměstí Svornosti (*Unity Square*). A little oddly shaped, yes, but a "square" nonetheless; Unity Square should be home base for your explorations. Pick a street and head off into the tiny alleys that fan out in all directions. There's no real sense in "planning" your route, simply choose a direction and go—you'll end up where you started eventually. Each turn seems to bring a new charming vista, and cute buildings and shops will amuse and keep shutterbugs busy. Don't forget to look up in the direction of the castle every once in a while; it pokes through in some amazing places. The actual square has a couple of notable buildings, including the Town Hall with its Renaissance friezes and Gothic arcades. ✉ *Cesk*ý *Krumlov.*

Regionální muzeum (*Regional Museum*). From the main square, a street called Horní ulice leads off toward the regional museum. A quick visit gets you acquainted with the history of the region from prehistoric times. A ceramic model of the city is one of the highlights. ✉ *Horní 152* ☎ *380–711–674* 🌐 *www.museum-krumlov.eu* 🎫 *50 Kč, discount with Český Krumlov Card.*

WHERE TO EAT

$$ CZECH Fodor's Choice ★ 🍴 **Na Louži.** Czech comfort food is served up every night at Na Louži. Lovingly preserved wood furniture and paneling lend a traditional touch to this warm, inviting, family-run pub. The food is unfussy yet satisfying. Look for the Czech specialties on the menu. (The 10 country-style rooms upstairs [$] are basic and cheap, perfect for a one-night stay; breakfast is included.) [$] *Average main: 200 Kč* ✉ *Kájovská 66* ☎ *380–711–280* 🌐 *www.hospodanalouzi.cz* 💳 *No credit cards* ✍ *Reservations essential.*

9

WHERE TO STAY

It seems you can't walk two blocks in Český Krumlov without stumbling over a pension or place offering private rooms. Even with this plethora, you'll need to book ahead May through September, when it's high season. Prices can be on a level with some Prague hotels, and definitely more expensive than in neighboring cities.

$ HOTEL 🏨 **Bellevue.** The façade of a 16th-century bakery gives way to a modern hotel with all the standard accessories. **Pros:** close to the castle; plentiful services available through the hotel. **Cons:** small breakfast room. [$] *Rooms from: 1400 Kč* ✉ *Latrán 77* ☎ *380–720–177* 🌐 *www.bellevuehotels.cz* 🛏 *59 rooms* 🍽 *Breakfast.*

$$ HOTEL 🏨 **Hotel Dvořák.** Wonderful views of the castle and river are the main selling points of this centrally located and quaint hotel. **Pros:** nice views; smack-dab central location. **Cons:** old-fashioned interior design; the

hotel restaurant could be better. [$] *Rooms from: 3900 Kč* ✉ *Radniční 101* ☎ *380–711–020* 🌐 *www.hoteldvorak.com* 🛏 *22 rooms, 4 apartments* 🍴 *Breakfast.*

$$ HOTEL Fodor's Choice ★ **Hotel Růže.** Converted from a Jesuit school, this excellent centrally located hotel with spacious rooms is a two-minute walk from the main square. **Pros:** central location; great views; quality restaurant. **Cons:** inconsistent bed layouts; baroque decorations are a bit overdone. [$] *Rooms from: 3050 Kč* ✉ *Horní 154* ☎ *380–772–100* 🌐 *www.hotelruze.cz* 🛏 *71 rooms* 🍴 *Breakfast.*

$ HOTEL **Hotýlek & Hospoda u malého Vítka.** Rooms are cleverly named after Czech fairy tales, with simple wooden furniture and fittings, and the folklore spirit extends throughout this hotel located between the main square and the castle. **Pros:** whimsical spirit; great value for the money. **Cons:** limited in-room amenities; rooms are simple and pared down; cramped bathrooms. [$] *Rooms from: 1600 Kč* ✉ *Radniční 27* ☎ *380–711–925* 🌐 *www.vitekhotel.cz* 🛏 *20 rooms* 🍴 *Breakfast.*

PERFORMING ARTS

Český Krumlov is a hotbed of cultural activity in summer. Events range from Renaissance fairs to music festivals. Activities to note include the International Music Festival held at the castle in July and August and summer performances at the open-air Revolving Theater. Opera and theater companies from České Budějovice perform here. Tickets can be prebooked (almost a necessity) by visiting 🌐 *www.otacivehlediste.cz*, or check with the tourist information offices in either Český Krumlov or České Budějovice. The website also has information on an app called Overtekst that allows people to follow a translation of the show's dialogue on a phone or tablet that runs an Android OS. The Český Krumlov office can also tell you about any other concerts or events happening while you are in town.

EN ROUTE

Hrad Rožmberk (*Rosenberg Castle*). This sprawling castle overlooks the Vltava River, about 20 km (12 miles) south of Český Krumlov. Inside, on the main tour, you'll see a mix of Romantic and Renaissance interiors; portraits of crusaders; and the Rosenberg Hall, dedicated to the family's history. The second route shows the apartments of aristocrats. The English Tower is a 200-step climb, and rewards with beautiful vistas of the countryside. English-language tours on Routes 1 and 2 are available for groups only. The basement has a Museum of Capital Justice, but the information is only in Czech. Buses run from Český Krumlov's main depot but are infrequent on weekends. Legend has it that the ghost of a White Lady appears from time to time. ✉ *Rožmberk nad Vltavou* ☎ *380–749–838* 🌐 *www.hrad-rozmberk.eu* 🎫 *Castle tours (in English): 180 Kč Route 1, 130 Kč Route 2. Museum of Capital Justice 50 Kč, tower 40 Kč* 🕒 *No Route 1 tour Mon., and Nov.–Mar.; no Route 2 tour Mon., and Dec. Museum of Capital Punishment closed Sept.–May.*

NIGHTLIFE

Cikánská jizba. If you're in town on a Friday night, head over to this tiny Romany-owned pub; the name translates to Gypsy Tavern. Romany musicians play and Czechs pack the place for locally made cold beer. It can get very crowded, but there are no reservations. ✉ *Dlouhá 31* ☎ ⊕ *www.cikanskajizba.cz.*

TÁBOR

90 km (54 miles) south of Prague.

Looking at Tábor now, it's hard to believe that this was once a counter-culture utopia and fortress. Lucky for visitors a few centuries later, the town has retained all this turbulent history in its design and buildings.

In the 15th century the town began as an encampment for religious reformers centered on the teachings of the anti-Catholic firebrand preacher Jan Hus. After Hus was burned at the stake in Constance, his followers came here by the thousands to build a society opposed to the excesses of Rome and modeled on the primitive communities of the early Christians. Tábor quickly evolved into the Hussites' symbolic and spiritual center, and along with Prague served as the bulwark of the religious reform movement.

The 1420s in Tábor were heady days for the reformers. Private property was denounced, and the many poor who made the pilgrimage to Tábor were required to leave their possessions at the town gates. Some sects rejected the doctrine of transubstantiation (the belief that the Eucharistic elements become the body and blood of Christ), turning Holy Communion into a bawdy, secular feast of bread and wine. Other reformers considered themselves superior to Christ—who by dying had shown himself to be merely mortal.

War fever in Tábor ran high, and the town became one of the focal points of the Hussite Wars (1419–34), which pitted reformers against an array of foreign crusaders, Catholics, and noblemen. Military general Jan Žižka led the charge fairly successfully, but the Church proved to be stronger and wealthier. Many of the reformists' victories were assisted by the strategic location of Tábor, which with its hilltop position and river boundary made it virtually impregnable. And what nature didn't provide, the residents did. The town was well fortified and there was an ingenious system of underground tunnels (whether they were used to hide in or to store food in is disputed). The streets were purposely laid out in a crooked and confusing manner to thwart invaders. Glimpses of this past can still be seen, and make Tábor one of the more interesting places to visit.

GETTING HERE

Direct buses and trains to Tábor are available, and both take about 1½ hours. Buses leave from the Florenc station and cost about 100 Kč; trains cost about 129 Kč and depart from Hlavní nádraží. By car, the distance is about 90 km (56 miles) and should take a little more than an hour. You'll take the E55 heading south toward České Budějovice.

9

Visitor Information Tábor Tourist Information. ✉ *Žižkovo nám. 2*
☏ *381–486–230* ⊕ *www.tabor.cz.*

TIMING

Tábor is rarely overrun with tourists, which makes it a relaxing place
to see. It's a popular spot with cyclists, and summers always bring a
few more people. The South Bohemian Music Festival is held each
July. There's also a Christmas market in December. Their big event is
the Tábor Meeting Days, held at the beginning of September. This fun
medieval festival is incredibly popular. Crafts, music, entertainers, and
food all pack into the main square; there's even a parade.

EXPLORING

Hrad Kotnov (*Kotnov Castle*). Rising above the river in the distance,
this castle dates to the 13th century and was part of Tábor's earliest
fortifications. After a fire in the early 1600s the castle was rebuilt as a
brewery. You can visit the tower, which the Hussites used for storing
artillery, as well as Bechyňská brána (Bechyně Gate). This is the last city
gate still standing, and has been preserved in its original High Gothic
style. Inside is an exhibit titled *Life and Work of Medieval Society.* Night
tours of the castle and tower are sometimes available. ✉ *Klokotská*
☏ *381–252–242* ⊕ *www.husitskemuzeum.cz* ▤ *Tower and gate 30 Kč*
⊙ *Closed Oct.–Apr.*

Husitské muzeum (*Hussite Museum*). You can find out all you ever
wanted to know about the Hussite movement and the founding and
history of the city. The museum is housed in the Old Town Hall, a
building that dates back to the early 1500s. You can also enter the
extensive labyrinth of tunnels below the Old Town here. A tour of the
tunnels takes about 20 minutes. There's also a Gothic Hall and occasional short-term exhibits. ✉ *Žižkovo nám. 1* ☏ *381–252–242* ⊕ *www.*
husitskemuzeum.cz ▤ *Museum tour 60 Kč, tunnel tour 50 Kč, Gothic*
Hall 20 Kč; combined tour 100 Kč ⊙ *Closed Sun.–Tues. Oct.–May.*

Pražská ulice. The main route to the newer part of town, this street is
delightfully lined with beautiful Renaissance façades. If you turn right
at Divadelní and head to the Lužnice River, you can see the remaining
walls and fortifications of the 15th century, evidence of the town's function as a vital stronghold.

Žižkovo náměstí (*Žižka Square*). There's no doubt who this square
belongs to—a bronze statue of Jan Žižka dominates the area and clearly
points to its Hussite past. The stone tables in front of the Gothic town
hall and the house at No. 6 date to the 15th century, and were used by
the Hussites to give daily communion to the faithful. Many fine houses
that line the square bear plaques describing their architectural style and
original purpose. Be sure to stroll the tiny streets around the square,
as they curve around, branch off, and then stop; few lead back to the
main square. This bemusing layout, created in the 15th century, was
designed to thwart incoming invaders. ✉ *Tábor.*

Side streets leading off Tábor's town square are purposely confusing in order to protect the center from incoming invasions.

WHERE TO EAT

$$ AMERICAN — 🍴 **Havana.** Right on the square, this café-bar has a superb atmosphere, if oddly resembling an English pub, and serves up tasty plates of steaks, grilled meat, burgers, and chicken. [$] *Average main: 200 Kč* ✉ *Žižkovo nám. 17* ☎ *381–253–383* 🌐 *www.kafehavana.cz.*

9

WHERE TO STAY

$ HOTEL — 🏨 **Dvořák.** A bit outside the city center, this former brewery building has been thoroughly renovated into one of the nicest places in town. **Pros:** modern rooms; efficient, helpful staff; on-site beer spa. **Cons:** can be busy during conferences. [$] *Rooms from: 1800 Kč* ✉ *Hradební 3037* ☎ *381–207–211* 🌐 *www.dvoraktabor.cz* 🛏 *72 rooms, 12 suites* 🍽 *Breakfast.*

$$ HOTEL Fodor's Choice ★ — 🏨 **Nautilus.** This tasteful boutique hotel on the edge of Tábor's charming central square exhibits touches of Bohemian craftsmanship in the architecture, beautiful antiques in the rooms, and elegant, original art on the walls (think shells). **Pros:** great eats; best address in town; rooms with genuine Bohemian flair. **Cons:** some rooms are a little dark; breakfast spread not as great as the food at the restaurant. [$] *Rooms from: 2850 Kč* ✉ *Žižkovo nám. 20* ☎ *380–900–900* 🌐 *www.hotelnautilus.cz* 🛏 *22 rooms* 🍽 *Breakfast.*

PÍSEK

44 km (28 miles) west of Tábor; 103 km (62 miles) south of Prague.
Písek is a bit of a surprise. It used to be that people came for one thing: Písek's 700-year-old Gothic bridge peopled with baroque statues. But a recent infusion of European Union funds has introduced some beautiful upgrades. The former mill and power station is now a museum dedicated to electricity, and a former malt house is a cultural house and art museum. There's a promenade that runs along the river beside the old city wall, and the square around the church is nothing short of lovely. They've changed the former Gothic moat into a tiny park, and even the city museum displays some interesting finds.

GETTING HERE
Buses leave from Prague's Na Knížecí station, and will take you there for around 100 Kč in approximately 90 minutes. Trains leave from Prague's Hlavní nádraží and cost 225 Kč, with the trip taking over two hours. If you drive, the trip should take no more than 90 minutes.

Visitor Information Písek Tourist Information. ⊠ *Velké nám. 113* ☎ *387-999-999* ⊕ *www.pisek.eu.*

TIMING
Písek means "sand," and back before the city was a city, people used to pan for gold in the river. From mid-May to the beginning of June the city displays sand sculptures honoring their namesake. There's a town festival every June and a folklore festival at the end of August.

EXPLORING

Gothic Bridge. Once the city's only claim to fame, this bridge is a site to see. It was built in the 1260s—making it the oldest bridge in the Czech Republic, surpassing Prague's Charles Bridge by 90 years. Not too shabby. Přemysl Otakar II commissioned it, seeking a secure crossing for his salt shipments over the difficult-to-ford Otava River. As early as the 9th century, Písek stood at the center of one of the most important trade routes to the west, linking Prague to Passau and the rest of Bavaria. In the 15th century it became one of five major Hussite strongholds. The statues of saints weren't added to the bridge until the 18th century. During the devastating floods of 2002 one of the statues was damaged, and all the paving stones washed away, but divers recovered most of the lost pieces. The statues on the bridge are not the originals. You can reach the bridge from třída Národní svobody on the left bank or Karlova Street from the right bank. ⊠ *Karlova St.*

Mariánský chrám (*Church of the Virgin*). Just off the main square, this church is the highlight of the recently renovated Bakaláře Square. You can't miss the 240-foot tower, which is open for a climb. Construction began in the late 1200s, about the time the bridge was built. The lone surviving tower was completed in 1487. On the inside, look for the *Madonna of Písek,* a 14th-century Gothic altar painting. On a middle pillar is a rare series of early-Gothic wall paintings dating from the end of the 13th century. ■ TIP➔ Ask about a tower visit at the Písek Tourist

Information Center. ✉ *Bakaláře at Leoše Janáčka* 🌐 *www.farnostpisek.cz.*

Prácheňské Muzeum. Inside a 13th-century castle's frescoed medieval halls, this museum documents the history of Písek and its surroundings, including the Czech fishing industry (with the additional original touch of live fish in large aquarium) and the history of local gold panning and mining in the nearby hills. There are two galleries devoted to temporary exhibits. Everything is in Czech, but ask for an info sheet in English. ✉ *Velké nám. 114* ☎ *382–201–111* 🌐 *www.prachenskemuzeum.cz* 🎟 *40 Kč, 20 Kč fee for photography* 🕓 *Closed Mon., and Jan. and Feb.*

FAMILY **Sladovna.** Písek has a brewing history dating back to the Middle Ages. This malt house was built in the 19th century, and continued producing malt for 100 years. In 2008 the city opened Sladovna, a cultural facility that houses two permanent exhibitions and five showrooms for temporary ones. There's a spot for inspired kids to color, a reading area, plus an igloo that shows fairy tales. It's all in Czech, but children should appreciate the bright colors and great graphics. ✉ *Velké nám. 113* ☎ *387–999–999* 🌐 *www.sladovna.cz* 🎟 *120 Kč.*

WHERE TO STAY

$ HOTEL 🏨 **Hotel Biograf.** A design-conscious hotel with an award-winning restaurant is a rare find in Písek; don't be put off by the plain exterior, the interior is surprisingly modern. **Pros:** large rooms; good location; all amenities. **Cons:** exterior low on charm; not a lot in the area to keep you overnight. [$] *Rooms from: 1800 Kč* ✉ *Gregorova 124* ☎ *380–425–510* 🌐 *www.hotelbiograf.com* 🛏 *44 rooms, 3 suites* 🍴 *Breakfast.*

EN ROUTE **Zvíkov.** In a country overrun with castles, Zvíkov lays claim to being the most famous early Gothic one. Everyone needs its marketing hook, but Zvíkov is interesting enough thanks to its location on two rivers and its authenticity. Unlike many other castles in Bohemia, this one survived the 18th and 19th centuries without renovation, and still looks exactly as it did 500 years ago. If you have the time, you can cycle here from Písek or jump on a boat and float downriver to another nearby castle, Orlík. ✉ *Rte. 138, 18 km (11 miles) north of Písek* ☎ *382–285–676* 🌐 *www.hrad-zvikov.eu* 🎟 *70 Kč* 🕓 *Closed Mon., and Nov.–Mar.*

TŘEBOŇ

48 km (28 miles) south of Tábor; 138 km (83 miles) south of Prague.

Třeboň, like Tábor, is off the international tourist trail, but it's a favorite with cyclists. And the town offers an appealing mix of adorable old buildings and authentic workaday local life.

Třeboň itself is a charming jewel box of a town. It was settled during the 12th century by the Wittkowitzes (later called the Rožmberks, or Rosenbergs), once Bohemia's noblest family. You can see their emblem, a five-petal rose, on castles, doorways, and coats of arms all over the region. Their official residence was 40 km (25 miles) to the southwest, in Český Krumlov, but Třeboň was an important second residence and repository of the family archives, which still reside in the town's châ-teau. The main square, Masarykovo náměstí, is a pleasing arrangement of baroque and Renaissance structures. Various markets pop up here all through the summer, and the Town Hall has notable frescoes.

To Czechs, Třeboň and carp are almost synonymous. If you're in the area in late autumn, you may be lucky enough to witness the great carp harvests, when tens of thousands of the glittering fish are netted from ponds in the surrounding area. Traditionally, they are served breaded and fried as the centerpiece of Christmas Eve dinner. But regardless of the season, you'll find carp on every menu in town. Don't be afraid to order it; the carp here are not the notorious bottom-feeders they are elsewhere, but are raised in clean ponds and served as a fresh catch with none of that muddy aftertaste.

One of the most pleasant activities here is a walk around the **Rybník Svět** (World Pond), an easy 12-km (7½-mile) trail that takes you through grassy fields and forests. When taking the walk (or as a destination itself), visit the Schwarzenberg Family Vault. Built in English Gothic style; it's a bit startling at first, but then seems to blend into its woody environs. If you'd rather not walk, 45-minute boat tours go around the lake about once an hour (in season and weather permitting). There's a variety of other walks and lots of cycle paths in the region; ask at the tourist information office for recommended routes and maps.

Along with the ponds, the region is known for its peat bogs. This has given rise to a local spa industry, and wellness weekends are popular attractions at the city's two main spas; **Bertiny Lázně** (☎ *384–754–111* ⊕ *www.berta.cz*) and **Lázně Aurora** (☎ *800–611–009* ⊕ *www.aurora.cz*). A variety of treatments are on offer, but both do peat massages. A dip in the iron-rich squishy substance is supposed to help with arthritis and other joint problems. But the sensation and smell are acquired tastes.

GETTING HERE
There is no direct bus service to Třeboň. Trains depart from the main station, and a change will be required in Veselí and cost around 190 Kč. Be sure to ask to go to the Třeboň lázné station versus the main Třeboň station, and save yourself a 20-minute walk into town.

Visitor Information Třeboň Tourist Information. ✉ *Masarykovo nám. 103* ☎ *384–721–169* ⊕ *www.itrebon.cz.*

EXPLORING

Bílý Koníček. Look for the Little White Horse, the best-preserved Renaissance house on the square, dating to 1544. It's now a modest hotel and restaurant—the perfect spot to enjoy some excellent local beer. ✉ *Masarykovo nám. 97* ☎ *384–721–213* ⊕ *bilykonicekhotel.cz.*

Kostel svatého Jiljí (*Church of St. Giles*). The Gothic style of South Bohemia is exemplified in this curious church. The unassuming exterior gives no clue to the vastness inside, nor the treasures it holds. Paintings in Czech Gothic style can be found by the main altar, also other artwork and frescoes dating as far back as the late 15th century. ✉ *Husova.*

Zámek Třeboň (*Třeboň Château*). The entrance to this château lies at the southwest corner of the square. From the outside the white walls make it appear restrained, but the inner courtyard is covered with *sgraffito*. There's a variety of tours of the interior, which boasts sumptuous re-creations of the Renaissance lifestyle enjoyed by the Rožmberks and apartments furnished in late-19th-century splendor. The gardens adjacent to the castle are well maintained and free to stroll in. The last of the Rožmberks died in 1611, and the castle eventually became the property of the Schwarzenberg family, who built their family tomb in a grand park on the other side of Svět Pond. It's now a monumental neo-Gothic destination for Sunday-afternoon picnickers. It's well worth the easy stroll along the lake to visit this tomb; summer concerts are held here occasionally. In the summer you can tour inside of a kitchen for preparing dogs' meals, a stable and casemates (part of the fortifications) with tunnels. The dogs' kitchen is a rarity and was for the noble family's pampered pets and working dogs. ✉ *Masarykovo nám.* ☎ *384–721–193* 🌐 *www.zamek-trebon.eu* 🎟 *Tour of family tomb 100 Kč with English explanation; tour of apartments 180 Kč; tour of renaissance interiors 180 Kč; casemates, stable, dog kitchen 70 Kč; Schwarzenberg tomb 60 Kč* 🕓 *Closed Mon., and Nov.–mid-Mar.; casemates closed Sept.–June.*

WHERE TO EAT

$$ MODERN EUROPEAN

🍴 **Šupinka.** In a city surrounded by fish; this is where the locals come to enjoy theirs. A stylish interior with floor-to-ceiling wooden arches and a small terrace serve as the backdrops to some creative cooking. There are some interesting chicken and pork dishes. Still, the majority of the menu focuses on *kapr* (carp), including a "demon" carp filled with Dijon mustard and chilies, and grass carp with lard and onions. There is a sister restaurant called Šupina nearby. [$] *Average main: 290 Kč* ✉ *Valy 56* ☎ *384–721–149* 🌐 *www.supina.cz* ✍ *Reservations essential.*

9

WHERE TO STAY

The tourist information center on the square is very helpful when it comes to booking rooms. They also offer a catalog of hotel options that includes amenities and prices to help narrow your choice.

$ HOTEL

🏨 **Romantick.** "Flower power" is the theme at this boutique hotel, as each room is named and designed after a flower; and some also offer nice views of the city. **Pros:** lots of amenities for this area. **Cons:** on the outskirts of the city, in an unattractive area; not all rooms have air-conditioning. [$] *Rooms from: 1390 Kč* ✉ *K Bertě 183* ☎ *725–135–888* 🌐 *www.romantick.cz* 🛏 *26 rooms* 🍽 *Breakfast.*

JINDŘICHŮV HRADEC

28 km (17 miles) southwest of Třeboň; 158 km (95 miles) south of Prague.

The ancient town of Jindřichův Hradec, which dates to the end of the 12th century, is mirrored in the reflective waters of the Vajgar Pond right in the town's center. Originally a market colony near the border between Bohemia and Moravia, the town acquired a castle to protect it, and it's the main attraction here as the third-largest castle in the country. (The interior, now an administrative center, is less interesting.) Other attractions include a town square with Gothic, Renaissance, and some baroque aspects, a regional museum, and excursions into the countryside.

Like other South Bohemian towns, this region is a popular spot for cyclists and hikers. If the countryside appeals to you but you're lacking the footpower to explore it, hitch a ride on the Narrow Gauge Railway (⊕ *www.jhmd.cz*). Trains depart daily in July and August from the city's main train station. The rails are a mere 760 millimeters apart, and the route winds south nearly to the border with Austria.

GETTING HERE

Jindřichův Hradec is about three hours from Prague. The train from Prague's Hlavní nádraží (main station) will require a change at Veselí. It costs about 215 Kč. There is no good direct bus connection.

Visitor Information Jindřichův Hradec Tourist Information. ⊠ *Panská 136* ☎ *384-363-546* ⊕ *infocentrum.jh.cz.*

TIMING

A laid-back vibe flows through Jindřichův Hradec. Winters feel isolated, but summers bring lots of cyclists to the area. The Day of the City festival is held at the castle every June, while the big summertime festivities happen during the Folk Rose Festival in mid-July.

EXPLORING

Jindřichův Hradec's Castle. As the third-largest castle in the Czech Republic, this is the dominant structure in town, holding 300 rooms and 10,000 pieces of art. Behind the courtyard and its elegant Italian arcades, the castle's core is pure Gothic splendor, reflected not only in its thick defensive walls and round tower but also in the **frescoes** covering interior corridors. Colorful examples of medieval coats of arms and a panorama depicting the legend of St. George date to 1338. Over the course of centuries, buildings of an adjoining Renaissance-era château were added to the early Gothic castle, together forming a large complex. There are three different marked routes through the castle for visitors to follow. Tour A is best for design lovers: you'll visit the Adam building, which includes glimpses of Renaissance, baroque, rococo, Empire, and classical styles, as well as see numerous paintings from a previous owner's vast collection. Tour B takes you to the castle's Gothic and medieval core, the Chapel of the Holy Spirit, and the Royal Hall. Tour C offers the opportunity to visit 18th- and 19th-century apartments as well as the Rondel, a bit of an architectural oddity set in this Gothic scene, designed by an Italian in the 16th century. The official term for the decor is "European Mannerism," but it really resembles a big pink cake with confectionary images of aristocratic dancers and musicians. Built as a ballroom, this space still hosts the occasional concert. Wander the exterior courtyards for free, or simply climb the Black

Tower for a view of the castle and surrounding area. ✉ *Dobrovského 1* ☎ *384-321-279* ⊕ *www.zamek-jindrichuvhradec.eu* ☙ *Castle tours (in Czech only): 100 Kč Tour A, 90 Kč Tour B, 90 Kč Tour C. Black Tower 30 Kč* ☉ *Closed Mon., and Nov.–Apr.*

Kostel Nanebevzetí Panny Marie (*Church of the Ascension of Our Lady*). Dating to the second half of the 14th century, this church and its tower are the other dominating features of the city's skyline. It's a Gothic triple-nave church with some interesting elements, including a Gothic Madonna from the beginning of the 15th century. By coincidence, the church straddles the 15th meridian, and you'll see a line marking the point. The city tower is also open for those wishing to scale 157 steps for an extensive view of the surrounding area. ✉ *Za kostelem* ☙ *Tower 20 Kč* ☉ *Tower closed Oct.–Mar., and weekdays in Apr., May, and Sept.*

Kostel svatého Jana Křtitele (*Church of St. John the Baptist*). The oldest church in town, built between the 13th and 16th centuries, this is an excellent example of Bohemian Gothic architecture. Inside, extensive frescoes in the clerestory date to the first half of the 14th century, and portray scenes from the lives of Christ, the Apostles, and various Czech saints. They also demonstrate the medieval necessity for pictorial narratives in educating the illiterate population. On the south side of the sanctuary you can see the Chapel of St. Nicholas, built in 1369. The vaulted ceiling is supported by a single central pillar; this is one of the earliest buildings using this construction in Bohemia. The church is open to the public in July and August; the adjacent monastery is now part of the city museum, and hosts temporary exhibitions. ✉ *Štítného* ☙ *30 Kč* ☉ *Closed Sept.–June.*

Muzeum Jindřichohradecka. Founded in 1882, this museum's big draw is its impressive Nativity scene. The huge, mechanical créche was built by one committed craftsman, Mr. Krýza, who dedicated more than 60 years to its creation in the latter part of the 19th century. The old mechanism has now been replaced with an electrical system, but the primitive charm of the moving figures remains. Amazingly, the scene contains 1,398 figures. Other exhibitions in the former Jesuit seminary include an apothecary. ✉ *Balbínovo nám. 19* ☎ *384-363-660* ⊕ *www.mjh.cz* ☙ *60 Kč, exhibitions 20 Kč* ☉ *Closed Mon. Apr.–Dec.*

Národní muzeum fotografie (*National Photography Museum*). This former Jesuit college now houses the foremost photography institution in the country. Reconstructed interiors rival the photos on display—the wall and ceiling frescoes have been lovingly restored. The permanent collection includes more than 200 photos donated by Czech photographers. Attached to the museum is the Chapel of St. Mary Magdalene, which occasionally hosts concerts. ✉ *Kostelní 20* ☎ *384-362-459* ⊕ *www.mfmom.cz* ☙ *90 Kč* ☉ *Closed Mon., and Jan.–Mar.*

WHERE TO STAY

$
HOTEL

▥ **Hotel Bílá paní.** Situated next to the castle, this cozy hotel takes its name from a ghost legend—and its otherwise comfortable rooms are alleged to be haunted. **Pros:** cheap and cheerful; castle views. **Cons:** rooms are sweet but spare; bathroom size and placement is a bit unorthodox.

9

Jindřichův Hradec has a cluster of historic buildings including a castle that features the European Mannerism style.

$ Rooms from: 1340 Kč ⊠ Dobrovského 5 ☎ 384–363–329 ⊕ www. hotelbilapani.cz ↗ 11 rooms ❢❍❢ Breakfast.

$ ☷ **Hotel Concertino.** Right on the town square, this historical-looking
HOTEL   hotel with a modern interior lets you spring directly into sightseeing
action. **Pros:** near the town square; expressive furnishings; plentiful
services for business travelers. **Cons:** decor is expressive but not necessarily cohesive; restaurant is hit or miss. $ Rooms from: 1350 Kč
⊠ Nám. Míru 141 ☎ 384–362–320 ⊕ www.concertino.cz ↗ 31 rooms,
3 suites ❢❍❢ Breakfast.

HLUBOKÁ NAD VLTAVOU

*17 km (10½ miles) southwest of Třeboň; 155 km (93½ miles) south
of Prague.*

Yes, Hluboká has a massive fairy-tale castle that can be seen for miles
around. But active outdoorsy types should come here for the excellent
sport center that offers tennis, golf, an adrenaline center, and more.
Cycling is easy for a brief nature break.

GETTING HERE

The journey from Prague to Hluboká—either by train from the Hlavní
nádraží (main station) or by bus from the Florenc station—is 2½ hours
unless you get one of the local connections that stops in every small
town (in which case the trip takes 3½ hours). The train ticket costs
about 250 Kč, the bus ticket 170 Kč; both require a change in České
Budějovice. There is also a direct bus from the Roztyly depot in Prague
for about 160 Kč. You may find it more convenient to stay overnight

in České Budějovice and see the castle in the morning after a 10-minute train trip. Alternatively, there's a 10-km (6-mile) cycle path.

Visitor Information Hluboká nad Vltavou Tourist Center. ✉ *Zborovská 80* ☎ *387–966–164* ⊕ *www.hluboka.cz.*

EXPLORING

FAMILY **Lovecká chata Ohrada** (*Ohrada Hunting Lodge*). Care for a brisk walk? Follow the yellow trail signs 2 km (1 mile) to the Ohrada Hunting Lodge, which houses a museum of hunting and fishing and is near a small children's zoo. ■**TIP**➜ **The lodge and the zoo have the same entrance.** ✉ *Zamék Ohrada 1, off Rte. 105* ☎ *387–965–340* ⊕ *www. nzm.cz/en/ohrada* ✉ *90 Kč, individual exhibits 50 Kč* ☉ *Closed Feb., Mar., Nov., and Dec., and Mon. Apr.–June, Sept., and Oct.*

Fodor's Choice **Státní zámek Hluboká** (*State Château Hluboká*). Hluboká's main focus
★ is its castle, with a cluster of white towers flanking its walls, and tour groups pop in and out regularly. Although the structure dates to the 13th century, what you see is pure 19th-century excess, perpetrated by the wealthy Schwarzenberg family attempting to prove their good taste. If you think you've seen this castle somewhere before, you're probably thinking of Windsor Castle, near London, which served as the template. Take a tour; the happy hodgepodge of styles in the interior reflects the no-holds-barred tastes of the time. On Tour A you'll see representative rooms, including the stunning morning salon and library. Tour B brings you into the private apartments and hunting salon, while Tour C takes you into the kitchen. Tour D is available daily only in July and August, and weekends only in June and September, and shows off the tower and chapel. Check out the wooden Renaissance ceiling in the large dining room, which was removed by the Schwarzenbergs from the castle at Český Krumlov and brought here. Also look for the beautiful late-baroque bookshelves in the library. The gardens are free to wander in. ✉ *Zamék 142* ☎ *387–843–911* ⊕ *www.zamek-hluboka.eu* ✉ *Tour A: 250 Kč. Tour B: 230 Kč. Tour C: 170 Kč. Winter tour: 230 Kč (tours with English commentary, audio headsets also available). Tour D: 40 Kč* ☉ *Closed Mon. Sept.–June.*

Galerie Mikoláše Alše (*Aleš Art Gallery*). Located near the chateau, the region's museum for art history displays a variety of works including sculpture, paintings, and porcelain. It's one of the most extensive collections of Gothic art in the country, and temporary exhibitions range from modern to contemporary. ✉ *Hluboká nad Vltavou čp. 144* ⊕ *www.ajg.cz* ✉ *70 Kč.*

Sportovně relaxační areál (*Sport-Relax Area*). Hluboká is working hard to offer visitors something beyond their castle, and this extensive sports complex is a complete change of pace. Here you can golf, play tennis or volleyball, rent Rollerblades or other sports equipment, test your bravery (and fitness level) in the "adrenaline park" (think a massive ropes course, unicycles, and a bungee trampoline), watch the local hockey team play in the stadium, or even catch a baseball game or soccer match. The park offers a playground for kids, plus a restaurant

Státní zámek Hluboká has echoes of England's Windsor Castle.

with a huge terrace. It backs up to the woods, so you can take off for a short hike as well. There's also a restaurant and a hotel. ⊠ *Sportovní 1276* ☎ *723–584–866* ⊕ *www.sport-hluboka.cz* ⊙ *Sports center closed Mon.–Thurs. Apr.–Oct.; restaurant closed Apr.–May and Mon. in Oct.*

ČESKÉ BUDĚJOVICE

26 km (16 miles) southwest of Třeboň; 164 km (99 miles) south of Prague.

České Budějovice is the largest city in Southern Bohemia, but it's more of a transportation hub and not nearly as charming as the neighboring towns. Still, a couple of interesting spots ensure that you won't be bored if you have a stopover, and you probably will. Schedule a couple of extra hours for a wander through the Old Town and a lunch break, and pause to sip the locally brewed Budvar.

The enormously proportioned main square, named after King Přemysl Otakar II, is lined with arcaded houses. The stunning Old Town Hall is from the 16th century. Designed by an Italian, it has bells in the tower that chime old South Bohemian tunes at the top of every hour. Another attraction is the central fountain from the 18th century. Be sure to look for the "magic stone," the lone cobblestone in the brick-covered square. Legend has it that if you step on this stone after 10 pm, you'll become lost. But the town's real claim to fame is its beer—the slightly sweet-ish Budvar.

GETTING HERE

The trip from Prague takes about two hours by either bus or train. Be careful to choose a *rychlík* (express train), not an *osobní* (passenger train), which would make your journey four hours. Trains leave from the Hlavní nádraží (main station) and cost about 165 Kč; buses leave from both Florenc and Na Knížecí and cost 165 Kč–170 Kč. Car travel (about 2½ hours) affords the greatest ease and flexibility. České Budějovice lies on the main artery through the region, the two-lane E55 south from Prague, which, though often crowded, is in relatively good shape.

Visitor Information České Budějovice Tourist Center. ⊠ *Nám. Přemysla Otakára II 2* 🕾 *386–801–413* ⊕ *www.c-budejovice.cz.*

EXPLORING

Budějovický Budvar brewery. Tours of the brewery start at the modern glass-enclosed visitor center. On the 60-minute route, you'll see the wells that source the water, the brew house, and other parts of the process up to the bottling plant. A beer tasting is included at the end of the tour. Advanced booking (online) is required. ⊠ *Karolíny Světlé 4* 🕾 *387–705–347* ⊕ *www.visitbudvar.cz* 🖃 *120 Kč* ☉ *Closed Sun.–Mon. Jan–Feb.*

Černá věž (*Black Tower*). To get a good view over the city, climb the 225 steps up to the Renaissance gallery of the Black Tower at the northeast corner of the square next to St. Nicholas's Cathedral. Don't look for a Black Tower; it's actually white, but got the nickname after a fire left some charred marks. ⊠ *Nám. Přemysla Otakara II* 🖃 *30 Kč* ☉ *Closed Nov.–Mar., and Mon. Apr.–Oct.*

Jihočeské Museum. You can't miss the imposing neo-Renaissance building of the Museum of Southern Bohemia. It was originally founded in 1877 in a small building next to the town hall, but generous donors flooded the facility with so many artifacts that the space had to be expanded. The major exhibits include theme collections portraying the history of the town and the region through an extensive variety of artifacts including metalwork, ceramics, glass, and furniture. A fascinating large-scale model shows the Old Town and its picturesque medieval walls and towers. A regular series of temporary exhibits also runs alongside the permanent ones. ⊠ *Dukelská 1* 🕾 *391–001–531* ⊕ *www.muzeumcb.cz* 🖃 *60 Kč* ☉ *Closed Mon.*

Koněspřežka. A source of pride for České Budějovice, Koněspřežka is the oldest railway station on the continent. Designed to transport salt to Bohemia from Linz in Austria, a horse-drawn railway was built between 1825 and 1832. One of the first major industrial developments in Europe, it reduced the journey between Linz and České Budějovice from two weeks to four days. Public transport was introduced soon afterward. The station is now a part of the city museum, and houses an exhibit dedicated to the horse-drawn railroad. You can also pick up a brochure from the tourist office that details other buildings throughout town that played a role in the transport. ✉ *Mánesova 10* ☎ *386–354–820* 🌐 *www.muzeumcb.cz* 🎟 *30 Kč* 🕒 *Closed Mon.*

WHERE TO EAT

$$ CZECH 🍴 **Masné krámy.** Operated by the Budvar brewery, the restaurant—a former butcher's market—aims for an upscale yet casual atmosphere with reasonably priced food and is now one of the best restaurants in town. It specializes in great Czech food and serves unpasteurized Budvar beer; fish and game are also on the menu. [$] *Average main: 200 Kč* ✉ *Krajinská 13* ☎ *387–201–301* 🌐 *www.masne-kramy.cz* ✍ *Reservations essential.*

WHERE TO STAY

$$ HOTEL 🏨 **Hotel Budweis.** Situated next to the river in a former mill, this beautifully restored grand hotel has exposed wooden beams, polished floors, and loads of natural light. **Pros:** nicest hotel in town. **Cons:** cheaper options available. [$] *Rooms from: 2990 Kč* ✉ *Mlýnská 6* ☎ *389–822–111* 🌐 *www.hotelbudweis.cz* 🛏 *59 rooms, 1 suite* 🍽 *Breakfast.*

PERFORMING ARTS

The city has its own theater, ballet, opera, and orchestra that put on a variety of performances throughout the year. The South Bohemian Theater is also the group that organizes the July and August performances at the Revolving Theater in Český Krumlov. Tickets sell out fast. You can reserve online at 🌐 *www.cbsystem.cz*. ✉ *Dr. Stejskala 23* ☎ *386–356–925* 🌐 *www.jihoceskedivadlo.cz.*

EN ROUTE

Holašovice. Peppered with small country homes and farmsteads, this traditional Czech village is so well preserved it's been designated a UNESCO World Heritage Site. Hardly touched by reconstruction or modern meddling, some of the houses date back to the town's founding in the 13th century. Don't expect grand chateaus or extensive decoration; this is "rural baroque," but every bit as picturesque with custard-yellow façades. The information center at No. 43 has a small exhibit about rural life. Budget about an hour for a visit, or longer if you'd like to enjoy traditional fare at **Špejchar u Vojty** (✉ Holašovice 3 ☎ *777–621–221*; 🕒 *May–Oct.*). Every July a "peasant" festival, Selské slavnosti, is held with traditional crafts and entertainment. ✉ *Holasovice, Holasovice* ☎ *387–982–145 for tourist office* 🌐 *www.holasovice.eu* 🕒 *Tourist Information Office closed Oct.–Mar., Mon. Apr.–Aug., and weekdays in Sept.*

WESTERN
BOHEMIA

WELCOME TO
WESTERN BOHEMIA

TOP REASONS
TO GO

★ **Take the waters:**
Wind through the Vřídlo
Colonnade, where
adventurous souls can
sip the waters.

★ **Book a spa day:** Try
the spa treatments,
either old-school health-
oriented treatments or
more familiar pampering.

★ **Catch the stunning view:**
Head up to Stag's Leap
for a sweeping vista.

★ **Walk the "main
streets":** Picturesque spa
towns Františkovy Lázně
and Mariánské Lázně
make a quaint stroll.

★ **Drink a Pilsner Urquell:**
Try this brew in the town
where it was born—Plzeň.

1 Karlovy Vary. Better
known to many as Karlsbad,
the largest of the spa towns
also hosts the country's
biggest film festival every
July.

2 Cheb. Proximity to
the German border brings
many bargain hunters for
shopping, while castle ruins
and a historical center add
some diversion.

3 Františkovy Lázně. The
smallest of the spa towns
in West Bohemia offers a
quiet escape to hotels with
mud baths and old-world
pampering.

4 Mariánské Lázně. In
this town's heyday, everyone
from Thomas Edison to Czar
Nicholas II came to take the
waters. Today visitors can
also enjoy golf and hiking.

5 Plzeň. The only major
Czech city to have been
liberated by U.S. forces at
the end of World War II, it's
also home to the country's
largest brewery.

Litvínov

Most

Vejprty

Chomutov

E442

Ostrov

Žatec

Karlovy Vary

Ohře

1

Bochov

E48

Bečov

E49

Toužim

4

Mariánské Lázně

Kralovice

Chodová Planá

Berounka

27

20

Stříbro

Plzeň **5**

Bor

Rokycany

Dobřany

Horšovský Týn

E53

26

Domažlice

Nepomuk

20

Klatovy

Horažďovice

Otava

GETTING ORIENTED

The natural springs of hot mineral water that dot the lands of Western Bohemia have made this region one of Europe's most important spa centers. These facilities near neighboring Germany have been renovated inside to meet international expectations during the last 25 years, but the exteriors of the colonnades and pavilions still reflect the styles of the 19th century. Because access to much of the border area was highly restricted in the communist era, the hills and forests still provide unspoiled natural settings for hiking and biking. The area also has a rich history of manufacturing luxury glassware and porcelain, which can be seen in downtown shops and factory stores. Farther south is the city of Plzeň, famous for inventing pilsner.

10

Updated by
Raymond
Johnston

Once upon a time, Western Bohemia was known as the playground of Central Europe's rich and famous. Its three well-known spas, Karlovy Vary, Mariánské Lázně, and Františkovy Lázně (also known by their German names, Karlsbad, Marienbad, and Franzensbad, respectively), were the annual haunts of everybody who was anybody: Johann Wolfgang von Goethe, Ludwig van Beethoven, Karl Marx, and England's King Edward VII, to name but a few.

The spas suffered dramatically, however, in the decades after World War II. The concept of a luxurious health spa was anathema to the ruling communist government, and many of the spa facilities were transformed into hospitals—in fact, the idea that these towns are where the sick should recuperate remains today. Pre-1989, some of the nicest properties were transformed into recuperation centers for workers.

The years since 1989 have been kinder to the spa resorts, and now the cities are home to the rich and famous once again. Karlovy Vary, as always, has the most recognition, and rebounded best of all. Helped by its annual international film festival and a heavy infusion of Russian private capital, Karlovy Vary is back on the map as an international spa destination. Františkovy Lázně, too, is on the comeback trail. The city officials have used bucketloads of Kaiser-yellow paint to spruce up those aging Empire facades, and the city's parks have gotten a much-needed makeover. Mariánské Lázně benefits from hordes of German day-trippers from just over the border.

In the Czech Republic spas have traditionally been seen as serious health treatments first, complete with physical examinations, blood tests, and various infusions to complement the waters, relaxation, and massage. This means for many visitors that the local concept of a spa differs from what they are used to back home (and explains in part the large number of elderly tourists shuffling about). Many hotels have added treatments—from Thai massages to pedicures—that fit the modern concept of a spa resort. For many places, though, "spa" still primarily means doctors, nurses, and lab coats, but this is changing as beer spas, wine spas, and other less traditional places pop up. The best place to inquire is at your hotel or the tourist information center.

Aside from the spas, the area is full of historic features stemming from the wealth it accrued as the district's important trade route into Germany and Italy. A strong Germanic influence can still be seen, particularly in towns like Cheb and Mariánské Lázně. Everywhere in the region you'll see Germans, mostly pensioners on coach tours dropping by for a walk around town and a slice of apple strudel before hitting the road back to Deutschland.

PLANNING

WHEN TO GO

The region's key cultural event is the Karlovy Vary International Film Festival, held in the first week in July. As strolling on the promenades of the spa towns is de rigueur, the summer months are the season. The winter months are fine if you want to spend all your time indoors getting massages and other luxury treatments. Most hotels do stay open during this season. But promenading around the colonnade will be a bit of a letdown in the cold, and there's less hobnobbing with fellow spa goers due to much smaller crowds.

GETTING HERE

By car, the D5 (E50) highway leads directly to Plzeň, while the R6 (E48) goes to Karlovy Vary and the spa towns in the northern part of the region. Some towns, lack direct train connections, making a direct bus a better choice. Buses to major hubs such as Plzeň are also faster and less expensive than trains.

GUIDED TOURS FROM PRAGUE

Guided one-day bus tours from Prague are available from several companies to the larger spa towns.

Martin Tours. One of the country's larger tour operators, Martin Tours offers regular trips to Karlovy Vary, including a glass factory, and the brewery in Plzeň for 1,500 Kč and 1,200 Kč each. The Plzeň trip includes beer tasting. ⊕ *www.martintour.cz.*

Tip Top Travel. Tip Top Travel offers a combined Karlovy Vary–Mariánské Lázně tour for 2,100 Kč. The tour lasts about 10 hours and the price includes a pickup at your hotel. ⊕ *www.tiptoptravel.cz.*

RESTAURANTS AND HOTELS

The quality of hotels in Western Bohemia is on a par with those in Prague (something that can't be said about some other parts of the country) and three- and four-star establishments have standard amenities, including satellite TV, room phones, and private bathrooms (and sometimes even Wi-Fi). One difference from the hotels in Prague: the peak season is shorter, running from May through September. Another difference: the staff tend to speak a very limited amount of English—German and Russian (particularly in Karlovy Vary) are much more common, in keeping with the majority of visitors. Prices have risen dramatically in

10

recent years, making private accommodations a more attractive offer. ■TIP➜ Be sure to read the fine print, as many spa hotels quote rates per person per night, rather than for double occupancy. The local tourist offices usually keep lists of pensions and private rooms. In addition to value-added tax (V.A.T.), there is also a "spa tax" of about 15 Kč per day for accommodations in spa facilities.

Hotel reviews have been shortened. For full information, visit Fodors. com.

	WHAT IT COSTS IN KORUNA			
	$	$$	$$$	$$$$
Restaurants	under 150 Kč	150 Kč–350 Kč	351 Kč–500 Kč	over 500 Kč
Hotels	under 2,200 Kč	2,200 Kč–4,000 Kč	4,001 Kč–6,500 Kč	over 6,500 Kč

Restaurant prices are the average cost of a main course at dinner, or if dinner is not served, at lunch. Hotel prices are the lowest cost of a standard double room in high season.

KARLOVY VARY

132 km (79 miles) west of Prague on R6 (E48).

Karlovy Vary—often known outside the Czech Republic by its German name, Karlsbad—is the most famous of the Bohemian spas. It's named for the omnipresent Emperor Charles IV, who allegedly happened upon the springs in 1358 while on a hunting expedition. As the story goes, the emperor's hound fell into a boiling spring and was scalded. Charles had the water tested and, familiar with spas in Italy, ordered the village of Vary to be transformed into a haven for baths. The spa reached its golden age in the 19th century, when aristocrats from all over Europe came for treatments. The long list of those who "took the cure" includes Peter the Great, Goethe, Schiller, Beethoven, and Chopin. Even Karl Marx, when he wasn't decrying wealth and privilege, spent time at the wealthy and privileged resort; he wrote some of *Das Kapital* here between 1874 and 1876.

Pulling off an extraordinary comeback after decades of communist neglect that left many buildings crumbling into dust behind beautiful facades, Karlovy Vary drips with luxury once again. Much of the reconstruction was led not by Czechs, but by Russians. Since the days of Peter the Great, Karlovy Vary has held a deep fascination for Russians, and many of them poured their newly gained wealth into properties here—so much so that Karlovy Vary's sleepy airport boasts nonstop service from Moscow several times a week, and four-fifths of the properties are actually Russian-owned. Don't be surprised to hear Russian spoken widely in the streets or see it used as the second language, after Czech, on restaurant menus.

Karlovy Vary's other vehicle in luring attention and investment has been its international film festival, which began in 1946. Every year during the first week of July, international stars and film fans flock here. Recent attendees include Oliver Stone, John Travolta, and Helen Mirren. If you're planning on visiting during the festival, line up your hotel room well in advance. Unless you're a true film buff, you're better off coming on a different week.

Whether you're arriving by bus, train, or car, your first view of the town approaching from Prague will be of the run-down section on the banks of the Ohře River. Don't despair: continue along the main road, following the signs to the Grandhotel Pupp, until you are rewarded with a glimpse of the lovely main street in the older spa area, situated gently astride the banks of the little Teplá ("Warm") River. (Drivers, note that driving through or parking in the main spa area is allowed only with a permit obtained at your hotel.) The walk from the new town to the spa area is about 20 minutes.

The Historická čtvrt (Historic District) is still largely intact. Tall 19th-century houses, with decorative and often eccentric façades, line the spa's proud riverside streets. Throughout, you can see colonnades full of people sipping the spa's hot sulfuric water from funny drinking cups with piped spouts.

GETTING HERE
Frequent bus service between Prague and Karlovy Vary makes the journey only about two hours each way, and the ticket costs about 160 Kč. The Prague–Karlovy Vary run takes longer—more than three hours by the shortest route—and costs about 170 Kč. If you're driving, you can take the E48 directly from Prague to Karlovy Vary, a drive of about 1½ hours in light traffic.

Visitor Information Karlovy Vary Tourist Information. ⊠ *Husovo nám. 2* ☎ *355–321–171* ⊕ *www.karlovyvary.cz.*

EXPLORING

TOP ATTRACTIONS

Fodor's Choice ★ **Jelení skok** (*Stag's Leap*). From Kostel svatého Lukáše, take a sharp right uphill on a redbrick road, then turn left onto a footpath through the woods, following signs to Jelení skok (Stag's Leap). After a while, steps lead up to a bronze statue of a deer looking over the cliffs, the symbol of Karlovy Vary. From here a winding path threads toward a little red gazebo opening onto a mythical panorama that's worth the strenuous hike to the top. ⊠ *Sovava trail in Petrova Výšina park.*

Mlýnská kolonáda (*Mill Colonnade*). This neo-Renaissance pillared hall, along the river, is the town's centerpiece. Built from 1871 to 1881, it has four springs: Rusalka, Libussa, Prince Wenceslas, and Millpond. ⊠ *Mlýnské nábř.*

Rozhledna Diana. Give your feet a rest. You won't need to walk to one of the best views of the town. Even higher than Stag's Leap sits this observation tower, accessible by funicular from behind the Grandhotel Pupp. There's an elevator to the top of the tower, and a restaurant at the tower's base. ⊠ *Výšina přátelství* ⊕ *www.dianakv.cz* ☎ *Funicular 45 Kč one-way, 80 Kč round-trip; tower free.*

10

Like Prague, Karlovy Vary also has a central river: the swirling Teplá.

Sadová kolonáda (*Park Colonnade*). Laced with white wrought iron, this elegant colonnade at the edge of Dvořákovy sady was built in 1882 by the Viennese architectural duo Fellner and Helmer, who sprinkled the Austro-Hungarian Empire with many such edifices during the late 19th century. They also designed the town's theater, the quaint wooden Tržní kolonáda (Market Colonnade) next to the Vřídlo Colonnade, and one of the old bathhouses. ⊠ *Dvořákovy sady.*

QUICK BITES

Jelení skok. After reaching the summit of Stag's Leap, reward yourself with a light meal at the nearby restaurant Jelení skok. There may be a cover charge if a live band is playing (prepare yourself for smooth rock by a synth-guitar duo). If you don't want to walk up, you can drive up a signposted road from the Victorian church. ⊠ *Pod Jelením skokem 884/2.*

Vřídelní kolonáda (*Vřídlo Colonnade*). Shooting its scalding water to a height of some 40 feet, the Vřídlo is indeed Karlovy Vary's hottest and most dramatic gusher. Built around it is the jarringly modern Vřídlo Colonnade. Walk inside the arcade to watch patients take the famed Karlsbad drinking cure. The waters (30°F–72°F) are said to be especially effective against diseases of the digestive and urinary tracts. They're also good for gout (which probably explains the spa's former popularity with royals). If you want to join the crowds and take a sip, you can buy your own spouted cup from one of the souvenir vendors throughout the town. ⊠ *Vřídelní ul., near Kosterní nám.*

WORTH NOTING

Hotel Thermal. Built in the late 1960s as the communist idea of luxury, this oversize modern hotel is the main venue of the Karlovy Vary International Film Festival in early July. Many people, though, consider it an eyesore that's out of step with the rest of the city. ⊠ *I. P. Pavlova 11* ☎ *359-001-111* ⊕ *www.thermal.cz.*

Kostel Maří Magdaleny (*Church of Mary Magdalene*). To the right of the Vřídlo Colonnade, steps lead up to the white Church of Mary Magdalene. Designed by Kilian Ignaz Dientzenhofer (architect of the two churches of St. Nicholas in Prague), this is the best of the few baroque buildings still standing in Karlovy Vary. ■TIP➔ **If it's open, try to visit the crypt.** ⊠ *Moravská ul.* ⊕ *www.farnost-kv.cz.*

■ NEED A BREAK

Elefant. On one of the town's main shopping streets is this resolutely old-fashioned, sophisticated coffeehouse, connected to Hotel Elefant. The apple strudel and coffee are quite good, and the outdoor terrace is a prime location for people-watching. ⊠ *Stará louka 30* ☎ *353-229-270* ⊕ *www.hotelelefant.cz.*

Kostel svatého Lukáše (*St. Luke's Church*). A five-minute walk up the steep Zámecký vrch from the Market Colonnade brings you to the Victorian, redbrick St. Luke's Church, once a gathering point for the local English community. ⊠ *Zámecký vrch at Petra Velikého.*

Kostel svatých Petra a Pavla (*Church of Sts. Peter and Paul*). Six domes top this splendid Russian Orthodox church. It dates to the end of the 19th century, and is decorated with paintings and icons donated by wealthy Russian visitors. ■TIP➔ **You can usually peek inside, daily 9-6.** ⊠ *Třída Krále Jiřího 26.*

WHERE TO EAT

The food in Karlovy Vary has improved due to the influx of Russians with money to spend. Pork and beer pubs are still the rule, though. Hotel food tends to be better.

$$ ITALIAN ✕**Pizzeria Capri.** This "riverfront" pizzeria became an institution during the annual film festival. The walls are decked out with photos of the owner smiling next to Hollywood stars. The pizza and fresh-fish dishes are passably good, and much improved by outdoor seating on a warm summer evening. Ⓢ *Average main: 250 Kč* ⊠ *Stará Louka 42* ☎ *353-236-090* ⊕ *www.pizzeriacapri.cz.*

$$$ CZECH ✕**Promenáda.** Although it's pricey, Promenáda is unquestionably the best place to eat in Karlovy Vary. The starchy vibe is "'70s French fussy," and meals are on the heavy side. However, the menu is constantly changing as the chef uses fresh, seasonal ingredients. There's also an impressive selection of Moravian wines and a staff who are efficient without hovering. Ⓢ *Average main: 400 Kč* ⊠ *Trziste 31* ☎ *353-225-648* ⊕ *hotel-promenada.cz* ⚘ *Reservations essential.*

$$ CZECH ✕**U Švejka.** Usually when a restaurant has the name "Schweik" in it—from the novel *Good Soldier Schweik*—it means one thing: tourist trap. But this local Schweik incarnation is a cut above its brethren. If you're

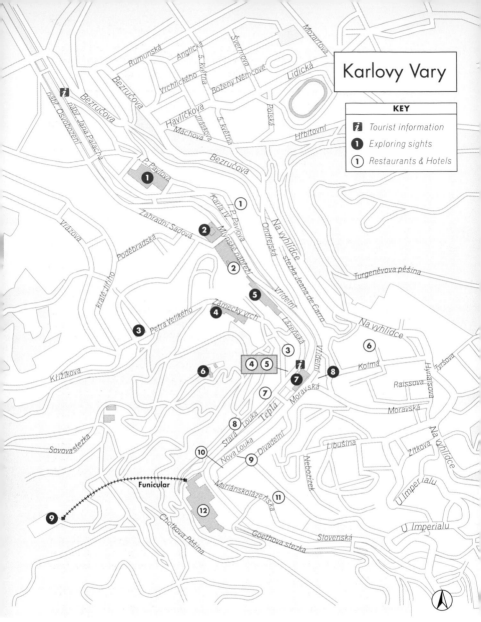

Karlovy Vary

KEY

🛈 Tourist information

❶ Exploring sights

① Restaurants & Hotels

Exploring ▼

Hotel Thermal **1**

Jelení skok **6**

Kostel Maří Magdaleny **8**

Kostel svatého Lukáše **4**

Kostel svatých
Petra a Pavla **3**

Mlýnská kolonáda **5**

Rozhledna Diana **9**

Sadová kolonáda **2**

Vřídelní kolonáda **7**

Restaurants ▼

Pizzeria Capri **8**

Promenáda **4**

U Švejka **7**

Hotels ▼

Carlsbad Plaza **11**

Grandhotel Pupp **12**

Hotel Dvořák **9**

Hotel Embassy **10**

Hotel Heluan **3**

Promenáda **5**

Růže Hotel **1**

Wellness Hotel
Jean de Carro **6**

Windsor Spa Hotel **2**

looking for a simple, decent Czech pub, with good local cooking and excellent beer, you've found it. [$] *Average main: 250 Kč* ✉ *Stará Louka 10* ☎ *353–232–276* 🌐 *www.svejk-kv.cz* 💳 *No credit cards.*

WHERE TO STAY

$$$ HOTEL 🏨 **Carlsbad Plaza.** A luxury hotel a stone's throw from the Grandhotel Pupp, Carlsbad Plaza is aimed at Karlovy Vary's wealthiest visitors. **Pros:** everything you could ever want; great wellness center. **Cons:** lots of things you probably don't—and you're paying for it all; some might find it fussy or distant. [$] *Rooms from: 6325 Kč* ✉ *Mariánskolázeňská 23* ☎ *352–441–111* 🌐 *www.carlsbadplaza.cz* 🛏 *126 rooms, 26 suites* 🍴 *Breakfast.*

$$$ HOTEL Fodor's Choice ★ 🏨 **Grandhotel Pupp.** The granddaddy of them all, this is one of Central Europe's most famous resorts, going back some 200 years. **Pros:** large rooms; living history; a sleek casino. **Cons:** costly extras; rooms are opulent but not that modern. [$] *Rooms from: 5100 Kč* ✉ *Mírové nám. 2* ☎ *353–109–631* 🌐 *www.pupp.cz* 🛏 *Grandhotel Pupp de Luxe: 111 rooms; Grandhotel Pupp First Class: 117 rooms* 🍴 *Breakfast.*

$$ HOTEL 🏨 **Hotel Dvořák.** The Austrian-owned hotel, which opened in 1990, occupies three renovated houses that overlook Nová louka and the Teplá River. **Pros:** efficient staff; large spa for the price point. **Cons:** some rooms are cramped. [$] *Rooms from: 2675 Kč* ✉ *Nová Louka 11* ☎ *353–224–145* 🌐 *www.hotel-dvorak.cz* 🛏 *126 rooms* 🍴 *Breakfast.*

$$ HOTEL Fodor's Choice ★ 🏨 **Hotel Embassy.** On a peaceful bend in the river, this family-run hotel includes spacious, well-appointed rooms. **Pros:** perfect for duffers; rooms offer a great value. **Cons:** small; no spa. [$] *Rooms from: 2950 Kč* ✉ *Nová Louka 21* ☎ *353–221–161* 🌐 *www.embassy.cz* 🛏 *29 rooms* 🍴 *Breakfast.*

$$ HOTEL 🏨 **Hotel Heluan.** A clean, safe bet if you've arrived in town without reservations and don't want to spend your savings on a room. **Pros:** inexpensive; friendly staff; completely no-smoking hotel. **Cons:** a bit of a hike uphill. [$] *Rooms from: 3000 Kč* ✉ *Tržiště 41* ☎ *353–321–111* 🌐 *www.heluan.eu* 🛏 *25 rooms* 🍴 *Breakfast.*

10

$$ HOTEL 🏨 **Promenáda.** The family-operated hotel is another good last-minute option right in the center of town, with pastel yellow rooms that are brightened by the occasional exposed wooden beam or windowsill flower box. **Pros:** beautiful pool; American-style spa; great restaurant; large rooms. **Cons:** dated fixtures; street noise on weekends. [$] *Rooms from: 3550 Kč* ✉ *Trziste 31* ☎ *353–225–648* 🌐 *www.hotel-promenada.cz* 🛏 *22 rooms* 🍴 *Breakfast.*

$$ HOTEL 🏨 **Růže Hotel.** More than adequately comfortable and well-priced given its location in the center of the spa district, the Růže also offers an array of modern spa services like bubble baths and Thai massage. **Pros:** nice views; good for large groups; new rooms. **Cons:** the modern interior lacks character. [$] *Rooms from: 3200 Kč* ✉ *I. P. Pavlova 1* ☎ *353–221–846, 353–221–853* 🌐 *www.hotel-ruze.com* 🛏 *54 rooms* 🍴 *Breakfast.*

$$ HOTEL 🏨 **Wellness Hotel Jean de Carro.** Framed on a hilltop off a side street above the spa, the Jean de Carro sits comfortably above the fray. **Pros:** great views; friendly staff. **Cons:** a bit of a hike; small rooms. [$] *Rooms from: 2990 Kč* ✉ *Stezka Jeana de Carro 4–6* ☎ *353–365–160* 🌐 *www.*

DID YOU KNOW?

Some of the water features in Karlovy Vary are decorative, like this central fountain, but most are practical taps that deliver the mineral-rich spring waters to spa patrons.

jeandecarro.com 🛏 *32 rooms* 🍴 *Breakfast.*

$ HOTEL 🏨 **Windsor Spa Hotel.** Neo-Gothic in style—on the outside, anyway—this spa hotel has fairly spartan rooms and a slight hospital vibe (it takes treatment rather seriously), but the location is excellent and treatments are gently priced. **Pros:** beautiful building; great location. **Cons:** austere rooms; limited amenities; medical feel. [$] *Rooms from: 1675 Kč* ✉ *Mlýnské nábř. 5* ☎ *353–242–569* 🌐 *windsor-carlsbad.cz* 🛏 *36 rooms* 🍴 *Breakfast.*

SIP WITH CAUTION

The waters from natural springs are loaded with minerals, which means they often have a sulfuric smell and taste—not necessarily the most appetizing thing. What's more, many of the waters speed the digestive process. You may want to sip at first as you get used to the flavor, and plan your day accordingly.

PERFORMING ARTS

Lázně III. If you're looking to get your high-culture fix, the Karlovy Vary Symphony Orchestra plays regularly at this hotel, a spa facility that doubles as an important cultural center for the town. Head to the Antonín Dvořák Music Hall on the first floor of the building to catch the concerts. The same building is also now home to Windsor Spa Hotel. ✉ *Mlýnské nábř. 5* ☎ *353–242–500* 🌐 *www.lazneiii.cz.*

Městské divadlo. Restored to its opulent 1890s glory, the Municipal Theater is home to live concerts of many kinds as well as theater performances. Interior paintings were done by well-known artists including a young Gustav Klimt. ✉ *Divadelní nám. 21* ☎ *353–225–621* 🌐 *www.karlovarske-divadlo.cz.*

NIGHTLIFE

Grandhotel Pupp. This upscale funhouse consists of the two nightclubs and the casino of the biggest hotel in town. You don't have to be James Bond to get in, so gamble the night away within the mirrored walls and under the glass ceiling of the Pupp Casino Club, or settle into a cocktail and some live music at the English-themed Becher's Bar. ✉ *Mírové nám. 2* ☎ *353–109–111* 🌐 *www.pupp.cz.*

SHOPPING

A cluster of exclusive stores huddles around the Grandhotel Pupp and back toward town along the river on Stará Louka. Lesser-known, high-quality makers of glass and porcelain can also be found on this street. If you're looking for an inexpensive but nonetheless singular gift from Karlovy Vary, consider a bottle of the bittersweet (and potent) Becherovka, a liqueur produced by the town's own Jan Becher distillery. Another thoughtful gift would be one of the pipe-shape ceramic drinking cups used to take the drinking cure at spas; you can find them along the colonnades. Boxes of tasty *oplatky* wafers, with various sweet fillings, can be found at shops in all the spa towns. (The most famous,

Kolonáda, is actually made in Mariánské Lázně.) The challenge is stopping yourself from eating it all before you give it as a gift.

Moser. To glass enthusiasts, Karlovy Vary is best known as the home of Moser, one of the world's leading producers of crystal and decorative glassware. ⊠ *Tržíště 7* ☏ *353–235–303* ⊕ *www.moser-glass.com.*

Moser Visitors Center. For people who want to see more of the process of glassmaking, the Moser Visitors Center has a museum and offers factory tours along with shopping. ⊠ *Kapitána Jarose 19* ☏ *353–416–242* ⊕ *www.moser.cz* ☞ *180 Kč combined admission for museum and glassworks.*

SPORTS AND THE OUTDOORS

Karlovy Vary is a town made for staying active in the outdoors. Exercise was often part of the treatment during the heyday of the resort, and the air quality here is markedly superior to that of Prague or other industrialized towns in the Czech Republic. Hiking trails snake across the beech-and pine-covered hills that surround the town on three sides. If you walk past the Grandhotel Pupp, away from the center, and follow the paved walkway that runs alongside the river for about 10 minutes, you'll discover a Japanese garden.

Karlovy Vary Golf Club. This course, opened in 1904, has been extensively modernized since 2004 to include a new clubhouse and redesigned holes, including two water traps. The clubhouse has a relaxation center and an indoor golf simulators. The club requires a golf association membership and a minimum handicap of 36 to make a reservation to use the course. Electric carts and clubs can be rented. The European ground squirrel, listed as a vulnerable species, lives on the course. ⊠ *Pražská 125* ☏ *353–331–001* ⊕ *www.golfresort.cz* 🖾 *1,200 for 9 holes; 2,000 Kč for 18 holes* 🏌 *18 holes; 6,773 yards; par 72* ☉ *Closed Nov.–Mar.*

CHEB

42 km (26 miles) southwest of Karlovy Vary; 174 km (105 miles) southwest of Prague.

Known for centuries by its German name of Eger, the old town of Cheb tickles the German border in the far west of the Czech Republic. The town has been a fixture of Bohemia since 1322 (when it was handed over to King Jan as thanks for his support of a Bavarian prince), but as you walk around the beautiful medieval square it's easy to forget you're not in Germany. The tall merchants' houses surrounding the main square, with their long, red-tile, sloping roofs dotted with windows like droopy eyelids, are more Germanic in style than anything else in Bohemia. You will also hear a lot of German on the streets from the day-trippers coming here from across the border.

Germany took possession of the town in 1938 under the terms of the notorious Munich Agreement. Following World War II, virtually the entire German population was expelled, and the Czech name of Cheb was officially adopted. During the Cold War, Cheb suffered as a communist outpost along the heavily fortified border with West Germany. Since then, thanks to German tourist dollars, Cheb has made an obvious economic comeback. The town center, with a lovely pedestrian zone, merits a few hours of strolling.

GETTING HERE
The journey from Prague to Cheb is about 3½ hours each way, whether you are taking the bus or the train; expect to pay more for the ride by train. The price for the bus trip is 200 Kč; the price for the train ride 300 Kč. The high-speed Pendolino train service goes to Cheb in 2½ hours, but seat reservations are required. Look for special deals on the Czech Railways website (⊕ *www.cd.cz*) that sometimes make the seat reservations free. If you're driving, you can take the E50 and then the 21 from Prague to Cheb, a drive of about 2½ hours, though traffic can sometimes be heavy.

Visitor Information Tourist Info Cheb. ⊠ *Jateční 2* ☎ *354–440–302* ⊕ *www. tic.mestocheb.cz.*

EXPLORING

Chebské muzeum (*Cheb Museum*). The building that houses this museum is just as interesting at its collection; it's known as the Pachelbel House, the setting for a murder during the Thirty Years' War. In 1634, General Albrecht von Wallenstein was executed in this house on the orders of Hapsburg emperor Ferdinand II. He was provoked by Wallenstein's increasing power and rumors of treason. According to legend, Wallenstein was on his way to the Saxon border to enlist support to fight the Swedes when his own officers barged into his room and stabbed him through the heart with a stave. Wallenstein's stark bedroom has been left as it was with its four-poster bed and dark red velvet curtains. (The story also inspired playwright Friedrich Schiller to write the *Wallenstein* trilogy; he planned the work while living at the top of the square at No. 2.) The museum is also interesting in its own right, with a Wallenstein family picture gallery, a section on the history of Cheb, and a collection of minerals (including one discovered by Goethe). There's also the stuffed remains of Wallenstein's horse. ⊠ *Nám. Krále Jiřího z Poděbrad 4* ☎ *354–400–620* ⊕ *www.muzeumcheb.cz* 🎫 *Full museum: 70 Kč; Wallenstein route only: 40 Kč; exhibition hall: 40 Kč* ⊗ *Closed weekdays in Jan. and Feb., Mon. and Tues. in Mar., Apr., and Oct.– Dec., and Mon. May–Sept.*

Chebský hrad (*Cheb Castle*). Built with blocks of lava taken from the nearby Komorní Hůrka volcano, this castle stands on a cliff overlooking the Ohře River. The castle—now a ruin—was built in the late 12th century for Holy Roman Emperor Frederick Barbarossa. Redbrick walls are 17th-century additions. Inside the castle grounds is the carefully restored double-decker **Romanesque chapel,** notable for the many lovely columns with heads carved into their capitals. The rather dark ground floor was used by commoners. A bright, ornate top floor was reserved for the emperor and his family, who entered via a wooden bridge leading to the royal palace. ⊠ *Dobrovského 21* ☎ *354–422–942*

10

🌐 *www.hrad-cheb.cz* 🎫 *80 Kč* ⏲ *Closed weekdays in Nov.–Mar., and Mon. Apr.–June, Sept., and Oct.*

Komorní Hůrka. Red markers indicate a path from Cheb's main square westward along the river and then north past this extinct volcano, now a tree-covered hill. Excavations on one side have laid bare the rock, and one tunnel remains open. Goethe instigated and took part in the excavations, and you can still—barely—make out a relief of the poet carved into the rock face. **■ TIP→ The volcano is about 2 miles out of town.** ✉ *Komorní dvůr.*

Kostel svatého Mikuláše (*Church of St. Nicholas*). The plain but imposing Church of St. Nicholas was begun in 1230, when the church belonged to the Order of Teutonic Knights. You can still see Romanesque windows on the towers; tinkering over the centuries added an impressive Gothic portal and a baroque interior. Just inside the Gothic entrance is a wonderfully faded plaque commemorating the diamond jubilee of Hapsburg emperor Franz Joseph in 1908. ✉ *Kostelní nám.* ☎ *354–422–458* 🌐 *www.farnostcheb.cz.*

"Roland" Statue. In the middle of the central square, náměstí Krále Jiřího z Poděbrad, this statue is similar to other Roland statues seen throughout Bohemia, attesting to the town's royal privileges. (Roland is a figure in medieval and Renaissance literature; his statues are found throughout Europe.) This one represents the town hero, Wastel of Eger. Look carefully at his right foot, and you can see a small man holding a sword and a head—this shows the town had its own judge and executioner. ✉ *Nám. Krále Jiřího z Poděbrad.*

Špalíček. In the lower part of náměstí Krále Jiřího z Poděbrad stand two rickety-looking groups of timbered medieval buildings (11 houses in all) divided by a narrow alley. The houses, forming the area known as Špalíček, date to the 13th century, and were once home to many Jewish merchants. **Židovská ulice** (Jews' Street), running uphill to the left of the Špalíček, served as the actual center of the ghetto. The small, unmarked alley running to the left off Židovská is called ulička Zavražděných (Lane of the Murdered). It was the scene of an outrageous act of violence in 1350: pressures had been building for some time between Jews and Christians. Incited by an anti-Semitic bishop, the townspeople chased the Jews into the street, closed off both ends, and massacred them. Now only the name attests to the slaughter. ✉ *Nám. Krále Jiřího z Poděbrad.*

WHERE TO EAT AND STAY

$$ CZECH
🍴 **Kavárna-Restaurace Špalíček.** The sameness of the restaurants lining the square can be a bit numbing, but this one offers a reasonably priced selection of standard pork and chicken dishes, with the added charm of being in the ancient Špalíček complex. [$] *Average main: 200 Kč* ✉ *Nám. Krále Jiřího z Poděbrad 50* ☎ *736–759–409* 🌐 *restaurace-spalicek.cz* 💳 *No credit cards.*

$ HOTEL
🏨 **Barbarossa.** One block from the main square, this charming family-run hotel is a favorite among visiting Germans, so book ahead, especially on weekends. **Pros:** near the main square; friendly staff. **Cons:**

DID YOU KNOW?

When you're in Cheb, it's easy to forget that you haven't actually crossed the border into Germany. The tall merchants' houses around the main square all demonstrate a Germanic style.

gets crowded; few amenities. [$] *Rooms from: 1800 Kč* ✉ *Jateční 7* ☎ *354–423–446* 🌐 *www.hotel-barbarossa.cz* 🛏 *21 rooms with bath* 🍴 *Breakfast.*

FRANTIŠKOVY LÁZNĚ

6 km (4 miles) north of Cheb; 180 km (109 miles) southwest of Prague.

Františkovy Lázně, or Franzensbad, is the smallest of the three main Bohemian spas. It isn't really in the same league as Karlovy Vary. The main spa area is only a few blocks, and aside from a dozen or so cafés in which to enjoy an apple strudel or ice cream, there isn't much to see or do. That said, the charm of its uniform, Kaiser-yellow Empire architecture grows on you. Gardens surrounding the main spa area—both the manicured "French" gardens and the wilder "English" parks—grow on you, too. They're as perfect for strolling now as they were 200 years ago. Summer is particularly pleasant, when a small orchestra occupies the gazebo in the Městkské sady (City Park) and locals and visitors sit in lawn chairs and listen.

The healing properties of the waters here were recognized as early as the 15th century, but Františkovy Lázně came into its own only at the start of the 19th century. Like Bohemia's other spas, Františkovy Lázně drew from the top drawer of European society, including one Ludwig Van Beethoven, who came here in 1812. But it remained in Cheb's shadow, and the spa stayed relatively small. In the years following World War II the spa declined. Most of the buildings were given over to factories and organizations to use as convalescent centers. Františkovy Lázně also developed a reputation for helping women with fertility problems, and Milan Kundera used it as the humorous, small-town backdrop for his novel *The Farewell Party*. Since 1989 the town has worked hard to restore the yellow facades to their former glory.

The best way to approach Františkovy Lázně is simply to find **Národní ulice,** the main street, and walk.

GETTING HERE

Expect to spend about four hours each way traveling between Prague and Františkovy Lázne via bus or train. As with other destinations, you'll pay more for riding the rails, and also make a few changes as there is little direct service. Costs are about 215 Kč one-way for the bus, about 310 Kč for a train with a change or 400 Kč without a change. Frequent buses run to and from Cheb. If you're driving, you can take the E50 and then the 21 from Prague to Františkovy Lázne, a drive of about three hours.

Visitor Information Františkovy Lázně Tourist Information. ✉ *Tři Lilie Hotel, Národní 3* ☎ *354–201–170* 🌐 *www.franzensbad.cz.*

EXPLORING

Františkův pramen. Under a little gazebo filled with brass pipes sits the town's main spring. The colonnade to the left once displayed a bust of Lenin that was replaced in 1990 by a memorial to the American liberation of the town in April 1945. To the right, in the garden, you'll see a statue of a small cherub holding a fish. The oval neoclassical temple just beyond the spring (amazingly, *not* painted yellow and white) is the **Glauberova dvorana** (Glauber Pavilion), where several springs bubble up into glass cases. ✉ *Národní ul. at nám. Miru.*

MOTHER AND CHILD

Františkovy Lázne has long been known as a refuge for women seeking help in fertility problems. Evidence of that can be seen in the main spring's statue of a small cherub holding a fish. In keeping with the fertility theme, women are encouraged to touch the fish to ensure their own fertility. You'll notice the statue is shiny from so many years of being rubbed.

Městské muzeum (*Town Museum*). A fascinating peek into spa culture is housed in this small museum, just off Národní ulice. There's a wonderful collection of spa-related antiques, including copper bathtubs and a turn-of-the-20th-century exercise bike called a Velotrab. The guest books provide insight into the cosmopolitan world of pre–World War I Central Europe. The book for 1812 contains the entry "Ludwig van Beethoven, composer from Vienna." There are also rotating exhibitions of graphic arts. ✉ *Dlouhá 4* ☎ *354–542–344* 🌐 *www.muzeum-frantiskovylazne.cz* 🎟 *35 Kč* 🕒 *Closed Mon., and mid-Dec.–mid-Jan.*

WHERE TO STAY

Most of the lodging establishments in town depend on spa patients, who generally stay for several weeks. Spa treatments usually require a medical checkup and cost substantially more than the normal room charge. Walk-in treatment can be arranged at some hotels or at the information center. Signs around town advertise massage therapy and other treatments for casual visitors.

$ HOTEL 🏨 **Rossini.** An alternative to the upscale spa hotels in the center, this small family-operated pension is in a more residential area and offers nine rooms, two with balconies. **Pros:** affordable and clean; free coffee throughout the day. **Cons:** no spa; outside of the town's main area. [$] *Rooms from: 1100 Kč* ✉ *Lidická 5* ☎ *603–156–760* 🌐 *www.rossini.cz* 🛏 *9 rooms* 🍴 *Breakfast.*

$$$ HOTEL Fodor's Choice ★ 🏨 **Tři Lilie.** "Three Lilies" is thoroughly elegant, from its brasserie to its guest rooms, some of which have balconies with French doors. **Pros:** glorious A/C; rooms with balconies; extremely efficient service. **Cons:** if you don't want spa services, much of its appeal is lost. [$] *Rooms from: 5800 Kč* ✉ *Národní 3* ☎ *354–208–900* 🌐 *www.frantiskovylazne.cz/cs/hotel-tri-lilie* 🛏 *31 rooms* 🍴 *Breakfast.*

MARIÁNSKÉ LÁZNĚ

30 km (18 miles) southeast of Cheb; 47 km (29 miles) south of Karlovy Vary.

Once Bohemia's star spa town, Mariánské Lázně now plays second fiddle to Karlovy Vary. Whereas the latter, with its glitzy international

DID YOU KNOW?

Walking Marianske Lazně's colonnades, it's easy to picture the town as it was when Goethe and Chopin came to "take the waters."

film festival and wealthy "New Russian" residents, has succeeded in luring investors, Mariánské Lázně seems to survive largely on the decidedly less glamorous (and much older) crowd coming over from Germany. Busloads of German retirees arrive daily. They walk the promenades and repair over ice cream and cake before boarding the coach to head back home. This trade keeps the properties in business but hardly brings the capital influx needed to overhaul the spa facilities.

> **MARIENBAD WITH A FRENCH TWIST**
>
> If the name "Marienbad" rings a bell, it may recall the groundbreaking 1961 French film *Last Year at Marienbad*. A collection of surreal vignettes, the movie explores the possible affair one French couple had in Marienbad through new-wave tricks like jarring jump cuts. But don't expect the manicured lawns and estates of this movie to reflect the landscape of the real Marienbad; it was shot in southern Germany.

The grounds have remained lush and lovely, especially the upper part of the town's spa area near the Grandhotel Pacifik. Here you'll find the colonnades and fountains and river walks you expect from a once-world-famous spa. And the woods surrounding the town are magnificent.

A hundred years ago Mariánské Lázně, or Marienbad as it was known, was one of Europe's finest resorts. It was a favorite of Britain's King Edward VII. Goethe and Chopin also came. Mark Twain, on a visit in 1892, couldn't get over how new everything looked. Twain—who had a natural aversion to anything too salubrious—labeled the town a "health factory."

The best way to experience the spa—short of signing up for a weeklong treatment—is simply to buy a spouted drinking cup (available at the colonnades) and join the rest of the sippers taking the drinking cure. Be forewarned, though: the waters from the Rudolph, Ambrose, and Caroline springs, though harmless, all have a noticeable diuretic effect. For this reason they're used extensively in treating disorders of the kidney and bladder. Unlike Karlovy Vary, the springs here are all cold water, and may be easier to stomach.

10

Walking trails of varied difficulty surround the resort in all directions, and one of the country's best golf courses lies about 3 km (2 miles) to the east of town. Hotel staff can also help arrange activities such as tennis and horseback riding. For the less intrepid, a simple stroll around the gardens, with a few deep inhalations of the town's clean air, is enough to restore a healthy sense of perspective.

GETTING HERE

Regular bus and train service between Prague and Mariánské Lázně makes the journey about three hours each way. Although similar in travel time, the train costs more than the bus. Expect to pay 184 Kč one-way for the bus, 255 Kč for the train. However, from Karlovy Vary, there is hourly train service for about 63 Kč. If you're driving, you can take the E50 and then the 21 from Prague to Mariánské Lázně, a drive of about two hours.

Visitor Information **Mariánské Lázně Tourist Information** (*Cultural and Information Center*). ✉ *Hlavní 47* ☎ *354–622–474* 🌐 *www.marianskelazne.cz.*

EXPLORING

OFF THE BEATEN PATH

Chodová Planá. Need a break from the rigorous healthiness of spa life? Chodovar Beer Wellness Land is a few miles south of Mariánské Lázně and offers a wellness hotel, two restaurants, and an underground complex of granite tunnels that have been used to age beer since the 1400s. Generous servings of Czech dishes can be ordered to accompany the strong, fresh Chodovar beer tapped directly from granite storage vaults. You can tour the brewery, but don't expect much English commentary. The brewery also offers a beer bath, massage and, unlimited consumption starting at 1290 Kč. The brewery promises it will cause a mild and gradual rise in heart activity and "scour away any unhealthy substances that may have accumulated." ■**TIP➔ There are brewery tours daily at 2 pm.** ✉ *Pivovarská 107, Chodová Planá* ☎ *374–617–100* 🌐 *www.chodovar.cz* 🎫 *Tour 85 Kč.*

WHERE TO EAT

$$ BRITISH

🍴 **Churchill's.** Dark-wood paneling, a serpentine bar, and a mixture of tables and booths give this restaurant a comfy British-pub vibe. It's in the same building as the Excelsior hotel, but with a separate entrance. British food isn't that far off from Czech—meat and potatoes are still front and center—but there are also decent pastas and salads to be had. Winston Churchill once visited Mariánské Lázně, which inspired its theme and name. [$] *Average main: 215 Kč* ✉ *Hotel Excelsior, Hlavní 121* ☎ *354–697–111* 🌐 *www.excelsiormarienbad.com* ✍ *Reservations essential.*

$$ CZECH

🍴 **Koliba.** An excellent alternative to the hotel restaurants in town, Koliba serves grilled meats and shish kebabs, plus tankards of Moravian wine (try the dry, cherry-red Rulandské červené), with traditional gusto. Occasionally fiddlers play rousing Moravian folk tunes. Exposed wooden ceiling beams add to the rustic charm of the inn's 15 rooms that face the surrounding nature preserve. [$] *Average main: 250 Kč* ✉ *Hotel Koliba, Dusíkova 592* ☎ *354–625–169* 🌐 *www.hotel-koliba.cz.*

WHERE TO STAY

Hotel prices have risen in recent years, and many properties are terribly overpriced for what is offered. Despite the glorious Empire and neoclassical facades of many of the hotels and spas, the rooms are a bit on the blah side—typical Central European bland for the most part—with a few exceptions listed below. Most of the hotels have ready-made packages with treatments, and if you plan to indulge in the spas anyway, they can offer some level of savings. Check the hotel's website for current offers. Private accommodations are usually cheaper than hotels, although with more limited amenities. The best place to look for a private room is along Paleckého ulice and Hlavní třída, south of the main spa area, or look in the neighboring villages of Zádub and Závišín.

$$$ HOTEL **Centrální Lázně.** Near the colonnade and Ambrose Spring, this egg-shell-white spa hotel offers unusual treatments such as magnetotherapy and peat packs. **Pros:** extensive therapies; central location (hence the name). **Cons:** not exactly a jumping scene; rooms are a bit spartan. [$] *Rooms from: 5250 Kč* ✉ *Goethovo nám. 1* ☎ *354–634–111* 🌐 *marianske-lazne.danubiushotels.cz* 🛏 *99 rooms* 🍴 *Breakfast.*

$$$ HOTEL **Grandhotel Pacifik.** This regal hotel at the top of Hlavní Street has been thoroughly renovated and now may be the best of the bunch, with a full range of spa and wellness facilities including a pool and a sauna. **Pros:** great views; prime location; extensive treatments. **Cons:** pricey; common areas a bit down at the heels. [$] *Rooms from: 4860 Kč* ✉ *Mírové nám. 84* ☎ *354–651–111* 🌐 *www.danubiushotels.com* 🛏 *102 rooms* 🍴 *Breakfast.*

$$ HOTEL **Hotel Bohemia.** As a cheaper alternative to some of the posher places in town, this late-19th-century hotel feels pleasantly down-to-earth. **Pros:** inexpensive compared with the other properties in town; friendly staff; beautiful fixtures. **Cons:** rooms a bit dark and grim; no spa. [$] *Rooms from: 3513 Kč* ✉ *Hlavní třída 100* ☎ *354–610–111* 🌐 *www.orea.cz/bohemia* 🛏 *Bohemia: 76 rooms; Dependence: 12 rooms* 🍴 *Breakfast.*

$$$ HOTEL **Hotel Grand Spa Marienbad.** The new kid on the block, this Austrian-owned hotel, made up of three interconnected buildings, boasts the most rooms and the biggest wellness center in Mariánské Lázně. **Pros:** huge spa; sleek rooms. **Cons:** officious staff; overly Teutonic vibe. [$] *Rooms from: 4380 Kč* ✉ *Ruska 123* ☎ *354–929–397* 🌐 *www.falkensteiner.com/en/hotel/marienbad* 🛏 *174 rooms* 🍴 *Some meals.*

$ HOTEL Fodor's Choice ★ **Hotel Koliba.** This hunting-style lodge is a perfect choice if you're here for just a day or two, puttering around town without an interest in lavish spa treatments. **Pros:** authentic charm; friendly staff. **Cons:** outside the center of town; a bit rustic. [$] *Rooms from: 1500 Kč* ✉ *Dusíkova 592* ☎ *354–625–169* 🌐 *www.hotel-koliba.cz* 🛏 *12 rooms* 🍴 *Breakfast.*

$$$ HOTEL **Hotel Nové Lázně.** This neo-Renaissance hotel and spa—opened in 1896—boasts an opulent façade and public spaces, but these give way to slightly austere rooms. **Pros:** beautiful façade; ideal for spa-fiends. **Cons:** not so ideal for the casual visitor; maintains a slight institutional feel. [$] *Rooms from: 6100 Kč* ✉ *Reitenbergerova 53* ☎ *354–644–111* 🌐 *www.danubiushotels.com* 🛏 *98 rooms* 🍴 *Breakfast.*

PERFORMING ARTS

The West Bohemian Symphony Orchestra performs regularly in the New Spa (Nové Lázně). The town's annual Chopin Festival each August brings in pianists from around Europe to perform the Polish composer's works.

NIGHTLIFE

Casino Bellevue. Open nonstop for those who want to try their luck, Casino Bellevue also caters to buses of tourists on shopping and gambling trips from Germany. ✉ *Anglická 281* ☎ *354–628–628* 🌐 *www.casino-bellevue.cz.*

Marianske Lazně's "Singing Fountain" sets off its water jets to accompanying music every hour.

PLZEŇ

92 km (55 miles) southwest of Prague.

Plzeň—or Pilsen in German, as it's better known abroad—is the industrial heart of Western Bohemia and the region's biggest city. To most visitors the city is known as a beer mecca. Anyone who loves the stuff must pay homage to the enormous Pilsner Urquell brewery, where modern Pils-style beer was first developed more than 150 years ago. Brewery tours are available and highly recommended. There's even a brewing museum here for intellectual beer aficionados.

Another item of interest—particularly for Americans—is historical. Whereas most of the Czech Republic was liberated by Soviet troops at the end of World War II, Plzeň was liberated by the U.S. Army, led by General George S. Patton. Under the communists this fact was not widely acknowledged. But since 1989 the liberation week celebrations held in May have gotten bigger and bigger each passing year. If you're traveling in the area at this time, it's worth stopping by to take part in the festivities. To this day Plzeň retains a certain "pro-American" feeling that other towns in the Czech Republic lack. There's even a big statue here emblazoned with an enthusiastic "Thank You, America!" written in both English and Czech. You'll find it, naturally, at the top of Americká Street near the intersection with Klatovská. You can learn all about the liberation at the Patton Memorial Museum.

GETTING HERE
Frequent bus and train service between Prague and Plzeň makes the journey about 1 hour 15 minutes each way. Expect to pay about 100 Kč for the bus, 105 Kč for the train. If you're driving, you can take the E50 directly to Plzeň, a drive of about one hour.

Visitor Information Plzeň City Information Centre. ⊠ *Nám. Republiky 41* ☎ *378–035–330* ⊕ *www.pilsen.eu/tourist.*

EXPLORING

TOP ATTRACTIONS

Náměstí Republiky (*Republic Square*). The city's architectural attractions center on this main square. Dominated by the enormous Gothic **Chrám svatého Bartoloměje** (Church of St. Bartholomew), the square is one of the largest in Bohemia. The church, at 335 feet, is among the tallest in the Czech Republic, and its height is rather accentuated by the emptiness of the square around it. There are a variety of other architectural jewels around the perimeter of the square, including the town hall, adorned with *sgraffiti* and built in the Renaissance style by Italian architects during the town's heyday in the 16th century. The **Great Synagogue,** which claims to be the second-largest in Europe, is a few blocks west of the square, just outside the green strip that circles the Old Town. Three very modern gold-colored fountains were added to the square in 2011; however, not everyone is a fan, as the fountains don't really mesh with the historic surroundings. ⊠ *Náměstí Republiky.*

Fodor's Choice
★
Pilsner Urquell Brewery. This is a must-see for any beer lover. The first Pilsner beer was created in 1842 using the excellent Plzeň water, a special malt fermented on the premises, and hops grown in the region around Žatec. (Hops from this area remain in great demand today.) Guided tours of the brewery, complete with a visit to the brewhouse and beer tastings, are offered daily. The brewery is near the railway station. The tour can be combined with a tour of the nearby Gambrinus brewery, the city's underground tunnels, and the Brewery Museum. ⊠ *U Prazdroje 7* ☎ *377–062–888* ⊕ *www.prazdrojvisit.cz* 🎫 *200 Kč (in English); 25% discount available for combined tours and Brewery Museum.*

QUICK BITES
Na Spilce. After a visit to the Pilsner Urquell Brewery, you can carry on drinking and find some cheap traditional grub at the large Na Spilce beer hall just inside the brewery gates. The pub is open weekdays and Sunday from 11 am to 10 pm, Friday and Saturday from 11 am to 11 pm. ⊠ *U Prazdroje 7* ⊕ *www.naspilce.com.*

Plzeň Historical Underground. Dating to the 13th century, this is a web of multilevel tunnels. Used for storing food and producing beer and wine, many of the labyrinthine passageways are dotted with wells and their accompanying wooden water-pipe systems. Tours last about 50 minutes. The entrance is in the Brewery Museum. ⊠ *Veleslavínova 6* ☎ *377–235–574* ⊕ *www.plzenskepodzemi.cz* 🎫 *120 Kč (in English); 25% discount available for combined tours and Brewery Museum.*

10

An old label of the local beer Pilsner Urquell, bottled in Plzeň

WORTH NOTING

Pilsen Beer Spa & Wellness Hotel Purkmistr. While Plzeň lacks the bitter thermal waters that are a draw in the spa region, it is better known for bitter Pilsner-style beer. So the opening of a beer spa was inevitable. You can bathe in a custom-made larchwood tub filled with warm beer for a 60-minute treatment. Potable beer is available from a barrel at the same time. The room is lined with stone tiles, and relaxing music plays in the background. The treatment can be combined with a beer massage, or a honey or chocolate massage. Other procedures are also available. The spa is a bit outside of the city center. ⊠ *Selská náves 21/2* ☎ *377–994–311* ⊕ *www.pilsenbeerspa.cz.*

Pivovarské muzeum (*Brewery Museum*). In a late-Gothic malt house, this museum sits one block northeast of náměstí Republiky. All kinds of fascinating paraphernalia trace the region's brewing history, including the horse-drawn carts used to haul the kegs. ■ TIP→ A phone app is available in place of an audio guide. ⊠ *Veleslavínova 6* ☎ *377–062–888* ⊕ *www.prazdrojvisit.cz* 📷 *90 Kč unguided (with English text), 30 Kč for audio guide, 25% discount when combined with brewery tour and underground.*

U.S. General George S. Patton Memorial. With exhibits and photos, this memorial tells the story of the liberation of Plzeň from the Nazis by U.S. soldiers on May 6, 1945. As the story goes, Patton wanted to press on from Plzeň to liberate Prague, but was prevented from doing so by the Yalta agreement between the United States and the Soviet Union that said Czechoslovakia was to remain under Soviet influence. U.S. aid to Czechoslovakia is also documented. The museum was dedicated in 2005 on the 60th anniversary of Plzeň's liberation. ✉ *Pobřežní 10* 📞 *378-037-954* ⊕ *www.patton-memorial.cz* 💲 *60 Kč* ◷ *Closed Mon.*

WHERE TO EAT

$
CAFÉ
✕ **Anděl Café.** In the evenings, this café, which offers affordable lunches and snacks, becomes a trendy bar. The emphasis is on fair trade items and food from local farmers who follow ecological practices. Formerly vegetarian, the bistro now serves some meat dishes. The interior is pleasant with that stripped-down modern look. 💲 *Average main: 110 Kč* ✉ *Bezručova 7* 📞 *777-022-235* ⊕ *www.andelcafe.cz.*

$
CAFÉ
✕ **Caffe Fellini.** This dessert spot is right across from St. Bartholomew Church. With an outdoor patio overlooking the square, it's a great place to cool down. Order some ice cream or a piece of cake and take in the front-row views. 💲 *Average main: 80 Kč* ✉ *Nám. Republiky 7* 📞 *776-151-429* ⊕ *www.caffefellini.cz* 💳 *No credit cards.*

$$
SPANISH
✕ **El Cid.** Strawberry-infused mojitos wash down excellent tapas dishes at this Spanish-style restaurant along the old town walls, just across from the Continental hotel. Pictures of bullfighters line the yellow walls, while a large patio overlooks the sprawling Křižíkovy Park. The menu also includes several types of paella, as well as pork neck marinated in olive oil and lobster cooked in wine and garlic. 💲 *Average main: 300 Kč* ✉ *Křižíkovy sady 1* 📞 *377-224-595* ⊕ *www.elcid.cz* ✍ *Reservations essential.*

$
PIZZA
✕ **Pizzerie Paganini.** Just off the main square on Rooseveltova, this cheery spot with red-and-white checked tablecloths serves up above-average thin-crust pies and pastas. Still, you're better off sticking with the simpler menu items rather than getting too fancy. 💲 *Average main: 120 Kč* ✉ *Rooseveltova 12* 📞 *377-326-604* ⊕ *pizza-paganini.cz.*

$$
MEDITERRANEAN
✕ **Rango.** Part of a hotel of the same name, the interior of Rango is a mash-up of medieval, baroque, and modern style—think Gothic arched ceilings and '60s modern light fixtures. Similarly, the cuisine ranges from Italy to Greece; in addition to pizzas and panini, they serve excellent mussels in white wine, and pork fillet in cream sauce with Parmesan and lemon. 💲 *Average main: 200 Kč* ✉ *Pražská 10* 📞 *377-329-969* ⊕ *www.rango.cz* ✍ *Reservations essential.*

$$
INTERNATIONAL
✕ **Slunečnice.** The sunny interior here echoes its name, which means "sunflower." This café bills itself as a health restaurant and offers some (but not exclusively) organic and vegetarian menu items in a variety of styles, from Indian to Italian. 💲 *Average main: 170 Kč* ✉ *Jungmannova 4* 📞 *377-236-093* ⊕ *www.slunecniceplzen.cz.*

$$
CZECH
✕ **U Mansfelda.** Fresh Pilsner Urquell and variations on classic Czech dishes draw diners to this Pilsner Urquell–sponsored restaurant. A gleaming copper hood floats above the taps in traditional pub style, and the patio invites visitors to spend the evening sipping cold beer and enjoying treats such as boar guláš with dumplings or roasted duck with red cabbage. The same space also has a wine bar (Vinárna). 💲 *Average main: 200 Kč* ✉ *Dřevěná 9* 📞 *377-333-844* ⊕ *umansfelda.cz* ◷ *Wine bar closed Mon. and Sat.*

10

WHERE TO STAY

$$ HOTEL **Courtyard Pilsen.** A surprising addition to the hotel scene in Plzeň, this sleek new property offers all the amenities a visiting American could hope for, right down to the flat-screen televisions and ice machines in the hallways on each floor. **Pros:** great amenities; a trusted name. **Cons:** doesn't feel especially local; extras such as breakfast are pricey. [$] *Rooms from: 2650 Kč* ✉ *Sady 5. kvetna 57* ☎ *373–370–100* 🌐 *www.marriott.com* 🛏 *195 rooms* 🍴 *No meals.*

$ HOTEL **Hotel Central.** This angular 1960s structure is recommendable for its sunny rooms, friendly staff, and great location, right on the main square. **Pros:** superlative staff; beautiful views of the main square; no-smoking restaurant; free Wi-Fi. **Cons:** the square can echo noise at night; very small bathrooms. [$] *Rooms from: 1566 Kč* ✉ *Nám. Republiky 33* ☎ *377–226–757* 🌐 *www.central-hotel.cz* 🛏 *77 rooms* 🍴 *No meals.*

$$ HOTEL **Hotel Gondola.** A superb choice, the Gondola is clean and quiet with cozy brick-walled rooms and modern facilities, including air-conditioning—all just a few steps away from the central square. **Pros:** incredible value; chockablock with add-ons. **Cons:** slightly odd location; limited business facilities. [$] *Rooms from: 2390 Kč* ✉ *Pallova 12* ☎ *377–994–211* 🌐 *www.hotelgondola.cz* 🛏 *20 rooms* 🍴 *Breakfast.*

$ HOTEL **Parkhotel Plzeň.** A 10-minute tram ride from the center, this large hotel built in 2004 near the Borský Park is perfect for anyone passing through town with a car. **Pros:** sleek new rooms; free Wi-Fi; golf course. **Cons:** outside the center; breakfast options rather limited. [$] *Rooms from: 1490 Kč* ✉ *U Borského parku 31* ☎ *378–772–977* 🌐 *en.parkhotel-czech.eu* 🛏 *150 rooms* 🍴 *Breakfast.*

NIGHTLIFE

House of Blues. House of Blues, related to the American chain in name only, showcases live blues and rock acts. Ignore the mirrored disco ball on the ceiling—ashtrays on every table let you know you're in a real joint. ✉ *Černická 10* ☎ *608–777–606* 🌐 *www.houseofblues.cz* 🕒 *Closed Aug.*

Jazz Rock Cafe. Jazz Rock Cafe gives you a license to party. Drop by on Wednesday to catch some live blues or jazz music. ✉ *Sedláčkova 18* ☎ *377–224–294* 🌐 *jazz.magicpoint.cz.*

Zach's pub. Zach's pub highlights various live acts, including Latin and blues, outdoors on its summer patio. The pub also serves reasonably priced Mexican food, and pets are welcome. ✉ *Palackého nám.* ☎ *377–223–176* 🌐 *www.zachspub.cz.*

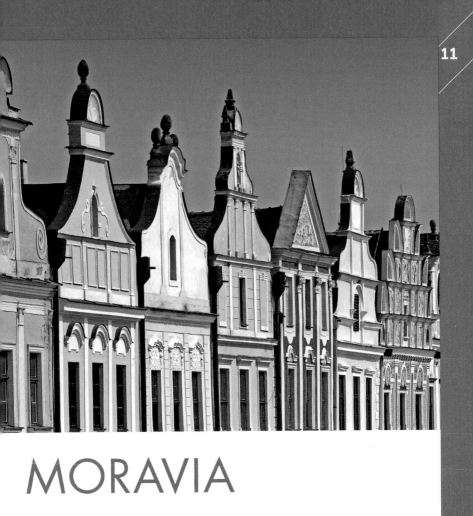

MORAVIA

WELCOME TO MORAVIA

TOP REASONS TO GO

★ **Circle the square:** In a country of town squares, Telč's is far and away the most impressive.

★ **See a classic castle:** When people think of castles, they imagine something like Hrad Bouzov.

★ **Spot colossal columns:** Olomouc's Trinity column is so amazing, it's under UNESCO protection.

★ **See the Château Lednice:** A delightful castle, with huge gardens and even a minaret out back!

★ **Uncover some new history:** It's exciting to watch Třebíč and Mikulov embrace their past by renovating and promoting their Jewish quarters.

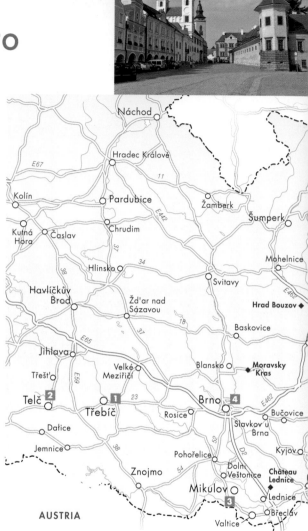

AUSTRIA

1 **Třebíč.** One of the best-preserved Jewish quarters in Central Europe, with a number of synagogues and a cemetery, this small town finds itself on the UNESCO World Heritage list. The city's dominant feature, however, is a looming Catholic basilica.

2 **Telč.** Time seems to have stopped several centuries ago in this town, almost unchanged since the Renaissance. Beautiful frescoes adorn the exteriors of most of the buildings in pastel colors or ornate black and white.

3 **Mikulov.** Moravia is wine country, and Mikulov is at

0   30 miles

0   30 km

O Jeseník

POLAND

Bruntál   Krnov

Opava O

Ostrava

Karviná

Český Těšín O

◆ **Hrad Šternberk**

O **Olomouc**

5

O Frýdek-Místek

Nový Jičín

O Přerov

Prostějov

Valašské Meziříčí

O Kroměříž

Zlín   49

Vsetín

Otrokovice O

Uherské Hradiště

SLOVAKIA

Uherské Brod

O Veselí

Hodonín

O Skalica

GETTING ORIENTED

The most obvious difference between Bohemia and Moravia is that the former is beer country and the latter is wine country. The divisions, while amicable, run much deeper. The people are also more in touch with their past, embracing folk costumes and music for celebrations. In smaller towns some older women still wear embroidered scarves and dresses, something you never see in Bohemia. The pace is also much slower, as agriculture and not industry has always been the driving force of life.

The castles and châteaux attest to the fact that the area was once quite wealthy, but in recent times development has been limited, leaving many areas still unspoiled. And because it's so far off the beaten path of Prague, you'll see far fewer tourists.

charm. That said, Brno also has a castle, a cathedral, and an Old Town Hall that would be on par with attractions in other European capitals.

5 Olomouc. The central city of Moravia was a major base for occupying Russian soldiers. Parts still have an abandoned feel, but the city is slowly waking up. The main square offers a truly monumental baroque column not far from a curious socialist-realist town clock built after World War II.

its center. Castles, châteaux, and sculpted parks dot the area, and vineyards cover many of the hills. Small wine cellars serve the best of the local beverages plus regional cuisine.

4 Brno. The capital of Moravia, Brno is a busy hub and the modern counterpoint to Prague's Old World

Updated by Raymond Johnston

The Czech Republic's other half, Moravia, is frequently overlooked by visitors. No cities here can compare with the noble beauty of Prague, and Moravia's gentle mountains suffer in comparison with the more rugged Tatras in Slovakia just to the east. Yet Moravia's colorful villages and rolling hills do merit a few days of exploration. Come here for good wine, good folk music, friendly faces, and the languid pace.

Despite sharing a common political union for more than 1,000 years with Bohemians, Moravians still consider themselves distinct from "Czechs" (though it must be said that those differences are not always apparent to visitors). The Moravian dialect of Czech is softer and—as Moravians insist—purer than that spoken in Bohemia. It's hard to generalize, but in a word the Moravians are "earthier" than their Bohemian cousins. They tend to prefer a glass of wine—or even better fiery *slivovice* (plum brandy)—to beer. Folk music, all but gone in Bohemia, is still very much alive in Moravia. And Catholicism is still a part of life here—particularly in cities like Olomouc—in a way that died out long ago in much of Bohemia.

Historically, Olomouc is one of its main centers. And it is still impressive today. Long a bastion of the Austro-Hungarian Empire—the city boasts two enormous central squares, a clock tower, and the country's largest Trinity column. In addition, southern Moravia has many small cities, including Mikulov, and a lovely wine region.

If your time is limited or you're just passing through, be sure to at least plan a stopover in the town of Telč in the south. Its enormous central square is like the backdrop of a film set.

PLANNING

WHEN TO GO

Wine harvest festivals, with the opportunity to taste the barely fermented young wine, hear folk songs, and eat local delicacies, are mainly in September. For some towns it is the only time they are truly crowded. But the summer months offer pleasant relaxation at outdoor cafés in an unhurried atmosphere. For bikers, many trails have opened up in the wine region, with spring and early summer being ideal for a tour. Winter should be avoided, especially in smaller towns, as many sights are closed and many shops still close for the weekend throughout the year.

GETTING HERE

Bus and train service makes much of Moravia easily accessible. A high-speed train to Olomouc makes it possible to go to there as a day trip, in just over two hours each way. And while trains do serve the smaller towns and cities, buses are usually more direct and faster. The D1 highway from Prague also leads into South Moravia and loops back up to end near Olomouc, but it gets heavy traffic at the start and end of the weekend.

GUIDED TOURS

Only a few tour providers offer day trips from Prague to Moravia, as it is farther than places in Bohemia. Guided tours are often available from tourist information centers in individual towns, but without transportation to and from Prague.

Travel agency Cesty za vínem. This travel agency creates customized small-group tours of the wine region, with transportation in a van from Prague or Brno, accommodations, and add-ons like live music and wine tastings. Note: It can be quite pricey. ⊕ *www.cestyzavinem.cz.*

Wittmann Tours. Wittmann Tours focuses on Jewish culture, and offers a trip to Třebíč. The trip is 2,900 Kč per person, plus entrance fees, in a group of five or more, or 10,000 Kč for a group of one or two. ⊕ *www. wittmann-tours.com.*

RESTAURANTS AND HOTELS

Compared with Prague, change has been slow to arrive in Moravia since 1990, especially beyond the major towns. The good news: food and hotels are priced lower. Service has improved but still lags behind Prague. Older hotel staff might not be proficient in English, but the younger generation has a functional level. And you might find menus in Czech and German, rather than English, especially in the south near the border. On the plus side, hotel and restaurant workers tend to be friendlier in Moravia and a bit more attentive than they are in Prague.

Cuisine in Moravia leans toward the heavy and the old-fashioned. Choices are sometimes limited to pork, chicken, and duck dishes, usually with lots of gravy. Slowly, a few places with healthier food and modern international cuisine are opening. Pizza places are also widespread. In mountainous areas, inquire locally about the possibility of staying in a *chata* (cabin). These are abundant, and they often carry a bit more of the Moravian spirit than faceless modern hotels. Many lack modern amenities, though, so be prepared to rough it a bit.

Hotel reviews have been shortened. For full information, visit Fodors. com.

WHAT IT COSTS IN KORUNA				
	$	$$	$$$	$$$$
Restaurants	under 150 Kč	150 Kč–350 Kč	351 Kč–500 Kč	over 500 Kč
Hotels	under 2,200 Kč	2,200 Kč–4,000 Kč	4,001 Kč–6,500 Kč	over 6,500 Kč

Restaurant prices are the average cost of a main course at dinner or, if dinner is not served, at lunch. Hotel prices are the lowest cost of a standard double room in high season.

TŘEBÍČ

35 km (21 miles) east of Telč; 151 km (91 miles) southeast of Prague.

UNESCO declared the looping streets of the Jewish Quarter and an ornate basilica in Třebíč both World Heritage Sites in 2003. The town is first mentioned in 1101, but it was almost completely destroyed in a war in 1468 and then rebuilt. Although known for its historic buildings, Třebíč also has a few modern ones in the art nouveau, cubist, and functionalist styles. Guided tours of the town are available in English from the information center at Karlovo náměstí 53. As in all small towns, very few shops are open on weekends.

If you arrive by bus or train from Prague, keep an eye out for the 19th-century windmill at the west edge of town. The town's tower **Městská věz** on Martinské Square provides a nice view of the whole city.

GETTING HERE

Ideally, you should combine Třebíč with a visit to Telč. Direct bus travel to Třebíč from Prague takes around 2½ hours and costs around 165 Kč. Train connections are not direct and are more expensive. Bus travel with a change in Jihlava, which has a nice square and town wall, is also possible; from Telč the bus trip takes less than 45 minutes and costs around 46 Kč.

Car travel from Telč is direct on Route 23 and takes about 20 minutes. From Prague it's fastest to get back on Highway E50 and go east to Velké Meziříčí. Then go south on Route 360; the trip should take less than three hours.

Visitor Information Třebíč Tourist information. ⊠ *Karlovo nám. 47* ☎ *568-847-070* ⊕ *www.visittrebic.eu.*

TIMING

Out of respect for Jewish traditions, some sites are closed on Saturday.

EXPLORING

11

Bazilika sv. Prokupa. The late Romanesque and early Gothic St. Procopius Basilica remains true to its original layout, from 1260. New sections were added as recently as the 1950s, but the oldest parts are easy to spot. Look for a very heavy style, with lots of stone and few windows. Two baroque towers at the front were added in the early 1700s by architect F. M. Kaňka. One of the oldest sections is the crypt, with Romanesque pillars and arches. The château next door has been fully renovated and houses the Vysočina Museum Třebíč. ⊠ Zámek 1 ☎ 568–610–022 ⊠ Basilica 100 Kč, museum 60 Kč.

Jewish Cemetery (Židovský hřbitov). The Jewish Cemetery has 3,000 tombstones dating from the Renaissance up to the 20th century. It's free to enter, but guided tours can be arranged. The cemetery is closed on Saturday, but almost all of it can be seen from the gate and the low wall. ⊠ Hrádek 14 ☎ 568–896–120 ⊠ Free ☉ Closed Sat.

Rear Synagogue. The Rear Synagogue has an exhibition of Jewish religious items and a wooden model of the ghetto as it was in the 1800s. A touch screen attached to the model provides audio information about the various buildings, with English as an option. Guided tours to the synagogue are available and also include a tour of the house of Seligmann Bauer. ⊠ Subakova 44 ☎ 568–610–023 ⊕ www.visittrebic.eu ⊠ 50 Kč, 120 Kč with a guide.

Židovská čtvrť (Jewish Quarter). A spiraling maze of winding streets, the Jewish Quarter has two synagogues and other buildings formerly used by the town's Jewish community. The **Front Synagogue** on Tiché náměstí is now used for Protestant services. Several houses in the district are intriguing, including a pink Renaissance house with an overhanging second floor at Pokorný 5. A trail of signs in English points out the remarkable spots. Remember your manners—most houses in this area are not museums, and people actually live in them. ⊠ Tiché náměstí ⊕ www.visittrebic.eu ⊠ Rear Synagogue 50 Kč, 120 Kč with a guide; Jewish Cemetery free; guided tour of Jewish Quarter 170 Kč (in English).

TELČ

35 km (21 miles) west of Třebič; 154 km (94 miles) southeast of Prague via Rte. 406.

Don't be fooled by the dusty approach to the little town of Telč or the unpromising, unkempt countryside surrounding the place. Telč is a knockout. What strikes the eye most here is not just its size but the unified style of the buildings. On the lowest levels are beautifully vaulted Gothic halls, just above are Renaissance floors and façades, and all the buildings are crowned with rich Renaissance and baroque gables.

A unified style is what makes Telč so lovely.

GETTING HERE

A car is your best option, and makes it easy to combine a trip to Telč with a stop in Třebič. From Prague, take Highway E50 and E59 south to Route 23 and then west to Telč. The trip takes about two hours without stops. Třebič is east on Route 23.

Direct bus service leaves from Prague's Florenc bus station and takes just under three hours; the fare is approximately 145 Kč. From Třebič a direct bus can take 42 minutes and costs around 46 Kč.

Train service from Prague requires several changes and takes more than four hours, so it isn't a practical option. It's recommended only for those who want the scenic route.

Visitor Information Telč Tourist Information. ✉ *Nám. Zachariáše z Hradce 10* ☎ *567–112–407* ⊕ *www.telc-etc.cz.*

EXPLORING

Kostel svatého Ducha (*Church of the Holy Spirit*). A tiny street leading off the main square takes you to the 160-foot Romanesque tower of the Church of the Holy Spirit, a solid tower finished off in conical gray peaks. This is the oldest standing structure in Telč, dating to the first quarter of the 13th century. The interior, however, is a confused hodgepodge, as the style was fiddled with repeatedly, first in a late-Gothic makeover and then refashioned again because of fire damage. ■**TIP**→ In the summer months, the tower is open for a small entrance fee. ✉ *Palackého ul.*

11

Fodor's Choice ★ **Náměstí Zachariáše z Hradce.** This main square is so perfect you feel like you've stepped into a painting, not a living town. Zacharias of Neuhaus, the square's namesake, allegedly created the architectural unity. During the 16th century, so the story goes, the wealthy Zacharias had the castle—originally a small fort—rebuilt into a Renaissance château. But the town's dull buildings clashed so badly that Zacharias had the square rebuilt to match the castle's splendor. Luckily for architecture fans, the Neuhaus dynasty died out shortly thereafter, and succeeding nobles had no desire to outfit the town in the latest architectural fashions.

If you've come by car, park outside the main walls on the south side of town and walk through the **Great Gate,** part of the original fortifications dating to the 13th century. As you approach on Palackého ulice, the square unfolds in front of you, graced with the château at the northern end and beautiful houses bathed in pastel ice-cream shades. Fans of Renaissance reliefs should note the *sgraffito* corner house at No. 15, etched like fine porcelain. The house at No. 61, across from the Černý Orel Hotel, also bears intricate details. ✉ *Náměstí Zachariáše z Hradce.*

Statní zámek Telč (*Telč château*). Credit the Italians for transforming this château from a Gothic castle into a refined Renaissance château. Grouped in a complex with the former **Jesuit college** and **Kostel svatého Jakuba** (Church of St. James), the castle was built during the 14th century, perhaps by King John of Luxembourg, the father of Charles IV. Renovation, overseen by Italian masters, took place between 1553 and 1568. In season you can tour the castle and admire the rich Renaissance interiors. Given the reputation of nobles for lively, lengthy banquets, the chastising *sgraffito* relief in the dining room depicting gluttony (in addition to the six other deadly sins) seems odd indeed. Other interesting rooms with *sgraffiti* include the Treasury, the Armory, and the Blue and Gold chambers. A curious counterpoint to all this Renaissance splendor is the castle's permanent exhibit of paintings by leading Czech modernist Jan Zrzavý. There are two tours: the first goes through the Renaissance chambers; the second displays the rooms that were used as recently as 1945. ✉ *Nám. J. Kypty* ☎ *567–243–943* 🌐 *www.zamek-telc.eu* 🎫 *Castle tours: 120 Kč Tour A (plus 100 Kč for English), 90 Kč Tour B (in Czech only). Underground 60 Kč, garden 10 Kč* ⏲ *Closed Mon.; no Tour B Oct.–Apr.*

QUICK BITES

Cukrárna u Mateje. Give in to your sweet tooth and indulge in good, freshly made cakes or an ice-cream cone at Cukrárna u Matěje, a little café and pastry shop at Na baště 2, on the street leading past the château to a small lake. ✉ ***Na baště 2.***

WHERE TO STAY

$ HOTEL 🏨 **Celerin.** Occupying a tiny corner of the square on the opposite side from the castle, this is the nicest hotel in town. **Pros:** central location on square; Wi-Fi connections. **Cons:** some rooms have limited views due to small (but historically accurate) windows; no elevator. [$] *Rooms from: 1530 Kč* ✉ *Nám. Zachariáše z Hradce 1/43* ☎ *567–243–477* 🌐 *www.hotelcelerin.cz* 🛏 *12 rooms* 🍴 *Breakfast.*

$ HOTEL 🏨 **Hotel U Černého orla.** In a lemon-yellow baroque house on the square, this is a decent older hotel that has nevertheless maintained suitably high standards. **Pros:** restored historic building right on the main square; free Wi-Fi access in rooms; pets can stay for free. **Cons:** lacks modern features such as A/C. [$] *Rooms from: 1800 Kč* ✉ *Nám. Zachariáše z Hradce 7* ☎ *567–243–222* 🌐 *www.cernyorel.cz* 🛏 *33 rooms* 🍴 *Breakfast.*

MIKULOV

60 km (37 miles) south of Brno; 283 km (174 miles) southeast of Prague.

In many ways Mikulov is the quintessential Moravian town, with pastel pink-and-yellow buildings and green rolling hills. For centuries it was one of the most important towns in the region—the seat of the Liechtenstein family in the late Middle Ages and then later the home to the powerful Dietrichstein family. The castle's size and splendor demonstrate Mikulov's onetime crucial position astride the traditional border between Moravia and Austria.

But Mikulov began an extended decline in the 19th century, when the main railroad line from Vienna bypassed the town in favor of Břeclav. Historically, Mikulov was the center of Moravia's Jewish community, growing to a population of several thousand at one point, but many Jews left to seek out life in bigger cities. The 20th century was especially cruel to Mikulov. The Nazis Aryanized many of the industries and deported remaining Jews. After the war, many local industries—including the all-important wineries—were nationalized. Mikulov stagnated as a lonely outpost at the edge of the Iron Curtain.

Recent years have seen a slow revival. Much of the wine industry is back in private hands, and standards have been raised, thanks in part to EU wine regulations. Day-trippers from Austria have spurred development of a nascent tourist industry. And after many decades of decline, the old Jewish Quarter is getting overdue attention. Although the Jewish community is still tiny—numbering just a handful of people—work is under way to try to preserve some of the remaining houses in the quarter. You can tour the quarter, where many of the houses are now marked with plaques explaining their significance. The Jewish cemetery is one of the largest in Central Europe, and a must-see if you're passing through.

Grape-harvesting time in October provides an ideal moment to visit and enjoy the local pastoral delights. Head for one of the many private *sklípeks* (wine cellars) built into the hills surrounding the town. If you visit in early September, try to hit Mikulov's renowned wine-harvest festival that kicks off the season with traditional music, folk dancing, and much guzzling of local Riesling.

GETTING HERE

Mikulov is easily reached by bus from Prague with a change at Brno's Zvonařka bus station. The trip takes a little more than 4 hours and costs about 270 Kč.

Main Square with the fountain and Holy Trinity Statue in Mikulov

Train service from Prague requires a change at Břeclav. It takes about 4½ hours and costs about 460 Kč.

By car, the trip is south of Brno on Highway E65 to Břeclav and then east on Route 40, and takes a little more than 30 minutes from Brno.

Visitor Information Mikulov Tourist Information. ✉ *Náměstí 1* ☎ *519–510– 855* ⊕ *www.mikulov.cz.*

EXPLORING

OFF THE BEATEN PATH

Château Lednice na Moravé. Just 12 km (7 miles) east of Mikulov is the Château Lednice na Moravé, a must-see if you happen to be in the area. The dining room alone, with resplendent blue-and-green silk wall coverings embossed with the Moravian eagle, makes the visit memorable. The grounds, not to be outdone by the sumptuous interior, have a 200-foot-tall minaret and a massive greenhouse filled with exotic flora. A horse-drawn carriage ride and a romantic boat ride are available, and are a great way to see the grounds. The absolute splendor of the palace and gardens contrasts sharply with the workaday reality of Lednice. ✉ *Zámek 1, Lednice* ☎ *519–340–128* ⊕ *www.zamek-lednice.com* 🎫 *Tours 180 Kč and 150 Kč each (2 circuits), plus 50 Kč per person for foreign language guide; Museum of Marionettes 150 Kč plus 50 Kč for foreign language guide; grotto 50 Kč; greenhouse 60 Kč; minaret 50 Kč; castle ruin 60 Kč* ☉ *Closed weekdays Nov.–May, and Mon. June–Sept.*

Fodor's Choice ★ **Jewish Cemetery** (*Židovský hřbitov*). Mikulov's massive and moving cemetery is not far from Husova ulice, just off Brněnská. The cemetery dates to shortly after 1421 when Jews were forced to leave Vienna and Lower Austria. The oldest legible stone is from 1605 and the most recent are from the 19th century, giving a wide range of stylistic flourishes. Stones for Moravian rabbis are among the most interesting. Step into the ceremonial hall to view an exhibit of the cemetery's history. The cemetery is open April to October, and during the rest of the year keys can be borrowed from the Tourist Information Center at Nám. 1. ✉ *Off Brněnská ul.* 🎟 *30 Kč* 🕓 *Closed Nov.–Mar., and Mon. in Apr. and Oct.*

Jewish Quarter (*Židovská čtvrt'*). Little of Mikulov's once-thriving Jewish Quarter still survives. The community once numbered several thousand people, and the town was the seat of the chief rabbi of Moravia from the 17th to the 19th century. Several respected Talmudic scholars, including Rabbis Jehuda Loew and David Oppenheimer, lived and taught here. What's left can be seen on a stroll down Husova ulice, which was once the center of the quarter. An information board near the corner with Brněnská ulice explains the significance of the community and what happened to it. The most important building still standing is the 16th-century Altschul. ✉ *Husova 11* 🎟 *Synagogue 50 Kč* 🕓 *Synagogue closed Mon.–Thurs. in Apr., Oct., and Nov., and Mon. in May and June.*

Mikulov zámek (*Mikulov Château*). Looming over the tiny main square and surrounding area is this arresting château. Built as the Gothic-era residence of the noble Liechtenstein family in the 13th century, the château later served as the residence of the powerful Dietrichsteins. Napoléon Bonaparte also stayed here in 1805 while negotiating peace terms with the Austrians after winning the Battle of Austerlitz (Austerlitz is now known as Slavkov, near Brno). Sixty-one years later, Bismarck used the castle to sign a peace treaty with Austria. The castle's darkest days came at the end of World War II, when retreating Nazi SS units set fire to it. Much of what you see today—though it looks deceptively ancient—is relatively new, having been rebuilt after World War II. The château holds the **Regionální Muzeum** (Regional Museum), exhibiting period furniture and local wine-making items, including a remarkable wine cask, made in 1643, with a capacity of more than 22,000 gallons. ■ **TIP→ There are four different tours that can be combined in various ways.** ✉ *Zámek 5* ☎ *519–309–019* 🌐 *www.rmm.cz* 🎟 *Full tour 150 Kč; history 80 Kč; cellar and barrel 50 Kč; wine history 50 Kč; Romans and Germans 50 Kč; chapel 30 Kč; night tours 150 Kč* 🕓 *Closed Nov.–Mar.*

WHERE TO STAY

$ HOTEL 🏨 **Hotel Tanzberg.** Prim and nicely renovated, this hotel sits in the middle of the former Jewish quarter, on Husova ulice. **Pros:** central location; historic building. **Cons:** few rooms; limited parking. [$] *Rooms from: 1250 Kč* ✉ *Husova ul. 8* ☎ *519–510–692* 🌐 *www.hotel-tanzberg.cz* 🛏 *14 rooms* 🍴 *Breakfast.*

BRNO

202 km (122 miles) southeast of Prague via Hwy. E65

Nicknamed the "Manchester of Moravia," Brno (pronounced "*burr-no*") has a different feel from other Czech or Moravian cities. Beginning with a textile industry imported from Germany, Holland, and Belgium, Brno became a leading industrial center of the Austro-Hungarian Empire during the 18th and 19th centuries. Some visitors search in vain for an extensive old town, pining for the traditional arcaded storefronts that typify other historic Czech towns. Instead, you'll see fine examples of the Empire and neo-Renaissance styles, their formal, geometric façades more in keeping with the conservative tastes of the 19th-century middle class.

In the 1920s and '30s, the city became home to some of the best young architects working in the early-modern, Bauhaus, and "international" styles. The architectural rivalry with Prague continues to this day, with Brno now claiming the country's tallest building. The AZ Tower beats Prague's City Tower by a mere six feet. When Prague roundly rejected a modern library designed by famed architect Jan Kaplický, a scale model of the façade was built as a bus stop on Okružní Street in Brno's Lesná district.

Experimentation wasn't restricted to architecture. Leoš Janáček, an important composer of the early modern period, lived and worked in Brno, as did Austrian novelist Robert Musil. That artistic support continues today, and the city is considered to have some of the best theater and performing arts in the country, as well as a small but thriving café scene. It has also become a high-tech development hub, with numerous software companies, several good science-oriented schools, and a government-backed support center.

And while the city has been reaching new heights with skyscrapers in its "Little Manhattan" area, it has also been reaching new depths by recently opening up an underground labyrinth as well as Europe's largest ossuary—a subterranean collection of human bones from several centuries.

Allow a couple of hours to fully explore the Špilberk Castle. Museum enthusiasts could easily spend a half day or more browsing through the city's many collections. Brno is relatively busy on weekdays, surprisingly slow on weekends. Avoid the city at trade-fair time (the biggest are in early spring and early autumn), when hotel and restaurant facilities are strained. If the hotels are booked, the tourist information center at the town hall will help you find a room.

GETTING HERE AND AROUND

Bus connections from Prague's Florenc terminal to Brno are frequent, and the trip is a half hour shorter than the train route. Most buses arrive at the main bus station, a 10-minute walk from the train station. Some buses stop next to the train station. Bus and train lines connect Brno and Vienna and run several times a day.

SAVED BY THE BELL

During the Thirty Years' War, Brno faced a fierce attack by Swedish troops. Brno's resistance was determined, and the Swedish commander decided that if the town couldn't be taken by noon the next day, they would give up the fight. Word of this reached the cathedral's bell ringer, and just as the Swedish troops were preparing their final assault, they rang the noon bells—an hour early. The ruse worked, and the Swedes decamped. The cathedral bells proved to be the final defensive strategy that saved the town from being taken. The new bullet-shape clock at Náměstí Svobody commemorates this by dropping a glass ball into a hole at 11 am every day.

Brno—within easy driving distance of Prague, Bratislava, and Vienna—is 196 km (122 miles) from Prague and 121 km (75 miles) from Bratislava. The E65 highway links all three cities.

Comfortable EuroCity or InterCity trains run six times daily, making the three-hour run from Prague to Brno's station. They depart either from Prague's main station, Hlavní nádraží, or the suburban nádraží Holešovice. Trains leaving Prague for Bratislava, Budapest, and Vienna normally stop in Brno (check timetables to be sure).

Trams are the best way to get around the city. Tickets start at 10 Kč for one zone with no transfer and go up to 86 Kč, depending on the time and zones traveled, and are available at newsstands and yellow ticket machines. A 25 Kč ticket allows for an hour of travel with changes. Tickets from the driver cost more. Single-day, three-day, and other long-term tickets are available. Most trams stop in front of the main station (Hlavní nádraží). Buses to the city periphery and nearby sights such as Moravský Kras in northern Moravia congregate at the main bus station, a 10-minute walk behind the train station. To find it, simply go to the train station and follow the signs to "čsad."

The nominal taxi fare is about 30 Kč per km (½ mile), on top of a 40 Kč initial fee. There are taxi stands at the main train station, Výstaviště exhibition grounds, and on Joštova Street at the north end of the Old Town, and other locations. Brush up on your Czech—dispatchers sometimes don't understand English.

Information Hlavní nádražní. ⊠ *Nádražní 1* ☎ *542–214–803* ⊕ *www.idos.cz.*
Main bus station (*ÚAN Zvonařka*). ⊠ *Zvonařka 1* ☎ *543–217–733.*

Visitor Information Brno Tourist Information. ⊠ *Radnická 8, Old Town Hall* ☎ *542–427–150* ⊕ *www.ticbrno.cz.*

EXPLORING

TOP ATTRACTIONS

Hrad Špilberk (*Spielberg Castle*). Once among the most feared places in the Hapsburg Empire, this fortress-cum-prison still broods over Brno behind menacing walls. The castle's advantageous location brought the early lords of the city, who moved here during the 13th century from neighboring Petrov Hill. Successive rulers gradually converted the old castle into a virtually impregnable fortress. Indeed, it successfully withstood the onslaughts of Hussites, Swedes, and Prussians over the centuries; only Napoléon, in 1809, succeeded in occupying the fortress. But the castle's fame comes from its gruesome history as a prison for enemies of the Austro-Hungarian monarchy and later for the Nazis' prisoners during World War II. Although tales of torture during the Austrian period are probably untrue (judicial torture had been prohibited prior to the first prisoners' arrival in 1784), conditions for the hardest offenders were hellish: they were shackled day and night in dank, dark catacombs and fed only bread and water. The castle complex is large, and the various parts generally require separate admissions. The **casemates** (passages within the walls of the castle) have been turned into an exhibition of the late-18th-century prison and their Nazi-era use as an air-raid shelter. You can see the entire castle grounds as well as the surrounding area from the **observation tower.** Aboveground, a **museum** in the fortress starts off with more displays on the prison era with detailed English texts. Included in the tour of the museum is an exhibition on the history of Brno, including several panoramic paintings of the city in the 17th century, and photos showing then-and-now views of 19th- and 20th-century redevelopment in the Old Town. One of the best of the permanent exhibitions focuses on the city's modern architectural heritage. You'll find room after room of sketches, drawings, and photographs of the most important buildings from the 1920s and '30s. Unfortunately, most of the descriptions are in Czech, but if you speak the language, you'll be in heaven. ■**TIP➜** Admission and opening hours vary according to what you want to see and where you want to go, i.e. entire complex, various combinations of exhibits, or individual castle sections. ✉ *Špilberk 1* ☎ *542–123–611* ⊕ *www.spilberk.cz* ✻*Entire complex 280 Kč; casemates 90 Kč; exhibitions and individual sections 150 Kč each; observation tower 50 Kč; south bastion 100 Kč* ۞ *Closed Mon. Oct.–Mar.*

Villa Tugendhat. Designed by Ludwig Mies van der Rohe and completed in 1930, this austere, white Bauhaus villa counts among the most important works of the modern period and is now a UNESCO World Heritage Site. Function and the use of geometric forms are emphasized. The Tugendhat family fled before the Nazis, and their original furnishings vanished. Replicas of Mies's cool, functional designs have been installed in the downstairs living area. Some of the original exotic wood paneling and an onyx screen remain in place. The best way to get there is to take a taxi or Tram No. 3, 5, or 11 to the Dětská nemocnice stop and then walk up unmarked Černopolní ulice for 10 minutes or so; you'll be able to see the modernist structure up on the hill. ■ **TIP➜ Reservations for tours are highly recommended, at least two months in advance, and can be made online.** The extended tour shows some of the building's infrastructure. ✉ *Černopolní 45* ☎ *545-212-118* ⊕ *www.tugendhat.eu* 🍴 *Basic tour 300 Kč, extended tour 350 Kč* ⊘ *Closed Mon. and Tues. in Jan. and Feb., and Mon. Mar.–Dec.*

WORTH NOTING

AZ Tower. As of April 2013, Brno has the tallest building in the Czech Republic. The AZ Tower rises 364 feet (111 meters), which is almost 7 feet taller than Prague's City Tower. It has mostly offices, with a few luxury apartments and a lower-level shopping mall. The wiggly-shape dark orange building has its critics, but many residents take beating Prague in the height contest as a point of pride. The tower also was planned to be ecological, with built-in solar panels and other green features. The roof, however, is not open to the public. Aside from shopping in the stores, there is little reason to go inside. ✉ *Pražákova* ☎ *543-236-244* ⊕ *www.aztower.org.*

Chrám svatých Petra a Pavla (*Cathedral of Saints Peter and Paul*). Best admired from a distance, the silhouette of slim neo-Gothic twin spires— added in the 20th century—give the cathedral a touch of Gothic dignity. Up close, the interior is light and tasteful but hardly mind-blowing. This is the church pictured on the face of the 10 Kč coin. ✉ *Petrov, at Petrská ul.* ⊕ *www.katedrala-petrov.cz* 🍴 *Free.*

Kostel Nalezení svatého Kříže (*Church of the Holy Cross*). If you've ever wondered what a mummy looks like without its bandages, this church will hold the answer. Formerly part of the Capuchin Monastery, the Church of the Holy Cross combines a baroque form with a rather stark façade. Enter the *krypta* (crypt) in the basement and the mummified remains of some 200 nobles and monks from the late 17th and 18th centuries are displayed, ingeniously preserved by a natural system of air circulating through vents and chimneys. The best-known mummy is Colonel František Trenck, commander of the brutal Pandour regiment of the Austrian army, who, at least in legend, spent several years in the dungeons of Špilberk Castle before finding his final rest here in 1749. Experts have concluded that his head is real, contrary to stories of its removal by a thief. A note of caution about the crypt: the graphic displays can be frightening to children (and even some adults), so ask at the admission desk for a small brochure (60 Kč) with pictures that preview what's to come, or look at the postcards for sale. Locals simply refer to the building as the Capuchin Church. ✉ *Kapucínské nám. 5* ☎ *542-213-232* ⊕ *www.kapucini.cz* 🍴 *70 Kč, plus 30 Kč to take pictures.*

Kostnice u sv. Jakuba (*St. James Ossuary*). Several basement rooms in the St. James Church are filled with neatly stacked bones, making it one of the largest ossuaries in Europe. Sealed up since the late 1700s, its contents were unearthed in 2001 and were cleaned after years of neglect before being opened to the public in 2012. Remains of some 50,000 people are estimated to be in the rooms, including victims of plagues, epidemics, and wars from the 13th to 18th centuries. It is much larger than the famous ossuary in Kutná Hora in Central Bohemia, which has bones in decorative designs. ✉ *Jakubské náměstí* ☎ *515–919–793* ⊕ *www.ticbrno. cz/en/podzemi/kostnice-u-sv-jakuba* 💰 *140 Kč, plus 50 Kč to take video (no fee for still photograpy)* ☾ *Closed Mon.*

Labyrint pod Zelným trhem (*Labyrinth under Zelný trh*). Some 2,296 feet of underground passages are filled with exhibits relating to alchemy, medicine, medieval punishment, and the more mundane aspects of life— like storing wine. Some of the old passages were rediscovered in the 1970s, and have undergone years of archeological research before opening to the public in 2011. Unfortunately, explanatory plaques are only in Czech. ✉ *Zelný trh 21* ☎ *542–212–892* ⊕ *www.ticbrno.cz* 💰 *160 Kč, plus 50 Kč to take video (no fee for still photography)* ☾ *Closed Mon.*

Mincmistrovský sklep (*Mintmaster's cellar*). The project to open up some of Brno's medieval underground includes access to the Mintmaster's cellar, which is under the house of Bruno, one of the city's coinmakers. The basement opened to the public in 2010 after being discovered during excavations in 1999. An exhibition in the vaulted rooms shows historical minting techniques. ✉ *Dominikánské nám. 1* ☎ *602–128–124* ⊕ *www.ticbrno.cz* 💰 *80 Kč, plus 50 Kč to take video (no fee for still photography)* ☾ *Closed Tues.*

Místodržitelský palác (*Governor's Palace*). Moravia's strong artistic ties to Austria can be seen in the impressive collection of painting and sculpture found in this splendid palace. The museum is divided into sections, but the most imprerssive part—art from the Gothic period to the 19th century—is on the first floor. The short-term exhibits are often a bit disappointing. ✉ *Moravské nám. 1A* ☎ *532–169–130* ⊕ *www. moravska-galerie.cz* 💰 *Permanent exhibits free, temporary exhibits vary* ☾ *Closed Mon. and Tues.*

Muzeum Romské kultury (*Museum of Romani Culture*). A small but singular museum devoted to the culture of the Roma, as Gypsies prefer to be called, is halfway between Brno's historical center and the high-rise housing projects. To bridge cross-cultural understanding (as Roma people are often the victims of discrimination), this museum is dedicated to their culture and history. Exhibits deal with traditional occupations, dress, and lifestyles. A study room has documents and photographs. ✉ *Bratislavská 67* ☎ *545–581–206* ⊕ *www.rommuz.cz* 💰 *80 Kč, English text 80 Kč* ☾ *Closed Mon. and Sat.*

Náměstí Svobody (*Freedom Square*). The best place to start any walking tour, this is the focal point of the city and a centerpiece for the massive effort to modernize the area. The square underwent extensive renovation in 2006, and adjoining streets feature some of the city's best shopping. Anyone who has been to Vienna might experience déjà vu here, as many of the buildings were designed by 19th-century Austrian architects. Especially noteworthy is the stolid Klein Palace at No. 15, built by Theophil Hansen and Ludwig Foerster, both prominent for their work on Vienna's Ringstrasse. A highly controversial clock—it's supposed to look like a bullet and remind people of a battle that happened in 1645—was added in 2010; most people, however, say it looks more like, ahem...a sex toy than a bullet. Also, you need a pamphlet to explain how to read the time on it. ⊠ *Náměstí Svobody.*

Pražákův palác (*Pražák Palace*). The largest collection of modern and contemporary Czech art outside of Prague lines the walls of this handsome, 19th-century neo-Renaissance building. If you've already seen these same artists represented in Prague's major galleries, you may be tempted to adopt a been-there-done-that attitude. But the emphasis here is on Moravian artists, who tended to prefer rural themes—their avant-garde concoctions have a certain folksy flavor. Modern and contemporary art is on the second floor; other sections have temporary exhibits. ⊠ *Husova 18* ☏ *542–215–758* ⊕ *www.moravska-galerie.cz* ⊡ *Permanent exhibits free, temporary exhibits vary* ☉ *Closed Mon. and Tues.*

▌NEED A
BREAK

Stopkova pivnice. After climbing to Špilberk Castle and touring several museums, what could be better than a nice cold beer? The Stopkova pivnice will set you up with one; if you're hungry, try the house guláš. Now part of the Kolkovna chain, there has been a pub on this site since the late 19th century. Its fame dates to the arrival of its new owner, the ingenious publican Jaroslav Stopka, who took over the original Jonákova pivnice in 1910. ⊠ *Česká 5* ⊕ *www.kolkovna.cz.*

Stará radnice (*Old Town Hall*). The oldest secular building in Brno exhibits an important Gothic portal. This door is the work of Anton Pilgram, architect of Vienna's St. Stephen's Cathedral. It was completed in 1510, but the building itself is about 200 years older. Look above the door to see a badly bent pinnacle that looks as if it wilted in the afternoon sun. This isn't the work of vandals, but was apparently done by Pilgram himself out of revenge against the town. According to legend, Pilgram had been promised an excellent commission for his portal, but when he finished, the mayor and city councillors reneged on their offer. Pilgram was so angered by the duplicity that he purposely bent the pinnacle and left it poised, fittingly, over the statue of justice.

Just inside the door are the remains of two other famous Brno legends, the **Brno Dragon** and the **wagon wheel**. The dragon—actually an alligator—apparently turned up at the town walls one day in the 17th century and began eating children and livestock. As the story goes, a gatekeeper came up with the idea of stuffing a freshly slaughtered goat with limestone. The dragon devoured the goat, swallowing the limestone as well, and when it drank at a nearby river, the water mixed with the limestone and burst the dragon's stomach (the scars on the preserved dragon's stomach are still clearly visible). The story of the wagon wheel, on the other hand, concerns a bet placed some 400 years ago that a young wheelwright, Jiří Birek, couldn't chop down a tree, form the wood into a wheel, and roll it from his home at Lednice (53 km [33 miles] away) to the town walls of Brno—all between sunup and sundown. The wheel stands as a lasting tribute to his achievement. (The townspeople, however, became convinced that Jiřì had enlisted the help of the devil to win the bet, so they stopped frequenting his workshop; poor Jiřì died penniless.)

No longer the seat of the town government, the Old Town Hall holds exhibitions and performances, and the town's tourist information office. To find out what's on, ask in the information center just inside Pilgram's portal. The view from the top of the tower is one of the best in Brno, but the climb (five flights) is strenuous. ⊠ *Radnická 8* ⊕ *www.kultura-brno.cz* ⊠ *Tower 50 Kč* ☾ *Closed Oct.–Mar.*

10-Z Fallout Shelter. A Cold War–era relic, this highly classified (hence the "10-Z" code name) shelter was designed to protect the political elite of the region in the event of a nuclear attack. Built during the Nazi occupation in World War II as a bomb shelter, between 1945 and '48 it was used by a wine wholesaler, after which it served as a secret shelter until 1989. Up to 500 people could have stayed inside if needed, but fortunately no one had to. It was declassified and opened to the public in 2015. There is an exhibition about the Cold War at the entrance with English text. Guided group tours of the whole complex with a flashlight (they provide them) take place as well, with some at night. On the tour you can see underground offices, a phone switchboard, heavy doors, and other curious infrastructure. The entrance is across the street from Husova 12. ⊠ *Husova* ⊕ *ticbrno.cz* ⊠ *Exhibition 79 Kč, guided tour 240 Kč. Tour tickets available at the Tourist Information Center at Radnické 8* ☾ *Closed Mon.*

Fodor'sChoice
★ **Uměleckoprůmyslové muzeum** (*Museum of Applied Arts*). Arts and crafts shine in this museum, which is without a doubt the Czech Republic's best venue to see applied arts. It has an assemblage of artifacts far more extensive than the truncated collection in Prague's museum of the same name. The collection includes Gothic, art nouveau, and Secessionist pieces, as well as an excellent, comprehensive overview of Bohemian and Moravian glass. Keep an eye out for the elegant furniture from Josef Hoffmann's Wiener Werkstätte (Vienna Workshop). Milan Knížák's jagged, candy-color table provides a striking example of contemporary work. ⊠ *Husova 14* ☎ *532–169–111* ⊕ *www.moravska-galerie.cz* ⊠ *Permanent exhibits free, temporary exhibits vary* ☾ *Closed Mon. and Tues.*

Zelný trh (*Cabbage Market*). Only in this Cabbage Market could Brno begin to look like a typical Czech town—not just for the many stands from which farmers still sell vegetables but also for the flamboyant **Parnassus Fountain** that adorns its center. This baroque outburst (inspiring a love-it-or-hate-it reaction) couldn't be more out of place amid the formal elegance of most of the buildings on the square. But when Johann Bernhard Fischer von Erlach created the fountain in the late 17th century, it was important for a striving town like Brno to display its understanding of the classics and of ancient Greece. Therefore Hercules slays a three-headed dragon, and Amphitrite awaits the arrival of her lover—all incongruously surrounded by farmers hawking turnips and onions. What could be more Czech? ⊠ *Zelný trh.*

WHERE TO EAT

$$ INDIAN 🍴 **Flavours.** This Indian eatery, formerly called Taj, is hidden upstairs in an atmospheric Victorian house. The dark wood furnishings are a bit out of character, but large windows help to brighten up the place. All-you-can-eat lunch and dinner buffets are available, in addition to a large menu of vegetarian and meat dishes. Be sure to point out if you want the food spicy, as Czechs tend to prefer blander versions. [$] *Average main: 200 Kč* ✉ *Běhounská 12/14* ☎ *725–372–595* 🌐 *www.flavoursbrno.cz.*

$$$ CZECH 🍴 **Pavillon Restaurant.** A contemporary re-creation of a landmark 1920s coffeehouse (the original was razed by the Communists to make way for a theater), this spot is high on flapper flair. Everything from the light fixtures to the furniture was faithfully copied from the original interior. In summer, the windows mechanically retract into the floor. Lofty ceilings provide pleasant, lilting acoustics, and the food lives up to the modern atmosphere. The restaurant now has trendy multicourse tasting menus in the evening, and offers gourmet Czech lunches during the day. [$] *Average main: 450 Kč* ✉ *Jezuitská 6, between Za Divadlem and Koliště* ☎ *541–213–497* 🌐 *www.restaurant-pavillon.cz.*

$$ CZECH 🍴 **Restaurace Špalíček.** This homey pub has a terrific central location right on the edge of the Zelný trh (Cabbage Market). The menu features the standard roast pork and dumplings kind of thing, but in a comfortable and merry setting. On a warm evening in summer sit outside and bask in the view on the square. [$] *Average main: 150 Kč* ✉ *Zelný trh 12* ☎ *542–211–526* 💳 *No credit cards.*

$$ CZECH 🍴 **U Královny Elišky.** With rooms named "The Musketeer" and "The Napoléon" and a menu full of wild game and fish, this 14th-century wine cellar turned restaurant remains true to its historic roots. In summer the historic ambience gets kicked up a notch as the garden becomes an arena for fencers in historical dress crossing swords, while spectators enjoy roast suckling pig or lamb. The adjacent pension ($) offers eight reasonably comfortable rooms at a good price (rates double during major trade fairs, however). [$] *Average main: 180 Kč* ✉ *Mendlovo nám. 1B* ☎ *543–212–578* 🌐 *www.ukralovnyelisky.cz* 🕓 *Closed Sun. and Mon.*

WHERE TO STAY

$$ HOTEL 🏨 **Grandhotel Brno.** The hotel dates to 1870, but got a thorough face-lift in the late 1980s and another upgrade in recent years, making it both comfortable and convenient, especially if you're traveling to Brno by train, as it's just across the street from the station. **Pros:** close to main transportation hub; air-conditioning. **Cons:** parking at the hotel is limited. [$] *Rooms from: 2500 Kč* ✉ *Benešova 18/20* ☎ *542–518–111* 🌐 *www.grandhotelbrno.cz* 🛏 *105 rooms* 🍽 *Breakfast.*

$$ HOTEL 🏨 **Hotel Pegas.** A little inn with a reasonable price and central location, Pegas has plain rooms that are snug and clean, with wood paneling and down comforters. **Pros:** on-site brewery; central location; Wi-Fi included in room fee. **Cons:** car access impossible due to pedestrian

zone; elevator does not reach ground floor. ⓢ *Rooms from: 2500 Kč* ✉ *Jakubská 4* ☎ *542-210-104* ⊕ *www.hotelpegas.cz* ⟿ *14 rooms* ⓸ *Breakfast.*

$$ **⌂ Royal Ricc.** Lovingly restored from a baroque town house, this bou-
HOTEL tique hotel retains period details, like exposed-beam ceilings. **Pros:** fine
Fodor's Choice detail in furniture and decoration make this an outstanding centrally
★ located hotel. **Cons:** hard to access by car since it's at the edge of a
pedestrian zone. ⓢ *Rooms from: 2450 Kč* ✉ *Starobrněnská 10* ☎ *542-
219-262* ⊕ *www.royalricc.cz* ⟿ *30 rooms* ⓸ *Breakfast.*

$ **⌂ Slavia.** The century-old Slavia, just off the main Česká ulice, feels a
HOTEL little dated, but the prices here are lower than at the comparable Grand
Hotel and the location is excellent. **Pros:** no-smoking rooms and rooms
for people with disabilities. **Cons:** rooms lack character. ⓢ *Rooms from:
1650 Kč* ✉ *Solniční 15/17* ☎ *542-321-249* ⊕ *www.slaviabrno.cz* ⟿ *84
rooms* ⓸ *Breakfast.*

PERFORMING ARTS AND NIGHTLIFE

Brno is renowned throughout the Czech Republic for its theater and
performing arts. Jacket-and-tie cultural events take place at a few main
venues slightly northwest of the center of town, a five-minute walk
from Náměstí Svobody. Check posted schedules at the theaters or on
their websites.

TICKETS

Divadlo Husa na provázku (*Goose on a String Theater*). One of the coun-
try's best-known fringe theater companies, Divadlo Husa na provázku,
has its home in Brno. ✉ *Zelný trh 9, at Petrská ulice* ☎ *542-211-630*
⊕ *www.provazek.cz.*

Janáček Theater. Opera and ballet productions are held at the modern
Janáček Theater. ✉ *Rooseveltova 7* ☎ *542-158-252* ⊕ *www.ndbrno.cz.*

Klub Alterna. A few blocks north of the city center, Klub Alterna hosts
good Czech jazz and folk performers. ✉ *Kounicova 48* ☎ *541-212-091*
⊕ *www.alterna.cz.*

Mahen Theater. The Mahen Theater is the city's principal venue for dra-
matic theater. ✉ *Rooseveltova 1* ☎ *542-158-252* ⊕ *www.ndbrno.cz.*

Předprodej vstupenek. In Brno you can buy tickets for performing arts
productions at individual theater box offices or at the central Předprodej
vstupenek. ✉ *Běhounská 17* ⊕ *vstupenky.ticbrno.cz.*

SHOPPING

Bright red, orange, and yellow flower patterns are the signature folk-
pottery look in Moravia. You can find these products in stores and hotel
gift shops throughout the region.

The shopping mall **Vaňkovka** (✉ *Ve Vaňkovce 1* ☎ *533-110-199*), link-
ing the main rail station and main bus station, has several restaurants
and stores for clothing.

Antikvariát Alfa. For rare books, art monographs, old prints, and a great selection of avant-garde 1920s periodicals, stop by Antikvariát Alfa. ✉ *Veselá 39* ☎ *542-211-947* ⊕ *www.antikalfa.cz* ☉ *Closed weekends.* **Galerie Ambrosiana.** For sophisticated artwork, including paintings and photography, stop by Galerie Ambrosiana. ✉ *Jezuitská 11* ☎ *542-214-439* ⊕ *www.ambrosiana.cz* ☉ *Closed weekends.*

OLOMOUC

77 km (48 miles) northeast of Brno; 275 km (165 miles) east of Prague.

Olomouc (pronounced "oh-loh-moats") is a handsome district capital, with some beautifully restored baroque houses along its broad central squares and the country's largest Trinity column, another UNESCO World Heritage Site. Its laid-back, small-town feel and the presence of a charming, inexpensive pension right in town make it an easy choice for an overnight stay.

Olomouc owes its relative prosperity to its loyalty to the Austro-Hungarian Empire. In the revolutionary days of the mid-19th century, when the rising middle classes throughout the empire were asserting their independence from the nobility, the residents of Olomouc remained true to the ruling Hapsburgs. During the revolutions of 1848, the royal family even fled here from Vienna for protection. Mozart, Mahler, and other famous composers stopped by on occasion, leaving behind a musical heritage that is still alive today with an active classical music scene.

The most prominent open space in Olomouc is the triangular Horní náměstí (Upper Square). Four of the city's half-dozen renowned **baroque fountains**, depicting Hercules (1687), Caesar (1724), Neptune (1695), and Jupiter (1707), dot the square and the adjacent other large square, Dolní náměstí (Lower Square) to the south.

A discount card called the **Olomouc Region Card** is valid for most tourist sights in and around the city, and for public transportation in the city, and is available at 240 Kč for 48 hours and at 480 Kč for five days. Admission to the Town Hall tower, botanical gardens, zoo, Hrad Bouzov, Hrad Šternberk, and other sites is included. The card also provides discounts at some restaurants, pools, fitness centers, and hotels. You can buy the card—and get more information on discounts and deals—at the main tourist information center at Horní náměstí 1 and at many hotels, travel agencies, and tourist venues. The information center also can tell you about local tour operators that organize half-day outings to the area's castles.

GETTING HERE

Traveling from Prague, in addition to driving, you can take either a train or a bus. By car, follow the D1 motorway south to Brno and then follow the signs and turnoffs to Olomouc from Brno. The trip will take about 3 hours in moderate traffic.

Direct train travel from Prague takes at least 2¾ hours, and costs around 220 Kč for the 250-km (150-mile) trip. High-speed Pendolino trains also serve Olomouc from Hlavní nádraží; seat reservations are required, often at no additional fee. Privately operated trains by Leo Express also travel here, with tickets starting at 169 Kč. Bus travel requires a change at Brno and takes over four hours.

Visitor Information Olomouc Tourist Information. ⌂ *Radnice, Horní nám.* ☎ *585-513-385* ⊕ *www.tourism.olomouc.eu.*

EXPLORING

TOP ATTRACTIONS

Arcidiecézní muzeum (*Archdiocesan Museum*). At this house in 1767 the young musical prodigy Wolfgang Amadeus Mozart, age 11, spent six weeks recovering from a mild attack of chicken pox and completed his Sixth Symphony. The 16-year-old King Wenceslas III suffered a much worse fate here in 1306, when he was murdered, putting an end to the Přemyslid dynasty. Now it houses treasures from the collections of the archdiocese, including golden monstrances, religious paintings, carved ivory objects, and a full-sized gilded coach. Modern art is also displayed in part of the building complex and included in the same admission, but is often a bit disappointing in comparison. ⌂ *Václavské nám. 3* ☎ *70 Kč (free Sun. and 1st Wed. of the month), includes Romanesque Bishop's Palace* ☉ *Closed Mon.*

OFF THE BEATEN PATH

Hrad Bouzov (*Bouzov Castle*). One of Moravia's most impressive castles, 30 km (18 miles) west of Olomouc, has been featured in several fairy-tale films. Its present romanticized exterior comes from a remodeling at the turn of the 20th century, but the basic structure dates back to the 1300s. Owned by the Order of Teutonic Knights from the late 1600s up to the end of World War II, it was later confiscated by the state. Inside, the knights' hall has extensive carved-wood decorations and wall paintings that look old, even if many are reconstructions. Other rooms have collections of period furniture. The castle kitchen, which was used until 1945, is one of the best-preserved examples. The castle offers several tours, some aimed at children and one that shows off the wedding hall and knight's hall. You can easily arrange a tour from the tourist information office in Olomouc; the castle is included in the Olomouc Card. ⌂ *Bouzov 8, Bouzov* ☎ *585-346-201* ⊕ *www. hrad-bouzov.cz* ⌂ *Classic tour 150 Kč (plus 190 Kč for English, min. 15 people), other tours 60 Kč-160 Kč* ☉ *Closed weekdays Nov.–Mar.*

Fodor'sChoice ★

Morový sloup (*Trinity Column*). In the northwest corner of Horní náměstí, this eccentric Trinity column is one of the best surviving examples of the Olomouc baroque style, which was prevalent in this region of Moravia after the Thirty Years' War in the 17th century. At 35 meters (115 feet), it's the tallest column devoted to victims of the plague in the Czech Republic. The column alone (not the rest of the square) is a UNESCO World Heritage Site. Its construction began in 1717, but it was not completed until 1754, long after the death of its principal designer, Václav Render, who left all his wealth to the city of Olomouc so that the column could be finished. Inside is a small chapel that, unfortunately, is never open. ⌂ *Horní nám.*

Románský biskupský palace (*Romanesque Bishop's Palace*). Next to the Cathedral of St. Wenceslas is a complex of buildings that for centuries were the center of the archdiocese. The oldest, commonly called Palác Přemyslovců (Přemyslid Palace), houses a museum where you can see early-16th-century wall paintings decorating the Gothic cloisters and, upstairs, a wonderful series of Romanesque windows and displays of sculpted stonework fragments. This part of the building was used as a schoolroom some 700 years ago, and you can still make out drawings of animals engraved on the walls by young vandals. ⊠ *Václavské nám. 4* 📖 *70 Kč, includes Archdiocesan Museum* ✪ *Closed Mon., and Oct.–Mar.*

WORTH NOTING

Chrám svatého Mořice (*Church of St. Maurice*). Nothing is left of the original Church of St. Maurice that stood just north of the Horní náměstí in 1257. This is a new church started in 1412 on the same site and remodeled many times. Its current fierce, gray exterior dates to the middle of the 16th century. A sculpture of Christ on the Mount of Olives dates to the 15th century. The baroque organ inside, the largest in the Czech Republic, originally contained 2,311 pipes until it was expanded in the 1960s to more than 10,000 pipes. An international organ festival takes place in the church every September. The tower is sometimes open to the public. ⊠ *Jana Opletalova ul.*

Dóm svatého Václava (*Cathedral of St. Wenceslas*). Between the main square and this cathedral lies a peaceful neighborhood given over to huge buildings, mostly belonging either to the university or the archbishop. The church itself is impressive, but to its Gothic appearance comes only from a 19th-century makeover. A plaque marks the fact that Pope John Paul II celebrated mass there in 1995. The crypt, open in the summer and fall, has a marble box with the heart of an archduke who otherwise is buried in Vienna. Some ecclesiastical treasures are also on display. ⊠ *Václavské nám.*

Kostel svatého Michala (*St. Michael's Church*). The interior of this tripledomed church casts a dramatic spell. The frescoes, the high and airy central dome, and the shades of rose, beige, and gray trompe-l'oeil marble on walls and arches work in concert to present a harmonious whole. The decoration followed a fire in 1709, only 30 years after the original construction. The architect and builder are not known, but it's surmised they are the same team that put up the Church of the Annunciation on Svatý Kopeček (Holy Hill), a popular Catholic pilgrimage site just outside Olomouc. ⊠ *Žerotínovo nám., 1 block uphill from Horní nám., along Školní ul.* ⊕ *www.svatymichal.cz.*

Radnice (*Town Hall*). Olomouc's central square is marked by the bright, spire-bedecked Renaissance town hall with its 220-foot tower. The tower was constructed in the late 14th century. The astronomical clock on the outside was built in 1422, and once rivaled the one in Prague. It was mostly destroyed by an artillery shell on the last two days of World War II. The modern socialist-realist mosaic decorations of the current clock date to 1955. Be sure to look inside the town hall at the beautiful stairway. You can also visit a large Gothic banquet room in the main building, with scenes from the city's history, and a late-Gothic chapel. Tours of the tower are given several times daily; tours of the rest of the building are by appointment. A tour called Olomouc in a Nutshell starts at the Information Center in the town hall and includes the town hall, tower, and main sights on the square. ✉ *Horní nám.* ☎ *585–513–385 for tourist office* 🌐 *www.tourism.olomouc.eu* 🎟 *Tower tour 30 Kč, Oloumoc in a Nutshell tour 70 Kč* 🕓 *No Oloumoc in a Nutshell tour Oct.–mid-June; tower closed in Jan. and Feb.*

QUICK BITES

Café Mahler. Wooden paneling and floral upholstery in the Café Mahler recall the taste of the 1880s, when Gustav Mahler briefly lived around the corner while working as a conductor at the theater on the other side of the Upper Square. It's a good spot for ice cream, cake, or coffee, or simply for sitting back and taking in the lovely view. ✉ ***Horní nám. 11.***

WHERE TO EAT AND STAY

$$ CZECH

🍴 **Hanácká Hospoda.** A low-key, relatively cheap dining option, this popular local pub serves staples like pork, chicken, and duck, but nicely turned out. A quieter no-smoking room is available at the back. According to an inscription on the outside of the house, Mozart stayed here as a young boy on a trip with his parents. [$] *Average main: 180 Kč* ✉ *Dolní nám. 38* ☎ *585–237–186* 🌐 *www.hanackahospoda.com.*

$$ CZECH

🍴 **Moravská restaurace a vinarná.** Traditional Moravian dishes like roast duck with cabbage, chicken breast stuffed with almond butter, roast piglet, or fried Olomouc cheese are served in a rustic interior. The wine cellar, open weekdays, is a bit homier than the street-level restaurant. The staff sometimes wear folk costumes, and live musicians occasionally perform folk music of the region. International wines, including rare vintages, are available alongside a large selection of Moravian wine. [$] *Average main: 290 Kč* ✉ *Horní nám. 23* ☎ *585–222–868* 🌐 *www.moravskarestaurace.cz.*

$$ HOTEL

🏨 **Arigone Hotel and Restaurant.** A renovated historic building blends a nice façade with modern rooms that have classic wooden furnishings. **Pros:** a good blend of historic and modern architecture; all rooms are no-smoking. **Cons:** parking is 300 yards away. [$] *Rooms from: 2290 Kč* ✉ *Universitní 20* ☎ *585–232–351* 🌐 *www.arigone.cz* 🛏 *53 rooms* 🍽 *Breakfast.*

$ HOTEL

🏨 **Flora.** The words "traditional communist-era hotel" don't generally evoke images of comfort, but this one was made much more inviting by a thorough makeover of the lobby and public areas. **Pros:** close to the main highways; lots of parking; several barrier-free rooms; spa and wellness services. **Cons:** unless you want to see a relic of eastern-bloc luxury, the hotel might not suit modern tastes. [$] *Rooms from: 1500 Kč* ✉ *Krapkova 34* ☎ *585–422–200* 🌐 *www.hotelflora.cz* 🛏 *140 rooms, 4 suites* 🍽 *Breakfast.*

$ HOTEL 🏨 **U Dómu.** Each of the rooms in this quiet, family-run pension just off Vaclavské náměstí sleeps up to four and has a small kitchenette. **Pros:** quiet; near the center. **Cons:** limited number of rooms; on a steep street. [$] *Rooms from: 1800 Kč* ✉ *Dómská 4* ☎ *585–220–502* 🌐 *www.hoteludomu.cz* 🛏 *6 rooms* 🍴 *Breakfast.*

TRAVEL SMART PRAGUE

GETTING HERE AND AROUND

Prague is divided into 10 major administrative districts (with numbers above 10 being used for administrative purposes for some of the larger public housing developments and outlying areas). Most visitors spend their time in "Prague 1," which encompasses the Old Town, Malá Strana, part of the New Town, and the Castle Area. Residents in conversation will often refer to the districts by number to orient themselves geographically ("x is in Prague 1" or "y is in Prague 7"). These district numbers correspond roughly to the city's traditional neighborhoods. The neighborhood of Vinohrady, which lies just to the east of Wenceslas Square, for example, is mostly in Prague 2. Other common neighborhoods and district numbers include Žižkov, Prague 3; Smíchov, Prague 5; and Holešovice, Prague 7. These names—along with the district numbers—appear on street signs.

∎ AIR TRAVEL

Prague is served by a growing number of budget carriers, which connect the Czech capital to several cities in the United Kingdom and across the European continent. These airlines are a great and cheap way to travel within Europe—though since the flights are popular, be sure to book well in advance. Budget carriers, however, are usually not much help in cutting costs when traveling from North America. Most of these carriers operate out of secondary airports (for example, Stansted in London instead of Heathrow, where most transatlantic flights land; Orly in Paris instead of the larger Charles de Gaulle airport). This means travelers must change not only airlines but also airports, which can add frustration and expense. Also, consider limits on both carry-on and checked baggage, which are often more stringent on budget carriers than on large international carriers. For flights within

NAVIGATING PRAGUE

Basic navigating vocabulary: *ulice* (street, abbreviated to ul.); *náměstí* (square, abbreviated to nám.); and *třída* (avenue). In Prague the blue signs mark the traditional street address, while the red signs are used to denote the number of the building for administrative purposes.

Europe, low-cost airlines are sometimes a viable alternative to bus and train travel.

The nonstop flight from New York to Prague takes about 8 hours, but the entire journey will take longer (12–15 hours) if you have to change planes at a European hub. The flight from London to Prague takes about 2 hours; the flight from Vienna to Prague takes less than an hour.

Airlines and Airports Airline and Airport Links.com. ⊕ *www.airlineandairportlinks.com.*

Airline Security Issues Transportation Security Administration. ⊕ *www.tsa.gov.*

AIRPORTS

Prague's Václav Havel Airport (formerly Ruzyně Airport) is the country's main international airport and lies about 15 km (10 miles) northwest of the city center. The airport has two main terminals—Terminal 1 (T1) and Terminal 2 (T2)—so make sure to read your ticket carefully to see where you are arriving and departing from. There is also a Terminal 3 for private and charter flights. The trip from the airport to the downtown area by car or taxi will take about 30 minutes—add another 20 minutes during rush hour (7–9 am and 4–6 pm).

Airport Information Václav Havel Airport. ☎ *220-111-888* ⊕ *www.prg.aero.*

GROUND TRANSPORTATION

There are several options for getting into town from the airport, depending on the amount of time you have, your budget, and the amount of luggage.

The cheapest option is Prague's municipal bus service, Bus No. 119, which leaves from just outside the arrivals area and makes the run to the Nádraží Veleslavín Metro station (Line A [green]) every 15 minutes or so during weekdays and less frequently on weekends and evenings. The 32 Kč ticket—plus an extra 16 Kč ticket if you have a large bag—can be purchased at the yellow vending machine at the bus stop and includes a transfer to the metro. A cheaper 24 Kč ticket allows for half an hour of travel, but that may not be enough to get all the way downtown. To reach Wenceslas Square, get off at Můstek station. ■TIP➜ It's important to buy your tickets before you get on the bus. Ticket inspectors ride the airport line often.

The Cedaz minibus shuttle links the airport with the central V Celnici street, adjacent to Náměstí Republiky (Republic Square), which is not far from the Old Town Square. It runs regularly between 7:30 am and 7 pm daily. The one-way fare to V Celnici is 150 Kč.

A taxi ride to the center will set you back about 600 Kč–900 Kč; the fare will be higher for destinations outside the center and away from the airport. Be sure to agree on the fare with the driver before leaving the airport. AAA Radiotaxi and FIX Taxi have an exclusive concessions to operate from the airport, but you can take any cab to the airport.

Prague Airport Shuttle offers transport to your hotel for a fixed price of 140 Kč per person to the center of Prague or a fixed rate to hotels that depends on the number of passengers (one to seven). The company promises to wait up to an hour from your originally scheduled arrival if your flight is delayed or if customs and immigration are slow. Reservations must be made in advance via email.

Contacts AAA Radiotaxi. ☎ 222–333–222 ⊕ *www.aaataxi.cz.* **Cedaz.** ☎ 220–111–111 ⊕ *www.cedaz.cz.* **FIX Taxi.** ☎ 220–113–892, 722–555–525 ⊕ *fix-taxi.cz.* **Prague Airport**

Shuttle. ☎ *602–395–421* ⊕ *praguetransport. com.*

FLIGHTS

Delta Airlines offers nonstop flights from the United States (from New York's JFK airport) to Prague in the summer (daily flights during the busiest season). No carrier offers direct service in the winter. Most major U.S.-based airlines fly to Prague through code-share arrangements with their European counterparts. However, nearly all the major European airlines fly there, so it's usually easy to connect through a major European airport (such as London–Heathrow, Paris, Amsterdam, or Vienna) and continue to Prague; indeed, flights between the United Kingdom and Prague are numerous and frequent, including some on cheap discount airlines, though in London most of these leave from Gatwick or Stansted airports rather than Heathrow, making them less attractive options for Americans. Fares from the United States tend to rise dramatically during the busy summer season, particularly from June through August or September. There are many discounts during the slow winter months.

Airline Contacts Delta Airlines. ☎ *800/221–1212 for U.S. reservations, 800/241–4141 for international reservations, 224–946–733 in Prague* ⊕ *www.delta.com.*

Budget Airlines in Europe EasyJet. ⊕ *www. easyjet.com.* **Eurowings.** ☎ *845/709–8332 in the U.S.* ⊕ *www.eurowings.com.* **Smart Wings.** ⊕ *www.smartwings.net.*

■ BUS TRAVEL

The Czech complex of regional bus lines known collectively as ČSAD operates its dense network from the sprawling Florenc station. For information about routes and schedules, consult the confusingly displayed timetables posted at the station, or visit the information window in the lower-level lobby, which is open daily from 6 am to 9 pm. The company's website will give you bus and train information in English (click on the British flag).

There are also private bus companies servicing routes between Czech towns and cities. Many of these have newer buses with added services and comfort, as well as competitive prices and seasonal deals. Most, but not all, buses use the Florenc station. Some buses—primarily those heading to smaller destinations in the south of the country—depart from above Roztyly Metro station (Line C [red]). You won't know beforehand which buses leave from Roztyly or one of several other hubs, so you will have to ask first at Florenc or check the website. There's no central information center at most other hubs; you simply have to sort out the timetables at the bus stops or ask someone.

Buses offer an easier and quicker alternative to trains for many destinations. The western Bohemian spa town of Karlovy Vary, for example, is an easy two-hour bus ride away. The same journey by train—because of the circuitous rail route—often takes three and a half hours.

ČSAD. ✉ *Florenc station, Křižíkova 4, Karlín* ☎ *900–144–444 (14 Kč per min)* ⊕ *www.idos.cz* Ⓜ *Lines B & C: Florenc.*

Flixbus. Private bus company with regional and international routes. ✉ *Florenc station, Křižíkova 4, Karlín* ⊕ *www.flixbus.cz* Ⓜ *Lines B & C: Florenc.*

Student Agency. Despite the name, you do not have to be a student to use this bus service that links Prague to many regional cities and has international routes. The company is rebranding to RegioJet to avoid confusion. ☎ *841–101–101* ⊕ *www.studentagency.eu.*

▌ CAR TRAVEL

Traveling by car has some obvious advantages: it offers much more flexibility and is often quicker than a bus or train. But these advantages can be outweighed by the costs of the rental and gasoline, as well as the general hassles of driving in the Czech Republic. Most roads in the country are of the two-lane variety, and are often jammed with trucks. And then there's parking. It's impossible in Prague and often difficult in the larger cities and towns outside the capital. If you do decide to rent a car and drive, don't set out without a large, up-to-date Český Autoatlas, available at gas stations and bookstores, or an updated map on your smartphone.

A special permit is required to drive on expressways and other four-lane highways. Rental cars should already have a permit affixed to the windshield. Temporary permits—for 10 days (310 Kč) or one month (440 Kč)—are available at border crossings, post offices, and service stations.

GASOLINE

Gas stations are plentiful on major thoroughfares and near large cities. Many are open around the clock. At least two grades of unleaded gasoline are sold, usually 91–93 octane (regular) and 94–98 octane (super), as well as diesel. Prices are per liter, and the average cost of gasoline is substantially higher than in the United States. The Czech word for gasoline is *benzin,* and at the station you pump it yourself.

PARKING

Finding a parking spot in Prague can be next to impossible. Most of the spaces in the city center, Prague 1, 2, 3, 7, and 10 are reserved for residents, so you'll have to look for public lots with machines that issue temporary permits (look for the big blue "P" on machines). To use the machines, insert the required amount of change—usually 20–30 Kč an hour—then place the ticket in a visible spot on the dashboard. Violators will find their cars towed away or immobilized by a "boot" on the tire. Some hotels offer parking—and this is a real advantage—though you may have to pay extra. A few streets also have meter parking that sells tickets to put in your window, but finding a spot is a virtual impossibility. Changes in the parking policy are pending, due to complaints from local businesses.

Parking is generally unrestricted in the outer areas of the city, though vacant spots can still be hard to find. If you have a car and you need to get rid of it, try parking it on one of the streets in Prague 5 or Prague 6. There's an underground lot at Náměstí Jana Palacha, near Old Town Square. There are also park-and-ride (p+r) lots at distant suburban Metro stations, including Skalka (Line A), Zličín and Černý Most (Line B), and Nádraží Holešovice and Opatov (Line C). These charge as little as 20 Kč per day, substantially cheaper than downtown parking.

RULES OF THE ROAD

The Czech Republic follows the usual Continental rules of the road. A right turn on red is permitted *only* when indicated by a green arrow. Signposts with yellow diamonds indicate a main road where drivers have the right of way. The speed limit is 130 kph (78 mph) on four-lane highways, 90 kph (56 mph) on open roads, and 50 kph (30 mph) in built-up areas and villages. Passengers under 12 years of age, or less than 150 cm (5 feet) in height, must ride in the backseat.

CAR RENTAL

Several major rental agencies have offices at the airport and also in the city. Prices can differ greatly, so be sure to shop around. Major firms like Avis and Hertz offer Western-style cars starting at around $45 per day or $300 per week, which includes insurance, damage waiver, and V.A.T. (value-added tax); cars equipped with automatic transmission and air-conditioning are available but are generally more expensive. Small-size "city cars," like Smart cars or Mini Coopers, are cheaper. It's best to reserve your rental car before you leave home, and it may be less expensive as well. Smaller local companies, on the other hand, can rent Czech cars for significantly less, but the service and insurance coverage may be inferior.

Drivers from the United States need no international driving permit to rent a car in the Czech Republic, only a valid domestic license, along with the vehicle registration. If you intend to drive across a border, ask about restrictions on driving into other countries. The minimum age required for renting is usually 21 or older, and some companies also have maximum ages; be sure to inquire when making your arrangements. The Czech Republic requires that you have held your driver's license for at least a year before you can rent a car.

Major Rental Agencies Avis. ☎ 810-777-810 in the Czech Republic, 800/230-4898 in the U.S. ⊕ www.avis.com. **Budget.** ☎ 800/472-3325 in the U.S. ⊕ www.budget. com. **Europcar.** ☎ 235-364-531 for reservations at Václav Havel Airport in Prague ⊕ www.europcar.com. **Hertz.** ☎ 225-345-000 in the Czech Republic ⊕ www.hertz.com.

Wholesalers Auto Europe. ☎ 888/223-5555 in the U.S. ⊕ www.autoeurope.com. **Europe by Car.** ☎ 212/581-3040 in New York, 800/223-1516 in the U.S. ⊕ www.europebycar. com. **Eurovacations.** ☎ 877/471-3876 in the U.S. ⊕ www.eurovacations.com. **Kemwel.** ☎ 877/820-0668 in the U.S. ⊕ www.kemwel. com.

▌PUBLIC TRANSIT TRAVEL

Prague has an excellent public transit system, which includes a clean and reliable underground subway system—called the Metro—as well as an extensive tram and bus network. Metro stations are marked with an inconspicuous "M" sign. A refurbished old tram (No. 91) travels through the Old Town and Lesser Quarter on summer weekends. Beware of pickpockets, who often operate in large groups on crowded trams and Metro cars and all other forms of transportation, including intercity buses.

The basic Metro, bus, and tram ticket costs 32 Kč. It permits 90 minutes of travel throughout the Metro, tram, and bus network. Short-term tickets cost 24 Kč and allow 30 minutes' ride on a tram, bus, or Metro. If you're carrying a big bag, you need to buy an additional 16 Kč ticket. Most local people have monthly or annual passes, so while it may look like almost everyone is riding for free, they do have tickets. A matter of politeness: Czechs keep to the right side of escalators, leaving the left side free to people who want to walk up or down. It just takes one person on the wrong side to block the entire escalator.

Tickets (*jízdenky*) can be bought at dispensing machines in Metro stations and at some newsstands. They can also be purchased via SMS over a mobile phone by calling ☎ 902–06–26 if you have an SIM card from a Czech service provider. If you send an SMS that says DPT24 or DPT32 to the number, you will receive a virtual ticket for 24 Kč or 32 Kč.

You can buy a one-day pass allowing unlimited use of the system for 110 Kč or a three-day pass for 310 Kč. Validated one- or three-day passes allow traveling with a child 6–15 years old for free. The passes can be purchased at main Metro stations, from ticket machines, and at some newsstands in the center. A pass is not valid until stamped in the orange machines in Metro stations or aboard trams.

The trams and Metro shut down around midnight, but special night trams (Nos. 50–59) and some buses run all night. Night trams run at 20- to 30-minute intervals, and all routes intersect at the corner of Lazarská and Spálená streets in the New Town, near the Národní třída Metro station. Schedules and regulations in English are on the transportation department's official website. Travel information centers provide all substantial information about public transport operation, routes, timetables, and so on. They are at major Metro stations and at both terminals at the airport.

Validate your Metro ticket at an orange stamping machine before descending the escalator. Trains are patrolled often; the fine for riding without a valid ticket is 1,500 Kč, but the fine is reduced to 800 Kč if you pay on the spot or within 15 days. Tickets for buses are the same as those used for the Metro, although you validate them at machines inside the bus or tram. Information about tickets, route changes, and fines is on the city transit company website.

Transit Information websites Dopravní Podnik. ⊕ *www.dpp.cz.*

Transit Information Centers Anděl.
☎ *296–191–817.* **Hradčanská.**
☎ *296–191–817.* **Můstek.** ☎ *296–191–817.*
Muzeum. ☎ *296–191–817.* **Nádraží Veleslavín.** ☎ *296–191–817.* **Václav Havel Airport.** ☎ *296–191–817.*

Lost and Found Lost & Found. ✉ *Ztráty a nálezy, Karoliny Světlé 5, Staré Mesto* ☎ *224–235–085.*

∎ TAXI TRAVEL

Taxis are a convenient way of getting around town, particularly in the evening, when the number of trams and Metro trains starts to thin out. But be on the lookout for dishonest drivers, especially if you hail a taxi on the street or from one of the taxi stands at heavily touristed areas like Wenceslas Square. Typical scams include drivers doctoring the meter or failing to turn the meter on and then demanding an exorbitant sum at the end of the ride. In an honest cab, the meter starts at 40 Kč and increases by 28 Kč per km (½ mile) or 6 Kč per minute at rest. Most rides within town should cost no more than 150–250 Kč. A loophole in the law allows drivers to set their own prices, even though the city has an official price. To counter this, the city has Fair Place stands with taxis that meet a minimum standard and agree to follow the set price list. Average prices are posted on a sign at each stand. The best way to avoid getting ripped off is to ask your hotel or restaurant to call a cab for you. If you have to hail a taxi on the street, agree with the driver on a fare before getting in. (If the driver says he can't tell you what the approximate fare will be, that's almost a sure sign he's giving you a line.) If you have access to a phone, a better bet is to call one of the many radio-operated companies, like AAA Taxi. The drivers are honest, and the dispatchers speak English.

Smartphone-based ride-share services like Uber are also available in Prague, but they are not regulated.

Taxi Companies AAA Radiotaxi.
☎ *222–333–222* ⊕ *www.aaa-taxi.cz.* **City Taxi.**
☎ *257–257–257* ⊕ *www.citytaxi.cz.* **Tick Tack.**
☎ *721–300–300* ⊕ *www.ticktack.cz.*

▮ TRAIN TRAVEL

Prague is serviced by two international train stations, so always make certain you know which station your train is using. The main station, Hlavní Nádraží, is about 500 yards east of Wenceslas Square via Washingtonova ulice. The other international station is Nádraží Holešovice, in a suburban area about 2 km (1 mile) north of the city center along the Metro Line C (red). Nádraží Holešovice is frequently the point of departure for trains heading to Berlin, Vienna, and Budapest. Two other large stations in Prague service mostly local destinations. Smíchovské Nádraží—southwest of the city center across the Vltava (on Metro Line B [yellow])—services destinations to the west, including trains to Karlštejn. Masarykovo Nádraží, near Náměstí Republiky in the center of the city, services mostly suburban destinations.

For train times, consult the timetables posted at the stations. On timetables, departures (*odjezd*) appear on a yellow background; arrivals (*příjezd*) are on white. There are two information desks at the main station, Hlavní Nádraží. The main Čedok office downtown can advise on train times and schedules.

On arriving at Hlavní Nádraží, the best way to get to the center of town is by Metro. The station lies on Metro Line C (red), and is just one stop from the top of Wenceslas Square (station: Muzeum)—travel in the direction of Haje station. You can also walk the 500 yards or so to the square, though the walk is not advisable late at night. A taxi ride from the main station to the center should cost about 100 Kč. To reach the city center from Nádraží Holešovice, take the Metro Line C (red) four stops to Muzeum; a taxi ride should cost roughly 200–250 Kč.

The state-run rail system is called České dráhy (ČD). On longer runs, it's not really worth taking anything less than an express (*rychlík*) train, marked in red on the timetable. Tickets are inexpensive: a second-class ticket from Prague to Brno (a distance of 200 km [124 miles]) costs about 220 Kč. A 40–60 Kč supplement is charged for the excellent international expresses, EuroCity (EC) and InterCity (IC), and for domestic SuperCity (SC) schedules. A 35 Kč supplement applies to reserved seats on domestic journeys, or up tp 250 Kč for the high-speed Pendolino train, which goes to Plzeň, Pardubice, Olomouc, and Ostrava. If you haven't bought a ticket in advance, you can buy one aboard the train, but for an extra fee. It's possible to book sleepers (*lůžkový*) or the less-roomy couchettes (*lehátkový*) on most overnight trains. You do not need to validate your train ticket before boarding.

Recently, private firms have been allowed to operate trains. Two companies, Leo Express and RegioJet, have routes from Prague to other major cities and also some international destinations. Tickets are not interchangable between companies.

The Eurail Pass and the Eurail Youthpass are valid for travel within the Czech Republic, and if you're traveling through to neighboring countries like Hungary, Austria, or Poland, it can be an economic way to bounce between the regions. (A three-country pass starts at €385 for adults or €253 for students.)

The European East Pass is also a good option for first-class travel on the national railroads of the Czech Republic, Austria, Hungary, Poland, and Slovakia. The pass allows five days of unlimited travel within a one-month period for €230 for first class and €158 for second class, and it must be purchased from Rail Europe before your departure. The many Czech rail passes available are useful chiefly by regular travelers. A discount applies to any group of 2–30 people traveling second class (*sleva pro skupiny*). It's always cheaper to buy a return ticket. Foreign visitors will find it easiest to inquire at the international booking offices of major stations for the latest discounts and passes that will apply to them. Rail schedules are available at ⊕ *www.idos.cz*.

Contacts Czech Railways. ⊕ *www.cd.cz.* **Eurail.** ⊕ *www.eurail.com.* **Leo Express.** ☎ *800–222–226* ⊕ *www.le.cz.* **Rail Europe.** ✉ *44 S. Broadway, White Plains* ☎ *800/622–8600 in the U.S.* ⊕ *www.raileurope.com.* **RegioJet.** ☎ *841–101–101* ⊕ *www.regiojet.cz.*

Information Čedok. ✉ *Na Příkopě 18, Nové Mesto* ☎ *800–112–112 (toll-free), 221–447–777* ⊕ *www.cedok.cz.*

ESSENTIALS

■ ACCOMMODATIONS

APARTMENT AND HOUSE RENTALS

International Agencies **Home Away.** ☎ 800/876-4319 ⊕ www.homeaway.com. **Interhome.** ☎ 800/882-6864 ⊕ www.inter-home.us. **Villas International.** ☎ 415/499-9490 in California, 800/221-2260 in the U.S. (toll-free) ⊕ www.villasintl.com.

HOME EXCHANGES

With a direct home exchange you stay in someone else's home while they stay in yours. Some outfits also deal with vacation homes, so you're not actually staying in someone's full-time residence, just their vacant weekend place. Home Exchange. com is $150 for a one-year membership.

Exchange Clubs **Home Exchange.com.** ☎ 800/877-8723 ⊕ www.homeexchange.com.

HOSTELS

Hostels offer bare-bones lodging at low, low prices—often in shared dorm rooms with shared baths—to people of all ages, though the primary market is young travelers, especially students. Prague has a reputation as a place for young people to party, and some independent hostels can be noisy and not very clean.

Many hostels are affiliated with Hostelling International (HI), an umbrella group of hostel associations with some 4,000 member properties in more than 80 countries. Other hostels are completely independent, and may be nothing more than a really cheap hotel.

Membership in any HI association, open to travelers of all ages, allows you to stay in HI-affiliated hostels at member rates. One-year membership costs about $28; hostels charge about $15–$90 per night, depending on location. Members have priority if the hostel is full; they're also eligible for discounts around the world, even on rail and bus travel in some countries.

Information **Hostelling International—USA.** ☎ 301/650-2100 in the U.S. ⊕ www.hiusa.org.

■ COMMUNICATIONS

INTERNET

Internet is widely available at hotels, and many provide Wi-Fi. Cafés with Internet stations can be found all over Prague, and you'll find you can check your email everywhere from the local bookstore to the Laundromat. Many Internet cafés allow Skype calling internationally.

PHONES

The good news is that you can now make a direct-dial telephone call from virtually any point on earth. The bad news? You can't always do so cheaply. Calling from a hotel is almost always the most expensive option; hotels usually add huge surcharges to all calls, particularly international ones. In some countries you can phone from call centers or even the post office. Calling cards usually keep costs to a minimum, but only if you purchase them locally. And then there are mobile phones (➪ see below), which are sometimes more prevalent—particularly in the developing world—than landlines; as expensive as mobile phone calls can be, they are still usually a much cheaper option than calling from your hotel.

The country code for the Czech Republic is 420. To call the Czech Republic from outside the country, dial the international access prefix, then "420," and then the nine-digit Czech number. To call from the United States, for example, dial "011–420–xxx–xxx–xxx."

CALLING WITHIN THE CZECH REPUBLIC

Most people in Prague have mobile phones, but a reasonable phone booth network still exists. Different pay phones accept Czech coins, euro coins, chip-based cards, or a combination of the three. Some phones allow for sending (but not receiving) SMSs and email. The special chip-based pay-phone cards called O2 Trick are available for 180 Kč and up at O2 service stores, some post offices, and newsstands. In almost all phones, instructions are written in English. A domestic call is 15 Kč per impulse from a coin-operated phone. SMS and email over a payphone is 5 Kč domestically and 10 Kč abroad. An impulse ranges from one minute to three minutes. International calls start at 15 Kč for 18 or 38 seconds, depending on the country called. International calling cards, usable on any phone, are much cheaper. Calls from a pay phone to a mobile phone can be quite expensive. The dial tone is a series of alternating short and long buzzes.

You can reach an English-speaking operator from one of the major long-distance services on a toll-free number listed in the instructions on the public phone. The operator will connect your collect or credit-card call at the carrier's standard rates. In Prague many phone booths allow direct international dialing.

There are no regional or area codes in the Czech Republic. Numbers that start with the first three digits running from 601 to 777, however, are mobile phones and the charge may be correspondingly higher. When calling a Czech number from within the Czech Republic, do not use the country code or any prefixes; simply dial the nine-digit number.

CALLING OUTSIDE THE CZECH REPUBLIC
When dialing out of the country, the country code is 1 for the United States and Canada. To dial overseas directly, first dial "00" and then the country code of the country you are calling. A call to the United States or Canada, for example, would begin with 001, followed by the U.S. or Canadian area code and number.

You can also ask the receptionist at your hotel to put the call through for you. In the latter instance, the surcharges and rates will probably be very high.

Access Codes AT&T. ☎ *800–222–55288.* **BT Direct.** ☎ *800–890–042.* **CanadaDirect.** ☎ *800–001–115.*

Other Contacts International Directory Assistance. ☎ *1181.*

CALLING CARDS
Newsstands carry cards with low rates for international calls, but these are no longer very common. Most brands are intended for discounts for calling Eastern Europe, Russia, Africa, and Asia.

MOBILE PHONES
If you have a multiband phone (some countries use different frequencies than what's used in the United States) and your service provider uses the world-standard GSM network (as do T-Mobile, AT&T, and Verizon), you can probably use your phone abroad. Roaming fees can be steep, however: 99¢ a minute is considered reasonable. And overseas you normally pay the toll charges for incoming calls. It's almost always cheaper to send a text message than to make a call, since text messages have a very low set fee (often less than 5¢).

If you just want to make local calls, consider buying a new SIM card (note that your provider may have to unlock your phone for you to use a different SIM card) and a prepaid service plan at your destination. You'll then have a local number and can make local calls at local rates. If your trip is extensive, you could also simply buy a new phone in your destination, as the initial cost will be offset over time. Some virtual mobile operators such as OpenCall offer SIM cards with no long-term commitment and very low international rates. Call prices within the European Union are regulated by law.

■**TIP→** If you travel internationally frequently, save one of your old mobile phones or buy a cheap one on the Internet; ask your mobile-phone company to unlock it for you, and take it with you as a travel phone, buying a new SIM card with pay-as-you-go service in each destination.

Contacts Cellular Abroad. ☎ 800/287–5072 ⊕ www.cellularabroad.com. Mobal. ☎ 888/888–9162 ⊕ www.mobalrental.com. Planet Fone. ☎ 888/988–4777 ⊕ www.planetfone.com.

■ CUSTOMS AND DUTIES

There are few restrictions on what you can take out of the Czech Republic. The main exception is items with special historical or cultural value. To be exported, an antique or work of art must have an export certificate. Reputable shops should be willing to advise customers on how to comply with the regulations. If a shop can't provide proof of the item's suitability for export, be wary. Now that the Czech Republic is in the Schengen zone, there should be no restrictions on bringing cigarettes and alcohol to neighboring countries. Austria, however, has cracked down on people with more than a carton of cigarettes due to the lack of required German-language health warnings. Large knives and martial-arts items, common in Czech tourist shops, are also illegal in much of Europe, even though border checks have been dropped.

Under certain circumstances you can receive a refund of 21% value-added tax (V.A.T.) payable on purchases over 2,001 Kč, provided the goods are taken out of the country soon after purchase. Ask about "Tax-Free Shopping" at the store when you purchase the goods, and make sure to collect all of the necessary stamps and receipts. You can get a cash refund at the airport. Many downtown stores specializing in fashion, glass, or other popular items have a "tax-free" sticker on the door, meaning they have the proper forms for reclaiming tax.

U.S. Information U.S. Customs and Border Protection. ⊕ www.cbp.gov.

■ ELECTRICITY

The electrical current in Eastern and Central Europe is 220 volts, 50 cycles alternating current (AC); wall outlets generally take plugs with two round prongs.

Consider making a small investment in a universal adapter, which has several types of plugs in one lightweight, compact unit. Most laptop and mobile-phone chargers are dual voltage (i.e., they operate equally well on 110 and 220 volts), so they require only an adapter. These days the same is true of small appliances such as hair dryers. Always check labels and manufacturer instructions to be sure. Don't use 110-volt outlets marked for shavers only for high-wattage appliances such as hair dryers.

Contacts Walkabout Travel Gear. ⊕ www.walkabouttravelgear.com.

■ EMERGENCIES

Doctors and Dentists American Dental. ⊠ Hvězdova 33, Pankrác ☎ 733–737–337 ⊕ www.americandental.cz.

Foreign Embassy U.S. Embassy. ⊠ Tržiště 15, Malá Strana ☎ 257–022–000 ⊕ www.usembassy.cz.

General Emergency Contacts Ambulance. ☎ 155. Autoklub Bohemia Assistance. ☎ 1240 ⊕ www.aba.cz. Prague City Police. ☎ 156. State Police. ☎ 158 ⊕ www.policie.cz. ÚAMK Emergency Roadside Assistance. ☎ 1230 ⊕ www.uamk.cz.

Hospitals and Clinics Na Homolce Hospital. ⊠ Roentgenova 2 ☎ 257–271–111 ⊕ www.homolka.cz.

Pharmacies Lékárna U Anděla. ⊠ Štefánikova 6, Smíchov ☎ 257–320–918. Lékárna U sv. Ludmily. ⊠ Belgická 37, Nové Mesto ☎ 222–519–731.

∎ HEALTH

Make sure food has been thoroughly cooked and is served to you fresh and hot. If you have problems, mild cases of traveler's diarrhea may respond to Imodium (known generically as loperamide) or Pepto-Bismol. Be sure to drink plenty of fluids; if you can't keep fluids down, seek medical help immediately.

Infectious diseases can be airborne or passed via mosquitoes and ticks and through direct or indirect physical contact with animals or people. Some, including Norwalk-like viruses that affect your digestive tract, can be passed along through contaminated food. Condoms can help prevent most sexually transmitted diseases, but they aren't absolutely reliable, and their quality varies from country to country. Speak with your physician and/or check the CDC or World Health Organization websites for health alerts, particularly if you're pregnant, traveling with children, or have a chronic illness.

OVER-THE-COUNTER REMEDIES

Pharmacies in Prague are well stocked with prescription and nonprescription drugs, though you may have trouble persuading a pharmacist to fill a foreign prescription. It's best to bring from home all of the prescribed medications you are likely to need. Pharmacies are generally open during regular business hours from 9 am to 6 pm, with some offering night and weekend service. A new law requires a standard 30 Kč fee per prescription. During off-hours, pharmacies will often post the name and address of the nearest open pharmacy on their doors. Pharmacies not only sell prescription medicines but are the only licensed dealers of typical over-the-counter products like pain relievers and cough medicines. Most standard U.S. over-the-counter products have Czech equivalents. Aspirin is widely available. However, items such as aspirin cannot be found outside pharmacies. The most common nonaspirin pain reliever is

Ibalgin (ibuprofen), sold in 200 mg and 400 mg doses.

∎TIP➜ Pharmacists may not speak English or know a drug's non-Czech brand name, but will certainly know the drug's generic name ("acetaminophen" for Tylenol, for example). Be sure to call a drug by its generic name when asking for it.

SHOTS AND MEDICATIONS

If you plan on doing a lot of hiking or camping, note that tick-borne Lyme disease is a serious risk in the woodlands of the Czech Republic. Schedule vaccinations well in advance of departure, because some require several doses, and others may cause uncomfortable side effects.

To avoid problems clearing customs, diabetic travelers carrying needles and syringes should have on hand a letter from their physician confirming their need for insulin injections.

∎ HOURS OF OPERATION

Though hours vary, most banks are open weekdays 8–5. Private currency exchange offices usually have longer hours, and some are open all night.

Gas stations on the main roads are open 24 hours a day.

In season (from May through September), most museums, castles, and other major sights are open Tuesday–Sunday 9–4. Hours vary at other times during the year, and some attractions in smaller, off-the-beaten-track places shut down altogether from November to March.

Most pharmacies are open weekdays 9–6, and are closed weekends. For emergencies, some pharmacies maintain weekend hours, though these can change from week to week. Ask someone locally for advice.

Some stores are open weekdays 9–6, but many are now are open to 11 pm. Some larger grocery stores open as early as 6 am, and a few of the hypermarkets in Prague (usually well outside of town along Metro lines) are open 24 hours. Department stores often stay open until 9 or even 10 pm. Outside Prague, most stores close for the weekend at noon on Saturday, although you may find a grocery store open at night or on the weekend.

HOLIDAYS

January 1; Good Friday, Easter Monday; May 1 (Labor Day); May 8 (Liberation Day); July 5 (Sts. Cyril and Methodius Day); July 6 (Jan Hus Day); September 28 (Day of Czech Statehood); October 28 (Czech National Day); November 17 (Day of a Struggle for Liberty and Democracy, aka Velvet Revolution Day); and December 24, 25, and 26 (Christmas Eve, Christmas Day, and Boxing Day).

■ MAIL

It takes about a week for letters and postcards to reach the United States. Remember to pay a little extra for airmail; otherwise your letters will be sent by ship. The opening hours of post offices vary—the smaller the place, the shorter the hours. Most large post offices are open weekdays 8–7. The main post office in Prague is open 22 hours, with a two-hour break after midnight. Orange post office boxes can be found around the city, usually attached to the side of a building.

At this writing, postcards and letters up to 50 grams in weight cost 27 Kč to send outside of Europe. You can buy stamps at post offices, hotels, newsstands, and shops that sell postcards.

If you don't know where you'll be staying, American Express mail service is a great convenience, available at no charge to anyone holding an American Express credit card or carrying American Express traveler's checks. There is an office in Prague. You can also have mail held *poste restante* (general delivery) at post offices in major towns, but the letters should be marked "Pošta 1," to designate the city's main post office; in Prague the poste restante window is at the main post office.

You'll be asked for identification when you collect your mail.

Information American Express. ⊠ *Na Příkopě 19, Nové Mesto* ☎ *222-800-333* ⊕ *www.americanexpress.com.*

Main Branch Prague Main Post Office. ⊠ *Jindřišská ul. 14* ⊕ *www.ceskaposta.cz.*

SHIPPING PACKAGES

The Czech postal service, Česká pošta, runs an Express Mail Service (EMS). You can post your EMS parcel at any post office, and Česká pošta can supply forms for customs clearance. Delivery times vary between one and five days, though material is often delayed by American customs. You may not send currency, travel checks, precious metals, or stones through Express Mail. Not every post office offers a pickup service.

Many other private international express carriers also serve the Czech Republic.

Some major stores can make their own arrangements to ship purchases home on behalf of their customers. A number of freight and cargo services operate international delivery services, and these can generally be relied upon. An average shipping time to the United States is 21 days (four days for air cargo). There's no reason not to use the reliable Česká pošta, which delivers anything up to 30 kg.

Express Services DHL. ☎ *800-103-000* ⊕ *www.dhl.cz.* **EMS.** ☎ *800-104-410* ⊕ *www. ceskaposta.cz.* **FedEx.** ☎ *800-133-339* ⊕ *www.fedex.com/cz_english.* **UPS.** ☎ *800-181-111* ⊕ *www.ups.com.*

■ MONEY

The Czech crown has been maintained at a level to promote foreign trade and tourism, though prices for some items are close to those of Western Europe. Many hotel prices are more realistic thanks to tough competition, and it's easy to find last-minute bargains. Prices at tourist resorts outside the capital are lower and, in the outlying areas and off the beaten track, very low. The story is similar for restaurants, with Prague being comparable to the United States and Western Europe, whereas outlying towns are much more reasonable. The prices for castles, museums, and other sights are rising, but still low by outside standards.

ATMs are common in Prague and most towns in the Czech Republic, and more often than not are part of the Cirrus and Plus networks, meaning you can get cash easily. Outside of urban areas, machines can be scarce, and you should plan to carry enough cash to meet your needs.

In Czech an ATM is called a *bankomat*, and a PIN is also a PIN, just as in English.

Prices throughout this guide are given for adults. Substantially reduced fees are almost always available for children, students, and senior citizens.

Banks in the United States never have every foreign currency on hand, and it may take as long as a week to order. If you're planning to exchange funds before leaving home, don't wait until the last minute.

ATMS AND BANKS

Your own bank will probably charge a fee for using ATMs abroad; the foreign bank you use may also charge a fee. Nevertheless, you'll usually get a better rate of exchange at an ATM than you will at a currency-exchange office or even when changing money in a bank. And extracting funds as you need them is a safer option than carrying around a large amount of cash.

■TIP➔ PIN numbers with more than four digits are not recognized at ATMs in many countries. If yours has five or more, remember to change it before you leave.

ATMs are safe and reliable, but there have been some incidents of stolen PIN numbers. Instructions are in English. If in doubt, use machines attached to established banks like Česká Spořitelna, Komerčni Banka, and ČSOB.

CREDIT CARDS

It's a good idea to inform your credit-card company before you travel, especially if you're going abroad and don't travel internationally very often. Otherwise, the credit-card company might put a hold on your card owing to unusual activity—not a good thing halfway through your trip. Record all your credit-card numbers—as well as the phone numbers to call if your cards are lost or stolen—in a safe place, so you're prepared should something go wrong. Both MasterCard and Visa have general numbers you can call (collect if you're abroad) if your card is lost, but you're better off calling the number of your issuing bank, since MasterCard and Visa usually just transfer you to your bank; your bank's number is usually printed on your card.

If you plan to use your credit card for cash advances, you'll need to apply for a PIN at least two weeks before your trip. Although it's usually cheaper (and safer) to use a credit card abroad for large purchases (so you can cancel payments or be reimbursed if there's a problem), note that some credit-card companies *and* the banks that issue them add substantial percentages to all foreign transactions, whether they're in a foreign currency or not. Check on these fees before leaving home, so there won't be any surprises when you get the bill.

■TIP➔ Before you charge something, ask the merchant whether he or she plans to do a dynamic currency conversion (DCC). In such a transaction the credit-card processor (shop, restaurant, or hotel, not Visa or MasterCard) converts the currency and charges you in dollars. In most cases you'll pay the merchant a 3% fee for this service in addition to any credit-card company and issuing-bank foreign-transaction surcharges.

Dynamic currency conversion programs are becoming increasingly widespread. Merchants who participate in them are supposed to ask whether you want to be charged in dollars or the local currency, but they don't always do so. And even if they do offer you a choice, they may well avoid mentioning the additional surcharges. The good news is that you *do* have a choice. And if this practice really gets your goat, you can avoid it entirely thanks to American Express; with its cards, DCC simply isn't an option.

Visa, MasterCard, and American Express are widely accepted by major hotels, restaurants, and stores, Diners Club less so. Smaller establishments and those off the beaten track, unsurprisingly, are less likely to accept credit cards.

Reporting Lost Cards American Express. *800/528-4800 in the U.S.* ⊕ *www.american-express.com.* **Diners Club.** *255-712-712 in the Czech Republic* ⊕ *www.dinersclub.com.* **MasterCard.** *800/627-8372 in the U.S., 636/722-7111 collect from abroad, 800-142-494 emergency number in the Czech Republic* ⊕ *www.mastercard.com.* **Visa.** *800/847-2911, 800-142-121 in the Czech Republic* ⊕ *www.visa.com.*

CURRENCY AND EXCHANGE

Although at some point in the future the Czech Republic is supposed to change to the euro, for now the unit of currency in the Czech Republic is the *koruna* (plural: koruny), or crown (Kč), which is divided into 100 *haléřů*, or hellers. The 50-heller coin, the last of the small denominations, was phased out in 2008, but prices are still marked in hellers. There are coins of 1, 2, 5, 10, 20, and 50 Kč; and notes of 100, 200, 500, 1,000, 2,000, and 5,000 Kč. Notes of 1,000 Kč and up may not always be accepted for small purchases. Notes for 50 Kč were phased out in 2011 and are no longer accepted.

Try to avoid exchanging money at hotels or private exchange booths, including the ubiquitous Chequepoint and Exact Change booths. They routinely take commissions of 8%–10%, in addition to giving poor rates. The best places to exchange money are at bank counters, where the commissions average 1%–3%, or at ATMs. The koruna is fully convertible,

which means it can be purchased outside the country and exchanged for other currencies. Of course, never change money with people on the street; not only is it illegal, but you will almost definitely be ripped off.

On arrival at the airport, your best bets for exchanging money are the ATM machines lined up in the terminal just as you leave the arrivals area. The currency-exchange windows at the airport offer rates similar to what you will find at exchange booths in town, but not quite as good as those at banks.

At this writing the exchange rate was around 24 Kč to the U.S. dollar.

■**TIP**➔ Even if a currency-exchange booth has a sign promising no commission, rest assured that there's some kind of huge, hidden fee. (Oh...that's right. The sign didn't say no fee.) And as for rates, you're almost always better off getting foreign currency at an ATM or exchanging money at a bank.

Exchange Services Exchange. ✉ *nám. Franze Kafka 2* ⊕ *www.exchange.cz.*

TIPPING

Service is not usually included in restaurant bills. In pubs or ordinary places, simply round up the bill to the next multiple of 10 (if the bill comes to 83 Kč, for example, give the waiter 90 Kč); in nicer places, 10% is considered appropriate for good food and service. Tip porters who bring bags to your rooms 40–50 Kč total. For room service, a 20 Kč tip is enough. In taxis, add 10%. Give tour guides and helpful concierges 50–100 Kč for services rendered.

■ PACKING

Prague's climate is continental, so in summer plan on relatively warm days and cool nights. Spring tends to be wet and cool; fall is drier but also on the chilly side. In winter, pack plenty of warm clothes and plan to use them. An umbrella is a good idea any time of year. Note that areas in higher elevations tend to stay very cool even in midsummer.

In general, pack for comfort rather than for style. Casual dress is the norm for everyday wear, including at most restaurants. Men will need a sport coat for an evening out at a concert or the opera. Shorts for men are not as common in Prague as they are in North America. In the evening, long pants are the norm, even in summer.

Many areas are best seen on foot, so take a pair of sturdy walking shoes and be prepared to use them. High heels can present considerable problems on the cobblestone streets of Prague.

Some items that you take for granted at home are occasionally unavailable or of questionable quality in Eastern and Central Europe, though the situation has been steadily improving. Toiletries and personal-hygiene products are relatively easy to find, but it's always a good idea to bring necessities when traveling in outlying areas, especially on weekends.

▌ PASSPORTS

Citizens of the United States need only a valid passport to enter the Czech Republic, and can stay for as long as 90 days without a visa. It's a good idea to make sure your passport is valid for at least six months on entry. If you plan on living or working in the Czech Republic, be advised that long-term and work visas must be obtained outside the country. Contact the Czech embassy or consulate in your home country well in advance of your trip. The Czech Republic is now part of the Schengen area, meaning that once a visitor enters one of the countries in the zone, which covers most of Europe, he or she will not have to show a passport at each border; a visitor's three-month stay begins upon the first point of entry into the Schengen area. Travelers are still required to have a valid passport, and spot checks still occur.

▌ RESTROOMS

Public restrooms are more common, and cleaner, than they used to be in the Czech Republic. You nearly always have to pay 5–10 Kč to the attendant. Restaurant and bar toilets are generally for customers only, but if you're discreet no one will care if you just drop by to use the facilities.

▌ SAFETY

Crime rates are relatively low in Prague, but travelers should be wary of pickpockets in crowded areas, especially on metros and trams, and at railway stations. Trams popular with tourists—like No. 22, which circumnavigates most of the major sites—are also popular with pickpockets. In general, always keep your valuables on your person; purses, backpacks, or cameras are easy targets if they are hung on or placed next to chairs.

Violent crime is extremely rare, and you shouldn't experience any problems of this sort. That said, you should certainly take the typical precautions you would take in any large city.

Although nothing is likely to happen, it is not wise for a woman to go alone to a bar or nightclub or to wander the streets late at night. When traveling by train at night, seek out compartments that are well populated.

As with any city popular with tourists, Prague has its share of scams. The most common rip-offs are dishonest taxi drivers, pickpockets in trams and on the Metro, and the ubiquitous offers to "change money" on the street. All these are easily avoided if you take precautions. If you have to hail a cab on the street, ask the driver what the approximate fare will be before you get in (if he can't tell you, that's a bad sign), and ask for a receipt (*paragon*) at the end of the ride. In trams and on the Metro watch your valuables carefully. And never exchange money on the street unless you want to end up with a handful of fake and worthless bills.

■ **TIP→** Distribute your cash, credit cards, IDs, and other valuables between a deep front pocket, an inside jacket or vest pocket, and a hidden money pouch. Don't reach for the money pouch once you're in public.

■ SPORTS AND THE OUTDOORS

Czechs are avid sportsmen and sportswomen. In the summertime, Prague empties out as residents head to their country cottages to hike or bike in clean air. In winter the action shifts to the mountains, a few hours to the north and east of the city, for decent downhill and cross-country skiing. If the ponds freeze over in Prague's Stromovka Park, kids nab their skates for pickup ice-hockey games—a national mania.

The most popular spectator sport, bar none, is ice hockey. Czechs are world hockey champions, and the Czech gold medal at the Nagano Winter Olympics in 1998 is held up as a national achievement practically on par with the 1989 Velvet Revolution. If you're here in wintertime, witness the fervor by seeking out tickets to an Extraliga game. The main Prague teams are Sparta and Slavia.

Soccer plays a perennial second fiddle to hockey, although the Czech national soccer team ranks among the best in the world. Prague's main professional team, Sparta, play their home games at Toyota Arena near Letná.

BICYCLING

Much of the Czech Republic is a cyclist's dream of gently sloping tracks for pedalers. The capital, however, can be unkind to bicyclers. Prague's ubiquitous tram tracks and cobblestones make for hazardous conditions—as do the legions of tourist groups clogging the streets. Nevertheless, cycling is increasingly popular, and there are now several adequate yellow-marked cycling trails that crisscross the city. From April to October two bike-rental companies provide decent bikes—as well as locks, helmets, and maps.

City Bike. City Bike runs guided tours leaving at 10:30, 1:30, and 4:30. Your English-speaking guides offer fun tidbits of history and point out architecture, but do not offer a full tour. The ride's pace is comfortable for those who haven't taken a spin in a while. ⚠ Be warned, Prague is not a bike-friendly city. ✉ *Královdvorská 5, Staré Mesto* ☎ *776–180–284* ⊕ *www.citybike-prague.com* Ⓜ *Line B: Nám. Republiky.*

Praha Bike. One of the multicultural teams from Praha Bike can casually guide you around several routes. The "classic" and "panoramic" are the most popular. There are also beer-garden and pub tours, a ride out of Prague to Karlštejn, and night tours. ✉ *Dlouhá 24, Staré Mesto* ☎ *732–388–880* ⊕ *www.prahabike.cz* Ⓜ *Line B: Nám. Republiky.*

HOCKEY

A feverish national fixation, ice hockey becomes a full-blown obsession during the World Championships (held every year in late spring) and the Winter Olympics.

The Czech national hockey league, Extraliga, is one of the most competitive in the world, and the best players regularly move on to the North American National Hockey League. Slavia Praha and Sparta are the two best teams, both in Prague. Hockey season runs from September to March. Tickets cost 160–900 Kč and are reasonably easy to get.

HC Slavia Praha. Although a relative giant in the Czech Republic, HC Slavia Praha usually finds itself chasing the leaders of the pack in international matches. ✉ *Zimní stadion Eden, Vladivostocká 1460/10, Vršovice* ☎ *267–311–417* ⊕ *www.hc-slavia.cz.*

HC Sparta Praha. HC Sparta Praha is routinely regarded as the premier team in an excellent local league—until players are lured across the Atlantic. Come to spot the next Jágr or Hašek. ✉ *O2 Arena, Českomoravská 2345/17, Karlín*

☏ *266–727–443*   ⊕ *www.hcsparta.cz*
Ⓜ *Line B: Českomoravská.*

PARKS AND PLAYGROUNDS

Praguers are gluttons for a sunny day in the park. A pleasant weekend afternoon brings out plenty of sun-worshippers and Frisbee-tossers, with their blankets, books, and dogs. Two of the city's best beer gardens can be found at Letná and Riegrovy Sady.

Kampa. Under the noses of the throng on Charles Bridge: take the steps off the bridge onto Na Kampě and follow the wide cobbled street to the end; Kampa is a diminutive gem hidden in the heart of Malá Strana. It's a location for lazing in the sunshine and resting your eyes from all the busy baroque architecture, with a playground for when the kids grow restless from the endless palaces and churches. ✉ *Malá Strana* Ⓜ *Tram to Malostranské nám.*

Letná. With killer views of the city across the river, this park is eternally busy. It has a huge restaurant and beer garden, for chilling like a local, located around Letenský zámeček, near the intersection of Kostelní and Muzejní. The large grassy northern plateau is also a great place to throw a Frisbee or kick a soccer ball. An excellent playground sits in the center near the tennis courts, just to the west of Letenský zámeček. Long-term construction projects in the area often hinder the tram routes. ✉ *Holešovice* Ⓜ *Tram to Sparta.*

Riegrovy Sady. This lush park climbs sharply up the slopes of Vinohrady. On the east side of the park, lovely landscaping surrounds a large beer garden and playground. A smaller and cozier beer stand with rooftop seating is in the center. It offers lavish views of Prague Castle on the distant horizon. It has become popular with exchange students and other English-speaking people. ✉ *Vinohrady* Ⓜ *Line A: Jiřího z Poděbrad.*

Stromovka. King of all Prague parks, these lands were formerly royal hunting grounds. Today the deer have been usurped by horse riders and dog lovers. Remarkably rustic for a city-based park, it's primarily a place for walking rather than loafing about. The racket from the ramshackle amusements at Výstaviště exhibition grounds (found at the park's eastern entrance where Dukelských hrdinů meets U Výstaviště) stresses the fact that you remain city-bound. ✉ *Holešovice* Ⓜ *Tram to Výstaviště.*

SKIING

Czechs are enthusiastic and gifted skiers, and the country's northern border regions with Germany and Poland hold many small ski resorts. Czechs generally acknowledge the Krkonoše Mountains, which straddle a border with Poland, to be the best. Experienced skiers may find the hills here a little small and the facilities not quite up to international standards. (Hard-core Czech skiers usually head to Austria or France.) Nevertheless, if you're here in midwinter and you get a good snowfall, the Czech resorts can make for a fun overnight trip from the capital. All the area ski resorts are regularly served by buses leaving from Florenc.

Černá Hora. Černá Hora is 180 km (112 miles, about a four-hour drive) east of Prague. The resort has a cable car, one chairlift, and a couple of drag lifts. The "Black Mountain" is not the biggest of ski resorts, but is often fairly quiet, meaning less waiting and a nice unofficial run, with plenty of forest to explore, directly under the cable car. ✉ *Cernohorská 265, Janské Lázne* ☏ *840–888–229* ⊕ *www. skiresort.cz/en.*

Harrachov. On weekends, when you want to take in some crisp mountain air and clap on a pair of skis, head for Harrachov. In the west of the Krkonoše, around 120 km (74 miles, a three-hour drive) from the capital, the resort offers red and blue runs served by two chairlifts and 11 rope tows. This small and friendly resort is ideal for beginners and intermediates. ✉ *Harrachov* ☏ *481–529–600 for town info center* ⊕ *www.harrachov.cz.*

Skiareal Špindlerův Mlýn. The biggest and most popular ski resort in the Czech Republic is Skiareal Špindlerův Mlýn, which is 160 km (99 miles, about a 3½-hour drive) from Prague. The twin slopes, Svatý Petr and Medvedín, gaze at each other over the small village and offer blue, red, and black runs served by four chairlifts and numerous rope tows. Weekends here are mobbed to a point well past frustration. ✉ *Špindleruv Mlýn* ☎ *499-467-101* ⊕ *www.skiarealspindl. cz.*

SOCCER

Games for the domestic Czech league, the ePojisteni.cz liga, run from August to May with a break in December and January. The games and the fans tend to be somewhat lackluster. Tickets are plentiful enough on match days (except for tournaments). International matches are hosted at Sparta's stadium.

AC Sparta Praha. AC Sparta Praha have an enthusiastic fan base, with the stadium roar to match. Although they have seen their fortunes dip a little recently, the team remain a domestic Goliath and a stone-slinging David in European competition. ✉ *Generali Arena, Milady Horákové 98, Letná* ☎ *296-111-400* ⊕ *www.sparta.cz* Ⓜ *Line A: Sparta.*

Bohemians 1905. Bohemians 1905 are back in the top league after a few difficult years. Fans are highly enthusiastic. ✉ *Doliček stadion, Vršovická 31, Vršovice* ☎ *245-005-014* ⊕ *www.bohemians.cz* Ⓜ *Tram to Vršovice Nám.*

SK Slavia Praha. Sparta's success is much to the chagrin of their bitter rivals SK Slavia Praha, who now play in the modern Eden Arena. ✉ *Eden Stadium, Vladivostocká 1460/10, Vršovice* ☎ *731-126-104* ⊕ *www.slavia.cz* Ⓜ *Tram No. 4, 7, 22, or 24 to Slavia.*

TENNIS

Tennis is one of the favorite local sports, but the national passion remains at a simmer instead of a rolling boil. The best-known Czech players have been Ivan

Lendl and, by ethnicity at least, Martina Navratilova. But there is a crop of younger players out there trying to crowd into the top 10. Prague is blessed with several public tennis courts; most are cinder or clay surface.

Česky Lawn Tennis Klub. Some of the city's best tennis courts can be found right next door to the tennis stadium, Česky Lawn Tennis Klub, which in its time has hosted ATP events. Open to the public for 310–660 Kč per hour are 10 outdoor courts and 6 indoor courts, all hard surface or clay, despite the name. ✉ *Ostrov Štvanice 38, Holešovice* ☎ *222-316-317* ⊕ *cltk.cz* Ⓜ *Line C: Vltavská.*

SK Hradčany. At SK Hradčany outdoor courts cost 180–255 Kč per hour. ✉ *Diskařská 1, Hradcany* ☎ *603-509-950* ⊕ *tenispraha.cz* Ⓜ *Tram No. 22 or 25 to Malovanka.*

▌TAXES

Taxes are usually included in the prices of hotel rooms, restaurant meals, and items purchased in shops. The price on the tag is what you'll pay at the register. The Czech V.A.T. is called DPH (daň z přidané hodnoty), and there are two rates. The higher one (21%) covers nearly everything—gifts, souvenirs, clothing, and food in restaurants. Food in grocery stores and books are taxed by 15%. Exported goods are exempt from the tax, which can be refunded. All tourists outside the EU are entitled to claim the tax back if they spend more than 2,000 Kč in one shop on the same day. Global Blue processes V.A.T. refunds in the Czech Republic and will give you your refund in cash (U.S. dollars or euros) from a booth at the airport; be aware that the Czech Republic does *not* provide postage-paid mailer for V.A.T. refund forms, unlike most other European countries.

When making a purchase, ask for a V.A.T. refund form and find out whether the merchant gives refunds—not all stores do, nor are they required to. Have the form stamped like any customs form by customs officials when you leave the country or, if you're visiting several European Union countries, when you leave the EU. After you're through passport control, take the form to a refund-service counter for an on-the-spot refund (which is usually the quickest and easiest option), or mail it to the address on the form (or the envelope with it) after you arrive home. You receive the total refund stated on the form, but the processing time can be long, especially if you request a credit-card adjustment.

Global Blue is a Europe-wide service with 240,000 affiliated stores and more than 700 refund counters at major airports and border crossings. Its refund form, called a Tax Free Check, is the most common across the European continent. The service issues refunds in the form of cash, check, or credit-card adjustment.

V.A.T. Refunds Global Blue. ☎ 866/706–6090 in the U.S., 800–700–755 in the Czech Republic ⊕ www.globalblue.com.

▌ TIME

The Czech Republic is on Central European Time (CET), one hour ahead of Greenwich Mean Time and six hours ahead of the Eastern time zone of the United States.

▌ TOURS

Major U.S. agencies often plan trips covering Prague and the Czech Republic. Abercrombie & Kent, Inc. is one agency that offers package tours to the area. The largest Czech agency, Čedok, also offers package tours.

GUIDED TOURS

Tours of Prague come under the supervision of Prague Information Service, which is reliable and always informative. The partly city-funded company organizes walking tours in Prague's city center and in the outskirts, including excursions from Prague. Many tailor-made tours can be arranged. Nonregistered guides can also be found, but unless they come with a personal recommendation from someone you trust, their services cannot be guaranteed. The Information Service rents GPS sets programmed with monument sites, restaurants, and cultural events for people who want to tour on their own; the price is 450 Kč for four hours (a deposit is required).

One small private company that does an excellent tour of the city is Custom Travel Services, operated by Jaroslav Pesta. The service offers a wide range of touring options. A full-day private walking tour of Prague with a boat ride for two or three people is 3,300 Kč, or 3,900 Kč for five to six people. The firm offers 100 different tours across the country, and also will customize a tour according to your interests.

Information Custom Travel Services. ☎ 608–866–454 ⊕ www.private-prague-guide.com. **Prague City Tourism.** ☎ 236–002–569 ⊕ www.praguecitytourism.cz/en.

WALKING TOURS

Themed walking tours are popular in Prague. You can choose from tours on medieval architecture, Velvet Revolution walks, visits to communist monuments, and any number of pub crawls. Each year, four or five small operators do these tours, which generally last a couple of hours and cost 150 Kč to more than 1,000 Kč. Inquire at Prague Information Service or a major ticket agency for the current season's offerings. Most walks start at the clock tower on Old Town Square.

A special guide service is available in the Czech Republic, designed to examine and explain the country's Jewish history. The company, Wittmann Tours, offers several different tours within Prague and also outside, including the Terezín concentration camp.

Information Wittmann Tours. ☎ 222–252–472 ⊕ www.wittmann-tours.com.

DAY TOURS AND GUIDES
BOAT TOURS

You can take a 30- to 60-minute boat trip along the Vltava year-round with several boat companies that are based on the quays near the Malá Strana side of the Charles Bridge. It's not really necessary to buy tickets in advance, though you can; boats leave as they fill up. One of the cruise companies stands out, and it's on the Old Town side of the bridge. Prague-Venice Cruises operates restored, classic canal boats from the late 19th century; the company operates one larger boat that holds 35 passengers and eight smaller boats that hold 12 passengers.

■**TIP➜** Take one of the smaller boats—particularly one of the uncovered ones—if you can, for a more intimate narrated cruise of about 45 minutes along the Vltava and nearby canals.

Refreshments are included in all cruises. You actually set sail from beneath the last remaining span of Judith's Bridge (the Roman-built precursor to the Charles Bridge). Look for the touts in sailor suits right before the bridge; they will direct you to the ticket office. Cruises are offered daily 10:30–6 from November through February, until 8 from March through June and September through October, and until 11 in July and August. Cruises cost 290 Kč.

Information Prague-Venice Cruises.
✉ *Křižovnické náměstí 3, Staré Mesto*
☎ 776–776–779 ⊕ *www.prague-venice.cz.*

BUS TOURS

Čedok offers a 3½-hour "Prague Castle in Detail" tour, a combination bus and walking venture that covers the castle and major sights around town in English. The price is about 950 Kč. Stop by the main office for information on other tours and tour departure points. You can also arrange a personalized walking tour. Times and itineraries are negotiable; prices start at around 400 Kč per hour.

Very similar tours by other operators also depart daily from Náměstí Republiky,

Národní třída near Jungmannovo náměstí, and Wenceslas Square. Prices are generally a couple of hundred crowns less than for Čedok's tours.

Information Čedok. ☎ 224–197–242 ⊕ *www. cedok.cz.* **Martin Tour.** ☎ 224–212–473 ⊕ *www.martintour.cz.* **Precious Legacy Tours.** ☎ 222–321–954 ⊕ *www.legacytours.cz.* **Premiant City Tour.** ☎ 224–946–922 ⊕ *www. premiant.cz.* **Wittmann Tours.** ☎ 222–252–472 ⊕ *www.wittmann-tours.eu.*

SPECIAL-INTEREST TOURS

One reason visitors come to the Czech Republic is to connect with their Jewish heritage. Wittmann Tours provides not only coverage of the main sights in Prague, but excursions to smaller Czech towns and to Trebíč.

Recommended Companies Čedok. ☎ 221–447–242 ⊕ *www.cedok.com.* **Wittmann Tours.** ☎ 222–252–472 ⊕ *www.wittmann-tours.com.*

■ VISITOR INFORMATION
ONLINE TRAVEL TOOLS

All About Prague Czech Tourist Authority. ⊕ *www.czechtourism.com.*

Currency Conversion Google. ⊕ *www. google.com.* **Oanda.com.** ⊕ *www.oanda.com.* **XE.com.** ⊕ *www.xe.com.*

Safety Transportation Security Administration (*TSA*). ⊕ *www.tsa.gov.*

Time Zones Timeanddate.com. ⊕ *www. timeanddate.com/worldclock.*

Weather Accuweather.com. ⊕ *www. accuweather.com.* **Weather.com.** ⊕ *www. weather.com.*

Other Resources CIA World Factbook. ⊕ *www.cia.gov/library/publications/the-world-factbook/index.html.*

VISITOR INFORMATION

Prague City Tourism maintains three helpful information offices—the most useful, and most overcrowded, is in the former Town Hall building (just to the left of the clock tower) on Old Town Square. The office can advise on walking tours, as well as answer basic questions and arrange accommodations.

Before You Leave Czech Tourist Authority.
⊕ *www.czechtourism.com.*

In Prague Eurolines. ☎ *224–218–680*
⊕ *www.eurolines.com.* **Prague City Tourism.**
✉ *Staroměstská radnice (Old Town Hall), Staré Mesto* ⊕ *www.praguecitytourism.cz.*

INDEX

A

Accessories shops, 193, 203
AghaRTA (jazz club), 163
Air travel, 302–303
Alchymist Grand Hotel and Spa
⊞ , 11, 131
Antiques shops, 177, 190
Apartment and house rentals,
    309
Archa Theater, 154
Arcidiecézní museum, 297
Aromi ✕ , 118
Art galleries, 177–178
Art galleries and museums.
    ⇨ See Museums and art
    galleries
Artěl (shop), 183
Arts. ⇨ See Nightlife; Perform-
    ing arts
ATMs, 314
Augustine, The ⊞ , 132
AZ Tower, 290

B

Banks, 314–315
Bars, 164–167, 169–171
Bazilika sv. Prokupa, 281
Bazilika svatého Jiří, 62
Basilika svatého Vavřince, 82
Beauty supplies, shopping for,
    178, 190
Beer, 156–157
Southern Bohemia, 245
Western Bohemia, 269–272
Betlémská kaple, 40
Bicycling, 317
Bílý Koníček, 238
Bio Zahrada ✕ , 118
Black–light theater, 150–154
Boat tours, 20, 26, 164–165,
    321
Bohemia. ⇨ See Southern
    Bohemia; Western Bohemia
Bohemia Bagel ✕ , 50
Bookstores, 179, 187, 191–192
Botanická zahrada, 90
Bretfeld Palace, 51
Breweries
Southern Bohemia, 245
Western Bohemia, 268,
    270–273
Bric a Brac (shop), 177
Bridges
Charles Bridge, 28–30, 50–51
Southern Bohemia, 229, 236
Brno, 277, 287–296

Brno dragon and the wagon
    wheel, 292
Budějovický Budvar brewery,
    245
Bus tours, 321
Bus travel, 303–304
Business hours, 12, 312–313
for nightlife, 160

C

Café au Gourmand ✕ , 37
Caffé Fresco ✕ , 77
Café Mahler ✕ , 299
Cafés, 108
Car rentals, 305
Car travel, 304–305
Casinos
Prague, 167
Western Bohemia, 259, 269
Castles and châteaux
day trips from Prague, 209,
    212, 214
Moravia, 282–283, 285–286,
    289, 291–292, 297–298
Nové Město and Vyšehrad, 78
Pražský hrad, 61–72
Southern Bohemia, 227–231,
    234, 240–241, 243
Western Bohemia, 261
Celetná ulice, 40
Cemeteries
Josefov, 46–47
Moravia, 281, 284, 286
Vinohrady and Žižkov, 82–84
Česká Kancelář, 69
Černá věž, 245
České Budějovice, 244–246
České Muzeum Stříbra, 204
Český Krumlov, 225–233
Český Šternberk, 213
Château Lednice na Moravé,
    285
Châteaux. ⇨ See Castles and
    châteaux
Cheb, 260–264
Chebské muzeum, 261
Chebský hrad, 261–262
Children's clothing, shopping
    for, 179
Chodová Planá, 268
Charles Bridge, 28–30, 50–51
Chrám svaté Barbory, 204
Chrám svatého Jakuba,
    204–205
Chrám svatého Mikuláše, 49
Chrám svatého Mořice, 298

Chrám svatého Víta, 62, 65–66
Chrám svatých Petra a Pavla,
    290
Church concerts, 141–142, 145
Church of the Assumption of
    the Virgin, 205
Churches. ⇨ See also Monas-
    teries and convents
day trips from Prague, 204–205
Hradčany, 58
Malá Strana, 49
Moravia, 281, 283, 290–292,
    298–299
Nové Město and Vyšehrad, 82
Pražský hrad, 62–66, 69
Southern Bohemia, 229,
    236–238, 241
Staré Město, 33. 40–42
Vinohrady and Žižkov, 83–84
Western Bohemia, 255, 262
Císařská konírna, 67
Clam–Gallas palác, 40–41
Classical music, 142–150
Clementinum, 33
Climate, 12
Clothing shops, 179–181,
    192–193, 195
Coin museum, 207
Convents. ⇨ See Monasteries
    and convents
Cotto Crudo ✕ , 102
Credit cards, 7, 314–315
Cubist buildings, 79
Cukrána u Matěje ✕ , 283
Cukrkávalimonáda ✕ , 110
Currency and exchange, 315
Customs and duties, 311

D

Dance, 154
Day trips from Prague,
    198–220
dining, 202, 207, 209, 211–
    213, 220
guided tours, 201
lodging, 202, 207–209,
    213–215
prices, 202
Department stores, 186,
    194–195
Dining, 7
best bets, 101
cafés, 108
cuisine, 92–96, 107, 109, 114,
    255

day trips from Prague, 202,
210, 209, 211–213, 220
Moravia, 280, 283, 294,
299–300
planner, 97–100
Prague, 91–122
prices, 99, 202, 225, 252, 280
Southern Bohemia, 225, 231,
235, 239, 246
symbols related to, 7
Western Bohemia, 251–252,
255–256, 262–264, 268, 273
Dóm svatého Václava, 298
Druhé nádvoří, 67
Dům U černé Matky boží, 33
Duties, 311

E
Egon Schiele Center, 227
Electricity, 311
Elefant ✕, 255
Emblem Hotel Prague ⏾, 127
Emergencies, 311

F
Festivals and seasonal events,
24–25, 148–150, 220
Film, 146–147
Food shops, 182, 193
Františkovy Lázně, 250,
264–265
Františkův pramen, 264–265
Franz Kafka Museum, 49–50
Front Synagogue, 281

G
Gardens
Letná, Holešovice, and Troja,
87–88
Malá Strana, 54–56
Pražský hrad, 67
Gask – Gallery of the Central
Bohemian Region, 205
Gay and lesbian clubs,
168–169
Glass shops, 183, 193
Golden Well ⏾, 132
Gothic Bridge, 229, 236
Grandhotel Pupp ⏾, 257
Great Gate, 283
Great Synagogue, 271
Greater Prague, nightlife in,
172

H
Haštal Hotel ⏾, 130
Health concerns, 259, 312
Hluboká nad Vltavou, 242–244

Hockey, 317
Holešovice (Prague neigh-
borhood). ⇨ See Letná,
Holešovice, and Troja
Holašovice (village), 246
Holidays, 313
Home decor shops, 183–184
Home exchanges, 309
Hostels, 137, 309
Hotel Embassy ⏾, 257
Hotel Koliba ⏾, 269
Hotel Le Palais ⏾, 137
Hotel Residence Agnes ⏾, 130
Hotel Růže ⏾, 232
Hotel Thermal, 255
Hotels. ⇨ See Lodging
Hrad Bouzov, 297
Hrad Kotnov, 234
Hrad Krumlov, 227, 229
Hrad Rožmberk, 232
Hrad Špilberk, 289
Hradčanské náměstí, 58
Hradčany (Castle Area)
dining, 113–114
exploring, 57–72
lodging, 133–134
nightlife, 166
shopping, 190
Husitské muzeum, 234

I
Ice hockey, 317
Icon Hotel Lounge ⏾, 136
Internet, 309
Itineraries, 22–23

J
Jan Hus monument, 33
Jazz clubs, 163, 165, 168, 171
Jazz Dock, 171
Jelení příkop, 67
Jelení skok, 254
Jelení skok ✕, 254
Jewelry shops, 184–185, 187,
193
Jewish Cemetery (Mikulov),
286
Jewish Cemetery (Třebíč), 281
Jewish heritage tours, 321
Jewish Quarter (Mikulov), 286
Jihočeské Museum, 245
Jindřichův Hradec, 239–242
Jindřichův Hradec's Castle,
240–241
John Lennon Peace Wall, 56
Josefov (Jewish Quarter), 14,
43–47
dining, 44, 109

exploring, 44–47
nightlife, 163–164

K
Kafka, Franz, 49–50, 80, 84
Kampa, 50, 318
Kaple svatého Kříže, 67
Kaple všech svatých, 69
Karlovo náměstí, 73–74
Karlovy Vary, 252–260
Karlštejn, 207–209
Karlštejn castle, 209
Karlův most, 28–30, 50–51
Klára Nademlýnská (shop),
181
Klášter Emauzy, 77–78
Klášter svaté Anežky České, 41
Klášterni pivovar Strahov, 166
Klausová synagóga, 44
Komorní Hůrka, 261–262
Koněspřežka, 245–246
Konopiště Castle, 214–215
Korunní komora, 65
Kostel Maří Magdaleny, 255
Kostel Matky Boží před Týnem,
33
Kostel Nalezení svatého Kříže,
290
Kostel Nanebevzetí Panny
Marie, 241
Kostel Nejsvětějšího Srdce
Páně, 83–84
Kostel Panny Marie vítězné, 50
Kostel svatého Ducha, 282
Kostel svatého Jiljí (Prague), 41
Kostel svatého Jiljí (Třeboň),
238
Kostel svatého Lukáše, 255
Kostel svatého Martina ve
zdi, 41
Kostel svatého Michala, 298
Kostel svatého Mikuláše
(Cheb), 262
Kostel svatého Mikuláše
(Prague), 41
Kostel svatého Víta, 229
Kostnice, 205–207
Kostnice u sv. Jakuba,
290–291
Královská zahrada, 67
Kralovské oratorium, 66
Královský letohrádek, 67
Křivoklát, 210–211
Křižikova fontána, 88
Kubista (shop), 177, 183–184
Kutná Hora, 202–208

L

La Finestra ✕, *106*
Labyrint pod Zelným trhem, *291*
Lapidárium, *89*
Last Judgment mosaic, *66*
Leopold Gate, *82*
Les Moules ✕, *44*
Letenské sady, *87–88, 172*
Letná, Holešovice, and Troja, *15, 318*
dining, *121–122*
exploring, *87–90*
L'Fleur
Libuše's Bath, *82*
Lidice, *215–216*
Lidice Memorial, *216*
Live music clubs, *163, 165, 168–169, 171*
Lobkovický palác, *68*
Lobkovicz Palace Café ✕, *68*
Lokál Inn 🏨, *133*
Lodging, *7, 309*
apartment and house rentals, *309*
best bets, *125*
budget boutique/hostels, *309*
day trips from Prague, *202, 207, 209, 213, 215*
home exchanges, *309*
Moravia, *283–284, 286, 294–295, 300*
planner, *124–126*
Prague, *124–138*
prices, *126, 202, 225, 252, 280*
Southern Bohemia, *225, 229, 231–232, 235, 237, 239, 241–242, 246*
symbols related to, *7*
Western Bohemia, *251–252, 256–257, 259, 262, 264–265, 268–269, 274*
Lokál Dlouááá ✕, *106–107, 161*
Lokál Inn 🏨, *128*
Loreta, *58*
Lovecká chata Ohrada, *243*
Lucerna music bar, *168*

M

Magdeburg Barracks, *217*
Mail and shipping, *313*
Maiselova synagóga, *45*
Malá Pevnost, *217–218*
Malá Strana (Lesser Quarter), *14*
dining, *50, 109–113*
exploring, *48–56*

lodging, *131–133*
nightlife, *165–166*
shopping, *187–190*
Malé náměstí, *41–42*
Malostranské náměstí, *50–51*
Mamaison Suite Hotel Pachtuv Palace 🏨, *138*
Mandarin Oriental Prague 🏨, *133*
Mariánské Lázně, *265–269*
Mariánský chrám, *236–237*
Marionette shops, *186, 190*
Markets, *176*
Masna Na kozím plácku (shop), *182*
Meet Factory, *171*
Mělník, *211–213*
Městské muzeum, *265*
Mikulov, *284–286*
Mikulov zámek, *286*
Mincmistrovský sklep, *291*
Místodržitelský palác, *291*
Mlýnská kolonáda, *253*
Monasteries and convents
Hradčany, *59*
Nové Město and Vyšehrad, *77*
Staré Město, *41*
Money matters, *314–316*
Moravia, *276–300*
dining, *279, 294–295, 299–300*
guided tours, *279*
lodging, *279, 286, 294–295, 299–300*
nightlife, *295*
prices, *280*
shopping, *290, 291, 296, 297*
Morový sloup, *297*
Morzin Palace, *51*
Mozart, Wolfgang Amadeus, *142*
Mucha, Alfons, *35, 64–65, 75*
Museum Kampa, *51*
Museum of the Terezín Ghetto, *217–218*
Museum Fotoatelier Seidel, *239*
Museums and art galleries
day trips from Prague, *204–205, 207, 217–218*
in Hradčany, *58*
in Josefov, *47*
in Letná, Holešovice, and Troja, *88*
in Malá Strana, *51*
in Moravia, *289–291, 293, 297*
in Nové Město and Vyšehrad, *74, 76–77*
in Southern Bohemia, *227, 229, 231, 234, 241, 243, 245*

in Staré Město, *32–42*
in Vinohrady and Žižkov, *83–84, 86*
in Western Bohemia, *261, 265, 271–272*
Music and musical instrument shops, *185, 193*
Muzeum Antonína Dvořáka, *74*
Muzeum hlavního města Prahy, *42*
Muzeum Jindřichohradecka, *241*
Muzeum Romské kultury, *291*

N

Na Louži ✕, *231*
Na Příkopě, *35*
Na Spílce ✕, *271*
Náměstí Republiky, *271*
Náměstí Svobody, *291–292*
Náměstí Svornosti, *231*
Náměstí Zachariáše z Hradce, *283*
Naplávka, *166*
Národní divadlo, *76, 149*
Národní muzeum, *77–78*
Národní muzeum fotografie, *241*
Národní technické muzeum, *88*
National Memorial on Vitkov Hil, *84, 86*
Nautilus 🏨, *235*
Nerudova ulice, *51*
Nightclub, *162–163, 168–171*
beer culture, *156–157*
Moravia, *291*
planner, *160*
Prague, *156–172*
Southern Bohemia, *233*
Western Bohemia, *259, 269, 274*
Noi ✕, *111*
Nové Město (New Town) and Vyšehrad, *14–15*
dining, *74, 77, 115–119*
exploring, *73–78*
lodging, *134–136*
nightlife, *166–169*
shopping, *190–195*
Novoměstská radnice, *78*
Nový Svět, *58–59*
Nový židovský hřbitov, *84*

O

Obecní dům, *35*
Obrazárna, *67*
Olomouc, *296–300*
One Room Hotel 🏨, *137*
Opera, *149*

326 <

P

Packing, 315–316
Palác Akropolis, 170
Palác Kinských, 35–36
Palaces
 Hradčany, 58
 Letná, Holešovice, and Troja,
  88–90
 Malá Strana, 51, 55
 Moravia, 283, 285–286,
  291–292
 Pražský hrad, 61–72
 Staré Město, 40–41
Památník národního písemnic-
 tví, 59
Památník Terezín, 218
Parks, 317–318
 Letná, Holešovice, and Troja,
  87–88, 90, 318
 Malá Strana, 50, 54–56
Passports, 316
Patchuv Palace ☲, 131
Patton Memorial, 272
Performance venues, 147–150
Performing arts
 planner, 141
 Prague, 140–154
 Southern Bohemia, 232, 246
 Western Bohemia, 269
Petřínské sady, 54
Philosophical Hall, 59
Pilsen Beer Spa Wellness Hotel
 Purkmistr, 272
Pilsner Urquell Brewery, 271
Pinkasova synagóga, 45–46
Písek, 236–237
Pivovarské muzeum, 272
Pivovarský dům ✕, 167
Playgrounds, 317–318
Plzeň, 270–274
Plzeň Historical Underground,
 271–272
Plaques, 80
Postal districts, 13
Prácheňské Museum, 237
Prašná brána, 36
Pravčická Brána, 219
Pražská ulice, 234
Pražskův palác, 292
Pražský hrad (Prague Castle),
 61–72
Prices
 day trips from Prague, 202
 Moravia, 280
 Prague dining, 99
 Prague lodging, 126
 Southern Bohemia, 225
 Western Bohemia, 252

Prints, shopping for, 179, 187
První nádvoří, 72
Prosekárna, 169
Public transit, 305–306
Pubs, 156–157, 169–171
Puppet shows, 147–150

R

Radnice (Olomouc), 298–299
Rear Synagogue, 281
Regionální Muzeum, 231
Restaurants. ⇨ See Dining
Restrooms, 316
Riegrovy Sady, 169, 318
Rock clubs, 162, 165–166,
 168–169, 171
"Roland" statue, 262
Romanesque chapel, 261–262
Romanesque rotunda, 82
Románský biskupský palace,
 298
Romanský palác, 69
Royal Ricc ☲, 295
Royal crypt, 65
Rozhledna Diana, 253
Rudolfinum, 46, 150

S

Sadová kolonáda, 254
Safety, 13, 160, 316
St. John of Nepomuk Sar-
 cophagus, 29, 52, 56
Sansho ✕, 117
Schönbornský palác, 55
Schwarzenberský palác, 58
Shoe shops, 180–181, 186,
 194, 196
Shopping
 Moravia, 290–291, 296–297
 Prague, 174–196
 Western Bohemia, 259–260
Shopping malls, 186, 194–195
Sightseeing tours and guides,
 24–26, 320–321
 day trips from Prague, 201
 Moravia, 280
 Southern Bohemia, 225
 Western Bohemia, 251
Skiing, 318–319
Sladovna, 237
Smíchov, 15
 dining, 120–121
 lodging, 138
 nightlife, 171
 shopping, 196
Soccer, 317, 319
Southern Bohemia, 222–246
 dining, 225, 231, 235, 239, 246

 guided tours, 225
 lodging, 225, 231–232, 235,
  237, 239, 241–242, 246
 nightlife, 233
 performing arts, 232, 246
 prices, 225
Špaliček, 262
Španělská synagóga, 47
Spas, 238, 254, 266–268, 272
Špička, 82
Sporting goods shops, 186,
 194
Sportovně relaxační areál,
 243–244
Sports and the outdoors, 260,
 317–319
Stag parties, 160
Stalin parties, 172
Stará radnice, 292
Stará sněmovna, 69
Staré Město (Old Town), 14
 dining, 35, 37, 34, 35, 100–109
 exploring, 22, 32–42
 lodging, 127–131
 nightlife, 158–171
 shopping, 176–186
Staroměstská radnice, 37, 40
Staroměstské náměstí, 29,
 36–37
Staronová synagóga, 46
Starý královský palác, 69
Starý židovský hřbitov, 46–47
Statní zámek Hlubaká, 243
Statní zámek Telč, 283
Statue of St. Wenceslas, 78
Stavovské divadlo, 42
Šternberský palác, 58
Stopkova pivnice ✕, 292
Strahovský klášter, 59
Street markets, 176, 185
Stromovka, 318
Svatová clavská Kaple, 65
Symbols, 7
Synagogues
 Moravia, 281
 Prague, 42–43, 44, 45
 Western Bohemia, 271

T

Tábor, 233–235
Tančící dům, 76–77
The Tavern ✕, 119
Taxes, 175, 319–320
Taxis, 306–307
Telč, 281–284
Telephones, 309
Tennis, 319
Terezín, 217–220
Terezín Memorial, 217–218

Theater, 147–150
Theater buildings, 42, 76
Thun–Hohenstein Palace, 51
Ticket outlets, 141, 295
Time, 320
Timing the visit, 12
Tipping, 315
Towers
  Moravia, 280, 290
  Southern Bohemia, 245
  Staré Město, 29, 33, 36, 40
  Vinohrady and Žižkov, 86
Town Hall Tower, 40
Toy shops, 186–187, 190, 194
Train travel, 307–308
Transportation, 302–308
Třebíč, 280–281
Třeboň, 237–239
Třeti nádvoří, 72
Tři Lilie ⛝, 265
Troja. ⇨ See Letná, Holešovice,
  and Troja
Truhlář Marionety (shop), 190

U

U Madré kachničky ✕,
  113–114
U Medvídků, 157, 161–162
U Zlatého Tygra, 162
Uměleckoprůmyslové museum
  v Praze, 47
Uměleckoprůmyslové muzeum,
  293

V

Václavské máměstí, 77
Valdštejnská Kaple, 66
Valdštejnská Zahrada, 54
Valkoun House, 51
Value–added taxes, 175,
  319–320
Veletržní palác, 88–89
Velkopřevorské náměstí, 56
Villa Tugendhat, 289–290
Vinohrady and Žižkov, 15
  dining, 118–120
  exploring, 83–86
  lodging, 136–137
  nightlife, 169–170
  shopping, 195–196
Visitor information, 61, 321
Vlašský dvůr, 207
Vojanovy sady, 56
Vrtbovská zahrada, 55, 56
Výtopna, 167
Vyšehrad ⇨ See Nové Město
  (New Town) and Vyšehrad
Vyšehrad Citadel, 78, 80

W

Walking tours, 26, 320
Weather, 12
Web sites, 321–322
Western Bohemia, 247–274
  dining, 251–252, 255–257,
  262, 268, 273

  guided tours, 251
  lodging, 251–252, 257, 259,
  262, 264–265, 268–269, 274
  nightlife, 259, 269, 274
  performing arts, 259, 269
  prices, 252
  shopping, 259–260
  sports and the outdoors, 260
Wine shops, 182, 193

Z

Zahrady pod Pražským hra-
  dem, 55
Zámek, 214
Zámek Konopiště, 214–215
Zámek Třeboň, 239
Zdenik's Oyster Bar ✕,
  108–109
Zelný trh, 293
Židovská čtvrť, 281
Židovská radnice, 47
Židovská ulice, 262
Žižka, Jan, 233–234
Žižkov. ⇨ See Vinohrady and
  Žižkov
Žižkov TV Tower, 86, 171
Žižkovo náměstí, 234
Zlatá ulička, 69, 72
Zlotá Praha, 164
Zoologická zahrada v Praze,
  90
Zoos, 90
Zvíkov, 237

PHOTO CREDITS

Front cover: Robert Harding / Alamy. [Description: Historic Center, Prague, Czech Republic]. 1, wrangel/iStockphoto. 2, lillisphotography/iStockphoto. **Chapter 1: Experience Prague:** 8-9, Matthew Dixon/iStockphoto. 16 (left), GrLb71/Shutterstock. 16 (top right), Ivo Brezina/Shutterstock. 16 (bottom right), Eugeny Shevchenko/iStockphoto. 17 (top left), atelier22/Shutterstock. 17 (bottom left), Anastazzo/Shutterstock. 17 (right), PHB.cz (Richard Semik)/Shutterstock. 18 (left), Brian K./Shutterstock. 18 (right), illisphotography/iStockphoto. **Chapter 2: Exploring Prague:** 27 and 28, Ekaterina Fribus /Shutterstock. 29 (bottom), Vladimir Sazonov/Shutterstock. 29 (top), Shchipkova Elena / Shutterstock.com. 30, courtyardpix/iStockphoto. 31, WH CHOW/Shutterstock. 32, Matthew Dixon/iStockphoto. 38-39, Dmitry Agafontsev/Shutterstock. 43, Roberto Gennaro/iStockphoto. 48, Kajano/Shutterstock. 52-53, courtyardpix/Shutterstock. 56, Nataliya Hora/Shutterstock. 57, Tupungato/Shutterstock. 60, Jozef Sedmak/Shutterstock. 61, hammondovi/iStockphoto. 64 and 68, Javier Larrea / age fotostock. 70-71, MATTES René/age fotostock. 73, Peter Zurek/Shutterstock. 76, Igumnova Irina/Shutterstock. 79, Vadim Balantsev/Shutterstock. 81, Razvan Chirnoaga/Shutterstock. 83, Martin Spurny/Shutterstock. 87, Ionia/Shutterstock. **Chapter 3: Where To Eat:** 91, magicinfoto/Shutterstock. 92, Tatiana Vorona/Shutterstock. 93 (bottom), Ivan Majtan/Shutterstock. 93 (top) Tobik/Shutterstock. 94, Ales Liska/Shutterstock. 95 (bottom) Sombra/Shutterstock. 95 (top), Kellydt | Dreamstime.com. 96, Courtesy of :C... LESTE Restaurant & Bar. 112, Frank Chmura / age fotostock. **Chapter 4: Where To Stay:** 123, Mandarin Oriental Prague. 124, Hotel Le Palais Prague. **Chapter 5: Performing Arts:** 139, Massimiliano Pieraccini/iStockphoto. 140, greynforty/Flickr. 143, David V./Shutterstock. 149, RENAULT Philippe / age fotostock. 151, Sergi Marin Casas/Flickr. 152-153, WOW Projects. **Chapter 6: Nightlife:** 155, Rglinsky | Dreamstime.com. 156, Dino/Shutterstock. 157 (bottom), jerrroen/Flickr. 157 (top), Courtesy of Company Pivovary Staropramen. 158, loopiss/iStockphoto. 159, robertpaulyoung/Flickr. **Chapter 7: Shopping:** 173, Annavee/Shutterstock. 174, Evdoha | Dreamstime.com. 176, Peter Zurek - Big Original/iStockphoto. 188-189, Javier Larrea / age fotostock. 191, jean schweitzer/Shutterstock. **Chapter 8: Day Trips From Prague:** 197, DEA / M BORCHI / age fotostock. 198, Pecold/Shutterstock. 199 (top), Filip Fuxa/Shutterstock. 199 (bottom), Jozef Sedmak/Shutterstock. 200, LWY/Flickr. 205, hornyak/Shutterstock. 206, Matt Ragen/Shutterstock. 215, Vaclav Ostadal / age fotostock. 219, Emmanuel Dyan/Flickr. **Chapter 9: Southern Bohemia:** 221, Elena Terletskaya/Shutterstock. 222, Roman Pavlik/Shutterstock. 223 (top), BESTWEB/Shutterstock. 223 (bottom), kohy/Shutterstock. 224, Ionia/Shutterstock. 230, Peter Zurek/Shutterstock. 235, julius fekete/Shutterstock. 242, Eleonoracerna/Shutterstock. 244, spfotocz/Shutterstock. **Chapter 10: Western Bohemia:** 247 and 248, Pavel Kosek/Shutterstock. 249 (top), Andrea Seemann/Shutterstock. 249 (bottom), Jita/Shutterstock. 250, Andrea Seemann/Shutterstock. 254, marchello_/Shutterstock. 258, Ionia/Shutterstock. 263, Alexander Cherednichenko/Shutterstock. 266, Pavel Kosek/Shutterstock. 270, Palis Michalis/Shutterstock. 272, Stefan Kiefer / age fotostock. **Chapter 11: Moravia:** 275, 1potter1/Shutterstock. 276, Beentree [CC BY-SA 3.0]. 277 (top), Pavel Kosek/Shutterstock. 277 (bottom), Karel Gallas/iStockphoto. 278, Sedlacek/Shutterstock. 282, Ales Liska/Shutterstock. 285, Prosiaczeq | Dreamstime.com. Back cover, from left to right: Lucertolone/Shutterstock; S.Borisov/Shutterstock; courtyardpix/Shutterstock. Spine: Brykaylo Yuriy / Shutterstock.

NOTES

NOTES

NOTES

NOTES

NOTES

NOTES

ABOUT OUR WRITERS

Raymond Johnston has worked in media for all of his professional career, hosting a popular radio show in the Midwest in the early 1990s before moving to New York to work for a company that published critical guidebooks on the Internet. In 1996 he moved to Prague, where he has worked as a film critic, a historical and linguistic consultant for TV programs, and a newspaper and magazine journalist and editor. Currently, he works for several websites with news, cultural and historical information about Prague. For this edition he updated the Western Bohemia, Southern Bohemia, Moravia, and Travel Smart chapters

Jennifer Rigby is a British journalist and writer who lived in Prague a few years ago and has since missed its beauty, delicious beer, and chilled-out vibe. She now lives and works in the slightly more hectic locations of Yangon, Myanmar, and London, England, writing for a number of leading international publications. But she continues to spend as much time in Prague as she can. In this edition, she wrote and updated the Where to Stay, Shopping, Day Trips, Performing Arts, and Nightlife chapters.

Will Tizard is a journalist and documentarian who has lived in Prague for more than 20 years, contributing travel news to several international guides and magazines, including the *Sunday Times Traveler,* and editing the *Time Out Prague* Guide. He has taught journalism and independent filmmaking at universities for a decade and is currently completing a master's in geopolitical studies at Charles University while producing and filming *Buried,* a documentary following the quest for the return of Torahs stolen by the Red Army during WWII. For this edition Will updated the Experience, Exploring, and Where to Eat chapters.

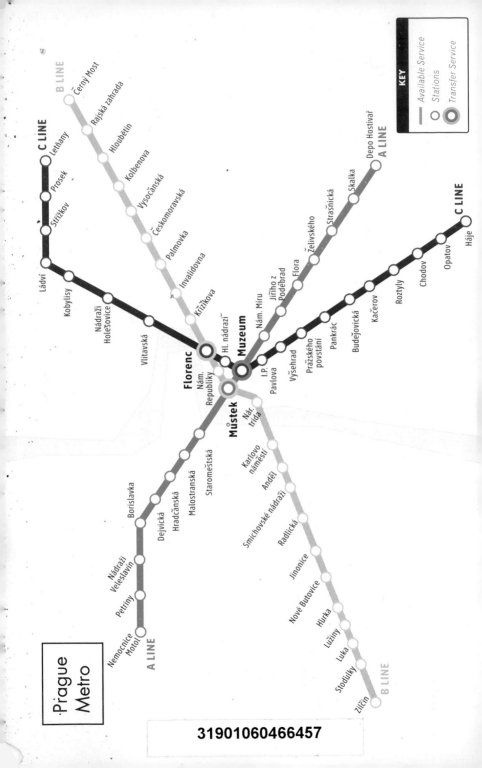

Prague Metro

B LINE
C LINE
A LINE
C LINE
A LINE
B LINE

KEY
— Available Service
○ Stations
◎ Transfer Service

Černý Most
Rajská zahrada
Hloubětín
Kolbenova
Vysočanská
Českomoravská
Palmovka
Invalidovna
Křížíkova

Letňany
Prosek
Střížkov
Ládví
Kobylisy
Nádraží Holešovice
Vltavská
Florenc
Nám. Republiky
Hl. nádraží
Muzeum
Můstek
Nám. Míru
Jiřího z Poděbrad
Flora
Želivského
Strašnická
Skalka
Depo Hostivař
Háje
Opatov
Chodov
Roztyly
Kačerov
Budějovická
Pankrác
Pražského povstání
Vyšehrad
I.P. Pavlova
Nár. třída
Karlovo náměstí
Anděl
Smíchovské nádraží
Radlická
Jinonice
Nové Butovice
Hůrka
Lužiny
Luka
Stodůlky
Zličín
Staroměstská
Malostranská
Hradčanská
Dejvická
Bořislavka
Nádraží Veleslavín
Petřiny
Nemocnice Motol

31901060466457